# Developmental Perspectives on Children With High-Incidence Disabilities

Edited by

Ronald Gallimore
Lucinda P. Bernheimer
*University of California, Los Angeles*

Donald L. MacMillan
*University of California, Riverside*

Deborah L. Speece
*University of Maryland*

Sharon Vaughn
*University of Texas, Austin*

**LEA** **LAWRENCE ERLBAUM ASSOCIATES, PUBLISHERS**
1999   Mahwah, New Jersey                    London

Lawrence Erlbaum Associates, Inc., Publishers
10 Industrial Avenue
Mahwah, NJ  07430

Cover design by Kathryn Houghtaling Lacey

**Library of Congress Cataloging-in-Publication Data**

Developmental perspectives on children with high-incidence
   disabilities / edited by Ronald Gallimore ... [et al.].
     p.  cm.—(The LEA series on special education and disability)
Papers in honor of Barbara K. Keogh.
   Includes bibliographical references and indexes.
ISBN 0-8058-2825-7 (alk. paper). — ISBN 0-8058-2826-5
   (pbk. : alk. paper).
   1. Learning  disabled  children—Education—United
States.  2. Handicapped  children—Education—United
States. 3. Learning disabilities—Research—United States. 4.
Special education—Government policy—United States.  5.
Keogh, Barbara K.  I. Gallimore, Ronald.  II. Series.
LC4705.D48   1998
371.92'6—dc21             98-24512
                           CIP

Printed in the United States of America
10  9  8  7  6  5  4  3  2  1

For Barbara K. Keogh
and all the children

# Contents

# Part II: Diagnosis, Classification, and Intervention

# Part III: Policy

# Part IV: Biographical

# List of Contributors

Lucinda Bernheimer, Department of Psychiatry, 760 Westwood Plaza, C9-752 NPI, University of California, Los Angeles, CA 90095-1759

Batya Elbaum, Department of Teaching and Learning, University of Miami, Coral Gables, FL 33124.

Margaret Faust, 1030 Columbia Avenue, Scripps College, Claremont, CA 91711

Steven R. Forness, Department of Psychiatry, 760 Westwood Plaza, University of California, Los Angeles, CA 90095-1759

Douglas Fuchs, Department of Special Education, Peabody College,Vanderbilt University Nashville, TN 37203

Lynn S. Fuchs, Department of Special Education, Box 328 Peabody College,Vanderbilt University Nashville, TN 37203

James J. Gallagher, 300 Nations Bank Plaza, STAGE/FPG, CB 8040, University of North Carolina, Chapel Hill, NC 27599

Ronald Gallimore, Departments of Psychiatry and Education, 760 Westwood Plaza, C8-881 NPI, University of California, Los Angeles, CA 90095-1759

Laura B. Jones, Department of Psychology, 2510 Lincoln Street, University of Oregon, Eugene OR 97405-2614

Martin J. Kaufman, School of Education, University of Oregon, Eugene, OR 97403-1215

Kenneth Kavale, College of Education, N259 Lindquist Center, University of Iowa Iowa City, IA 52242

Linda M. Lewis, School of Education, University of Oregon, Eugene, OR 97403-1215

Carol Keogh Lindsay, Department of Social and Behavioral Sciences, 3091 Spring View, North Idaho College, Coeur D' Alene, ID 83814

Reid Lyon, Human Learning and Behavior Branch, Room 4B05, 6100 Executive Blvd., National Institute of Child Health and Human Development (NICHD), Bethesda, MD 20892

Donald L. MacMillan, School of Education, 900 University Avenue, University of California, Riverside, CA 92521

Mary Rothbart, Department of Psychology, 2510 Lincoln Street, University of Oregon, Eugene OR 97405-2614

Carol E. Smith, 2615 Crest Drive, System Development Corporation, Manhattan Beach, CA 90266

Deborah Speece, Department of Education, 1308 D Benjamin Bldg., University of Maryland, College Park, MD 20742

Annette Tessier, California State University, 305 19th Place, Manhattan Beach, CA 90266

Joseph K. Torgesen, Department of Psychology, Florida State University, Tallahassee, FL 32306-1051

Sharon Vaughn, Department of Special Education, 306 SZB, University of Texas, Austin, Texas 78712

Hill M. Walker, Center on Human Development, Clinical Services Building, University of Oregon, Eugene, OR 97403-1211

Thomas S. Weisner, Departments of Psychiatry and Anthropology, 760 Westwood Plaza, C8-881 NPI, University of California, Los Angeles, CA 90095-1759

Emmy Werner, 123 AOB IV, University of California, Davis, CA 95616

Bernice Wong, Department of Education, 8888 University Drive, Simon Fraser University, Burnaby, B.C. V5A 1S6, Canada

# Preface

This volume has two purposes. The first is to summarize, substantiate, and extend current knowledge of the development of children with high-incidence disabilities, most notably learning disabilities, behavioral disorders, and mild mental retardation. Especially for younger children, some categorical labels fail to recognize that those described as displaying behavioral disorders (BD) and others presenting externalizing problem behaviors overlap with mild mental retardation (MMR) and learning disabilities (LD). Essentially, *high-incidence disabilities* is the intersection of MMR, LD, and BD as a subset of a continuum of behavior problems ranging from socialized delinquency to mild BD to seriously emotionally disturbed (SED). Most children displaying high-incidence disabilities who are referred for special education services represent an undifferentiated general category in the primary grades, becoming differentiated into more homogeneous groups later in their school careers when more certain "calls" can be made based on history as opposed to psychometric profiles. The first purpose of this volume is to summarize what is known about developmental constructs in the study of high-incidence disabilities and to cast this knowledge in a form that identifies significant research challenges.

The second purpose is to honor the career of Professor Barbara K. Keogh and her contributions to the developmental study of children with high-incidence disabilities. Internationally recognized for her accomplishments, Professor Keogh is esteemed for originality and clarity of thought. For nearly 40 years, she has set an extraordinary model of analytic rigor combined with a kind and generous manner that inspires, supports, and sets an exacting standard of scholarship. The contributing authors to this volume represent only a fraction of the students and scholars touched by her distinguished career.

In conceiving this volume, the editors sought to represent the topics, problems, and issues to which Professor Keogh has devoted herself. We invited chapters that summarize what we know about the high-incidence handicapping conditions that her research has mainly addressed. We also sought to reflect the probing, questioning style that she brings to her own work. In light of her characteristic modesty and distaste for self-aggrandizement, we believed she would be more comfortable if we encouraged contributors to begin with issues she has addressed in her career but then use the opportunity to add something new, clarifying, and challenging to scholarly discourse.

The audience for this volume includes scholars, policymakers, and graduate students in special education and associated disciplines who seek to stay current on this wide-ranging topic of high-incidence disabilities. We hoped to construct a volume that Barbara would buy for her library, recommend to colleagues, and assign to students. Those who know her will appreciate what a high standard this sets.

We are grateful to the contributors for their good efforts and for being timely in meeting the deadlines that we set. At UCLA, substantial thanks are due Rhodora Maliksi-Farmer for coordinating communications among the editors and contributors, and for her contributions to the preparation of the manuscript. Dr. Lindsay Clare, in her final days as a graduate student at UCLA, copyedited all chapters, taking great care to meet the publisher's requirements for manuscript preparation. Dr. Michele D. Crockett undertook the exhaustive work of indexing and proofing the final copy, doing an excellent job, for which the editors are deeply grateful.

Dr. Jack Keogh is thanked for his successful efforts to keep both his wife in the dark about this project and the editors enlightened regarding crucial details of her schedule. To surprise her, the editors planned an invitational conference at UCLA to be held May 17th, 1997. When she learned of the conference 3 months prior to that date and who was coming, Professor Keogh invited the editors and others to a party at her home to meet her new granddaughter, Lily. When she issued the invitations she thought the editors were simply coming to a conference. She learned of the volume only a few days before the conference. As a result, hours after the volume was announced, she hosted us at a party in her home, for which Jack had made all arrangements. Besides the humor she saw in this ironical turn of events, nothing conveys more about her than the question of which she appreciated more: Learning that a volume was to be published in her honor, or the opportunity to show off her new granddaughter?

—*Ronald Gallimore*
—*Lucinda P. Bernheimer*
—*Donald L. MacMillan*
—*Deborah L. Speece*
—*Sharon Vaughn*

# Developmental Perspectives on Children With High-Incidence Disabilities

# PART I

## Developmental Foundations and Extensions

# 1 Three Parallels Between the Development of Special Education and the Career of Professor Keogh

**Ronald Gallimore**
*University of California, Los Angeles*

A long, distinguished research career relates to an investigator's chosen field in three ways. First, there are discernible parallels between the development of fields themselves and the evolving interests and activities of distinguished investigators. The parallels are expectable because distinguished researchers are shaped by and, in turn, shape their fields of inquiry both during their work lives and into the future, defining the second and third ways careers and fields relate: The contributions of distinguished scholars guide and goad a field forward during their career, and their visions for the future define the questions and challenges for the next generation of researchers. Thus, it is for the field of special education research and the career of Professor Barbara K. Keogh (BKK).

## PARALLELS BETWEEN DEVELOPMENT OF SPECIAL EDUCATION RESEARCH AND BARBARA K. KEOGH'S CAREER

One of Professor Keogh's first professional positions was on the psychology staff of the juvenile court and probation office of Oakland, California. Her clients were incarcerated children and adolescents, some abandoned, many abused, and a few who had committed violent felonies. Common to both boys and girls, who otherwise had profoundly different problems, was a "history of early and continuing school problems and a deep antipathy toward school and teachers" (Keogh, in press, p. 6). These observations—the distinct developmental problems (and presumably histories) of boys and girls and their shared distaste for schooling—anticipate career-long interests that parallel evolution of special education research from Keogh's early days in the court and proba-

**3**

tion office to her continuing and active research program at UCLA as the century comes to a close. She wrote in an autobiographical chapter:

> I think my experience as a clinician was invaluable as it provided a solid "real world" base for interpreting psychological theory and for understanding problem behaviors. It also underscored the complexities and individual variations in the development and expression of problems and the seeming weakness of many therapeutic approaches. Over time I found that information collected in clinical protocols was often irrelevant to the problem being considered, and sometimes unnecessarily invaded areas of personal privacy. I also came to realize that many clinical practices were often inefficient and redundant, based on beliefs rather than on evidence of efficacy. These were discouraging observations which were reinforced when I became involved in special education, as there are many controversial and poorly tested interventions with exceptional children. I also found much of the practice of school psychology to be basically psychometric, limited by legalistic school district requirements and by school psychologists' strong testing orientation. I recognized the importance of interventions, but I became increasingly skeptical that we were getting the results we sought, be it in clinical or school settings (Keogh, in press, pp. 7–8).

This skepticism, she noted, helped move her into an academic career of research and teaching. What clinicians were doing in the late 1950s and early 1960s had value, she believed, but it was necessary to develop a research base. As Keogh's academic career began, research in special education began to emerge from numerous strands and in several disciplines. When she accepted a faculty position at UCLA in 1966, few faculty were formally trained in special education, per se, (e.g., Peabody, Illinois, Syracuse were among the few institutions). Into this context, BKK brought her training in developmental psychology, providing a perspective in which children with disabilities were viewed through "developmental lenses." Regardless of their categorical designation, Keogh insisted that they be viewed first and foremost as children who, like nondisabled children, developed in presumably predictable ways.

Looking back now, we can see that her research career unfolded in parallel with the development of special education research. In fact, Keogh's research career roughly spans the same period of time that the field of learning disabilities (LD) has been formally recognized. What Torgesen (chap. 8, this volume) writes with respect to gains in learning disabilities research can be said about the field of special education in general:

> Over the past 2 decades, our general faith in a scientific approach to the study of learning disabilities has borne considerable fruit. During that time, Keogh's voice (Keogh, 1993, 1994; Keogh & MacMillan, 1983) has been both strong and consistent in urging us to frame our questions about learning disabilities from a developmental perspective and answer them using the methods of science. (Torgesen, chap. 8, this volume, p. 157)

A principal example of the parallel development of the field and Keogh's career is the growing appreciation of a developmental perspective. For example, in the past and too often in the present many studies of LD and other special education populations ignored developmental factors (Lyon, chap. 13, this volume). Many investigations examined only one point in time without accounting for developmental differences within a sample, even when they existed. A developmental perspective is required, because patterns of growth and change may vary widely among subgroups of children with high-incidence disabilities. Moreover, human development is seldom linear, and only longitudinal designs permit the investigator to capture the irregular course in developmental trajectories. Understanding how the many personal and social contributions to development and to the expression of disability interact and transact over time requires commitment to longitudinal, developmental research designs.

Because *high-incidence disabilities* are the intersection of mild mental retardation (MMR), learning disabilities (LD), and behavior disorders (BD) [a continuum ranging from socialized delinquency to mild BD to severely emotionally disturbed (SED)], longitudinal efforts should take into account the range of difficulties (comorbidities) manifested by each child. Forness, Kavale, and Walker (chap. 7, this volume) offer compelling evidence that ignoring comorbid conditions can be counterproductive. For instance, in some cases several years pass before a severe emotional or behavioral disorder is recognized as such, very possibly because most children with severe disorders had either premorbid or comorbid conduct or oppositional defiant disorders that masked the symptoms of more serious psychiatric disorders. Such differences can, and often are, easily obscured when categorical affiliation is the independent variable in an investigation. In many instances, parents or guardians may have been aware that something was seriously amiss in their child's social or emotional development as early as preschool. Forness et al.'s discussion speaks eloquently to the idea, often expressed by Keogh, that the study of children with disabilities requires an appreciation of the individual differences among those grouped into disability categories. Forness et al.'s review suggests a rich avenue of research, and reinforces the importance of longitudinal developmental studies of what differential assessment, classification, early intervention, or remediation might be required, depending on the type and manifestations of problems, and the developmental status of the individual.

Werner (chap. 2, this volume) argues that longitudinal developmental research with at-risk children made us cognizant of the following: (a) predictions of future outcomes are more accurate for groups rather than for individuals within groups, (b) outcomes vary according to the time and content of assessment, and (c) at any time, risk conditions may be buffered by the presence of protective factors. Thus, the probability of adverse consequences is not fixed or the same across individuals with developmental disabilities. These caveats apply to all types of research undertaken with a developmental perspective: that is, research that focuses on predisposing risk factors (i.e., parental psychopathology); research that monitors the consequences of an adverse event in the pre-, peri-, and post-natal period (i.e., preterm birth); and research with infants and young children with identified problems (e.g., Down syndrome).

The steady accumulation of *research-based, developmentally sensitive knowledge* is strong evidence that special education research has moved beyond where it was when Professor Keogh worked in a juvenile court. For example, the studies reviewed by Werner (chap. 2, this volume) alert us to a point that Professor Keogh has consistently argued for decades—there are large individual differences among high-risk children in their responses to both negative and positive circumstances in their environment. These variations can, in turn, be expected to show up in evaluation studies of the effects of intervention programs for children with developmental disabilities (Werner, chap. 2, this volume). Beyond what Professor Keogh imagined for special education in the early 1960s, there is now wide appreciation that "research and intervention programs seem to be most useful if they are based on a life-span perspective that goes beyond the narrow confines of the school or therapy setting and demonstrate how effectively individuals with childhood disabilities manage the developmental tasks of adulthood in a world of rapid technological advances and complexity" (Werner, chap. 2, this volume, pp. 28–29). The individual differences that BKK observed in those days at the Oakland court and probation office have turned out to be fundamental scientific issues for special education researchers of today. As the field develops, we can expect developmentally sensitive research that can lead to more individually tailored and effective treatment and intervention efforts.

An understanding of children with high-incidence disabilities and the effective treatment of such children requires an appreciation of the contextual nature of disabilities. For years, Professor Keogh stressed that children develop in a multitude of different environments, but their disability is specifically linked to only one—the school or classroom—and even that context is analyzed inadequately for effects on development. The importance of school, home, peer group, and neighborhood as environments in which development occurs has implications for the study of these children as well as their treatment. Fuchs and Fuchs (chap. 10, this volume) alert us to the effects school-reform efforts, as reflected by the adoption of performance assessments, may have on children with high-incidence disabilities. They note the policy and research implications of this contextual issue, and warn:

> It remains unknown whether schools, in light of constraints on available knowledge and resources, can deliver on promises associated with the implementation of performance assessments. The first order of business is to design technically defensible assessments that can satisfy internal as well as external testing purposes. The second obstacle is to develop methods for helping teachers use these assessments to improve their instructional planning. The third challenge is to identify fair, clear policies that permit students with high-incidence disabilities to participate in these assessment programs in ways that do not threaten their simultaneous, and

sometimes competing, need to accomplish more fundamental skills—such as achieving literacy (Fuchs & Fuchs, chap. 10, this volume, p. 216).

Definitional problems troubled special education when Professor Keogh began her career, and they trouble it still. Lyon (chap. 13, this volume) notes, for example, that the ambiguity inherent in extant definitions of LD leaves the diagnostic and identification process open for wide interpretation and misinterpretation. Imprecise diagnostic decision-making criteria allow some children to be identified as having learning disabilities when they do not, when others with LD are overlooked. Keogh and her colleagues (Keogh, Major-Kingsley, Omori-Gordon, & Reid, 1982) pointed out over 15 years ago that children with LD may differ radically from one another across identifications and programmatic variables, depending on the setting or state from which the sample is collected. Because many research studies have been done with children identified as LD according to these varying and ambiguous criteria (i.e., "school-identified subjects"), our knowledge of LD has reflected ambiguity as well.

Definitional reliability alone is not sufficient, however. MacMillan and Speece (chap. 6, this volume) remind us of Keogh's (1987) view that "definition has meaning only when tied to purpose. Because there are multiple purposes in the LD field, there will continue to be multiple definitions" (Keogh, 1987, p. 97). However, because multiple definitions impede policy, research, and practice, it is folly to try to understand learning disabilities by studying children who are school-identified as LD (Keogh, 1987; Keogh & MacMillan, 1983). The reverse is also true: Studying groups identified by research criteria that bear no resemblance to school-identified children with LD produces findings that cannot possibly inform practitioners about the population they serve. The implications for future research and practice may be disconcerting for some. Because public schools are not in the business of providing pristine samples, researchers, if they are to achieve meaningful progress, must be prepared to bear greater research costs in order to increase the precision of sample selection. It is probably accurate to say that definitional issues are discussed in more sophisticated terms than they were 40 years ago, but definitive statements and consensus continue to elude the field, as MacMillan and Speece's (chap. 6, this volume) discussion suggests.

## BARBARA K. KEOGH'S CONTRIBUTIONS
## TO SPECIAL EDUCATION RESEARCH

The second parallel between the development of a field of research and an individual's career is the contributions of the latter to the former. Distinguished researchers leave their marks, which can be seen in major dimensions of work in the field. Another mark of the most prominent marks BKK left was her introduction of developmental psychology constructs and measures to the study of problems exhibited by children in high incidence categories. One was her interest in some of Jerome Kagan's work on cognitive styles, particularly on impulsivity-reflection studied with the matching familiar figures test. In some ways, this interest was prophetic, given the current interest in the role of impulsivity as a contributing factor in Attention Deficit/Hyperactivity Disorder (ADHD).

A third of BKK's marks concerned the study of temperament. Rothbart and Jones (chap. 3, this volume) note that Professor Keogh has been one of the leaders in research on childhood temperament. Although her work has been particularly focused on the individual child and teacher in the classroom, her contributions to the field extend beyond that setting. She was instrumental in the extension of Thomas and Chess' concept of "goodness of fit" into the classroom. Keogh (1986) argued that "goodness of fit" of the child to the classroom can refer to both curriculum (the tasks presented to the child) and social interactions (peer and teacher).

Keogh's influence on research in social development of children with high-incidence handicaps is apparent in several respects. Rather than looking for convergence on social outcomes across all students with learning disabilities, Keogh has guided us to look for subtypes of students with particular patterns of difficulty and to examine social, cultural, and environmental explanations for these differences. If we are truly going to provide the most effective services for students and their families with special needs, it will only occur when we understand individual differences.

Students with and without learning disabilities overlap considerably on many measures of social functioning, including domains of self-perception, peer acceptance, and friendships. This overlap provides support for Keogh's suggestion that we study children along common dimensions rather than based on school-identified categories. Torgesen (chap. 8, this volume) writes that Professor Keogh helped us think about ways to deal with the problem of heterogeneity among children and adults who are categorized as "learning disabled." Because of the variety of learning disabilities manifested by children and adults, it is not possible to make coherent theoretical or empirical statements about the class as a whole (Keogh et al., 1982; Torgesen, 1993), but rather we should narrow our focus to specific types of learning disabilities (such as disabilities in learning to read,) rather than the larger category of learning disabilities in general.

Finally, in the late 1970s, Professor Keogh began a strand of research that is still in place—the study of children with early developmental delays of uncertain etiology, whose diagnoses and prognoses were ambiguous. In Project REACH (Keogh & Kopp, 1982) children between the ages of 25 and 42 months and their families were recruited; in the most recent follow-up (Bernheimer & Keogh, 1996) they were between 17 and 19 years of age. Project CHILD, begun a decade later (Gallimore, Weisner, Nihira, Keogh, & Bernheimer, 1983), replicated the REACH sampling strategy and enrolled 103 children, who are currently 14 and 15 years of age. In this research, Keogh and her colleagues have addressed a number of issues with which her career is identified: the application of a developmental perspective to children with high-incidence disabilities; the individual differences in patterns of development over time and their predictors (Keogh, Bernheimer, & Guthrie, 1997);

and the range in educational and personal-social outcomes for children with nonspecific developmental delays (Keogh, Coots, & Bernheimer, 1995). Keogh's work in Project CHILD extended to family outcomes as well as child outcomes (Keogh, Bernheimer, Weisner, & Gallimore, 1998), with recent work examining the goodness of fit of main effect and transactional models for testing the influences of family accommodations on child status over time (Keogh, Bernheimer, Garnier, & Gallimore, 1997). Since the passage of Individuals With Disabilities Act (IDEA), the states are increasingly identifying children for services under the developmental delay criteria. Thus, in addition to contributing to research in special education, this body of work has important policy implications. Keogh's research provides compelling evidence that the majority of these children do not "outgrow" their delays and will continue to need services as they get older.

Perhaps Keogh's most indelible contribution to the field of special education research is not widely recognized, because it is seen only in personal contact—her skill in mentoring graduate students and younger colleagues. Her legacy includes a generation of scholars who have been touched by her kind words, encouragement, and tough questions. For example, Sharon Vaughn (personal communication, December 9, 1997) noted:

> As a young researcher who was just beginning my career, I heard a speech by Keogh in which she urged the research community to consider issues regarding the conduct of research from a developmental, longitudinal perspective. In response, my colleague Anne Hogan and I began a 5-year prospective study of a cohort of kindergartners. We were particularly interested in their social functioning prior to and following identification for special education. This initial speech by Keogh, and subsequent conversations, influenced a line of research that has lasted more than 12 years.

Most important, through her mentoring Barbara K. Keogh instills a code of the highest integrity and is not concerned with personal aggrandizement. She was once asked if her children realized how famous she was. Barbara seemed almost startled by the question, as though "fame" had never occurred to her. In typical fashion she replied, "Oh, you know, to them I'm just Mom."

## DEFINING CHALLENGES
## FOR THE NEXT GENERATION

A final parallel between developing fields and distinguished careers lies in the future. In her 1994 paper entitled, "What the Special Education Research Agenda Should Look Like in the Year 2000" (Keogh, 1994b), Professor Keogh set three major challenges for the field. Although she referred to the end of this century, her challenges are sufficiently robust to last well into the 21st century. The three challenges are:

- To amass a solid and comprehensive data base which provides basic descriptive, developmental data on problem conditions—data which could inform prevention and intervention.

- To expand our understanding of at least some of the many individual and contextual influences which impact the development and competence of disabled individuals.

- To document the effectiveness of interventions and the interactions of interventions with individual variations within and across problem conditions.

To meet these challenges, there is much to be done. Happily, Professor Keogh provided us a road map adapted from her 1994 paper, along with some additional comments kindly prepared for this volume:

> First, ... there are many solid and worthwhile studies and projects, but what has *not* emerged to date is a solid body of generalizable evidence that allows us to address practice or which informs needed changes in policy. After several decades of research in special education, we have little definitive to say about prevention and intervention, about developmental data on problem conditions, about competing models of intervention, about the ways in which school programs affect outcomes for exceptional children. My charge to both policy people and researchers is to develop and support a systematic research agenda that brings focus and coherence to our studies.

> Second, I argue that it is essential for researchers to recognize the need for careful and accurate description of problem conditions, of the populations and samples they study ... Opportunistic samples, for example, clinic rosters, school system identified pupils, and volunteer subjects come from essentially unknown or inadequately defined populations, and may not represent an accurate nor complete expression of particular problem conditions—thus, the limits on generalization and inference, as well as on implications for interventions. For those who know me this is a familiar refrain, because it is central to the notion of the need for an accepted marker system for describing study samples. Closely related, considerable evidence documents that variations within cultural groups may be greater than variations between cultures. Thus, summarizing demographics such as socioeconomic, ethnic, and cultural status provides only limited insights into the functioning of families and schools. Ethnicity and culture might productively be considered as independent variables in research with special populations.

> Third, it is increasingly clear that to understand problem conditions and what to do about them we must take into account the context in which they occur. Schools and classrooms are complex social systems that differ in the physical organization of space; the demands of the curriculum; the "mix" of children; and the attitudes, beliefs, and competencies of teachers. Thus, it is clearly an error to assume that "schooling," like ethnicity or culture, is a common effect. We need methods and measures to describe both families and schools at proximal levels.

Fourth, it follows from the last point that at least part of our effort must be put into research and development carried out in the field. Traditional academic research is almost by definition theory based and context free. Its goal is propositional knowledge that can be generalized across settings and time. This is a worthwhile and important scientific goal, yet students are instructed in schools that are bound by local conditions and local cultures that drive practice. To affect practice, then, it is necessary to understand and appreciate local knowledge. Special education research from this perspective is not simple to carry out, and will not be quick. There will be many failed projects and negative findings, but these will inform us if they are part of a coherent program of work.

Fifth, both policymakers and researchers together must determine what problems represent necessary and legitimate topics for study. What policies require evidence, and what policies stand on social value alone? Expressed differently, how much evidence is needed before we offer services to exceptional individuals? Do all policy decisions require comprehensive research evidence? The answer is probably no, because both empirical findings and common sense support action in many areas as for example, educational programs for young, at-risk children. The role of research in such instances is to develop and test implementation efforts, to determine what works for whom and why in what conditions, to find better and more effective ways to achieve the policy goals, and to provide evidence that can inform policy (Keogh, 1994b).

Finally, special education has a relatively long history, one filled with good intentions and strong advocacy. We have seen a range of methods and approaches to interventions with children with special needs, many of these controversial and lacking systematic tests. Indeed, many programs have been based on strongly held beliefs rather than on evidence of effectiveness. In my view, the field has matured to a point that we are ready to move beyond advocacy to evidence, to test our treatments with data, and to draw reasoned generalizations and inferences. From a developmental perspective, we have gotten through adolescence and moved into adulthood. It is time that our research reflects our growing maturity as a field (Keogh, private communication, January 15, 1998).

These challenges represent an investigative agenda for the next generation of researchers in special education. They also reflect habits of mind that we would do well to take up at the same time we ponder her challenges. Her students, colleagues, and friends know that Professor Keogh is a very nice person in possession of a very tough mind. There are legends surrounding her ability to pose a question that unhinges even the most confident researcher or graduate student. She is modest about this question-posing skill, because to her it merely reflects the residue of what it is that researchers ought to be doing more often. In her challenge to the field to face the issues of the next century, and in her characteristically generous manner, she reveals the origin of the legendary questions and urges us all to visit there more often.

We are only seven years away from the year 2000 and we have a long way to go in a short time. I am reminded again of the observation of Donald Broadbent (1973), an eminent British experimentalist, who summarized a set of studies carried out in his Cambridge laboratory. He then added "experiment having failed, I decided it was necessary to start thinking" (p. 72). ... We are now in a time of enormous change, and the potential for progress is real. At the same time there are many threats to progress, some from social/political and economic conditions, others from conflicts and dissensions within our profession. Real progress requires that we address both policy and research issues. As a start I paraphrase Broadbent and suggest that we are forced to think. (Keogh, 1994b, p. 68)

## REFERENCES

Bernheimer, L. P., & Keogh, B. K. (1996). *Project REACH follow-up report.* Los Angeles: University of California.

Broadbent, D. E. (1973). *In defense of empirical psychology.* London: Metheun.

Gallimore, R., Weisner, T. S., Nihira, K., Keogh, B. K., & Bernheimer, L. P. (1983). *Ecocultural opportunity and family accommodation to developmentally delayed children.* Research proposal submitted to the National Institute of Child Health and Human Development. Sociobehavioral Research Group, Mental Retardation Research Center, University of California, Los Angeles.

Keogh, B. K. (1986). Future of the LD field: Research and practice. *Journal of Learning Disabilities, 19,* 455–460.

Keogh, B. K. (1987). A shared attribute model of learning disabilities. In S. Vaughn & C. Bos (Eds.), *Research in learning disabilities: Issues and future directions* (pp. 3–18). Boston: College-Hill.

Keogh, B. K. (1993). Linking purpose and practice: Social-political and developmental perspectives on classification. In G.R. Lyon, D.B. Gray, J.F. Kavanagh, & N.A. Krasnegor (Eds.), *Better understanding learning disabilities: New views from research and their implications for education and public policies* (pp. 311–323). Baltimore: Brookes.

Keogh, B. K. (1994a). A matrix of decision points in the measurement of learning disabilities. In G.R. Lyon (Ed.), *Frames of reference for the assessment of learning disabilities: New views on measurement issues* (pp. 15–26). Baltimore: Brookes.

Keogh, B. K. (1994b). What the special education research agenda should look like in the year 2000. *Learning Disabilities Research & Practice, 9*(2), 62–69.

Keogh, B. K. (in press). A professional life in family context. In L.T. Hoshmand (Ed.), *Creativity and moral vision in psychology: Narratives on identity and commitment in a postmodern age* (pp. 00-00). Thousand Oaks, CA: Sage.

Keogh, B. K., Bernheimer, L.P., Garnier, H.E., & Gallimore, R. (1997). *Models of change for children with developmental delays: Child-driven or transactional?* Manuscript submitted for publication.

Keogh, B. K., Bernheimer, L. P., & Guthrie, D. (1997). Stability and change over time in cognitive level of children with delays. *American Journal on Mental Retardation, 101,* 365–373.

Keogh, B. K., Bernheimer, L. P., Weisner, T. S., & Gallimore, R. (1998). Child and family outcomes over time: A longitudinal perspective on developmental delays. In M. Lewis & C. Feiring (Eds.), *Families, risk, and competence* (pp. 269–287). Mahwah NJ: Lawrence Erlbaum Associates.

Keogh, B. K., Coots, J. J., & Bernheimer, L. P. (1995). School placement of children with nonspecific developmental delays. *Journal of Early Intervention, 20,* 65–78.

Keogh, B. K., & Kopp, C. B. (1982). *Project Reach final report.* Los Angeles: University of California.

Keogh, B. K., & MacMillan, D. L. (1983). The logic of sample selection: Who represents what? *Exceptional Education Quarterly, 4,* 84–96.

Keogh, B. K., Major-Kingsley, S., Omori-Gordon, H., & Reid, H. P. (1982). *A system of marker variables for the field of learning disabilities.* Syracuse, NY: Syracuse University Press.

Torgesen, J. K. (1993). Variations on theory in learning disabilities. In R. Lyon, D. Gray, N. Krasnegor, & J. Kavenagh (Eds.), *Better understanding learning disabilities: Perspectives on classification, identification, and assessment and their Implications for education and policy* (pp.153–170). Baltimore, MD: Brookes.

# 2 ✤ Risk and Protective Factors in the Lives of Children With High-Incidence Disabilities

**Emmy E. Werner**
*University of California, Davis*

Barbara Keogh, whose distinguished contributions to special education we honor in this volume, reminds us that effective programs of assessment, prevention and intervention need to consider not only the risk factors in the lives of children with developmental disabilities, but also the protective factors that allow some of these individuals to make a successful transition into adolescence and adulthood (Keogh & Weisner, 1993). Longitudinal research with "at-risk" children has made us cognizant of the fact that (a) predictions of future outcomes are more accurate for groups rather than for individuals within groups, (b) outcomes vary according to the time and content of assessment, and (c) at any time risk conditions may be buffered by the presence of protective factors. Thus, the probability of adverse consequences is not fixed or the same across individuals with developmental disabilities. These caveats apply to all types of research undertaken with a developmental perspective: that is, research that focuses on predisposing risk factors (e.g., parental psychopathology); research that monitors the consequences of an adverse event in the pre-, peri-, and postnatal period (e.g., preterm birth); and research with infants and young children with identified problems (e.g., Down syndrome).

Because of major technological advances, risk research is currently paying increased attention to genetic and prenatal risk factors, and to the small-for-gestational-age (SGA) survivors of neonatal intensive care. Attention to psychosocial postnatal risk factors (such as child abuse) has increased as well. The impact of poverty—the major risk factor for one out of four children in the United States today—has remained a persistent concern, especially for behavioral scientists who focus on the lives of minority children. Table 2.1 lists some of the more common risk factors.

**15**

## TABLE 2.1
### Risk Factors Associated With High-Incidence Disabilities
### in Children

| Prenatal Period | Perinatal Period | Postnatal Period |
| --- | --- | --- |
| Chromosomal abnormalities | Anoxia | Cerebral trauma |
| Inborn errors of metabolism | Congenital defects | Encephalitis |
| Harmful drugs | Disorders of labor and delivery | Micronutrient deficiencies |
| Nutritional deprivation | Low birthweight | Toxic substances |
| Maternal infections | Infections | Family dysfunction |
| Metabolic disorders | Metabolic disorders | Parental mental illness |
| Radiation | Neonatal intracranial hemorrhage | Parental substance abuse |
| Toxic agents | | Child abuse |

Longitudinal studies in North America and Europe that have followed young children over extended periods of time have consistently demonstrated that the negative effects of many biological risk factors diminish with the passage of time, and that the developmental outcome of virtually every risk condition ever studied in children depends on the quality of the caregiving environment, and on how the child himself or herself affects that environment (Werner & Smith, 1992).

We know now that individuals with developmental disabilities do not simply react to their environment. Instead, they are actively engaged in an attempt to organize and structure their world and to seek their niche in it. There is also a growing awareness of the importance of monitoring the development of such children within the various social contexts in which they grow up, taking account of the changing demands made on them within a variety of settings, such as the hospital, the home, the neighborhood, the school, and the community at large (Werner, Randolph, & Masten, 1996).

## METHODOLOGICAL ISSUES

Methodological issues that have confronted researchers who study the buffering process of protective factors in the lives of children and youth with high-incidence developmental disabilities include the selection of age- (or stage-) appropriate measures of adaptation, the need to use multiple criteria to determine "successful outcome," the need for normal control groups, and the need to observe individuals at multiple measurement points in time. Age at first identification of the developmental disability; severity and chronicity, and the developmental stage at which the follow-ups take place all may play a role in determining the impact of the disability and the likelihood of a more or less successful outcome (Spekman, Goldberg, & Herman, 1993).

Just as risk factors and stressful life events may co-occur within a particular population of individuals with developmental disabilities or within a particular developmental period, protective factors are also likely to occur together to some degree (Seifer & Sameroff, 1987). Assessing the overall pattern of external and internal resources alerts us to the possibility of one resource substituting for another in successfully coping with a developmental disability. The task of delineating such interconnections should become an important agenda in future longitudinal studies of the life course of individuals with developmental disabilities and in the evaluation of intervention programs.

Garmezy, Masten, and Tellegen (1984) hypothesized that protective factors may operate through three different mechanisms: compensation, challenge, and immunization. In the compensatory model, risk factors and protective factors are seen as combining in the prediction of (good or poor) outcome. In the challenge model, a high-risk condition can become a potential enhancer of competence (provided that the degree of stress it causes is not excessive), and the relationship between the effects of risk and protective factors may therefore be curvilinear. In the immunity model, there is a conditional relationship between risk and protective factors: Such factors may buffer the stressful impact of a developmental disability on the quality of an individual's adaptation, but may have no detectable effects in the absence of a disability.

Keogh and Weisner (1993) tested the predictive power of alternate models using data from two ongoing longitudinal studies of children with mild developmental delays (Project CHILD and REACH). In their preliminary data analyses that extend from early to middle childhood, the compensatory model yielded the highest association with outcome. The strongest association was between Stanford Binet IQ scores and the compensatory model scores. The compensatory, challenge, and immunity models may not be mutually exclusive; they may operate simultaneously or successively in the adaptive repertoire of individuals with developmental disabilities, depending on the nature of the disability and developmental stage. The impact of specific risk and protective factors may vary relative to the child's age, to the severity of the problem condition, and possibly to the child's gender. This is an important issue for future research.

## FOLLOW-UP STUDIES INTO ADULTHOOD

There are only a few studies that have looked at the interplay between risk and protective factors in the adult lives of children with behavioral disorders, learning disabilities, and mild mental retardation. Among a handful of investigations with a life-span perspective is the Kauai Longitudinal Study with which I have been associated during the past 3 decades.

This study has involved a team of pediatricians, psychologists, and public health and social workers who have monitored the impact of a variety of biological and psychosocial risk factors, stressful life events, and protective factors on the development of a multiethnic cohort of 698 children, born in 1955 on the "Garden Island" in the Hawaiian chain. These individuals were followed, with relatively little attrition, from birth to ages 1, 2, 10, 18, 32, and, most recently, age 40. A detailed description of the methodology, database and results of this study can be found in *Overcoming the Odds: High Risk Children from Birth to Adulthood* (Werner & Smith, 1992).

We were able to obtain follow-up data in adulthood (at ages 32 and 40) on some 80% of the individuals in this cohort who had been diagnosed as having behavior disorders, learning disabilities, or mild mental retardation at ages 10 and/or 18. Our criteria for evaluating the quality of their adult adaptation were based on two perspectives: the individual's own account of success and satisfaction with work, family and social life, and their state of well-being; and on their records in the community. The latter included court records; records from the state departments of health and mental health, social service and vocational rehabilitation agencies, and the U.S. Veterans Administration (for men and women who had served in the Armed Forces).

The following criteria were used to define successful coping in adulthood:

*School/work*: Is employed and/or is enrolled in school; is satisfied with work and/or school achievement.

*Relationship with spouse/mate*: Is married or in long-term committed relationship; is satisfied with partner and reports little or no conflict. No record of desertion, divorce, or spouse abuse in court files.

*Relationship with children*: Evaluates children positively; is satisfied with parental role. No record of child abuse or delinquent child-support payments in court files.

*Relationship with peers*: Has several close friends who provide emotional support when needed; is satisfied with those relationships. No record of assault, battery, rape, or other criminal offenses in court files.

*Self-assessment*: Is (mostly) satisfied with present state of life; reports no dependency on alcohol or drugs; no psychosomatic illnesses. No record of psychiatric disorders in Mental Health Register.

## CHILDREN WITH BEHAVIOR DISORDERS

*At age 10*, 25 youngsters in this cohort (some 3.5%) had been identified by diagnostic tests and observations of clinical psychologists and child psychiatrists as having serious behavior disorders that interfered with their school achievement. Twenty (80%) of these children had conduct problems and displayed overt antisocial behavior. Among the other five were two diagnosed as adjustment reactions to childhood, and one each with a diagnosis of childhood neurosis, schizoid personality, and sociopathic personality.

*By age 18*, the number of individuals with serious behavior disorders had grown to 70 youths (some 10% of the cohort, including 23 males and 47 females). Their diagnoses ranged from problems of sexual identity to neurotic symptoms; hysteria; severe depression (including two suicide attempts); obsessive compulsive behavior; and paranoid, schizoid behavior. Half of the males and one third of the females in this group also had records of juvenile offenses. For both sexes, a combination of moderate to severe perinatal stress, a low standard of living, and distressing temperamental traits in infancy were predictive of serious behavior disorders in middle childhood. A combination of serious behavior and learning problems with a moderate to marked physical handicap by age 10 was, in turn, the most powerful set of predictors of behavior disorders by age 18. The predictability of behavior disorders improved considerably from the early to the middle childhood years, especially for children of the poor.

*By age 32*, a significant shift in life trajectories from risk to adaptation had taken place in about half of the individuals who had been diagnosed as having behavior disorders in their childhood or youth. The proportion of "troubled" youths who showed spontaneous recovery in adulthood in this Pacific Asian cohort are identical with those reported by Robins (1978) in her follow-up studies of "deviant" Black and White children in St. Louis, and by Magnusson (1988) in his longitudinal study of a cohort of Swedish youngsters who were of approximately the same age as the children of Kauai.

Only a minority of the troubled youths needed mental health services or vocational rehabilitation by the time they reached their early 30s, but a higher proportion of males than females in this group had grown into adults who had difficulties finding and keeping a job, who had marriages that ended in divorce, who were delinquent in child or spouse support, and who had criminal records.

*By age 40*, a third of those with behavior disorders in their childhood or teens had some continuing midlife problems, including difficulties with finding and keeping a job during a period of economic recession on the island, and problems in marital relationships. The overwhelming majority, however, were in stable marriages and jobs, were satisfied with their relationships with their spouses and teenage children, and were responsible citizens in their community.

Looking back at the lives of the men and women who had made a successful adaptation to adulthood, we noted a number of protective factors in the individuals and their families that appeared to have contributed to positive changes in their life trajectories. Such persons tended to be first-born or only children who had been considered cuddly and affectionate infants. Most had been active babies who had shown normal physical development in early childhood. None had suffered any central nervous system impairment. None had any physical handicaps, and few suffered from serious childhood illnesses. By age 10 they had higher mean scores on a nonverbal measure of problem-solving ability than did youths who grew into a troubled adulthood.

Most of the youths whose behavioral problems persisted into adulthood had grown up in single-parent households during their teens, whereas youths who had recovered grew up in homes where both parents were present. The majority had household chores to attend to, and their parents provided structure and rules for them.

Only a third of the individuals with behavior disorders in childhood and/or adolescence had received some counseling or psychotherapy by the time they reached adulthood. A significant minority (one out of five men, one out of three women) had converted to fundamentalist religions that assured them salvation, security, and a sense of mission. The most significant turning point for the majority of adults with childhood behavior disorders, however, was meeting a supportive friend or marrying an accepting spouse.

Overall, the outlook in adulthood for individuals who had been shy and lacked confidence as children was considerably better than for youths who displayed antisocial behavior, or for children whose parents had chronic mental health problems, and who had been exposed to serious perinatal complications. Similar findings have been reported from studies with other ethnic groups on the U.S. mainland and in Europe (Caspi, Elder, & Bem, 1988; Mednick, Cudeck, Griffith, Talovis, & Schulsinger, 1984; Patterson, DeBaryshe, & Ramsey, 1989).

At both age 32 and age 40, less than 10% of the individuals with behavior disorders in childhood or adolescence rated mental health professionals as helpful in times of stress or crisis. For the two adulthood follow-ups, mental health professionals ranked 12th among 14 sources of support, far behind spouses/mates, parents, siblings, members of the extended family, friends, co-workers, teachers/mentors, ministers, and faith and prayer. Only self-help organizations and pets were chosen by a slightly lower percentage of respondents as helpful in difficult and/or stressful times.

## CHILDREN WITH LEARNING DISABILITIES AND ATTENTION DEFICIT HYPERACTIVE DISORDERS

Among the 1955 cohort of the Kauai Longitudinal Study were 22 children (13 males; 9 females) who had been diagnosed as learning disabled on the basis of the following criteria:

1. Evidence of serious reading problems (i.e., reading more than one grade below age expectancy), despite average or above-average performance on the Wechsler Intelligence Scale for Children (WISC).

2. WISC subtest scores characterized by a great deal of scatter, with a discrepancy of more than one standard deviation between Verbal and Performance IQ.

3. Behavior checklists, completed independently by teachers and parents, that noted that the child was persistently "distractible," "hyperactive," and/or "unable to concentrate."

A combination of low birthweight (< 2,500 gm), a congenital defect, and a low standard of living and maternal education were the most powerful early predictors for the girls in this group. A combination of moderate-severe perinatal stress, maternal ratings of high activity level and low social responsiveness at age 1, and a home rated low in family stability in early childhood were the most effective early predictors for the boys in this group.

In the time span between ages 10 and 18, four fifths of the youths diagnosed as learning disabled had some contacts with community agencies. Rates for contacts with the Department of Education's Office of Special Services, the high school counselors, the Department of Health, and the judiciary system (police and Family Court) were significantly higher than for youths of the same age and gender who were not learning disabled.

Group tests, administered in Grade 12, confirmed a picture of poor scholastic performance and serious underachievement. At age 17/18, these individuals scored significantly lower than did their peers on measures of self-assurance and interpersonal adequacy, socialization and responsibility, achievement motivation, and intellectual efficiency.

Had we concluded our follow-up of the learning disabled at the threshold of adulthood, we would have come up with an overwhelmingly negative prognosis (see Kavale, 1988). Only one out of four learning-disabled children, identified by age 10, had improved their lot by age 18; the few lucky ones who did gave credit to the sustained emotional support of family members, peer friends or elders who bolstered their self-esteem. In contrast, most of the learning-disabled teenagers considered intervention by counselors, mental health professionals, and special education teachers "of little help."

During our two follow-ups in adulthood, at ages 32 and 40, we were able to obtain interview data (about work, family, and social life), an assessment of their state of health and well-being, as well as community records from 80% of the learning-disabled individuals. By age 32, the life course of *most* adults diagnosed as learning disabled in childhood had considerably improved. Less than 10% had criminal records or persistent mental health problems—in contrast to 27% with delinquency records and 32% with serious mental health problems in adolescence. Their marriage and divorce rates were similar to the 1955 cohort as a whole, as was their employment rate. None were unemployed or relied on welfare payments. The majority worked in service jobs or as skilled technicians.

One half of the individuals with learning disabilities went on to obtain additional schooling after high school. Three out of four were judged to have made a successful adaptation to the demands of work, marriage, and family life at age 32. Eight years later, at age 40, the same proportion, three out of four, among the individuals with childhood learning disabilities were making an adequate to good adaptation to midlife. Despite a downturn in the economy, none were unemployed, although one out of four worried about their job security and stress-related health problems.

Several clusters of protective factors appeared in the interviews and records of individuals with learning disabilities who had made a successful adult adaptation:

Cluster 1 included temperamental characteristics of the individual that helped him or her to elicit positive responses from a variety of caring persons: parents, teachers, friends, spouses, and coworkers.

Cluster 2 included special skills and talents as well as the motivation to use efficiently whatever abilities they had; faith that the odds could be overcome, realistic educational and vocational plans, and regular chores and domestic responsibilities assumed as children and teenagers.

Cluster 3 included characteristics and caregiving styles of the parents, especially the mother, that reflected competence and fostered self-esteem in their offspring, and structures and rules in the household that gave their children a sense of security.

Cluster 4 consisted of supportive adults who fostered trust and acted as gatekeepers for the future. Among these "surrogate" parents were grandparents, elder mentors, youth leaders, and members of church groups.

Cluster 5 consisted of openings of opportunities at major life transitions—from high school to the workplace, from civilian to military life, from single to married status and parenthood—that turned the life trajectories of the majority of individuals with learning disabilities on the path to a successful adult adaptation.

There are only a handful of other studies in the literature that have focused on protective factors in the lives of individuals with learning disabilities who have made a successful transition into adulthood (Brooks, 1994; Miller, 1996). Some of the key factors that enabled them to "overcome the odds" included self-understanding and acceptance, realistic goal setting, and perseverance, as well as supportive adults in their family and/or community. Spekman, Goldberg, and Herman (1992) found that, in early adulthood, successful men and women with learning disabilities expressed a strong sense of being in control of their fate. They believed that they were not passive victims of their disabilities, but agents capable of changing their lives. They were able to "dose challenges" for themselves, and had developed effective strategies for coping and reducing stress. They also sought, accepted, and appreciated the support and counsel provided by members of their family and/or community.

Reiff, Gerber, and Ginsberg (1997) identified a nearly identical set of factors in their study of learning-disabled adults who "exceeded expectations." Their model of success focused on their ability to take control—a set of conscious decisions to take charge of their lives, to adapt to changing circumstances and to move ahead. A realistic goal orientation, persistence, and "learned creativity" (i.e., reliance on special talents and skills they had developed to cope with their learning disability) enabled these men and women to attain a remarkable degrees of personal, social and vocational success. Rogan and Hartman (1990) and Vogel, Hruby, and Adelman (1993) reported that such compensatory strategies and high-achievement motivation were related to both educational and employment success in college students with learning disabilities.

In a review of long-term outcomes of children with attention deficit hyperactive disorders (ADHD), Hechtman (1991) noted that individuals with positive outcomes in adulthood shared a number of protective factors that had been found in other follow-up studies of successful men and women with learning disabilities. They tended to have higher initial IQ scores and lower initial scores on hyperactivity and distractibility, had the ability to tolerate frustration, and grew up in a home environment that fostered emotional stability in the child.

In addition to these personal qualities within the individual that served a protective function, a support network within the family and community enhanced the likelihood of successful outcomes. Successful adults with learning disabilities and ADHD actively sought and utilized the advice and support of family members, teachers, friends, employers, or coworkers (Reiff et al., 1997; Spekman et al., 1992; Weiss & Hechtman, 1986). In addition, they purposefully selected their mentors, and help was provided by a supportive spouse.

In sum: Studies of the adult lives of individuals with learning disabilities inform us that a substantial number (but by no means all!) are enjoying satisfying, successful, and meaningful lives. They alert us to the need to look beyond the horizons of special education to ways in which we can provide a continuum of services to them that reduce the likelihood of negative chain reactions associated with a learning disability, promote self-esteem and efficacy, and offer second chances in later life (Werner, 1993).

## CHILDREN WITH MILD MENTAL RETARDATION

Among the children in the Kauai Longitudinal Study, those diagnosed with mild mental retardation had fewer prospects of positive adaptation in adulthood than did most children with behavior disorders or learning disabilities. There were 19 individuals (approximately 3% of the surviving children in the 1955 birth cohort) who were diagnosed as having mild mental retardation by age 10 and placed in classes for the educable mentally retarded before federal legislation mandated their inclusion in regular classroom activities.

An infant test score (Cattell IQ) below 80 at age 2, when all children received pediatric and psychologic examinations as part of the study, was the most powerful predictor of mild mental retardation at age 10. The predictive power of the results of the infant test increased with the addition of information on pre-perinatal biological factors for the girls (i.e., the presence of a congenital defect) and with the inclusion of information on the early caregiving environment (family instability; a mother with little education who had experienced psychological trauma during pregnancy) for the boys. The majority of the children with mild mental retardation at age 10 (three out of four) had grown up in poverty.

In adulthood, we were able to obtain follow-up data on 75% of the mildly mentally retarded. Eight percent had died by age 40, and 8% were unemployed—rates twice as high as those for the cohort as a whole. Most of the mildly mentally retarded women were housewives; the mildly retarded men tended to hold unskilled or semi-skilled jobs as service workers. Most of these jobs were in the tourist industry on the island that was negatively affected by a series of economic recessions and by hurricane Iniki that devastated Kauai in the early 1990s.

Only a third of the individuals in this group managed to make a satisfactory midlife adaptation. The quality of their adaptation seemed to be related to their level of intelligence: The two thirds with poor adaptation (at work and in family life) at age 40 had IQ scores at age 10 that were significantly lower than those with adequate to good adaptation in mid life (55 vs. 68). Personality and motivational factors also appeared to make a difference, such as getting along with others, having a pleasant, "easygoing" personality, and support of an extended family, especially siblings.

Our numbers are small, but our findings complement the results of a study of 19-year-old Swedish men by Granat and Granat (1978). These investigators noted that only about half of the persons with IQs below 70 had been identified as being mentally retarded. Others, who were equally impaired intellectually, only became identified after taking IQ tests when drafted into the army. The features that distinguished the two groups were personality and motivational factors, such as social skills, being "upbeat," being prompt, and staying on task at school or on the job.

Recent work in the United States has also pointed to the importance of personality-motivational factors as determinants of life success among the mildly mentally retarded. In a study of individuals with IQs between 70 and 84 (borderline mental retardation) during the year following high school, Zetlin and Murtaugh (1990) found that many of these young adults were performing poorly in work and school. Some of their problems were due to disagreements with bosses or coworkers, an inability to persist at job or school over many months, and other motivational problems.

Issues related to personality and motivation will become more critical over the next few years, as public schools continue to declassify students who previously had been identified as mentally retarded, and who then tend to fall between the cracks in the educational and vocational rehabilitation system. We urgently need to understand how personality and motivational characteristics help or hinder these individuals as they look for a place within our society (Hodapp & Zigler, 1995).

## PROTECTIVE FACTORS: A SUMMARY

Despite the heterogeneity of the developmental disabilities that have been the focus of this review, one can begin to discern a common core of individual dispositions and sources of support that act as protective buffers in the lives of the men and women who have made a successful transition into adulthood. They have been reported in studies of African-Americans, Whites, and Pacific Asians, who grew up in poverty as well as relative affluence, and among indi-

### TABLE 2.2
### Protective Factors Within the Individual Replicated in Two or More Follow-Up Studies of Children With High-Incidence Disabilities

| Protective Factors | Developmental Period |
|---|---|
| "Easy," engaging temperament | Infancy-childhood |
| Age-appropriate self-help skills | Early-middle childhood |
| Practical problem solving skills | Childhood-adulthood |
| Special talents | Childhood-adulthood |
| Positive self-concept | Childhood-adulthood |
| Impulse control | Childhood-adulthood |
| Achievement motivation | Childhood-adulthood |
| Planning, foresight | Adolescence-adulthood |
| Persistence | Adolescence-adulthood |
| Faith, a sense of coherence | Adolescence-adulthood |
| Internal locus of control | Adolescence-adulthood |

viduals who resided in countries with different health and educational policies (the United States, Canada, Denmark, and Sweden). These protective buffers appear to transcend ethnic, social class, and geographic boundaries. Tables 2.2 and 2.3 examine these buffers more closely.

Several clusters of protective factors have emerged as recurrent themes in follow-up studies of children with developmental disabilities who managed to grow into competent and confident adults. Some protective factors are internal resources that help the individual to cope successfully with his or her disability; others are external sources of support in the family and community.

Such individuals tend to be engaging to other people, elders and peers alike. They have good communication and practical problem-solving skills, including the ability to actively recruit substitute caregivers and mentors. They have a talent or special skill that is valued by the community, they are motivated to do the best they can with the abilities they have, and they have faith that their own actions can make a positive difference in their lives.

They also have supportive family members who provide them with affectional ties that encourage trust, autonomy, and initiative. Among them are parents, grandparents, siblings, and spouses. There are also supportive

## TABLE 2.3
### Protective Factors Within the Family and Community Replicated in Two or More Follow-Up Studies of Children With High-Incidence Disabilities

| Protective Factors | Developmental Period |
| --- | --- |
| Low birth order | Infancy |
| Small family size (three or fewer children) | Infancy |
| Maternal competence | Infancy-adolescence |
| Close bond with primary caregiver | Infancy-adolescence |
| Supportive grandparents | Infancy-adolescence |
| Supportive siblings | Childhood-adulthood |
| Structure and rules in household | Childhood-adolescence |
| Assigned chores ("required helpfulness") | Childhood-adolescence |
| Supportive teachers | Preschool-adulthood |
| Mentors (elders or peers) | Childhood-adulthood |
| Success experiences in school or extracurricular activities | Childhood-adulthood |
| Supportive spouse or mate | Adulthood |
| Supportive friends | Adulthood |
| Supportive co-workers or boss | Adulthood |
| Supportive church community | Adulthood |

teachers, mentors, and friends in the community at large that reinforce and reward their efforts and provide them with positive role models.

## THE SHIFTING BALANCE BETWEEN VULNERABILITY AND RESILIENCY

Just as the degrees of vulnerability among individuals with developmental disabilities is relative, depending on complex interactions among constitutional factors and life's circumstances at different points in the developmental cycle, so their resilience is governed by a similar dynamic interaction among the internal and external resources from which they can draw. Longitudinal studies, like ours, that have followed "at-risk" children from birth to adulthood have found a shifting balance between stressful life events that heighten children's vulnerability and protective factors that enhance their resilience. This balance changes not only with the different stages of the life cycle, but also varies with gender. During the first decades of life, boys tended to be more vulnerable and "at risk" for developmental disabilities; in the second decade of life more girls were susceptible, especially for behavior disorders associated with teenage pregnancies. In the third and fourth decade of life, however, more women than men appeared to make a successful transition into early adulthood and midlife.

However, a significant proportion of those individuals who had "recovered" expressed a persistent need to detach themselves emotionally from parents and siblings whose domestic problems still threatened to engulf them. This was especially true for adult children of alcoholics, some of whom had been physically and emotionally abused when they were growing up (Werner & Smith, 1992). The balancing act between forming new attachments to loved ones of their choice and the loosening of old family ties that evoked painful memories exacted a toll in their adult lives. The price they paid varied from stress-related health problems to a certain aloofness in interpersonal relationships, especially among the men, some of whom were still single at age 40.

On the positive side, we found that the opening of opportunities at major life transitions (entry into the world of work, marriage, parenthood) enabled the majority of the youths with learning disabilities and behavior disorders to rebound in their 20s and 30s. Among the most potent second chances for such individuals were adult education programs, military service, active participation in a church community, and a supportive friend or spouse.

## LINKS BETWEEN PROTECTIVE FACTORS
## AND SUCCESSFUL ADULT ADAPTATION
## OF INDIVIDUALS WITH DEVELOPMENTAL DISABILITIES

When we examined the links between protective factors within the individual and outside sources of support, we noted that children with developmental disabilities who made a successful transition into adulthood had certain dispositions that led them to select or construct supportive environments that rewarded their efforts and sustained their motivation and perseverance. Although parental competence and the sources of support available to them in their family were modestly linked to the quality of their adult adaptation, these factors made less of a contribution to a successful outcome in adulthood than did the individuals' competencies, self-esteem, and temperamental dispositions. Many of the high risk youths left adverse conditions in their homes and their island community after high school and sought environments that they found more compatible. In short, they picked their own niches (Scarr & McCartney, 1983).

Protective factors within the individuals (e.g., a pleasing, easy-going temperament, practical problem-solving skills, a positive self-concept, and an internal locus of control) tended to make a greater impact on the quality of adult adaptation for females with childhood disabilities. Outside sources of support (both in the family and community) tended to make a greater difference in the lives of the males with developmental disabilities (Werner, 1993; Werner & Smith, 1992).

## IMPLICATIONS FOR RESEARCH AND INTERVENTION

It needs to be emphasized that most of the studies reviewed here include children with developmental disabilities that were diagnosed before Public Law 99-457 and IDEA (Public Law 101-476) were passed by the U.S. Congress. In the past 10 years, many more "at-risk" children and their families have been served by early childhood intervention programs (Kirk, Gallagher, & Anastasiow, 1997). It is to be hoped that the Individual Family Service Plan (IFSP) and the Individualized Education Plan (IEP) mandated by federal legislation will focus not only on ameliorating or eliminating risk factors in the lives of developmentally disabled children, but also strengthen and increase the number of protective factors from which they can draw. These include competencies and sources of informal support that already exist in the family and community that can be utilized to enlarge a child's repertoire of problem-solving skills, and can enhance his or her self-esteem.

Certainly the studies reviewed here provide us with a more hopeful perspective than can be gleaned from reading only the literature on children who succumb to the negative consequences of biological insults and/or caregiving deficits. They alert us to the fact that there are large individual differences among high-risk children in their responses to both negative and positive circumstances in their environment—variations that we will, no doubt, also discover in evaluation studies of the effect of intervention programs for children with developmental disabilities.

Research and intervention programs for individuals with developmental disabilities require an ecological perspective that takes into account the different demands made on the young person in the context of the home, the school, the neighborhood, the world of work, and the community at large. It requires interdisciplinary cooperation to forge a chain of protective factors that reduce the negative impact of a childhood disability, increase an individual's efficacy, and open up opportunities for success. Such intervention necessitates the professional skills of pediatricians, psychologists, special educators, and therapists. But it also must rely on the cooperation of members of the extended family, caring neighbors, and mentors who can play an enabling role in the lives of the child with a developmental disability. These informal ties need to be encouraged and strengthened, not displaced by formal intervention programs.

Research and intervention programs seem to be most useful if they are based on a life-span perspective that goes beyond the narrow confines of the school or therapy setting and demonstrate how effectively individuals with childhood disabilities manage the developmental tasks of adulthood in a world of rapid technological advances and complexity. Such questions can only be answered by long-term follow-up studies that can inform us about the benefits, the cost, and—ultimately—the limits of intervention (Pless & Stein, 1994; Werner, 1994).

Both research and intervention programs need to pay more attention to ecological context variables that mediate the expression of potentially harmful biological and psychosocial events over time. Such an approach calls for the application of statistical techniques (both in research and evaluation programs) that capture the reciprocal nature of the interactions between the child with a developmental disability and the changing contexts in which he or she lives. It requires a synthesis of the perspectives of the clinician who sensitively monitors the behavior of the child, and that of the ethnographer who carefully observes the world in which the child's life unfolds.

Future research that focuses on the life course of developmentally disabled children in the context of their families also could profit from the use of behavior genetic strategies. Many stressful experiences, such as parental mental illness or substance abuse, impinge differently on different siblings in the same family. Therefore, we need to look more carefully at the contributions of shared versus nonshared family environments to the vulnerability and resiliency of children with developmental disabilities, especially those with behavior disorders (Rende & Plomin, 1993). Ultimately, the most powerful tests about the effects of protective factors in the lives of developmentally disabled children may come from intergenerational and sibling studies and from evaluation studies of intervention programs. Both types of studies should have high priority in the next decade.

## REFERENCES

Brooks, R. B. (1994). Children at risk: Fostering resilience and hope. *American Journal of Orthopsychiatry, 64,* 545–553.

Caspi, A., Elder, G. H., & Bem, D. J. (1988). Moving away from the world: Life course patterns of shy children. *Developmental Psychology, 24,* 824–831.

Garmezy, N., Masten, A. S., & Tellegen, A. (1984). The study of stress and competence in children: A building block for developmental psychopathology. *Child Development, 55,* 97–111.

Granat, K., & Granat, S. (1978). Adjustment of intellectually below-average men not identified as mentally retarded. *Scandinavian Journal of Psychology, 19,* 41–51.

Hechtman, L. (1991). Resilience and vulnerability in long-term outcomes of attention deficit hyperactivity disorders. *Canadian Journal of Psychiatry, 36,* 415–421.

Hodapp, R. M., & Zigler, E. (1995). Past, present, and future issues in the developmental approach to mental retardation and developmental disabilities. In D. Cicchetti & D. J. Cohen (Eds.), *Developmental psychopathology, Vol. 2: Risk, disorder, and adaptation.* New York: Wiley.

Kavale, K. A. (1988). The long-term consequences of learning disabilities. In M. Wang, M. C. Reynolds, & H. J. Walberg (Eds.), *Handbook of special education: Research and practice* (pp. 303–344). Oxford, England: Pergamon.

Keogh, B. K., & Weisner, T. (1993). An ecocultural perspective on risk and protective factors in children's development: Implications for learning disabilities. *Learning Disabilities Research and Practice, 8,* 3–10.

Kirk, S. A., Gallagher, J. J. & Anastasiow, N. J. (1997). *Educating exceptional children.* Boston: Houghton Mifflin.

Magnusson, D. (1988). *Individual development from an interactional perspective.* Hillsdale, NJ: Lawrence Erlbaum Associates.

Mednick, S. A., Cudeck, R., Griffith, J. J., Talovis, S. A., & Schulsinger, F. (1984). The Danish high risk project: Recent methods and findings. In N. S. Watt, E. J. Anthony, L. C. Wynne, & J. E. Roff (Eds.), *Children at risk for schizophrenia: A longitudinal perspective* (pp. 21–42). Cambridge, England: Cambridge University Press.

Miller, M. (1996). Relevance of resilience to individuals with learning disabilities. *International Journal of Disability, Development, and Education, 43,* 255–269.

Patterson, G. R., DeBaryshe, B., & Ramsey, E. (1989). A developmental perspective on antisocial behavior. *American Psychologist, 44,* 329–335.

Pless, I. B., & Stein, R. K. (1994). Intervention research: Lessons from research on children with chronic disorders. In R. J. Haggerty, L. R. Sherrod, N. Garmezy, & M. Rutter (Eds.), *Stress, risk and resilience in children and adolescents: Processes, mechanisms, and interventions* (pp. 317–353). New York: Cambridge University Press.

Reiff, H. B., Gerber, P. J., & Ginsberg, R. (1997). *Exceeding expectations: Successful adults with learning disabilities.* Austin, TX: Pro-Ed.

Rende, R., & Plomin, R. (1993). Families at risk for psychopathology: Who becomes affected and why? *Development and Psychopathology, 5,* 529–540.

Robins, L. (1978). Study of childhood predictors of adult outcomes: Replications from longitudinal studies. *Psychological Medicine, 8,* 611–622.

Rogan, L. L., & Hartman, D. (1990). Adult outcomes of learning disabled students ten years after initial follow-up. *Learning Disabilities Focus, 5,* 91–102.

Scarr, S., & McCartney, K. (1983). How people make their own environments: A theory of genotype → environment effects. *Child Development, 54,* 424–435.

Seifer, R., & Sameroff, A. J. (1987). Multiple determinants of risk and invulnerability. In E. J. Anthony & B. J. Cohler (Eds.), *The invulnerable child* (pp. 51–69). New York, N.Y.: Guilford Press.

Spekman, N. J., Goldberg, R. J., & Herman, K. L. (1992). Learning disabled children grown up: A search for factors related to success in the young adult years. *Learning Disabilities Research and Practice, 7,* 161–170.

Spekman, N. J., Goldberg, R. J., & Herman, K. L. (1993). An exploration of risk and resilience in the lives of individuals with learning disabilities. *Learning Disabilities Research and Practice, 8,* 11–18.

Vogel, S. A., Hruby, P. J., & Adelman, P. B. (1993). Educational and psychological factors in successful and unsuccessful college students with learning disabilities. *Learning Disabilities Research and Practice, 8,* 35–43.

Weiss, G., & Hechtman, L. T. (1986). *Hyperactive children grown up.* New York: Guilford.

Werner, E. E. (1993). Risk and resilience in individuals with learning disabilities: Lessons learned from the Kauai Longitudinal Study. *Learning Disabilities Research and Practice, 8,* 28–34.

Werner, E. E. (1994). Programs that foster resilience among children at risk. In *International encyclopedia of education* (2nd ed., pp. 4775–4780). Oxford, England: Pergamon.

Werner, E. E., Randolph, S., & Masten, A. S. (1996, March). *Fostering resilience in kids: Overcoming adversity.* Paper presented at a Congressional Breakfast Meeting, Consortium of Social Science Associations, Washington, DC.

Werner, E. E., & Smith, R. S. (1992). *Overcoming the odds: High risk children from birth to adulthood.* Ithaca, NY: Cornell University Press.

Zetlin, A., & Murtaugh, M. (1990). What happened to those with borderline IQ's? *American Journal of Mental Retardation, 94,* 463–469.

# 3 ✤ Temperament: Developmental Perspectives

**Mary K. Rothbart**
**Laura B. Jones**
*University of Oregon*

For the past two decades Barbara Keogh has been one of the leaders in research and thinking on temperament in childhood. Although her work has been particularly focused on the individual child and teacher in the classroom, her contributions to the field extend far beyond that setting. In this chapter, we describe some of Keogh's major contributions to the temperament area, and use her research and thinking as a starting point to discuss some continuing issues in temperament and education. We then address questions about the structure of temperament and its development. We argue that the shorter list of temperament dimensions under current study makes it feasible for educators to consider temperament-related classroom strategies that will apply to groups of children rather than to single individuals. Finally, we discuss the applicability of concepts of temperament to the schooling of children with developmental disabilities.

## TEMPERAMENT AND "GOODNESS OF FIT"

Ideas about temperament have an ancient history. In the Western tradition, they go back at least 2,000 years to the Greco-Roman physicians who described a fourfold typology of temperament. This behavioral typology was, in turn, linked to the physiology of the individual as it was understood at that time, in terms of the humors of the body (Diamond, 1974). The irritable choleric individual was described as having a preponderance of yellow bile; the sad and anxious melancholic person, a preponderance of black bile; the positive and outgoing sanguine individual, a preponderance of blood; and the slow-to-arouse phlegmatic person, a predominance of phlegm.

Over the centuries, one of the identifying features of thinking about temperament has been the links made between temperamental behavior and experience and the individual constitution. Attempts to link physiology to

**33**

temperament have continued to the present time. It is not surprising that recent advances in the neurosciences have led temperamental individuality to
be increasingly related to variability in brain structure, and to neural and
neuroendocrine functioning (Gunnar, 1994; Rothbart, Derryberry, & Posner,
1994). By temperament, researchers refer to individual differences in emo-
tionality, activity and attention that are constitutionally based and show some
stability over time (Rothbart & Bates, 1998).

Even in the historically earliest views of temperament, the relation of individual temperament to behavior in the social environment was considered. In
medieval woodcuts, we see the sanguine individual serenading his beloved,
the melancholic as a distraught lover, the choleric as a spouse beater, and the
phlegmatic sleeping long after his wife has been up and about. The fourfold
typology of temperament was employed in psychological and medical thinking throughout the Middle Ages and up to this century, and a few typologies remain in current thinking. Kagan (1994), for example, describes two
temperamental types, the inhibited child and the uninhibited child.

The majority of recent work on temperament in childhood, however, has
been built on dimensions identified in the pioneering research of Thomas,
Chess, and colleagues in the New York Longitudinal Study (NYLS; Thomas &
Chess 1977; Thomas, Chess & Birch, 1968; Thomas, Chess, Birch, Hertzig, &
Korn, 1963). Thomas, et. al. (1963) collected extensive data from interviews
with parents of infants 2 to 6 months of age, identifying nine dimensions of infant temperamental variability through a content analysis of parents' descriptions. The nine dimensions they identified included activity level, intensity,
and threshold of reaction, mood, approach-withdrawal to novelty,
rhythmicity, adaptability to new situations, persistence, and distractibility. We
discuss these dimensions, and more recent revisions of this NYLS list, in the
sections that follow.

Thomas and Chess also developed the important concept of "goodness of
fit." In their view, temperamental characteristics affect developmental outcomes through transactions with the social environment. *Goodness of fit* refers
to how well children's characteristics, capacities, and temperament meet the
expectations and demands of the environment (Keogh, 1994; Thomas &
Chess, 1977; Thomas et al., 1968). Goodness of fit can apply when a person is
making an adaptation to a new task or a new social group. For the young child,
for whom much is new, much adaptation is required, and adults vary in the extent to which they are willing to accommodate the child in this adaptation. The
goodness-of-fit idea provides a framework for thinking about significant interactions between children and their social world, and, in mutual accommodation, stresses the reciprocity of influence in social development (Sameroff &
Chandler, 1975).

Potential for adult–child conflict in the family can develop when a task is difficult to perform, given the child's temperamental characteristics (e.g., sitting
quietly in the grocery cart on a shopping trip), or when the child fails to meet
the parents' expectations over an extended period. Quiet and reserved parents
of a highly active and curious child, for example, might have difficulty accept-

ing their child's "unregulated" behavior, whereas a less active and more inhibited child might fit comfortably into their home environment. Lack of fit can lead to parent attributions of poor motivation or ill will to the child, and can maintain conflictual and angry interactions, although it need not, depending on the parents' acceptance and knowledge about the child.

Just as the understanding of goodness of fit has provided a unique and helpful approach to thinking about child development in the family, Keogh and other educational researchers have extended this idea into the classroom, another major setting for children's adaptations (Hegvik, 1984; Keogh, 1982, 1986, 1989, 1994; Martin, Nagle, & Paget, 1983). Keogh (1986) argued that goodness of fit of the child to the classroom can refer to both curriculum (the specific tasks presented to the child) and social interactions (with peer and teacher). The goodness-of-fit idea presents a significant challenge to the educator: How can an adult working with a number of children deal with temperamental characteristics of the individual child that provide a poor fit with the requirements and expectations of the school setting?

In the classroom, children are presented with somewhat different demands and expectations for behavior than in the home. Conduct that may be considered appropriate in the home, such as boisterous activity or direct expressions of frustration, might be viewed as disruptive at school. Extremes in children's activity level, persistence, emotional reactivity, and flexibility may not be in accordance with classroom demands or the teacher's expectations (Keogh, 1989, 1994). In addition, just as a poor fit between child and parent in the home can lead to conflict, classroom situations resulting in poor fit can also lead to peer–child or teacher–child conflict, and to teachers' negative attributions about the child. This is especially true if the teacher believes the child is purposefully behaving in a difficult or uncooperative manner (Pullis, 1989).

In a research program designed to examine goodness of fit in the classroom, Pullis and Keogh developed a teacher report measure of child temperament (Keogh, Pullis, & Cadwell, 1982). They began with an examination of the validity and reliability of Thomas and Chess' (1977) 64-item Teacher Temperament Questionnaire (TTQ), and then developed a revision of the NYLS-based measure. Factor analysis of the TTQ was performed, and 23 items with the largest factor loadings were retained. Items clustered into three factors. The first factor, task orientation, included activity level, persistence, and distractibility items. The second, personal and social flexibility, contained adaptability, approach-withdrawal, and positive mood items. The third, reactivity, included items assessing a tendency to react negatively in stressful or frustrating situations, taken from negative mood, intensity, and threshold scales. Keogh et al.'s (Keogh, 1982; Pullis, 1979, cited in Keogh, Pullis, & Caldwell, 1982) psychometric work was important, because the structure of temperamental characteristics it revealed has proven to be quite similar to the structure of temperament identified in both teacher (see Keogh, 1986) and parent reports (Rothbart & Bates, 1998). This structure is discussed later in the chapter.

## TEMPERAMENT AND THE CLASSROOM

Keogh's research then examined an important aspect of goodness of fit by assessing teachers' ideas about the teachable child. Keogh noted that teachers screen information about individual students through their expectations of what students ought to be like (Keogh, 1982, 1989; Kornblau & Keogh, 1980). Teachers have a priori ideas about the qualities of a model student. Students are seen as highly teachable if their characteristics closely match this a priori view, but less teachable the further they are from the model. Keogh measured "teachability" with the 33 item Teachable Pupil Survey questionnaire developed by Kornblau (1982), another 3-factor scale. The first factor, cognitive/motivational characteristics, contained items related to children's thinking processes (e.g., logical-rational, clear-thinking, bright). The second, school appropriate behaviors, included items about children's behavior in the classroom (e.g., completes work on time and follows directions). The third, personal and social skills, contained items about the child's level of friendliness, sincerity, and sense of humor.

Keogh found strong agreement among teachers about what defines teachability (Keogh, 1994). In addition to the Teachable Pupil Survey, teachers completed the Teacher Temperament Questionnaire (TTQ). Keogh compared "ideal" teachability scores with children's actual scores to formulate a discrepancy score representing degree of fit between the child and the model. Students with similar ideal and actual ratings (a good fit) were also rated as high in temperamental attention span, adaptability and approach, and low in activity and reactivity in the TTQ. We can picture children with these characteristics sitting attentively at their desks or tables, persisting until a task is completed, flexibly responding to changes in the environment and approaching the teacher with questions only when it is appropriate. Interestingly, these temperamental attributes seem to contribute more than high IQ and/or lack of academic deficiencies (Keogh, 1982) to prediction of teachers' beliefs about students' potential.

In a further examination of how views of teachability corresponded to children's temperament, Keogh and Kornblau (Keogh, 1994) had teachers rate children from both regular and special education classes using the Teachable Pupil Survey and the TTQ. Regular education students were rated higher than special education students on all three teachability factors. The strongest relationships for both regular and special education students were positive ones between children's task orientation scores and their school appropriate behaviors. Ratings of positive mood and moderate intensity were also positively associated with personal/social skills scores.

In another study, strong relations between children's temperament and teachers' views of their teachability were again found in a group of learning-disabled subjects (Keogh, 1994). School-appropriate behaviors and personal/social skills were positively associated with temperamental task orientation. In addition, temperamental flexibility was positively related to the cognitive/emotional teachability factor. A strong negative relationship was found between temperamental task orientation and children's behavior checklist (CBL; Achenbach & Edelbrock, 1986) ratings of overall number of problems, intensity of problems, and externalizing (but not internalizing) problems. Teachers' views of teachability and children's problem scores on the CBL were also highly negatively correlated. Overall, in these studies, temperamental task orientation appeared to be most closely linked to teachability.

Temperamental variables were also related to teachers' management decisions and interactions with children (Keogh, 1989). One study involving students with learning disabilities also found temperamental task orientation to be of particular importance. The higher a child was rated in task orientation, the less teachers monitored their behavior (Pullis, 1985). Reactivity was also related to teacher's monitoring decisions; highly reactive children received increased monitoring, especially during unstructured play situations and transitions.

The tone of teacher–child interaction may differ as well. Martin (1989) found that teachers tend to criticize children who are distractible and low in attention. In some cases, teachers' criticism might stem from mistaken attributions such as a belief that the child purposefully behaves in an uncooperative manner. Pullis (1985) found that when teachers thought students with behavioral disorders were capable of but not practicing self-control, they were more likely to respond with the use of punitive and coercive discipline techniques.

Although we do not know the direction of influence in these studies, caregivers and teachers of children lower in sustained attention and persistence tend to take on a substantial share of the responsibility for monitoring the behavior of these children. This is understandable in the context of a classroom environment, where maintenance of order is important. Efforts to maintain order in the short run, however, may deprive students of opportunities to practice and develop skills that are essential components of self-regulation. We discuss this issue further later in the chapter. We now consider ways in which an understanding of temperament may improve classroom conditions and children's learning.

An important step to breaking negative cycles in teacher-student interaction appeared to be to encourage teachers to realize that a behavior is not necessarily purposeful, so that they could proceed with a plan to reduce conflict and help the child build control capacities (Pullis, 1985). Sensitivity to temperamental differences can be extremely helpful in moving the focus from attributions of purposeful misbehavior to plans for reestablishing a positive relationship with the child.

Huntington and Simeonsson (1993) argued that understanding children's temperament can foster a caregiver's appreciation of children's individuality. Keogh (1994) also noted that as teachers become aware of the reality of temperamental differences, they can look beyond motivational explanations for children's behavior (e.g., "She's purposefully disrupting the classroom"), and instead focus on redefining the child's behavior in the context of the classroom (e.g., "She really likes to be active—how can I get her to be more involved in academic activities?"). Research on caregiver–child relationships has indicated that, when caregivers attribute good and helpful characteristics to their children, the children respond with more compliance, even in the absence of the caregiver (Kuczynski, 1981, cited in Maccoby & Martin, 1938).

Can a temperament approach to the classroom offer more, however, than changing teachers' views about the purposefulness of children's problem behavior? We believe it can, but only if we can develop an understanding of basic dimensions of child variability, and their relation to adaptations or problems. Appropriate strategies can then be developed for dealing with problems in relation to the temperament dimensions involved. In the next section, we therefore put forward a short list of temperament characteristics, and some of their implications for the classroom. The advantage of working from a short list is recognizing that temperamental variability in children does *not* mean that every child will require his or her individual curriculum. Instead, there are limited sets of problems and possibilities that adults can come to recognize and with which they can work.

This point is related to our need to achieve an appropriate balance in applying temperament constructs. Removing blame from the child for not "fitting" our requirements does not thereby remove adults' responsibility for advancing the child's functioning. In addition, it is important to recognize that temperamental characteristics have a developmental history and they interact with each other. In particular, temperamental control systems of fear and executive attention develop over time and are open to experience. The executive attention system, related to task orientation in Keogh's research, appears to be particularly important in the classroom, and strategies for both providing and training control in children are therefore a major priority for educators. We now turn to a discussion of our current understanding of temperament dimensions and their development.

## STRUCTURE AND DEVELOPMENT OF TEMPERAMENT

The past 2 decades of research have refined our view of basic dimensions of temperament, suggesting important revisions in the NYLS list (Martin, Wisenbaker, & Huttunen, 1994; Rothbart & Bates, 1998; Rothbart & Mauro, 1990). The revision is needed in part because we are increasingly aware that the structure of temperament changes with development. The NYLS was developed on the basis of individual differences observed by parents in behavioral reactions of infants early in the first year of life, yet major developments in temperament occur in the months and years following this period (Rothbart, 1989b; Rothbart & Bates, 1988). We have characterized these changes as moving from initial individual differences in emotional, motor, and attentional reactivity to increasing self-regulation of the child's responses (Rothbart & Derryberry, 1981), including possibilities for increasing self-control over behavior and emotion through the development of attention. Development of self-regulating capacities is essential to effective socialization of the child in both home and school. We now undertake a brief discussion of the structure and early development of temperamental systems.

## BROAD FACTORS OF TEMPERAMENT FOUND
## IN QUESTIONNAIRE ASSESSMENTS

Temperament is seen by researchers as a disposition or tendency of a child, measurable across contexts that share eliciting features (novel situations or strange persons, e.g., are eliciting conditions for fear). Temperamental dispositions are assessed in scales using multiple items (Rothbart & Bates, 1998). In developing a temperament scale, we aggregate items across a wide range of appropriate eliciting situations, allowing us to capture variability in children's behavior that is shared across situations. Contributions of other variables to individual item scores are expected to cancel each other out as psychometric "noise" as we aggregate across items. When it is not possible to identify shared variability across items, however, we are not able to assess a given dimension of temperament. For some NYLS scales (e.g., intensity and threshold), it has proven very difficult to find sufficient generality across a range of stimulating situations and children's responses to develop internally reliable scales (Rothbart & Mauro, 1990).

Thomas and Chess (1977) also did not attempt to conceptually differentiate their dimensions from one another. Scales assessing temperament in the NYLS system have thus often overlapped in both definition and item content. An item such as "Becomes positive after a few minutes in a new situation," for example, might conceptually belong on the mood, adaptability and approach-withdrawal scales. Given this lack of differentiation of scale dimensions, scale scores and correlations among scores become difficult to interpret.

To clarify this situation, item-level factor analyses have been carried out in Sweden (Bohlin, Hagekull, & Lindhagen, 1981) and Australia (Sanson, Prior, Garino, Oberklaid, & Sewell, 1987) on large sets of questionnaire data. Factors extracted from these analyses have led to a shorter list of temperament dimensions than the original NYLS list (Rothbart & Bates, 1998; Sanson & Rothbart, 1995). Moreover, the shorter list has proven to be conceptually similar to lists of temperament dimensions developed that were based on behavioral genetic and animal studies of temperament (Buss & Plomin, 1975; Rothbart 1981). The shorter list for infants includes dimensions of fear, irritability/anger, positive affect/approach, activity level, and persistence (Rothbart & Mauro, 1990). The Australian temperament study also found a very small threshold factor that was not widely generalizable.

In this shorter list, positive affect is differentiated from two forms of negative affect, and adaptability items are combined with approach items. Bipolar scales with positive affect and approach at one pole and negative affect and avoidance on the other do not emerge in these analyses. This is very important, because the structure of temperament indicates that distress proneness does *not* preclude a proneness to experience positive affect. In other words, a child who tends to be negative can also be positive. This point is very important for parents, caregivers, and teachers: Changes in a situation can allow us to accentuate the child's positive tendencies, while at the same time diminishing negative reactions that could lead to discouragement or conflict.

For example, a fearful child who prefers to play alone, interacting primarily with puppets and play figures in the classroom, might typically balk at her teacher's request to read aloud in front of a group. One helpful approach might be to introduce her indirectly to public speaking. The student could begin as the voice of a puppet in a class puppet show; this opportunity builds on her well-developed creative skills and, given the opportunity to speak for the puppet, the child can gradually increase her skills and confidence in public speaking. For the highly anxious child, unpredictable classroom transitions can also lead to negative reactions. A clear routine with added signals to the child that an activity is about to change can decrease negative reactions while building ordered mental scripts and expectations for classroom activity in the child.

Analyses of the structure of temperament have also been carried out for older children. For children age 3 years and above, the shorter list of temperament characteristics extracted from scale and item-level factor analyses includes broad factors of surgency (positive affect, activity level, and approach), fear, and irritability/anger, with the latter two sometimes combined into a higher-order negative affectivity factor (Rothbart & Bates, 1998). These are very similar to the infant dimensions.

An important additional factor has been found in the assessment of temperament in older children, however; we have called this dimension effortful control. It includes children's ability to shift and focus attention, their inhibitory control, and perceptual sensitivity. Although based on attention, effortful control is not identical to the reactive orienting of attention seen early in infancy and beyond (see Ruff & Rothbart, 1996). Reactive orienting in infancy appears to be related to interest or disinterest. By the preschool period, however, children come to demonstrate increased executive function involving inhibitory control, planning, and attentional control. In all of our research, higher effortful control scores have been found to be related to lower negative reactivity and possibly the control of negative emotions. This factor is extremely important, because children with executive capacities are not only affected by reactive approach to positive stimuli and avoidance of negative ones; these children can be socialized to delay and to choose less favorable alternatives in accordance with internalized rules and principles. For children who have not yet developed these capacities or whose executive attention systems are compromised, reward and punishment may continue to be more important.

Keogh's factor of task orientation identified in the classroom appears to map onto the broad factor of effortful control found in other temperament studies. In addition, Keogh's reactivity factor maps on negative affectivity. It is less clear the degree to which the personal and social flexibility factor maps on surgency, although there is clearly some overlap. Our current, shorter lists of temperament characteristics will certainly become longer as we learn more about variability in temperament, but, for now, they provide a shared basis for thinking and investigation of temperament in childhood, in the home, and in the classroom. They also prepare us to consider developmental issues in the study of temperament.

## DEVELOPMENT OF TEMPERAMENT

In our work, we have defined temperament as individual differences in constitutionally based reactivity and self-regulation (Rothbart & Derryberry, 1981). Reactivity refers to the latency, intensity, and duration of emotional, motor, and attentional reactions to stimulation; self-regulation refers to processes serving to modulate this reactivity, including attentional controls. We see temperament as including dispositions toward emotional, motor, and attentional reactions, as well as self-regulative capacities such as executive attentional control. In our developmental model of temperament, individual differences in reactivity precede the development of self-regulatory processes (Rothbart & Derryberry 1981), with different self-regulative systems developing at different times during the early years.

From the earliest days of life (and for some variables, like activity level, during intrauterine development), emotional and attentional reactivity can be assessed through measures of the latency, intensity, recovery time and duration of emotional, motor, and attentional responses (Rothbart & Derryberry, 1981). Newborns vary in their tendency to distress, activity levels, and attentional reactivity, and there is organization among these early reactions. Infants can become very active, then distressed. A distressed infant also shows lower levels of orienting (see review by Rothbart, 1989b), and when 3-month-old infants orient to an external stimulus, their distress can be at least temporarily relieved (Harman, Rothbart, & Posner, 1997). There is some evidence of stability of individual differences in negative reactivity from the newborn period up to 2 years of age (Riese, 1987). In addition, at 4-months of age, distress and motor reactivity combine to predict behavioral inhibition and fearfulness during the second year of life (Kagan, 1994).

Positive reactivity develops during the first 6 months of life, and the expression of positive affect is also positively linked to motor reactivity. Infants who show a greater disposition to positive affect will also more rapidly approach exciting objects or people (Rothbart, 1988), and they are more subject to frustration. Calkins, Fox, and Marshall (1996) found that a combination of positive affect and motor reactivity in 4-month-old infants predicts later extraverted or outgoing behavior. After the first year of life, individual differences in extraverted reactions show considerable stability over age (Rothbart, 1989). It is interesting to note that a number of the reactive systems identified in infant temperament are very similar to evolutionarily conserved systems of affect and motivation in other animals. These systems include attentional orienting and interest, irritability, fearfulness and behavioral inhibition, and positive reactivity and approach.

Children who are highly approaching, with little fear or attentional control, can create problems in the classroom, disrupting the flow of classroom activities. Teachers may therefore find it helpful to channel the child's high approach tendencies. The child might serve well as "classroom ambassador," greeting classroom visitors and new students and providing tours of the room. He or he might help to create a book about classroom rules and schedules. Emphasis could then be placed on an important aspect of the child's job as ambassador: modeling appropriate behavior and adherence to classroom routines. As the child experiences reinforcement for desired behaviors in a style that complements his or her behavioral tendencies, rather than opposing them, the student can positively contribute to the flow of classroom activity.

By 8 to 10 months, signs of fearful inhibition of approach are seen. Some infants at that age begin to inhibit approach to new and exciting objects or persons (Rothbart, 1988). This inhibited reaction appears to be part of the fear system, and does not develop until late in the first year. Behavioral inhibition serves an important function in individuals' response to danger, and the brain circuits underlying fearfulness and inhibition are among those best understood by the neurosciences (LeDoux, 1996). Fear or shyness also acts as a control on impulsive behavior, but it is important to note that this is an emotionally reactive form of regulation.

Behavioral inhibition as a form of fearfulness has been extensively studied by Kagan (1994) and his colleagues. Inhibition shows considerable individual stability across time, and has been observed in children's responses to novel situations, strangers, and conditioned signs of punishment. Because novelty reactions generally wane over time, however, initial shyness in children can be gradually replaced by comfortable interaction if the situation is a nonpunishing one. Asendorpf, for example, assessed shyness in longitudinal studies of German children across their school years (Asendorpf, 1993). Children's initial levels of shyness to strangers showed considerable longitudinal stability from one year to the next, but initially shy children often made adaptations to their new setting, becoming less withdrawn as the school year progressed. They also tended to become less shy over the years if they also scored higher on intelligence assessments and teacher's judgments of social competence (Asendorpf, 1994).

On the other hand, some children who were initially more outgoing in Asendorpf's study became more withdrawn over the course of the year. Children who became secondarily withdrawn also proved to be the children more likely to show problems later in development. Asendorpf (1993) suggested that secondary shyness may be due at least in part to negative experiences with other children, and these experiences can sometimes result from less self-regulated social behavior in more outgoing children.

Temperamental shyness has important implications for the teaching situation. Shy children may become easily overwhelmed by stimulation, and classroom structures allowing them a chance to seek occasional refuge from excitement are helpful. Gentle encouragement is also important for children who become easily discouraged or tend to become retiring. Allowing for a slow approach to novelty is often useful for these children, and their cognitive skills may best be demonstrated when they come to feel comfortable in a situation. Developing skills that are not compatible with shyness is an important complementary approach: speaking, singing, acting, and other performance skills allow shy children to adapt more comfortably to new situations. It is important that shy children not be ignored because they are causing few problems in the classroom.

On the other hand, shy children show considerable positive resources. They may observe other children for a long enough time to make cautious adaptation a new situation. Moreover, they already possess a control system that can support early socialization by teacher or parent. Kochanska (1995) identified links between early temperamental fearfulness and the development of conscience in children. She further discovered that gentle means of their mother's socialization work best for more fearful children in their internalization of conscience. The child who tends to rush into new situations, on the other hand, may be less sensitive to fear-related socialization, and also may be at risk for stress reactions in connection with the lack of self-regulation (Gunnar, Larson, Hertsgaard, Harris, & Brodersen, 1992).

Kochanska (1995) also found mechanisms for socialization that appear to be effective for more fearless children. When mother and child show a relationship characterized by warm and mutually receptive interactions and positive motivation for action, the child is more likely to show internalization of conscience. Other studies have found that even caregiver responsivity in a single situation can lead to an environment in which children will enthusiastically embrace the caregiver's message (Parpal & Maccoby, 1985). Although not directly involving teacher–student interactions, this research supports the idea that children are more receptive to internalization in an environment characterized by acceptance and sensitivity.

The executive control system will later be added to fear control as a mechanism for socialization. This system does not have the reactive qualities of fearful inhibition, and it is not specifically tied to any emotion, although emotional systems can influence and be influenced by it. We have also called this the *second* or *executive attention system* (Posner & Rothbart, 1991; Ruff & Rothbart, 1996). The second or executive attentional system is involved when the child inhibits a dominant activity in order to perform a subdominant activity. This effortful control of attention and action is related to the capacity to deliberately focus and shift attention, and the ability to plan and delay action.

The development of this system can be seen first in the behavior of older infants who are able to restrain their reaching tendencies (Diamond, 1974). When a 6-month-old watches an experimenter place an object into the open front of a four-sided Plexiglas box, the infant will nevertheless reach for it along the line of sight, and will be prevented by the Plexiglas cover from obtaining it. With development, infants are able to inhibit reaching along the line of sight, instead reaching at the location where they saw the object placed, even if this location has been at the opposite side of the box. Children's memory of where the object has been placed is now linked to inhibition of their tendency to make a habitual reaction along the line of sight. Initially, this motor inhibition appears to be preverbal. Later, the ability to inhibit a dominant response in order to perform a subdominant response will be linked to verbal instructions.

Capacities for children's verbally based self-regulation develop over the preschool years, and we suggested that these capacities are linked to the maturation of anterior brain systems, including the anterior cingulate and nearby structures (Posner & Rothbart, 1991). In studies in our laboratory, Gerardi (1997; Gerardi, Rothbart, Posner, & Kepler, 1996) has traced development of attentional control over the ages of 2 to 3 years in a task identified as a marker for executive attention function. The Stroop task requires adults to report the color of ink in which a word is printed, even though the printed word may signify a different color name. Thus, the adult must identify red as the ink color even though the word written in red ink is "blue," and there is a strong tendency to read the word rather than naming the color. Stroop tasks are particularly likely to activate those brain structures in adults that are associated with executive control (Posner & Raichle, 1994).

Our Stroop-like task for young children creates conflict between the location and identity of the correct response. Pictures of animals or objects are presented to the right or left of a computer display, and children are asked to press the button that matches the picture. The correct button is located either directly under the stimulus (compatible) or on the other side (incompatible condition). Children are both slowed and less accurate in the incompatible location; adults are also slowed by this condition. In tracing the development of performance on this task, Gerardi (1997) found that 24-month-olds are more accurate for compatible than incompatible conditions, but their performance is close to chance. Children from 30 to 36 months of age perform much more accurately on this task, but show clear slowing in their performance on the incompatible condition. Like the adult Stroop task, this conflict task requires children to inhibit a dominant response (pressing the button below the picture) in order to perform a subdominant response (matching the identity of the picture).

We also addressed whether children's performance in this laboratory task would be related to parents' reports about their children's temperamental characteristics. Indeed, children who performed more accurately at the conflict task and/or were less slowed by the incompatible condition were reported by their mothers in the Children's Behavior Questionnaire to be better able to focus attention, to inhibit action when requested to do so, and to behave less impulsively. These findings indicate that the child's laboratory task performance linked from brain function is also linked in important ways to real-world behavior.

In Gerardi's task, children apply a single rule that requires inhibition of a dominant response and performance of a subdominant response. In older children, between the ages of 3 and 5 years, we observed children's development of the ability to follow two different rules for behavior that depend on context, with one rule conflicting with the other (Jones, 1997; Reed, Pien, & Rothbart, 1984). The task involves a Simon-Says game, where children are first asked to demonstrate their knowledge of commands like "touch your nose," and "shake your feet." Children are then told that when one stuffed animal gives an instruction, they are to perform it; when the other stuffed animal gives the instruction, they are to inhibit the action. Children's performance on this Simon-Says task is related to their skills on other tasks requiring inhibition of action, such as a pinball game where the child is asked to inhibit releasing the plunger for varying periods of time (Reed et al., 1984).

Questions of children's motivation are clearly important when we assess these self-regulative capacities: Children may have the capacity but not the inclination, to perform an act that requires effort. Jones obtained some preliminary evidence that when mothers report low levels of temperamental control, but children actually perform well on the laboratory task, patterns of conflict appear to have developed in the home so that the mother has difficulty enlisting her child's cooperation. We are now investigating this possibility systematically.

## TEMPERAMENT IN CHILDREN WITH DEVELOPMENTAL DISABILITIES

As discussed earlier, the nature and frequency of teacher–student interactions differ with respect to the student's temperamental characteristics, particularly with respect to task orientation or executive control. These findings may be especially important for children with learning disabilities. Children identified as learning disabled in the first grade have been found to exhibit increasingly maladaptive classroom behavior over the next three years (McKinney & Speece, 1991, cited in Keogh & Speece, 1996). These findings may be related to the development of executive control functions. As other children come to control their actions and emotions, children lacking in controls may lag further behind. Because temperamental task orientation is an especially salient characteristic of teachability in the classroom, a developmental lag could interact with the school environment, including teachers' expectations and decisions, and result in long-term consequences for children with developmental disabilities.

Effortful control of attention facilitates children's ability to plan, shift, and focus attention and action, and delay gratification. Children low in task orientation and/or highly reactive may experience more difficulty utilizing these skills. For example, a highly fearful child, low in effortful control, might find it very difficult to persist in a boisterous group activity. Faced with the need to maintain order, it is easy to see how a teacher might decide to behave more directively with this child (e.g., "Come over here right now!"). These immediate decisions, however, may have subtle, long-term influences on the development of attentional control.

Silverman and Ippolito (1995) argued that as children perform tasks requiring persistence and sustained attention, responsibility for managing behavior is gradually transferred from adult to child. They further proposed, as we suggested earlier, that the development of this attentional ability is strengthened when children are given opportunities to practice self-regulating skills, and when adults avoid taking over this responsibility and instead provide encouragement and assistance. This raises another very important issue concerning temperament and development: To what extent are temperamental characteristics themselves subject to experiential influence? Much more research is needed in this area.

Variations in the timing of development of executive function and variations in the capacity to control attention and action are important in both home and school, and may be particularly important in the development and education of special populations of children (Ruff & Rothbart, 1996). Research groups studying temperament in children with developmental disabilities have varied in their thinking about these issues. Huntington and Simeonsson (1993), for example, stressed the variability that exists *within* populations of children with developmental disabilities. They argued that "temperament is a characteristic idiosyncratic to each child and is not specifically defined by developmental status or disabling condition" (Huntington & Simeonsson, p. 58). Their work highlights the importance of temperament assessment for meeting the educational needs of individual children.

Another group of researchers (Wagner, Ganiban, & Cicchetti, 1990) took a somewhat different, but in our opinion, complementary view. They suggested that there may be important ways in which children in one diagnostic group differ from children in other groups, and that these differences may be related to basic developmental processes, such as aspects of arousal or attention. Evidence exists, for example, that children with Down syndrome tend to show less inhibitory and attentional control when matched for mental age with children without disability (Kopp, 1990; Wagner et al., 1990). In our view, both positions described previously are helpful. There may be group differences across populations as well as variability among children in a given diagnostic group that will be important for structuring the classroom situation.

Children with autism are members of another diagnostic group having characteristics in common. One feature of autism includes rigidity of thought and behavior; even small environmental changes or breaks in routine can lead to anxiety for a child with autism (Jordan & Powell, 1995). Equipped with knowledge about this specific challenge, teachers can build a curriculum to help their students become familiar with the daily sequence of events. For example, highly structured transition times and picture schedules are often helpful. Subtle changes in the teachers' approach can often lead to substantial improvements in children's behavior. Many children with Asberger's syndrome resist a command made to them directly, but will comply if a rule is stated generally (Jordan & Powell, 1995). Knowledge about specific disabilities can lead to adaptations in the classroom addressing the needs of a particular student, but the changes may also benefit the class as a whole. Class rules displayed with symbols and/or words may particularly benefit the student with Asberger's syndrome, but can serve as a helpful reference for other students as well.

Finally, it is important to note that although temperamental variability exists on a number of dimensions, that number is not so large as to overwhelm our capacity to devise temperament-based strategies for working with children, and to recognize children to whom these strategies apply. Mistakes will be made in choice of strategy and identification of child characteristics, but if our strategies do not succeed, we can go back to a diagnosis of the child–situation fit, trying a different strategy for the future.

## THE CLASSROOM

The relationship between personal characteristics and school-appropriate behavior is influenced by classroom structure, social demands, and curriculum (Keogh, 1994). Keogh defined *classrooms* as "complex social systems with particular constraints and requirements that interact with a range of individual abilities and characteristics" (Keogh, 1994, p. 247). Classroom structure can be defined by either physical requirements (e.g., children must remain seated) or social expectations (e.g., children will take turns and share). Some classrooms require children to sit at desks for extended periods of time, whereas other settings favor a more open approach. Differing temperamental characteristics can lead to varying learning outcomes in each of these situations (Keogh, 1989).

Children high in activity might have difficulty sitting for extended periods, and highly reactive children might feel very uncomfortable in a crowded classroom. In the social realm, relationships have been found between adaptability and teachers' perceptions of children's adjustment and social abilities (Feuerstein & Martin, 1980, cited in Keogh, 1989). Finally, a given curriculum comes with a set of instructional expectations. Temperamental variables are especially important when repetitive tasks require sustained attention and persistence (Hall & Cadwell, 1984, cited in Keogh, 1989), and the application of the executive attention system.

Consistent with the idea that goodness of fit includes the interaction of individual differences *and* the environment Keogh noted that traditional assessment approaches tend to focus on the individual child, and virtually ignore information about the school environment (Keogh & Speece, 1996). Keogh and her colleagues proposed that a given classroom experience can be substantially different for "at-risk" children. These differences in turn can be reflected in teachers' beliefs and attitudes about achievement potential for students with learning disabilities, teachers' instructional and management techniques, and teacher–pupil interactions.

Children identified as at risk, or requiring special educational assistance, show some striking consistencies with respect to the temperamental variables of task orientation and reactivity. In a study of children with developmental delays, Keogh (1994) found few significant differences between children placed in regular education programs and those placed in special education programs, except that children placed in special education programs were rated lower in task orientation and frustration tolerance. Pullis and Cadwell (1985) compared a group of children identified as at risk by classroom teachers to a group of matched "nonrisk" students. Teachers rated the at-risk children as significantly higher in reactivity and significantly lower in task-orientation and adaptability.

Pullis (1985) examined the relationship between individual differences in behavior strategies used by mainstream and resource teachers. Teachers completed a three-part questionnaire in which they ranked their classroom management strategies (ranging from *ignoring* to *corporal punishment*) for individual children, and rated the children on temperament (TTQ) and classroom competence. Differences in estimates of children's competence, temperament, and management strategies were found between mainstream and resource teachers. Although both groups rated children with learning disabilities as lower in academic performance, the mainstream teachers rated them significantly lower on these estimates. In addition, compared to resource teachers, mainstream teachers rated students with learning disabilities significantly lower in intellectual ability and motivation. Pullis cites evidence that teachers' low-ability expectations can further lead to differential treatment with respect to quality of curriculum, instructional pacing, and interactions (Brophy, 1982, cited in Pullis, 1985). Teacher's reactions toward students whom they perceive as less motivated also tend to be characterized by more extreme disappointment and frustration (Brophy & Rohrkemper, 1981, cited in Pullis, 1985).

Differences between mainstream and resource teachers were also found in classroom management decisions. Mainstream teachers indicated that children with learning disabilities required significantly more monitoring during whole-class instruction and free-play activities. Modes of discipline also differed: Mainstream teachers tended to resort to more punitive discipline approaches (e.g., referring students to the office or sending them home) compared to resource teachers. Pullis suggested that these decisions may be a reflection of the stress that mainstream teachers experience due to the inclusion of children with learning disabilities in the classroom. General classroom teachers report they do not have enough time, support, or training to serve children with handicaps (Hudson, Graham, & Warner, 1979, cited in Pullis, 1985), and they are reluctant to make changes requiring planning, instructional, or environmental adaptations (Vaughn & Schumm, 1996).

With respect to temperament, mainstream teachers rated students with learning disabilities as significantly lower in task orientation and reactivity. Pullis suggested that children with learning disabilities are more likely to withdraw in a mainstream situation and, consequently, to display less disruptive behavior. He proposed that these characteristics might also contribute to teachers' perceptions of students with learning disabilities as being less motivated. Pullis' idea had empirical support from Vaughn and Schumm (1996), who studied general education teachers of grades 3 through 12 over a period of 5 months. Vaughn and Schumm found that students with learning disabilities in a general education classroom initiated significantly fewer bids for help from the teacher, engaged less in class discussions, and showed significantly less negative behavior toward peers.

In another study, Schumm and Vaughn (1991, cited in Vaughn & Schumm, 1996) asked general education teachers about adaptations they would be willing to make for children with learning disabilities included in their classroom. Strategies teachers do not find desirable or feasible are not likely to be adopted (Vaughn & Schumm, 1996). Teachers indicated instructional adaptations or physical restructuring of the classroom as least desirable and practical. Changes teachers found most feasible included providing reinforcement and encouragement, establishing a personal relationship with the student, involving the student in whole class activities, respecting the mainstreamed student as an individual, establishing appropriate routines, and adapting classroom management strategies. Teachers were also more likely to prefer strategies that could be used for all students in the classroom.

How might temperament be considered in the context of the changes that classroom teachers appear willing to implement? Three of these strategies—providing reinforcement and encouragement, establishing a personal relationship with students, and respecting mainstreamed students as individuals—all facilitate positive interactions with students. As indicated earlier, Kochanska's work has shown that one mechanism of internalization for children who are not easily controlled by fear of punishment is a reciprocal relationship between mother and child characterized by warm, mutually receptive interactions (Kochanska, 1995). Inherent in caregiver supportiveness, sensitivity, and empathy toward children is respect for children as individuals.

With large student populations, the classroom is a very busy place. Teachers are continually challenged with the need to make quick judgments and decisions about students' behavior, and these judgments and decisions powerfully influence their interactions with students. Teachers' sensitivity to students' individual differences can help them develop more positive frames for viewing children who vary in reactivity and capacities for self-control. In addition, teachers' awareness of the relation between specific temperament characteristics and particular problems, allows the application of strategies for improving children's performance, and bettering the fit between child and classroom. We hope that future research on the plasticity of reactive and executive attention systems will also provide increasing aid for teachers and the students in their care.

## REFERENCES

Achenbach, T. M., & Edelbrock, C. S. (1986). *Manual for the teacher's report form and teacher version of the child behavior profile.* Burlington: University of Vermont, Department of Psychiatry.

Asendorpf, J. B. (1993). Beyond temperament: A two-factor coping model of the development of inhibition during childhood. In K. H. Rubin, & J. B. Asendorpf (Eds.), *Social withdrawal, inhibition, and shyness in childhood* (pp. 265–289). Hillsdale, NJ: Lawrence Erlbaum Associates.

Asendorpf, J. B. (1994). The malleability of behavior inhibition: A study of individual development functions. *Developmental Psychology, 30,* 912–919.

Bohlin, G., Hagekull, B., & Lindhagen, K. (1981). Dimensions of infant behavior. *Infant Behavior and Development, 4,* 83–96.

Buss, A. H., & Plomin, R. (1975). *A temperament theory of personality development.* New York: Wiley.

Calkins, S. D., Fox, N. A., & Marshall, T. R. (1996). Behavioral and physiological antecedents of inhibition in infancy. *Child Development, 67,* 523–540.

Diamond, S. (1974). *The roots of psychology.* New York: Basic Books.

Gerardi, G. (1997). *Development of executive attention and self-regulation in the third year of life.* Unpublished doctoral dissertation, University of Oregon, Eugene.

Gerardi, G., Rothbart, M. K., Posner, M. I., & Kepler, S. (1996, April). *The development of attentional control: Performance on a spatial Stroop-like task at 24, 30, and 36–38 months of age.* Poster session presented at the annual meeting of the International Society for Infant Studies, Providence, RI.

Gunnar, M. R. (1994). Psychoendocrine studies of temperament and stress in early childhood: Expanding current models. In J. E. Bates & T. D. Wachs (Eds.), *Temperament: Individual differences at the interface of biology and behavior* (pp. 175–198). Washington, DC: American Psychological Association.

Gunnar, M. R., Larson, M., Hertsgaard, L., Harris, M., & Brodersen, L. (1992). The stressfulness of separation among 9-month-old infants: Effects of social context variables and infant temperament. *Child Development, 63,* 290–303.

Harman, C., Rothbart, M. K., & Posner, M. I. (1997). Distress and attention interactions in early infancy. *Motivation and Emotion, 21,* 27–43.

Hegvik, R. L. (1984, October). *Three year longitudinal study of temperament variables, academic achievement and sex differences.* Paper presented at the St. Louis Conference on Temperament in Educational Process, St. Louis, MO.

Huntington, G. S., & Simeonsson, R. J. (1993). Temperament and adaptation in infants and young children with disabilities. *Infant Mental Health Journal, 14,* 49–60.

Jones, L. B. (1997). *Voluntary attentional control in young children.* Unpublished master's thesis, University of Oregon, Eugene.

Jordan, R., & Powell, S. (1995). *Understanding and teaching children with autism.* New York: Wiley.

Kagan, J. (1994). *Galen's prophecy: Temperament in human nature.* New York: Basic Books.

Keogh, B. K. (1982). Children's temperament and teacher's decisions. In R. Porter & G. M. Collins (Eds.), *Temperamental differences in infants and young children* (pp. 269–278). London: Pitman.

Keogh, B. K. (1986). Temperament and schooling: What is the meaning of goodness of fit? In J. V. Lerner & R. M. Lerner (Eds.), *New directions for child development: Temperament and social interaction in infants and children* (pp. 89–108). San Francisco: Jossey Bass.

Keogh, B. K. (1989). Applying temperament research to school. In G. A. Kohnstamm, J. E. Bates, & M. K. Rothbart (Eds.), *Temperament in childhood* (pp. 437–450). New York: Wiley.

Keogh, B. K. (1994). Temperament and teachers' views of teachability. In W. B. Carey & S. C. McDevitt (Eds.), *Prevention and early intervention: Individual differences as risk factors for the mental health of children* (pp. 246–256). New York: Brunner/Mazel.

Keogh, B. K., Pullis, M., & Cadwell, J. (1982). A short form of the teacher temperament questionnaire. *Journal of Educational Measurement, 19,* 223–230.

Keogh, B. K., & Speece, D. L. (1996). Learning disabilities within the context of schooling. In D. L. Speece & B. K. Keogh (Eds.), *Research on classroom ecologies: Implications for inclusion of children with learning disabilities* (pp. 1–14). Mahwah, NJ: Lawrence Erlbaum Associates.

Kochanska, G. (1995). A longitudinal study of the roots of preschooler's conscience: Committed compliance and emerging internalization. *Child Development, 66,* 1752–1769.

Kopp, C. B. (1990). The growth of self-monitoring among young children with Down syndrome. In D. Cicchetti & M. Beeghly (Eds.), *Children with Down syndrome: A developmental perspective* (pp. 231–251). New York: Cambridge University Press.

Kornblau, B. W. (1982). The Teachable Pupil Survey: A technique for assessing teachers' perceptions of pupil attributes. *Psychology in the Schools, 19,* 170–174.

Kornblau, B. W., & Keogh, B. K. (1980). Teacher's perceptions and educational decisions. In J. J. Gallagher (Ed.), *New directions for exceptional children: No. 1. the ecology of exceptional children* (pp. 87–101). San Francisco: Jossey-Bass.

LeDoux, J. E. (1996). *The emotional brain: The mysterious underpinnings of emotional life.* New York: Simon & Schuster.

Maccoby, E. E., & Martin, J. A. (1983). Socialization in the context of the family: Parent-child interaction. In P. H. Mussen (Series Ed.) & E. M. Hetherington (Vol. Ed.), *Handbook of child psychology: Vol. 4. Socialization, personality, and social development* (pp. 1–101). New York: Wiley.

Martin, R. P. (1989). Activity level, distractibility, and persistence: Critical characteristics in early schooling. In G. A. Kohnstamm, J. E. Bates, & M. K. Rothbart (Eds.), *Temperament in childhood* (pp. 451–461). New York: Wiley.

Martin, R. P., Nagle, R., & Paget, K. (1983). Relationships between temperament and classroom behavior, teacher attitudes, and academic achievement. *Journal of Psychoeducational Assessment, 1,* 377–386.

Martin, R. P., Wisenbaker, J., & Huttunen, M. (1994). Review of factor analytic studies of temperament based on the Thomas-Chess structural model: Implications for the Big Five. In C. F. Halverson, Jr., G. A. Kohnstamm, & R. P. Martin (Eds.), *The developing structure of temperament and personality from infancy to adulthood* (pp. 157–172). Hillsdale, NJ: Lawrence Erlbaum Associates.

Parpal, M., & Maccoby, E. E. (1985). Maternal responsiveness and subsequent child compliance. *Child Development, 56,* 1326–1334.

Posner, M. I., & Raichle, M. E. (1994). *Images of mind.* New York: Scientific American Library.

Posner, M. I., & Rothbart, M. K. (1991). Attentional mechanisms and conscious experience. In M. Rugg & A. D. Milner (Eds.), *The neuropsychology of consciousness* (pp. 91–122). London: Academic.

Pullis, M. (1985). Students' temperament characteristics and their impact on decisions by resource and mainstream teachers. *Learning Disability Quarterly, 8,* 109–122.

Pullis, M. (1989). Goodness of fit in classroom relationships. In W. B. Carey & S. C. McDevitt (Eds.), *Clinical and educational applications of temperament research* (pp. 117–120). Amsterdam, The Netherlands: Swets & Zeitlinger.

Pullis, M., & Cadwell, J. (1985). Temperament as a factor in the assessment of children educationally at risk. *The Journal of Special Education, 19,* 91–102.

Reed, M. A., Pien, D. P., & Rothbart, M. K. (1984). Inhibitory self-control in preschool children. *Merrill-Palmer Quarterly, 30,* 131–147.

Riese, M. L. (1987). Temperament stability between the neonatal period and 24 months. *Developmental Psychology, 23*, 216–222.

Rothbart, M. K. (1981). Measurement of temperament in infancy. *Child Development, 52*, 569–578.

Rothbart, M. K. (1988). Temperament and the development of inhibited approach. *Child Development, 59*, 1241–1250.

Rothbart, M. K. (1989a). Biological processes of temperament. In G. Kohnstamm, J. Bates, & M. K. Rothbart (Eds.), *Temperament in childhood* (pp. 77–110). Chichester, England: Wiley.

Rothbart, M. K. (1989b). Temperament and development. In G. Kohnstamm, J. Bates, & M. K. Rothbart (Eds.), *Temperament in childhood* (pp. 187–248). Chichester, England: Wiley.

Rothbart, M. K., & Bates, J. E. (1998). Temperament. In W. Damon (Series Ed.) & N. Eisenberg (Vol. Ed.), *Handbook of child psychology: Vol. 3. Social, emotional and personality development* (5th ed., pp. 105–176). New York: Wiley.

Rothbart, M. K., & Derryberry, D. (1981). Development of individual differences in temperament. In M. E. Lamb & A. L. Brown (Eds.), *Advances in developmental psychology* (Vol. 1, pp. 37–86). Hillsdale, NJ: Lawrence Erlbaum Associates.

Rothbart, M. K., Derryberry, D., & Posner, M. I. (1994). A psychobiological approach to the development of temperament. In J. E. Bates & T. D. Wachs (Eds.), *Temperament: Individual differences at the interface of biology and behavior* (pp. 83–116). Washington, DC: American Psychological Association.

Rothbart, M. K., & Mauro, J. A. (1990). Questionnaire approaches to the study of infant temperament. In J. W. Fagen & J. Colombo (Eds.), *Individual differences in infancy: Reliability, stability and prediction* (pp. 411–429). Hillsdale, NJ: Lawrence Erlbaum Associates.

Ruff, H. A., & Rothbart, M. K. (1996). *Attention in early development: themes and variations.* New York: Oxford University Press.

Sameroff, A. J., & Chandler, M. J. (1975). Reproductive risk and the continuum of caretaking casualty. In F. D. Horowitz (Ed.), *Review of child development research* (Vol. 4, pp. 187–244). Chicago: University of Chicago Press.

Sanson, A. V., Prior, M., Garino, E., Oberklaid, F., & Sewell, J. (1987). The structure of infant temperament: Factor analysis of the Revised Infant Temperament Questionnaire. *Infant Behavior and Development, 10*, 97–104.

Sanson, A. V., & Rothbart, M. K. (1995). Child temperament and parenting. In M. Bornstein (Ed.), *Parenting* (Vol 4, pp. 299–321). Hillsdale, NJ: Lawrence Erlbaum Associates.

Silverman, I. W., & Ippolito, M. F. (1995). Maternal antecedents of delay ability in young children. *Journal of Applied Developmental Psychology, 16*, 569–591.

Thomas, A., & Chess, S. (1977). *Temperament and development.* New York: Brunner/Mazel.

Thomas, A., Chess, S., & Birch, H. G. (1968). *Temperament and behavior disorders in children.* New York: New York University Press.

Thomas, A., Chess, S., Birch, H. G., Hertzig, M. E., & Korn, S. (1963). *Behavioral individuality in early childhood.* New York: New York University Press.

Vaughn, S., & Schumm, J. S. (1996). Classroom ecologies: Classroom interactions and implications for inclusion of children with learning disabilities. In D. L.

Speece & B. K. Keogh (Eds.), *Research on classroom ecologies: Implications for inclusion of children with learning disabilities* (pp. 1–14). Mahwah, NJ: Lawrence Erlbaum Associates.

Wagner, S., Ganiban, J. M., & Cicchetti, D. (1990). Attention, memory, and perception in infants with Down syndrome: A review and commentary. In D. Cicchetti & M. Beeghly (Eds.), *Children with Down syndrome: A developmental perspective* (pp. 147–179). New York: Cambridge University Press.

# 4 *✦* Family Life Is More Than Managing Crisis: Broadening the Agenda of Research on Families Adapting to Childhood Disability

**Ronald Gallimore**
**Lucinda P. Bernheimer**
**Thomas S. Weisner**
*University of California, Los Angeles*

This chapter reviews efforts to broaden research on families adapting to childhood disability and delay. First, we briefly review and critique the long-standing emphasis in family research on crisis, stress, coping, and the restoration of emotional well-being. Second, to broaden family research to include capacities other than crisis management, we revisit what Rueben Hill (1949) called the "established routines" of family life and what families do to sustain them. Third, we review contemporary research on families adapting to childhood disability for evidence that sustaining a daily routine of life is a function distinguishable from those attendant to crisis and stress. Finally, we examine the intervention and research implications of the idea that an enduring family project is creation and maintenance of a sustainable daily routine of life.

## INTRODUCTION

Recent initiatives underscore a needed expansion of the scope and content of research on families adapting to children with special needs. The 1989 legislation (Amendments to the Individual With Disabilities Education Act, or IDEA), mandating development of individual family service plans (IFSPs), codified the idea that families can be recruited as proactive agents in interventions for children with disabilities (Harbin, 1993). The wording of the legislation refers to "enhancing the capacity of families to meet the special needs" of their children with handicaps (Gallagher, 1989, p. 388). Among other intentions, this wording encouraged professionals to regard families as partners to be empowered as active co-decision-makers rather than as cases to be managed.

These initiatives resonate with many contemporary social trends and are no longer the subject of debate. However, this is an instance of legislation and policy ahead of science, because many family functions remain largely unexamined. One exception is the capacity to manage the demands, strains, and stresses associated with childhood disability (Beresford, 1994b). Many significant contributions have been made in the study of crisis management, including family systems (Olson, Sprenkle, & Russell, 1979), family stress (McCubbin & Patterson, 1983), Patterson's Family Adjustment and Adaptation Response (FAAR) model extended to health issues (1988), and family life-cycle theory (Turnbull, Summers, & Brotherson, 1986). Many of these contributions owe a debt to Rueben Hill's (1949) classic study of family response to war separations in which he presented the ABCX model (A=stressor event; B=family's crisis-meeting resources; C=family's definition of stressor; C interacts with A and B to produce X (crisis)). The ABCX model was based on yet earlier studies of family adaptation to the Great Depression. Preceding adoption by the disability field, other foci of family stress research included effects of alcoholism and bereavement. Thus, the family model borrowed from sociology framed the rearing of a child with disabilities in terms of the stress and reactions attending crisis or disturbance of the family's homeostasis. Many efforts focused on the impact of initial diagnosis and entry into services rather than on daily life. The appeal and value of crisis-centered family theories is understandable, given the demands of childhood disability. The early emphasis on psychopathological reaction (Farber, 1959; Holt, 1958) reflected long-standing trends in social and behavioral research.

The stress/coping focus had many good effects: It helped justify services for parents dealing with childhood disability, documented that these families needed assistance, and called attention to the need for more funding. However, so exclusive a focus on crises, stress, and psychological reactions also perpetuated the notion "that a family with a child who has a disability is a family with a disability" (Glidden, 1995). Many studies focus on how much stress such families face, what they do about it, and how negative or psychopathological the consequences are. One problem, as Glidden (1995) noted, is the failure to distinguish between *demands* and *stressors*. The failure to maintain this distinction is explicitly contrary to the Lazarus and Folkman (1984) formulation, which insisted that demands are experienced differently in different families and environments, and that high demands do not inevitably produce high stress and therefore higher probabilities of negative reactions. Because *demands* are certainly higher in families dealing with childhood disability, failure to distinguish them from stressors "has tended to perpetuate the perception of maladjustment in families rearing children with developmental disabilities" (Lazarus & Folkman, 1984, p. 483). In addition, much of the research in the area has been carried out by researchers interested in psychological application and it is understandable that they may have focused on psychopathological problems families face in crisis and how professionals can help. Finally, because of the pathological perspective on families, much of the research has been conducted without reference to general research on families in the social sciences. As a result, families of children with disabilities continued to be viewed by implication or by default (if not explicitly) as different, more prone to pathology, and by implication, less competent (Byrne, Cunningham, & Sloper, 1988).

The past decade has seen a call to broaden research perspectives on families of children with disabilities to include adaptation and adjustment. Although there is a continuing interest in family stresses associated with childhood disabilities, there is also increasing recognition that families of children with problems are faced with the same tasks as are families with typically developing children (Barnett & Boyce, 1995; Byrne et al., 1988; Freedman, Litchfield, & Warfield, 1995; Hodapp & Zigler, 1993; Turnbull et al., 1986). All working parents, for example, struggle to balance values/goals, personal needs, work and home responsibilities, and to find and keep affordable child care, health care, and flexible and supportive environments.

The call to broaden research perspectives beyond crisis response comes from many sources. One of the most compelling is from the families of children with disabilities who in recent years have joined the dialogue and in some cases become partners in the search for new perspectives on family capacities. A recent volume included numerous first-person accounts of coping with childhood disabilities, many of which suggested that families are concerned with more than crises and their management (Turnbull et al., 1993). Indeed, many volumes in the personal account genre suggest families dealing with childhood disabilities do not think their lives and functions can be understood solely in terms of periodic crises breaking long paragraphs of everyday living (e.g. Kaufman, 1988). Some parents of children with disabilities have forcefully objected to researcher and practitioner focus on stress and coping (Vohs, 1993). Some suggest that we ask additional questions: "Professionals kept asking me what my 'needs' were. I didn't know what to say. I finally told them, 'Look, I'm not sure what you're talking about. So let me just tell you what happens from the time I get up in the morning until I go to sleep at night. Maybe that will help'" (remark made by parent panelist at a 1989 HCEEP conference on Parent-Professional Partnerships, reported in Bernheimer, Gallimore, & Kaufman, 1993, p. 267).

Parents such as this mother are talking about concerns beyond the emotional costs of daily demands and strains. They are telling researchers what they do to sustain a daily routine of life that—besides being emotionally tolerable—takes account of other realities and interests they have at stake. These parents are telling us to revisit Hill's ABCX model—a foundation of contemporary family research in the disability field—and remember that he defined stress-producing family crises as "disruptions of *established routines*" (Hansen & Johnson, 1979, p. 584, emphasis added). As some parents and researchers have suggested, the "established routines" of families and how they are created and sustained have been unwisely treated as background to more dramatic phenomena (Hansen, 1993; Weisner, 1984; Whiting & Edwards, 1988). It is not surprising that dramatic responses associated with crisis/stress/coping capture more attention than do established routines. For everyone, including researchers, "Most of our day-to-day behavior in families is routine: We act in a well established manner, and think about our actions—if we think about them at all—only after the fact" (Hansen, 1988, p. 54).

What some researchers have theorized about creating and sustaining a daily routine as an essential family function has direct relevance to IDEA's challenge regarding family capacities (Hansen, 1993; Weisner, 1984, 1998). Knowing what families do in crisis or how they handle emotional costs of dealing with childhood disability are necessary but not sufficient indicators of their functioning. We also need to conceptualize and research how families construct and sustain unremarkable times—the times of family life between episodes of crises and problems, when there is established routine, balance, homeostasis, and equilibrium. There is more to family life than crises that punctuate long passages of living; sustaining an established daily routine is an achievement worthy of respect and scientific inquiry. If family coping in times of stress is an important family capacity, ability to sustain a daily routine of life that is viable all the rest of the time deserves serious study and recognition. It represents a potentially important indicator of family functioning that is not tied to stress and psychopathological theories and models, and is related to many factors in addition to childhood disabilities. This is the central claim of our chapter. What are the implications of this claim for theory, research, and policy?

## A FAMILY PROJECT: CONSTRUCTING A SUSTAINABLE DAILY ROUTINE

All families must construct and maintain a daily routine, but not all daily routines are possible. A sustainable family routine is a compromise among the constraints we must live with, the values we hold, and the characteristics of individual family members. We do not arbitrarily choose when to go to work or shop or cook dinner; it is not irrelevant to deeply held values that families schedule meals so that parents and children are usually present; we do not participate in carpools to get children to special activities or services because we like the incidental social interactions involved in organizing them. Sustaining routines to reconcile many competing factors is an enduring family project, not just an occasional mobilization of coping strategies in response to stress.

Daily routines evolve over time and are neither static, rigid, arbitrary, optimized, nor entirely voluntary. Although routines change, they are not easily altered because the sustainability of the routine is the product of so many trade-offs. Some changes are a consequence of crisis and stress, but many are the reorganizing and fine-tuning of daily and weekly schedules that are familiar to every family. Sustainability rests in part on how congruent a family's routine is with the numerous factors that it must accommodate. When a family describes its daily routine much more is involved than may be manifest in brief narratives. Like everyday concepts, *patterns* of everyday life are experience-near, transparent, and taken for granted as the way things are and must be. As Geertz (1984) noted, "People use experience-near concepts spontaneously, unselfconsciously ... they do not, except fleetingly and on occasion, recognize that there are any concepts at all. That is what experience-near means—that ideas and the realities they inform are naturally and indissolubly bound up together. What else could you call a hippopotamus? Of course the gods are powerful, why else would we fear them" (p. 125).

Of course, many pieces of our routines are the way they are; how could they be otherwise? Naturally, we do not mention the redundant constraints and multiple purposes our routines reflect. They are both ordinary and transparent, and do not make as a good a conversation topic as do more dramatic episodes of our lives. The established routine and its constraints are the ground on which the figure of dramatic events occur. The relative lack of attention to routines is evidence for their power in everyday life, a power so pervasive that it goes without saying. What factors influence the shape and sustainability of the family daily routine?

## Factors Affecting Sustainability

*Ecological Features.*     The features of the ecological niche in which a family lives are a powerful constraint on what routines can be sustained. One of the most powerful features, as Whiting and Edwards (1988) documented, is the means by which the family's living is earned. In many parts of the world, daily routines are shaped by how far mothers must travel to fetch water or harvest their subsistence crops. In many societies, the 40-hour work week and the length of the daily commute ripple through a family and child's day, forcing compromises and choices that may be necessary but not always desirable. Whatever else must be accommodated by the family's routine, subsistence activities—whether in wage jobs or otherwise—have influence that places them first among equals. In addition to earning a living, in some environments, health or safety factors greatly influence family routines (e.g., in neighborhoods where children must be protected from violence, racial discrimination, and other urban ills). Transportation and communication required for work or other health, safety, and support requirements are also important features shaping routines. According to cross cultural research, another major factor affecting the organization of a family's routine is the number and complexity of domestic chores, including child care (Whiting & Edwards, 1988; Wishart, Bidder, & Gray, 1981). The reciprocal costs as well as benefits of social support networks also shape routines in many niches (Beresford, 1994b; Kazak & Wilcox, 1984; Trute & Hauch, 1988b; Waisbren, 1980).

*Values and Goals.*     Just as not all routines are possible, not all are acceptable even if possible. To be sustainable, a daily routine must not only be congruent with competing ecological factors, it must also be meaningful enough to the family that it is honored and defended (Weisner, Beizer, & Stolze, 1991). Thus, parents with strong familistic values will have difficulty sustaining a routine that is driven primarily by the demands of their high-pressure careers. Families of children with disabilities may find it easier to sustain a hectic schedule of transporting the child to a variety of community activities if they have strong "normalization" values. Parents who believe that all children, delayed or not, move through different, largely unrelated "stages" in life each of which is unique and special, may be less likely to sustain a routine directed at long term outcomes reached far in the future. Such cultural goals and moral values for child development and parenting play important roles in how daily routines are lived out in a community, by providing the end points, the purposes for parenting and development, as well as the appropriate scripts for how to achieve those goals (Harkness, Super, & New, 1996). In spite of the importance of parental goals, values, and moral commitments, little empirical work exists on the role played by values and goals in families with special needs children. Studies of meaningfulness have focused largely on religious values, which contribute to sustainability in two ways: by serving as a means of interpreting and giving meaning to the disability (Weisner et al., 1991), and by providing a system of support to help cope with the day-to-day realities of raising a child with problems (Fewell, 1986). It should be noted that religious beliefs can lead to negative as well as positive interpretations of parents' circumstances. For example, parents may evaluate their family circumstances as either punishment or reward, extensions of God's will, or lessons from God (Haworth, Hill, & Glidden, 1996). Religious belief systems are generally regarded as having a positive impact, however, because they provide a valuable interpretive framework (Haworth et al., 1996) and, by implication, contribute to a more sustainable daily routine.

*Personal Characteristics.*    Characteristics of family members are another factor that must be accommodated by the daily routine. For our purposes in this chapter, a good but not only example is the impact of a child's disabilities on the daily routine. Whereas earlier investigators suggested that the impact of the disability varies according to child diagnosis or cognitive level (Cummings, 1976; Holroyd & McArthur, 1976), more contemporary work confirms that it is the burden of care that matters to families (Byrne et al., 1988; McDonald, Couchonnal, & Early, 1996; Quine & Pahl, 1985). Thus, a child with limited independent living skills has the potential to cause more disruption (e.g., major financial expenditures associated with altering the home environment), daily hassles (e.g., complications in daily transportation), and disability-related problems (e.g., finding suitable leisure activities for the child) than does a child with better skills (Wallander, Pitt, & Mellins, 1990). Families adapting to disability often describe in substantial detail the measures they take to accommodate perceived child characteristics in order to sustain a routine (Gallimore, Weisner, Kaufman, & Bernheimer, 1989). Hence, one of the challenges of parents is to create and sustain a routine that balances the inevitably competing and varied competencies and personal characteristics of family members as well as care of the child with disabilities.

## A Sustainable Daily Routine and Other Family Projects

Sustaining a routine over the long haul and managing time-limited crises may be distinguishable projects, but they are always connected in experience. Some changes are initiated by crisis or emotional discomfort, but not all changes in the daily routine (or perhaps even most), are provoked by what is stressful or discomforting. Some are driven by strongly held beliefs about the way life should be lived. For example, Weisner et al. (1991) compared religious and nonreligious families regarding their adaptations to a child with early developmental delays. Although results were mixed for the impact of religion, there was some evidence that religious convictions mobilized noncrisis-related daily routine adjustments that were partly related to incorporating a child with delays into family life.

In other cases, a period of crisis may initiate a long rebuilding of the routine to restore sustainability in response to new circumstances. For example, Gallimore et al. (1989) presented a case of a family who bought a new home, in part to reduce stress on the family caring for two children, one with delays. Purchasing the house required the mother to take employment to pay the mortgage, which led to many other changes (including domestic role arrangements and increased access to child services) that the mother's paycheck also provided. In other cases, changes in the routine are made as small, unnoticed adjustments so mundane and ordinary that only through extended interviewing or observation would they be detected—because the families themselves do not encode them as important adaptations. Examples include a subtle change in dinner schedules, the quiet giving up of career goals by some mothers, or increases in child care by fathers that go unremarked.

As personal experience and stress research suggest (Beresford, 1994a), no family routine is sustainable if it takes too great a toll on any single individual. The disability literature is filled with accounts, for example, of mothers taken to the breaking point trying to sustain a routine that might optimize developmental gains for a child with disabilities (Featherstone, 1981; Kaufman, 1988; Park, 1982). No matter how much is gained in a child's development and safety, in domains of family functioning, or the instantiation of values into everyday life, if the emotional or social costs are too great a routine cannot be sustained.

However, in many instances the emotional and psychological well-being of parents and children are only one set of costs that families take into account. Gallimore et al. (1989) used case studies to illustrate how sustaining a daily routine depends on balancing multiple factors, including emotional well-being. For most of the 93 families followed over more than 10 years, emotional costs were not the pre-eminent factor driving parents' choices and efforts—the *sustainability* of their daily routine was often the focus of their efforts

(Gallimore, Coots, Weisner, Garnier, & Guthrie, 1996; Keogh, Bernheimer, Gallimore, & Weisner, in press; Weisner, Matheson, Coots, & Gallimore, 1997). The parents recognized that no matter how tired or stressed they individually or jointly felt at some time, life had to go on, and that often the best way to "feel better" and restore family harmony was a sustainable routine. Although it might not be perfect or optimized for every individual, it was "good enough" and, most important, it could be maintained over the long term. Many spoke of how they would "like it to be," but quickly added that what they were sustaining was as close as they were likely to get to their ideal—give or take a few adjustments here and there.

The daily routine project is often superordinate to emotional well-being, in part because individuals in a family are in conflict over resources, material and otherwise (Weisner, 1984). This is a familiar tension "expressed in the aged Hobbesian problem of a rational order of free individuals: If all pursue their own rational interests, how can order be maintained" (Hansen, 1993, p. 75). If each did, then the sustainability of a family's routine would be put at too great a risk by self-interest.

Several family models subsume the problem of self-interest conflict among individuals within a superordinate family-level process. Systems theory, for example, is based on the hypothesis that there are two central processes of family life: adaptability (communication and role flexibility) and cohesion (emotional bonding of individuals in family; Olson et al., 1979). Such family-level processes help mediate the conflictive potential of self-interest and its disruptive impact. However, to restore smooth function or to sustain it, Olson (1986) also argued that the family must preserve *a familiar sense of order and maintain balance between inevitable interpersonal conflicts* (emphasis added). This comes very close to saying that in addition to mediating conflict that arises among members, strengthening family bonds, and restoring emotional harmony, the family has a superordinate, and enduring project—constructing a *sustainable* daily life in which personal and interfamilial relations can be nurtured and mended. Constructing an emotionally and physically tolerable daily routine that accommodates everyone's needs and concerns, yet is sustainable given their ecological circumstances, is one way to preserve a sense of order and balance individual conflicts.

The theory and definition of adaptation itself leads us to consider ongoing systematic demands, rather than focusing on perturbations of the family's homeostasis. Adaptation is the *diminishing* responsiveness to repeated and continued stimulation (Helson, 1964), not continuous high responsiveness. Its functions are homeostasis and regulation of information. Adaptations enhance the relative ability to survive in a particular niche. Excessive focus on the immediate response to change due to stress, then, misses the deeper activity of adaptation, which is the routinization and balance of the person or family within the everyday routine and environment, not the dramatic changes. But what is the evidence that constructing a sustainable routine is a distinguishable, enduring project for families adapting to childhood disability?

## CONTEMPORARY FAMILY LITERATURE: LOCATING THE DAILY ROUTINE

In this section, we review selected literature for evidence that sustaining the daily routine is a family project distinguishable from coping with stress, a project that is described, implicitly or explicitly, by researchers, practitioners, and parents. The review is not confined to the mental retardation and developmental disabilities (MR/DD) field; we have also included publications from psychology, pediatrics, nursing, social welfare, and social work in addition to those from mental retardation. In some of this literature, the daily routine project and the family efforts to sustain it are relegated to the background by the focus on a stress model, or by an emphasis on individual coping. In other literature, the daily routine project is itself the focus, and sustaining it is an end in itself, not just a means of reducing stress or increasing individual well-being. We begin by examining two models of family functioning in households of children with disabilities, both of which refer to periods of balance, homeostasis, or stability: Patterson's FAAR model (Family Adjustment and Adaptation Response) and Turnbull et al.'s (1986) application of family life-cycle theory to disability.

Patterson (Patterson, 1988, 1991, 1995a, 1995b) recognized that crises and their management do not represent a full accounting of adaptation to childhood disability. Whereas a model of stress and coping underlies the FAAR, Patterson focuses on adaptation and adjustment, following Hill's (1949) definition of crises as "disruptions of *established routines*." The FAAR model is constructed around three domains: sources of stress, mediators of stress, and outcomes of stress:

> The sources of stress are termed *demands,* and can emerge from individual members, the family unit, or from the community. The mediators of stress are called *capabilities,* and also found in any of these systems. The family attempts to maintain balanced functioning by using capabilities (resources and coping behaviors) to meet demands (stressors, strains, and daily hassles). The meanings the family attributes to their situation (demands and capabilities) are a critical factor in achieving balanced functioning. ... The outcome of the family's efforts to achieve balanced functioning is called family *adjustment* or family *adaptation.* ... Good outcomes are reflected in (1) positive physical and mental health of individual members, (2) optimal role functioning of individual members, and (3) maintenance of a family unit that can accomplish its life cycle tasks. (Patterson, 1995a, p. 50)

One does not have to look any further to recognize that the task of constructing a sustainable routine is central if not featured in Patterson's conception. Family and community-level demands and capabilities are compatible with ecological *resources* and *constraints;* a positive outcome requires a *balance* between demands and capabilities. Family *meanings* serve as facilitators or inhibitors of balanced functioning. Like the sustainable daily routine described earlier in this chapter, Patterson's definition of *adjustment* constitutes relatively stable periods during which only minor changes are made in response to the daily demands of life. Patterson comments that during *adjustment* periods the organization of day-to-day family life incorporates the child's disability, but the disability does not become a focal point around which all else revolves (Patterson, 1991). Said differently, the daily routine is not solely child-driven. There is a balance between the needs of the child, the needs of other family members, and, by implication, all the other factors that must be accommodated to achieve a sustainable routine. In the FAAR model, the organization of day-to-day family life is not an end in itself, however. Of greater importance is the positive physical and emotional health of *individual* family members, and the optimal role functioning of *individual* members. Good outcomes are recognized at the level of the individual. At the family-level, the daily routine functions to accomplish its life cycle tasks.

Turnbull et al. (1986) also addressed life-cycle tasks. Applying family life-cycle theory to disability, they noted that families with mentally retarded members must adapt to chronic demands as well as life-cycle transitions. Although these transitions occasion change, discontinuity, and stress, within developmental stages routines are established that contribute to stability—until the next stress-producing transition. An extensive list of "chronic" family functions that Turnbull et al. assembled (generating income, health care and maintenance, food purchasing and preparation, to name a few) is distinguished as much by its applicability to everyday periods of stability and ordinariness as its relevance at times of transition, disruption, and crisis. These "chronic" functions that contribute to stability are not featured as targets of investigation themselves, but instead are viewed as "products or outcomes of family interaction, because they represent the results of interaction in terms of the ability to meet the individual needs of the family members" (Turnbull et al., 1986, p. 51).

Like the Patterson and Turnbull et al. contributions, many studies we reviewed come close but never explicitly explore routine sustainability as a distinguishable family function. Several investigators referenced family efforts to sustain their daily routine in studies of individual and family responses to the stress of parenting a child with disabilities. As example, Bradley, Parette, and VanBiervliet (1995) identified additions to family routines in homes with technology-dependent children: daily battery charging and cleaning, keeping a protected space clean for the ventilation system, and dealing with size/portability of the equipment when transporting the child.

Leyser (1994) conducted a 4-year follow-up interview study of families of children with disabilities and found that significantly fewer mothers in Year 5 than in Year 1 reported that the child had a negative impact on family life. At the same time, there were no differences in mothers' perceptions of the time needed to care for the child, or in perceptions of child behavior problems. In discussing the decreased negative impact, Leyser implicated three factors that have a direct impact on the daily routine's sustainability: subsistence, domestic workload, and support. Fewer mothers at follow-up reported financial hardships, more fathers were in better-paying jobs, and more mothers were in the work force. Regarding workload and support, more mothers reported weekly and daily contact with grandparents, who provided "help with daily routines, preparation of meals, and respite care" (Leyser, 1994, p. 383). The latter results suggest that focusing on the daily routine project would provide a more satisfying lens through which to examine changes during the 4 years that Leyser et al. followed these families. Additional glimpses of the daily routine project in studies of family stress may be found in Hornby and Seligman (1991); Quine and Pahl (1985); Sloper, Knussen, Turner, and Cunningham (1991); Tunali and Power (1993); and Wallander et al. (1990).

In other studies of positive parent outcomes, a sustainable daily routine can be identified as a background goal. Examples of positive outcomes include satisfaction (Byrne et al., 1988; Sloper & Turner, 1993), improved mental health (Beresford, 1994a; Quine & Pahl, 1985), and positive adaptation (Trute & Hauch, 1988a). In these studies, there is reference to a balance between resources and constraints and values, (e. g. mother and father roles in domestic and childcare task; Trute & Hauch, 1988b), or amount of time a mother has for herself and participation of other family members in household tasks (Byrne et al., 1988). In their study, McDonald et al. (1996) recorded parents' views of major pleasant events in the past year. Glimpses of daily routine concerns were visible in some reports: "C's behavior improved at home. I was able to remain in the car while he went into the local store and made purchases appropriately" (McDonald et al., 1996, p. 506).

Like this quotation from McDonald et al., in the literature cited thus far the daily routine project is treated implicitly and either obscured by the stress model or confounded with improving individual well-being (usually the mother's). In a comprehensive review on coping in families of children with disabilities, Beresford (1994b) examined research findings using the process model of coping (Lazarus & Folkman, 1984) as a theoretical ground. In this model, Beresford made a distinction between two kinds of coping resources: personal and socioecological. A close look at Beresford's description of socioecological resources reveals evidence of families working to sustain their routines (e.g., the marital relationship, social network, functional resources, and economic circumstances). However, in the studies reviewed these socioecological resources were evaluated for their instrumental contributions to coping with stress and restoring well-being.

The literature reviewed by Beresford extended also to the means by which families achieve a sustainable daily routine. For example, Quine and Pahl (1985) reported that many of the mothers of severely handicapped children in their interview study were sleep deprived because their children woke frequently at night. They noted that some mothers found the only solution was to sleep with the child so as to be able to attend to his or her needs without disturbing other family members. The implication is that as costly as this solution was to the mother, it was more costly to have the entire family's sleep disturbed. In a later study Quine and Pahl (1991) found a significant correlation between financial resources and lower maternal stress. Beresford's comment on this finding seems to acknowledge the impact of making a daily routine more sustainable, although the implications are filtered through focus on stress-induced emotional costs: "Money can buy practical resources such as child-minding, laundry equipment, and cleaning services, thus relieving parents of certain care and household tasks" (p. 189). That the routine might be made more sustainable was not noted as an explicit end in itself.

In summarizing an ethnographic study by Bregman (1980), Beresford clearly implicated sustainability of the daily routine as a family outcome worthy of consideration. The data were obtained by Bregman, who spent several days with each of six families whose child had a progressive neuromuscular disease. Beresford (1994b) described this study as a "fascinating, and perhaps unique" (p. 192) account of coping strategies:

> First, the families adopted a "take each day as it comes" philosophy and focused on the present. This was reflected in the ways their lives were organized. Daily activities were planned and completed. The children experienced interesting and exciting activities while they were still able to enjoy them. The families avoided pre-empting a need, preferring to deal with it when it actually arose. Second, parents aimed to maintain a lifestyle that was as normal as possible. Various strategies were used to attain this goal, including modifying clothing so the child could dress him or herself, and ensuring the child maintained social contacts with healthy children. … Third, the parents sought to minimize their family's vulnerability by reducing the risk of crises. This was done by keeping well informed, seeking out the best options for the child's health care and education, trouble-shooting, and monitoring the standard of services. Finally, Bregman noted that an important aspect of parental coping was to maintain and develop coping resources. Parents developed and capitalized their personal strengths. They believed they were caring for their children well and acknowledged their successes. Coping with the emotional strains of care included recreation and releasing emotions by crying. In addition, the parents drew on informal and formal support networks, including financial, emotional, and practical support. (Beresford, 1994b, pp. 192–193)

In Bregman's work, the treatment of the daily routine project is more explicit. There are references to meaningfulness, in the parents' goal of maintaining a normal lifestyle, and in the parents' beliefs that they were providing quality care to their children. We can also see evidence of congruence, in terms of the parents planning activities that their ill children could still enjoy, while using recreation and support to meet their own needs. Although Bregman's study is explicitly concerned with coping strategies, the focus on adaptation at the family level revealed snapshots of their everyday life. She brought explicitly into focus not only the central importance to families of constructing sustainable routines, but also some of the actions they took to sustain them.

Bregman's work suggested that one capacity of families worthy of investigation is their efforts to incorporate a child with disabilities into the families' routines. Such efforts would have to take account not only the child's needs and the emotional well-being of parents, but all the other factors that affect routine sustainability. In a longitudinal study that inquired directly about family efforts to construct sustainable routines, these efforts were defined as *accommodations* (Gallimore et al., 1989; Gallimore, Goldenberg, & Weisner, 1993; Gallimore, Weisner, Guthrie, Bernheimer, & Nihira, 1993; Keogh et al., in press; Weisner et al., 1997). In this study, family accommodations were presumed to occur in response to both serious concerns and mundane problems of daily life.

Using an ecocultural model as a framework (Weisner, 1984), in-depth interviews gave parents an extended opportunity to describe their daily routines and what they did to achieve sustainability, including the kind and intensity of accommodations made in response to the child with delays. Asking parents directly produced a wealth of reports about efforts made to sustain their daily routines. Using a rating system checked for reliability by independent, blind coders, each family was assessed for number and intensity of accommodations made at three child ages. From preschool to late childhood, 93 families reported a substantial, statistically significant increase in the number of accommodations made: 749, 891, and 1,388 at ages 3, 7, and 11, respectively. Ratings of intensity, or how much effort families put into their accommodations, on the other hand, showed little change over the same period (Gallimore et al., 1996). Accommodations were reported by parents in 10 different ecological and cultural domains, including those pertaining to health and safety, family subsistence, domestic chores, and social and emotional relationships. Most of the accommodations reported have parallels in Beresford's (1994a) "socio-ecological coping resources" of social support, support from spouse, extended family, and formal agencies, marital status, and socio-economic circumstances. In addition, they were similar in many respects with those reported by other researchers, for example Sloper and Turner's (1993) study of physically disabled children and their families. Sloper and Turner suggested that parent resources and coping strategies include material resources, employment, housing, social and family resources, social networks and support systems, family environment, and marital relationship; as well as psychological resources such as personality, control orientation and problem-solving, and help-seeking skills and strategies. Although many of these coping resources no doubt serve to secure or restore emotional well-being, they are also plausibly used to sustain a daily routine.

Although much remains to be explored, available literature (and every reader's own everyday experience) provides some support for our contention that sustaining a daily routine is a major family function. Often treated as given, once featured it is relatively easy to find hints and hard signs in the research literature that it is a family function distinguishable from crisis response and management functions. It is a candidate for the broadened agenda that the research community has been challenged to develop, an agenda that includes the positive as well as the psychopathological forms of family adaptation to developmental disabilities. How the sustainable routine project might aid intervention planning, and what more we need to learn about it are the subjects of the next section.

## INTERVENTION AND RESEARCH IMPLICATIONS

Intervention Issues

Legislated changes and increased awareness of the importance of families in the lives of children with disabilities have had a significant impact on clinical practice (Bailey & Simeonsson, 1988; Guralnick, 1989; Krauss & Jacobs, 1990). The change in emphasis from child to family is epitomized in the shift from Individual Education Programs (IEPs) to Individual Family Service Plans (IFSPs). Desired outcomes of intervention programs, once conceptualized solely in terms of child characteristics, now include parent empowerment (Dunst, Trivette, & Deal, 1988; Johnson, McGonigel, & Kaufmann, 1989), and parent satisfaction (McBride, Brotherson, Joanning, Whiddon, & Demmitt, 1993; McWilliam et al., 1995). The traditional interpretation that a child with problems means a family with problems has received serious and healthy challenge (Dyson, 1993; Glidden, 1993; Innocenti, Huh, & Boyce, 1992; Mahoney, O'Sullivan, & Robinson, 1992; Shonkoff, Hauser-Cram, Krauss, & Upshur, 1992). From these and other sources, professionals are now urged to recognize and build on family capacities in order to design interventions that will best meet the needs of the child in the context of the family.

Not surprisingly, the shift to family-focused intervention has encountered some difficulties. Many IFSP plans fail to be fully implemented or sustained by parents (Meyer & Bailey, 1993). Clinicians frequently complain that parents do not follow through on what seem to be well-thought-out intervention plans. Bernheimer and Keogh (1995) observed that the gap between professional advice and parental practice is common and gives pause—why aren't well-designed plans always implemented and sustained? One possibility is suggested in preceding sections of this chapter—family-focused interventions may not always be consistent with, and embedded in, the everyday routines of family life. This possibility is clearly indicated in recent literature emphasizing the importance to parents of professionals who "consider unique family environments and routines" (Brotherson & Goldstein, 1992, p. 519; see also Affleck & Tennen, 1993; Bosch, 1996; Herman, Marcenko, & Hazel, 1996).

There is also some indication that attention to a family's daily routine increases the likelihood that more precise treatment plans will be developed. Reflecting on the lack of an empirical rationale for services to children with severe disabilities, Quine and Pahl (1985) described these services as a "mixture of expediency, idealism, and consumer demand" (p. 501). They advocated translating detailed research about the everyday challenges faced by parents into services, noting that such an approach is important in terms of deciding what services should be provided, and which families should be given priority if services are limited.

The issue then becomes the most effective (and least intrusive) way to identify problems with and challenges to intervention plans. Byrne et al. (1988) stressed the importance of not simply asking parents if there are problems and accepting their replies at face value. Rather, parents should be given time to think about how things really are, and should be asked specific questions in order to help them do this. The aim is "not to discover a problem come what may, but to obtain a valid picture" (p. 53). When parents describe their daily lives, they are providing professionals with a picture of something that implicates intervention planning. Assessments that precede intervention planning must address a wide range of characteristics describing family functioning, including what the daily routine represents and what it reflects.

## Finding, Adapting, and Creating "Slots" for Intervention in the Daily Routine

> Where is that fifteen minutes [to carry out the intervention plan] going to come from? What am I supposed to give up? Taking the kids to the park? Reading a bedtime story to my eldest? Washing the breakfast dishes? Sorting the laundry? Grading students' papers? Because there is no time in my life that hasn't been spoken for, and for every fifteen-minute activity that is added, one has to be taken away. (Featherstone, 1981, p. 78)

As Featherstone suggested, finding a place in a family's routine for something new, such as changes that might be involved in an intervention, nearly always requires trade-offs. Whether the child comes to a center or clinic for treatment, or the professional visits the home, the family's daily routine must accommodate the intervention. To get to services, the child must be transported by somebody, usually a parent who may have to adjust and alter his or her schedule. A schedule alteration may require the assistance of others, such as a neighbor or relative who will supervise the other siblings in the family, or an employer who agrees to flexible work hours. The family that implements a plan at home must make parallel accommodations. Some time, place, and person must be found in the daily routine to do the treatment that has been planned. Said differently, there must be a "slot" in the daily routine to which the intervention can be "fitted."

If all that is involved is finding a slot, then little more is entailed than a common sense appraisal of whether an intervention can be carried out by the family. But if a slot has to be adapted or created, in many instances the daily routine must be more thoroughly examined to determine what the family is already trying to do. Despite its ordinary and mundane nature, the daily routine of family life is an arena in which parents seek and in fact have some control. Many families use what control they have over their routine to achieve the kind of daily life they desire within the constraints under which they live. Thus, the sustainable daily routine that a clinician sees or has described by the parents is fitted not only to material factors such as income and work hours, but also to the values and goals of the family. Changing that routine or adapting it to accommodate an intervention may be far more difficult, and have more rippling effects than might at first seem likely. Consider this case reported by Bernheimer, Gallimore, and Weisner (1990):

> Todd was one of four children. His parents ran a mom and pop grocery store, and placed a high premium on quality family time, although it was difficult getting everyone together. One daily period of togetherness was the dinner hour. Because Todd was very withdrawn socially, the intervenor felt the dinner hour would be an excellent opportunity for intensive family input for Todd. The parents were initially enthusiastic, because the intended outcome—a more socially appropriate Todd—would enhance the quality of "family time." The unintended outcome was quite different, however. In addition to being socially withdrawn, Todd was very disruptive; throwing his food on the floor, leaving his seat and running around the table in circles. Thus "family time" became chaotic and stressful. The parents designed a new intervention: Todd was fed early, and during dinner, he was seated in front of the television to watch tapes of "Sesame Street," an activity he would stay with for a good half hour. The family dinner was salvaged as "quality time" for the other members of the family, while Todd was engaged in an age-appropriate activity [REACH, Case 401]. (p. 229 )

Neither the clinicians nor parents fully realized when they designed this intervention that the daily routine followed by the family was not only fitted to work schedules, but to strongly held values. Their evolved, multiply determined routine balanced many considerations, so that attempts to change it tampered with considerations that the parents did not always fully appreciate were at stake. The intervention could not be continued as planned because it threatened the sustainability of their routine that, in the end, they wished to defend.

Does knowledge about the daily routine ensure that professional interventions will be successfully implemented in all families? Clearly, no, some families faced with overwhelming external pressures will always challenge the professionals who plan interventions. The daily routine in these families is likely to be composed of activities that seem unrelated to the child (e.g., keeping up with the rent, making food stamps stretch until the end of the month, coping with substance abuse). Yet making "a sensitive examination of the … context … that receives an intervention" (Gallimore, Goldenberg, & Weisner, 1993, p. 553) should help practitioners understand what needs to happen in order for an intervention to be implemented. It should also prevent practitioners from introducing additional stress to a multiply challenged family.

Currently, there is no consensus about how best to assess the family context that receives an intervention. Although assessment of the daily routine represents a promising approach conceptually, a long operational road lies ahead in terms of developing procedures that complement existing measures of stress and coping. Time use and diary measures, or time allocation methods, are available, but have not been used for this purpose to our knowledge, and may be too clock-based and difficult for parents to complete (Gross, 1984; Juster & Stafford, 1985). Global ratings of daily routine sustainability have been reliably obtained (Weisner et al., 1997) as have ratings of family accommodations (Gallimore et al., 1989, 1993, 1996). However, these ratings have so far been used only in research, and remain unexamined as tools of intervention assessment.

Examining a family's efforts to shape their daily routines offers a window into one form of functional instrumentality that resonates with legislative calls to "strengthen family capacity." However, "enhancing the capacity of families to meet the special needs" of their children (Gallagher, 1989, p. 388) by attending to the daily routine requires clinicians to recognize that families are already doing something. It requires listening more closely to parents' accounts and concerns, and what they do to sustain their routines. Listening means probing and understanding the complex balancing of ecological constraints, values, and individual characteristics that are encoded into the accommodations that sustain the family's daily routine. By knowing the accommodations a family makes, and the many factors that are balanced by them, parents and clinicians can jointly construct "successful interventions...that can be woven back into the daily routine. They are the threads that provide professionals with the tools to reinforce, rather than fray, the fabric of everyday life" (Bernheimer & Keogh, 1995, p. 430).

## Implications for Research

In the past several years, a growing chorus of investigators have noted that there are families of children with disabilities who are managing very well (Bernheimer & Keogh, 1995; Byrne et al., 1988; Hanson & Hanline, 1990; Keogh et al., in press; Trivette, Dunst, Deal, Hammer, & Probst, 1990). As the shift to family-focused interventions has challenged practitioners to chart new territories, so has the shift to family adaptation and adjustment challenged researchers to ask new questions. Increasing numbers of investigators have replaced the question "How sick are these families?" with the question "How healthy are these families?" Family outcomes of stress, marital discord, maladjustment, and malaise are being replaced by outcomes of adaptation, satisfaction, marital harmony, and positive adjustment.

Ironically, this second generation of research is plagued by many of the same issues that were identified for the preceding one. Summers (1988) observed that positive family outcomes are defined as generally as are negative family outcomes. Broad constructs are used (e.g., acceptance, adjustment, adaptation), and various investigators define these constructs differently. The benefit of a focus on family strengths rather than pathologies is clear; but the continued focus on responses to stress due to the child with disabilities, even if now focused on the positive end of the continuum of family responses, has many of the same problems as the earlier work.

A second issue noted by Summers is the need to consider multiple impacts of a child with disabilities on the family. She noted that even a "clean" stress (or adaptation) measure will not provide a comprehensive picture of the impact of a disability on families. A family might be adapting through the use of one coping strategy or another, but also failing to accomplish some essential task. Perhaps there is very little parental time available for siblings or, perhaps, family life revolves around the child with problems to the extent that parents have little time for their own relationship. Summers advocates developing measures that define several domains of family functioning and evaluating the degree to which each family member feels his or her needs are being met in each area.

A third issue is related to the question being asked with increasing frequency: "Why is it that some families appear to be doing better than others?" Although several investigators have measured the relation between factors such as child characteristics, perceptions of family life, or family structure variables and the well-being of family members, few have examined the processes through which these factors may influence family functioning (Harris & McHale, 1989; Quittner, Opipari, Regoli, Jacobsen, & Eigen, 1992; Reddon, McDonald, & Kysela, 1992). For example, a mother's education is often strongly correlated with her children's cognitive development, although many studies leave unexamined the mediating mechanisms between the static and developmental variables.

In our view, research on the daily routine and associated family functions responds to these three issues. First, a new positive outcome can be defined and operationalized as a sustainable daily routine that measures the effective fit among resources, goals, and competing individual interests in the family's social ecology. In presenting this point of view, Weisner et al. (1997) argued that assessing routine sustainability opens new lines of investigation that complement the historic focus on crisis and stress. By not confounding family and individual outcomes, this approach does not assume that successful family outcomes necessarily converge with best or optimal outcomes for any single individual. Rather, this approach explicitly defines a "good family outcome" as one that sustains all members in a routine that creates and supports resilient responses to threat and challenge (Lancaster & Lancaster, 1983).

Second, the issue of multiple impacts is addressed by the fact that family accommodations that maintain a daily routine are distributed across 10 different ecological and cultural domains (Gallimore et al., 1989; Weisner, 1984). Thus, it is possible to identify multiple domains affected by a child with disabilities and thereby obtain a more differentiated assessment of child impact on family functioning. At the same time, the pattern of family accommodations illuminates the processes through which child characteristics or family structure influence family functioning. Support for this notion is found in the work of Boyce, Jensen, James, and Peacock (1983), whose research with families of children with respiratory illnesses demonstrated that family routines constitute an important moderator in the general relationship between stress and illness. They concluded that "family routines appear to be both a rich source of information about an individual family and a sensitive indicator of similarities and differences among families" (p. 194). Thus, it might be possible to identify characteristic patterns of accommodation that differentiate families adapting to distinctly different kinds of disabilities—a prediction that depends on a parallel impact on the daily routine.

The third point concerns the relationship between child characteristics and family functioning. A main impetus for the shift to family-focused interventions was the acknowledgment of families as a context for early child development. It seems ironic, then, that the bulk of family research casts child characteristics (e.g., IQ, specific diagnosis, severity of the disability) as independent variables, and family status or functioning (e.g., stress level or marital satisfaction) as dependent variables. When the research question concerns the impact of the family on the child, measures of family stress and satisfaction and other characteristics are not sufficient: We need to identify how those relatively global characteristics affect the everyday routine of development-sensitive activities that influence the child. For example, Baldwin, Baldwin, and Cole's (1990) study of stress-resistant families and children showed that "proximal and distal risk variables differ from one another in the degree to which they directly impinge on the child" (pp. 257), and, we would add, on the family. A major mediator of impingement, according to cross-cultural studies, is the way families organize children's daily lives, who they are with, what they are doing, and the meaning attributed to it by those involved (Weisner, in press).

## Final Thoughts on Broadening the Research Agenda

Although well-being is often thought of as a psychological state, there is a sociocultural parallel: competence and engagement in established daily routines and activities (Weisner, 1984; Weisner et al., 1997). Well-being is enhanced through participation in sustainable routines, in addition to whatever enhanced well-being comes from specific kinds of interactions, work roles of parents, stimulation in the home, and so forth. A sociocentric conception of well-being is better fitted to the everyday achievement of families in creating a routine, than are individualistic, psychological conceptions of happiness or coping skills. There is robust evidence that sustaining a daily routine is an enduring and valued project for families in all cultures—a project with major impact on child development in addition to well-being (Weisner, 1984; Weisner et al., 1997). Broadening the research agenda to focus on this sociocultural family project is one way to meet the challenge to enhance the adaptive capacity of families of children with handicaps (Gallagher, 1989).

Finally, some research approaches make implicit assumptions about what constitutes "good or better" families and family life. Some of these assumptions are as unexamined as the ones held in our culture about the ideal family of two parents and a few children living in separate households with distanced kin relations. Sometime in the past, unacknowledged cultural models shaped investigations, so that variations in family structure and lifestyle were defined as deviations (Keogh et al., in press). Happily, the growing appreciation of diversity in our society has raised awareness that families come in varying forms, sizes, and styles. In disability research, there has been a parallel challenging of implicit assumptions: Many now question whether managing crises and coping with stress are the only useful lens for studying families rearing children with disabilities, just as many question the overemphasis on decontextualized cognitive and verbal assessments as the central outcome for assessing individual child competencies. Parents, policymakers, practitioners, and researchers have begun to insist that other family matters be added to the investigative agenda. Vohs, a single parent of a child with developmental disabilities, voiced this insistence as well as anyone: "To me, [coping] has always connoted a sense of putting up with, or enduring, an undesirable situation. I personally decided many years ago that the possibility of a life gauged against a standard of coping as the highest value did not inspire me" (Vohs, 1993, p. 51).

## ACKNOWLEDGMENTS

The writing of this chapter was supported by grants from the National Institute of Child Health and Human Development (HD19124 and HD11944). Thanks are due to Jennifer Coots and Marty W. Krauss for comments on an earlier draft. The authors gratefully acknowledge the support of Robert B. Edgerton and their other colleagues in the Sociobehavioral Research Group of UCLA's Mental Retardation Research Center and the Division of Social Psychiatry. During the year in which this chapter was prepared, Weisner was at the Center for Advanced Study in the Behavioral Sciences with support provided by National Science Foundation Grant #SBR-9022192 and the William T. Grant Foundation Grant #95167795.

## REFERENCES

Affleck, G., & Tennen, H. (1993). Cognitive adaptation to adversity: Insights from parents of medically fragile infants. In A. P. Turnbull, J. M. Patterson, S. K. Behr, D. L. Murphy, J. G. Marquis, & M. J. Blue-Banning (Eds.), *Cognitive coping, families, and disability.* (pp. 135–150) Baltimore: Paul H. Brookes.

Bailey, D. B., & Simeonsson, R. J. (1988). Assessing needs of families with handicapped infants. *Journal of Special Education, 22,* 117–129.

Baldwin, A. L., Baldwin, C., & Cole, R. E. (1990). Stress-resistant families and stress-resistant children. In J. Rolf, A. S. Mastem, D. Cicchetti, K. H. Nuechterlein, & S. Weintraub (Eds.), *Risk and protective factors in the development of psychopathology* (pp. 257–281). Cambridge, England: Cambridge University Press.

Barnett, W. S., & Boyce, G. C. (1995). Effects of children with Down Syndrome on parents' activities. *American Journal on Mental Retardation, 100,* 115–127.

Beresford, B. A. (1994a). Easing the strain: Assessing the impact of a Family Fund grant on mothers caring for a severely disabled child. *Child: Care, Health, and Development, 19,* 369–378.

Beresford, B. A. (1994b). Resources and strategies: How parents cope with the care of a disabled child. *Journal of Child Psychology and Psychiatry, 35,* 171–209.

Bernheimer, L. P., Gallimore, R., & Kaufman, S. Z. (1993). Clinical assessment in a family context: A four group typology of family experiences with young children with developmental delays. *Journal of Early Intervention, 17(3)*, 253–269.

Bernheimer, L. P., Gallimore, R., & Weisner, T. S. (1990). Ecocultural theory as a context for the Individual Family Service Plan. *Journal of Early Intervention, 14(3), 219–233.*

Bernheimer, L. P., & Keogh, B. K. (1995). Weaving interventions into the fabric of everyday life: An approach to family assessment. *Topics in Early Childhood Special Education, 15(4)*, 415–433.

Bosch, L. A. (1996). Needs of parents of young children with developmental delays: Implications for social work practice. *Families in Society: The Journal of Contemporary Human Services, 77*, 477–486.

Boyce, W. T., Jensen, E. W., James, S. A., & Peacock, J. L. (1983). The family routines inventory: Theoretical origins. *Social Science and Medicine, 17*, 193–200.

Bradley, R. H., Parette, H. P., & VanBiervliet, A. (1995). Families of young technology-dependent children and the social worker. *Social Work in Pediatrics, 21*, 23–37.

Bregman, A. M. (1980). Living with progressive childhood illness: Parental management of neuromuscular disease. *Social Work in Health Care, 5*, 387–408.

Brotherson, M. J., & Goldstein, B. L. (1992). Time as a resource and constraint for parents of young children with disabilities: Implications for early intervention services. *Topics in Early Childhood Special Education 12*, 508–527.

Byrne, E. A., Cunningham, C. C., & Sloper, P. (1988). *Families and their children with Down's Syndrome.* London: Routledge.

Cummings, S. T. (1976). The impact of the child's deficiency on the father: A study of fathers of mentally retarded and or chronically ill children. *American Journal of Orthopsychiatry, 46*, 246–255.

Dunst, C., Trivette, C., & Deal, A. (1988). *Enabling and empowering families.* Cambridge, MA: Brookline.

Dyson, L. (1993). Response to the presence of a child with disabilities: parental stress and family functioning over time. *American Journal on Mental Retardation, 98*, 207–218.

Farber, B. (1959). Effects of a severely mentally retarded child on family integration. *Monographs of the Society for Research on Child Development, 24* (Whole No. 71).

Featherstone, H. (1981). *A difference in the family.* London: Penguin.

Fewell, R. R. (1986). Supports from religious organizations and personal beliefs. In R. R. Fewell & P. F. Vadasy (Eds.), *Families of handicapped children: Needs and supports across the life span* (pp. 297–316). Austin, TX: Pro-Ed.

Freedman, R. I., Litchfield, L. C., & Warfield, M. E. (1995). Balancing work and family: Perspectives of parents of children with developmental disabilities. *Families in Society: 76*, 517–514.

Gallagher, J. J. (1989). A new policy initiative: Infants and toddlers with handicapping conditions. *American Psychologist, 44*, 387–391.

Gallimore, R., Coots, J. J., Weisner, T. S., Garnier, H. E. & Guthrie, D. (1996). Family responses to children with early developmental delays II: Accommodation intensity and activity in early and middle childhood. *American Journal on Mental Retardation, 101* (3), 215–232.

Gallimore, R., Goldenberg, C. N., & Weisner, T. S. (1993). The social construction and subjective reality of activity settings: Implications for community psychology. *American Journal of Community Psychology, 21* (4), 537–559.

Gallimore, R., Weisner, T. S., Guthrie, D., Bernheimer, L. P., & Nihira, K. (1993). Family responses to young children with developmental delays: Accommodation activity in ecological and cultural context. *American Journal on Mental Retardation, 98* (2), 185–206.

Gallimore, R., Weisner, T. S., Kaufman, S. Z., & Bernheimer, L. P. (1989). The Social construction of ecocultural niches: Family accommodation of developmentally delayed children. *American Journal on Mental Retardation, 94,* 216–230.

Geertz, C. (1984). "From the native's point of view": On the nature of anthropological understanding. In R. A. Shweder & R. LeVine (Eds.), *Culture theory: Essays on mind, self, and emotion* (pp. 123–136). Cambridge, England: Cambridge University Press.

Glidden, L. M. (1993). What we do *not* know about families with children who have developmental disabilities: Questionnaire on resources and stress as a case study. *American Journal on Mental Retardation, 97,* 481–495.

Gross, D. R. (1984). Time allocation: A tool for the study of cultural behavior. *Annual Review of Anthropology, 13,* 519–558.

Guralnick, M. J. (1989). Recent developments in early intervention efficacy research: Implications for family involvement in PL 99–457. *Topics in Early Childhood Special Education, 9,* 1–17.

Hansen, D. A. (1988). Schooling, stress, and family development: Rethinking the social role metaphor. In D. M. Klein & J. Aldous (Eds.), *Social stress and family development* (pp. 44–78). New York: The Guildford Press.

Hansen, D. A. (1993). The child in family and school: Agency and the workings of time. In P. A. Cowan, D. Field, D. A. Hansen, A. Skolnick, & G. E. Swanson (Eds.), *Family, self, and society: Toward a new agenda for family research.* (pp. 69–102) Hillsdale, NJ: Lawrence Erlbaum Associates.

Hansen, D. A., & Johnson, V. A. (1979). Rethinking family stress theory: Definitional aspects. In W. R. Burr, R. Hill, F. I. Nye, & I. L. Reiss (Eds.), *Contemporary theories about the family: Research-based theories* (Vol. l, pp. 582–603). New York: Free Press.

Hanson, M. J., & Hanline, M. F. (1990). Parenting a child with a disability: A longitudinal study of parent stress and adaptation. *Journal of Early Intervention, 14,* 234–248.

Harbin, G. L. (1993). Family issues of children with disabilities: How research and theory have modified practices in intervention. In N. J. Anastasiow & S. Hamel (Eds.), *At-risk infants: Interventions, families and research* (pp. 101–111). Baltimore: Brookes.

Harkness, S., Super, C., & New, R. (Eds.). (1996). *Parents' cultural belief systems.* New York: Guilford.

Harris, V. S., & McHale, S. M. (1989). Family life problems, daily caregiving activities, and the psychological well-being of mothers of mentally retarded children. *American Journal on Mental Retardation, 94,* 231–239.

Haworth, A. M., Hill, A. E., & Glidden, L. M. (1996). Measuring religiousness of parents of children with developmental disabilities. *Mental Retardation, 34,* 271–279.

Helson, H. (1964). *Adaptation-level theory: An experimental and systematic approach to behavior.* New York: Harper & Row.

Herman, S. E., Marcenko, M. O., & Hazel, K. L. (1996). Parents' perspectives on quality in family support programs. *Journal of Mental Health Administration, 23,* 156–169.

Hill, R. (1949). *Families under stress.* New York: Harper & Row.

Hodapp, R. M., & Zigler, E. (1993). Comparison of families of children with mental retardation and families of children without mental retardation. *Mental Retardation, 31,* 75–77.

Holroyd, J., & McArthur, D. (1976). Mental retardation and stress on the parents: A contrast between Down's syndrome and childhood autism. *American Journal of Mental Deficiency, 80,* 431–436.

Holt, K. S. (1958). The home care of severely retarded children. *Pediatrics, 2,* 744–755.

Hornby, G., & Seligman, M. (1991). Disability and the family: current status and future developments. *Counseling Psychology Quarterly, 4,* 267–271.

Innocenti, M. S., Huh, K., & Boyce, G. C. (1992). Families of children with disabilities: Normative data and other considerations on parenting stress. *Topics in Early Childhood Special Education, 12,* 403–427.

Johnson, B. H., McGonigel, M. J., & Kaufmann, R. K. (1989). *Guidelines and recommended practices for the individualized family service plan.* Chapel Hill, NC: National Early Childhood Technical Assistance System.

Juster, F. T., & Stafford, F. P. (Eds.) (1985). *Time, goods, and well-being.* Ann Arbor, University of Michigan Press: Institute for Social Research.

Kaufman, S. (1988). *Retarded isn't stupid, Mom!* Baltimore: Brookes.

Kazak, A. E., & Wilcox, B. L. (1984). The structure and function of social support networks in families with handicapped children. *American Journal of Community Psychology, 12,* 645–661.

Keogh, B. K., Bernheimer, L. P., Gallimore, R., & Weisner, T. S. (1998). Child and family outcomes over time: A longitudnal perspective on developmental delays. In M. Lewis & C. Feiring (Eds.), *Families, risk, & competence.* Mahwah, NJ: Lawrence Erlbaum Associates.

Krauss, M. W., & Jacobs, F. (1990). Family assessment: Purposes and techniques. In S. Meisels & J. P. Shonkoff (Eds.), *Handbook of early childhood intervention* (pp. 303–325). Cambridge, England: Cambridge University Press.

Lancaster, J. B., & Lancaster, C. S. (1983). Parental investment: The hominid adaptation. In D. Ortner (Ed.), *How humans adapt: A biocultural odyssey* (pp. 333–399). Washington, DC: Smithsonian Institution Press.

Lazarus, R. S., & Folkman, S. (1984). *Stress, appraisal, and coping.* New York: Springer.

Leyser, Y. (1994). Stress and adaptation in orthodox Jewish families with a disabled child. *American Journal of Orthopsychiatry, 64,* 376–385.

Mahoney. G., O'Sullivan, P., & Robinson, C. (1992). The family environments of children with disabilities: Diverse but not so different. *Topics in Early Childhood Education, 12,* 386–402.

McBride, S. L., Brotherson, M. J., Joanning, H., Whiddon, D., & Demmitt, A. (1993). Implementation of family-centered services: Perceptions of families and professionals. *Journal of Early Intervention, 17,* 414–430.

McCubbin, H. L., & Patterson, J. M. (1983). The family stress process: The double ABCX model of family adjustment and adaptation. In H. McCubbin, M. Sussman, & J. Patterson (Eds.), *Social stress and the family: Advances and developments in family stress theory and research* (pp. 7–37). New York: Haworth.

McDonald, T. P., Couchonnal, G., & Early, T. (1996). The impact of major events on the lives of family caregivers of children with disabilities. *Families in Society: The Journal of Contemporary Human Services, 75,* 502–514.

McWilliam, R. A., Lang, L., Vandiviere, P., Angell, R., Collins, L., & Underdown, G. (1995). Satisfaction and struggles: Family perceptions of early intervention services. *Journal of Early Intervention, 19,* 43–60.

Meyer, E. C., & Bailey, D. B. (1993). Family-centered care in early intervention: Community and hospital settings. In J. L. Paul & R. J. Simeonsson (Eds.), *Children with special needs: Family culture, and society* (pp. 181–209). Orlando, FL: Harcourt Brace Jovanovich.

Olson, D. H. (1986). Circumplex model VII: Validation studies and FACES III. *Family Process, 26,* 337–351

Olson, D. H., Sprenkle, D. H., & Russell, C. (1979). Circumplex model of marital and family systems. I: Cohesion and adaptability dimension, family types and clinical applications *Family Process, 18,* 3–28.

Park, C. C. (1982). *The siege.* Boston: Little, Brown.

Patterson, J. M. (1988). Families experiencing stress. I. The Family Adjustment and Adaptation Response Model. II. Applying the FAAR Model to health-related issues for intervention and research. *Family Systems Medicine, 6* (2), 202–237.

Patterson, J. M. (1991). Family resilience to the challenge of a child's disability. *Pediatric Annals, 20,* 491–499.

Patterson, J. M. (1995a). Promoting resilience in families experiencing stress. *Pediatric Clinics of North America, 42,* 47–63.

Patterson, J. M. (1995b). The role of family meanings in adaptation to chronic illness and disability. In A. P. Turnbull, J. M. Patterson, S. K. Behr, D. L. Murphy, J. G. Marquis, & M. J. Blue-Banning (Eds.), *Cognitive coping, families, and disability* (pp. 221–238). Baltimore: Brookes.

Quine, L., & Pahl, J. (1985). Examining the causes of stress in families with severely mentally handicapped children. *British Journal of Social Work, 15,* 501–517.

Quine, L., & Pahl, J. (1991). Stress and coping in mothers caring for a child with severe learning difficulties: A test of Lazarus' transaction model of coping. *Journal of Community and Applied Psychology, 1,* 57–70.

Quittner, A. L., Opipari, L. C., Regoli, M. J., Jacobsen, J., & Eigen, H. (1992). The impact of caregiving and role strain on family life: Comparisons between mothers of children with cystic fibrosis and matched controls. *Rehabilitation Psychology, 37,* 275–290.

Reddon, J. E., McDonald, L., & Kysela, G. M. (1992). Parental coping and family stress I: Resources for and functioning of families with a preschool child having a developmental disability. *Early Child Development and Care, 83,* 1–26.

Shonkoff, J. P., Hauser-Cram, P., Krauss, M. W., & Upshur, C. C. (1992). Development of infants with disabilities and their families. *Monographs of the Society for Research in Child Development, 57* (6, Serial No. 230).

Sloper, P., Knussen, C., Turner, S., & Cunningham, C. (1991). Factors related to stress and satisfaction with life in families of children with Down's Syndrome. *Journal of Child Psychology and Psychiatry, 32,* 655–676.

Sloper, P., & Turner, S. (1993). Risk and resistance factors in the adaptation of parents of children with severe physical disability. *Journal of Child Psychology and Psychiatry, 34,* 167–188.

Summers, J. A. (1988). Family adjustment: Issues in research on families with developmentally disabled children. In V. B. van Hasselt, P. S. Strain, & M. Hersen (Eds.), *Handbook of developmental and physical disabilities* (pp. 79–90). New York: Pergamon.

Trivette, C. M., Dunst, C. J., Deal, A. G., Hammer, A. W., & Probst, S. (1990). Assessing family strengths and family functioning style. *Topics in Early Childhood Special Education, 10,* 16–35.

Trute, B., & Hauch, C. (1988a). Building on family strength: A study of families with positive adjustment to the birth of a developmentally disabled child. *Journal of Marital and Family Therapy, 14,* 185–193.

Trute, B., & Hauch, C. (1988b). Social network attributes of families with positive adaptation to the birth of a developmentally disabled child. *Canadian Journal of Mental Health, 7,* 5–16.

Tunali, B., & Power, T. G. (1993). Creating satisfaction: A psychological perspective on stress and coping in families of handicapped children. *Journal of Child Psychiatry and Psychology, 34,* 945–957.

Turnbull, A. P., Patterson, J. M., Behr, S. K., Murphy, D. L., Marquis, J. G., & Blue–Banning, M. J. (Eds). (1993) *Cognitive coping, families, and disability.* Baltimore: Brookes.

Turnbull, A. P., Summers, J. A., & Brotherson, M. J. (1986). Family life cycle: Theoretical and empirical implications and future directions for families with mentally retarded members. In J. J. Gallaher & P. M. Vietze (Eds.), *Families of handicapped persons: Research, programs, and policy issues* (pps. 45–65). Baltimore: Brookes.

Vohs, J. (1993). On belonging. In A. P. Turnbull. J. M. Patterson, S. K. Behr, D. L. Murphy, J. G. Marquis, & M. J. Blue-Banning (Eds.), *Cognitive coping, families, and disability* (pp. 51–66). Baltimore: Brookes.

Waisbren, S. (1980). Parents' reaction to the birth of a developmentally disabled child. *American Journal of Mental Deficiency, 84,* 345–351.

Wallander, J. L., Pitt, L. C., & Mellins, C. A. (1990). Child functional independence and maternal psychosocial stress as risk factors threatening adaptation in mothers of physically or sensorially handicapped children. *Journal of Consulting and Clinical Psychology, 58*(6), 818–824.

Weisner, T. S. (1984). Ecocultural niches of middle childhood: A cross-cultural perspective. In W. A. Collins (Ed.), *Development during middle childhood: The years from six to twelve* (pp. 335–369). Washington, DC: National Academy of Sciences.

Weisner, T. S., Beizer, L., & Stolze, L. (1991). Religion and the families of developmentally delayed children. *American Journal on Mental Retardation, 95* (6), 647–662.

Weisner, T. W., Matheson, C., Coots, J. J., & Gallimore, R. (1997, April). *Sustainability of daily routines as a family outcome.* Paper presented at Society for Research in Child Development, Washington, DC.

Weisner, T. S. (1998). Human development as a culturally organized adaptive project. In D. Sharma & K. Fischer (Eds.), *Socio-emotional development across cultures. New directions in child development* (pp. 69–85). San Francisco: Jossey-Bass.

Whiting, B., & Edwards, C. (1988). *Children of different worlds: The formation of social behavior.* Cambridge, MA: Harvard University Press.

Wishart, M. C., Bidder, R. T., & Gray, O. P. (1981). Parents' report of family life with a developmentally delayed child. *Child: Care, Health, and Development, 7,* 267–279.

# 5 ❧ The Self-Concept and Friendships of Students With Learning Disabilities: A Developmental Perspective

**Sharon Vaughn**
*University of Texas–Austin*

**Batya Elbaum**
*University of Miami*

Social competence is a broad construct that represents a number of critical factors comprising (a) social skills, (b) relationships with others, including friendships and peer acceptance, (c) age-appropriate social cognitions, including self-concept, and (d) behaviors that suggest adjustment or the absence of behaviors associated with maladjustment (e.g., acting out, severe attention problems; Vaughn & Hogan, 1990). For students with learning disabilities (LD), two of these factors—self-concept and friendship—seem particularly important in that they provide insights as to how students perceive themselves and their closest relationships with individuals outside of their families.

By far, the majority of studies examining children's self-concept and peer relations have been conducted in school settings. Newer research focusing on friendships has begun to move beyond the classroom in order to provide a broader perspective on the social functioning of school-age children and adolescents. This broader perspective is particularly important with respect to students with LD, since their academic self-perceptions and the friendships they form with classmates are likely influenced by their low academic performance in the school setting.

Thus, the aim of this chapter is to briefly synthesize the knowledge base on two aspects of the social functioning of students with LD—self-concept and friendship—and to provide a developmental context for interpretation of these

**81**

findings. This chapter also addresses key methodological, conceptual, and practical issues related to the research, and suggests implications for future research.

## SELF-CONCEPT

The terms *self-concept*, *self-perception*, and *self-esteem* have been used interchangeably to refer to how people judge themselves and how self-satisfied they feel. Often the self-perceptions people form are an appraisal of themselves based on their own expectations or the expectations of significant others (e.g., parents). Self-perceptions have been the focus of considerable interest in education and psychology because they provide a gauge of the effects of academic and social difficulties on students' emotional well-being and sense of self (Haager & Vaughn, 1997).

The construct of self-concept is of interest with regard to students with LD for several reasons. First, students with LD demonstrate significant difficulties in academic areas, as well as frequent problems in social areas. Second, students with LD are identified and generally provided with special education. How these factors influence the self-concept of students with LD has been the topic of considerable research. Furthermore, most students with LD are educated for some or all of the school day in classes with their non-LD peers; thus, students with LD often have two reference groups that are relevant to their self-comparisons: non-LD students and other students with LD. The reference groups that students with LD most identify with and how this influences their self-perception has also been investigated. Also, students with LD are distinct from other students with academic difficulties (e.g., low achievers, mentally retarded) in that they are characterized as having average or above cognitive abilities. The extent to which students with LD make distinctions in their evaluations of their cognitive abilities and academic performance has also been of interest and is reviewed in this chapter.

### Self-Concept: A Multidimensional Construct

Since the work of James (1963), the importance of self-perception has been well recognized. James was one of the first to highlight how an individual's aspirations and accomplishments relate to his or her self-esteem. As a result of James' work, researchers learned to consider the extent to which individuals perceive that they have achieved their goals as evidence for predicting their self-concepts. However, disparities between achievements and self-perceptions are not necessarily a sign of maladjustment. In fact, individuals who have been extremely successful in society often display considerable self-image disparity (Achenbach & Zigler, 1963).

Harter's widely known model of self-perception has been influenced by the theories of both James and Cooley (Harter, 1985). Fundamentally, Harter agreed with James that one's overall feelings of self-worth are influenced by the ways in which achievements correspond with aspirations (James, 1963). Harter also agreed with Cooley's version of self-perception whereby one's self-perception is influenced by the perceptions of others (Cooley, 1902). Essential, however, to Harter's model of self-concept is the notion of multidimensionality. Harter identified six domains of self-perception: scholastic, social, athletic, physical, behavioral, and global self-worth. This notion of multiple domains of self-perception is supported by other researchers (e.g., Marsh, 1988; Shavelson, Hubner, & Stanton, 1976).

The view that self-concept is multidimensional is based on the premise that individuals may not view themselves equally across different domains of functioning such as athletic ability, academic competence, or social competence (Harter & Pike, 1984). There is evidence that self-evaluations are domain-specific (Harter & Pike, 1984), and that measures of self-concept differ depending on whether the self-appraisal is tapping perceptions of general self-worth or perceptions about specific domains of development. For example, one's appraisal of one's physical attractiveness may differ considerably from one's appraisal of one's academic success. Because students with LD are distinguished from their non-LD peers by low academic performance, consideration of their academic self-perceptions independent from global self-worth or any other domain is essential. Thus, in the following sections we consider self-perceptions in the academic and social domains separately, followed by more global self-perceptions. We then discuss factors that influence self-concept and its measurement.

*Academic Self-Perceptions.*   When the domain of academic self-perception is examined independently from other domains of self-perception, students with LD exhibit significantly lower scores than do their non-LD classmates (e.g., Cooley & Ayers, 1988; Hiebert, Wong, & Hunter, 1982; Kane, 1979; Kifer, 1975; Kistner, Haskett, White, & Robbins, 1987; Montgomery, 1994; Pickar & Tori, 1986; Winne, Woodlands, & Wong, 1982). According to Hagborg (1996), 70% of students with LD demonstrate significantly lower self-perceptions in the academic domain than do their non-LD peers. In Chapman's (1988b) review of the academic self-concept of students with LD, academic self-perception was significantly lower for students with LD in 19 of 20 studies, with students with LD scoring in the 19th percentile on academic self-perception. These findings are unsurprising in light of the fact that the academic performance of students with LD is typically below that of their non-LD classmates.

Although their academic self-perceptions tend to be low, students with LD consistently rate themselves as being as smart as other students (Bear & Minke, 1996; Renick & Harter, 1989). Given that students with LD are often identified by the co-occurrence of low academic achievement with cognitive abilities in the average range, these self-perceptions of cognitive ability appear to be fairly accurate. Because students with LD often display memory problems, it is interesting that they also perceive themselves to be more forgetful (Bear & Minke, 1996). Thus, studies across several areas provide converging evidence that students with LD have relatively accurate self-appraisals of their academic performance and ability.

*Social Self-Perceptions.*     In the social domain, studies have yielded more contradictory findings than in the academic domain for students with LD. Students with LD often demonstrate low social competence, yet self-perceptions of their social functioning do not show a consistent pattern, in contrast to their low self-perceptions in the academic area. Some researchers reported no differences between students with and without LD on social self-perception (e.g., Colangelo, Kelley, & Schrepfer, 1987; Kistner et al., 1987; Montgomery, 1994). Other researchers reported lower social self-perceptions for students in the LD group (e.g., Cielesz, 1983; Hildreth, 1987; LaGreca & Stone, 1990; Renick & Harter, 1989; Rosenberg & Gaier, 1977). Still others reported lower social self-perceptions when students with LD are compared to average-to-high achievers, but not when they are compared to low achievers (Haager & Vaughn, 1995; Vaughn, Haager, Hogan, & Kouzekanani, 1992). One study even reported higher social self-perceptions for students with LD (Winne et al., 1982).

Interestingly, self-perception of social acceptance for students with LD is significantly related to depression. Students with LD who have high ratings of depression also rate themselves very poorly on self-perceptions of social acceptance (Heath & Wiener, 1996). Moreover, students with LD have been shown to demonstrate higher levels of depression than do non-LD students (Heath & Wiener, 1996). This finding is congruent with other research linking low self-esteem and depression (Leahy, 1985).

*Global Self-Perceptions.*     Students with LD often maintain positive feelings of global self-worth despite their significant difficulties in the academic domain. In a study comparing the self-perceptions of students with LD and a normally achieving comparison group (Cooley & Ayers, 1988), the self-concept of students with LD was found to approximate that of non-LD students when items that related to academic self-concept were removed from the scale.

There are a number of explanations for this. One is that students with LD may receive adequate social support from teachers and parents, and this support bolsters their global self-perception (Forman, 1988; Kloomok & Cosden, 1994). This explanation is somewhat difficult to support at the school level since many teachers appear to hold negative perceptions of students with LD (e.g., Priel & Leshem, 1990). However, where teachers were self-identified as accepting of students with LD, the students with LD were well accepted by their peers (Vaughn, McIntosh, Schumm, Haager, & Callwood, 1993), suggesting that the teachers had established an accepting environment for their students with LD. Another explanation is that students are aware that they have academic problems but perceive that they are competent in other areas (Kloomok & Cosden, 1994). For example, students may perceive that they excel in nonacademic activities and that their performance in these areas offsets their poor academic performance (Chapman, 1988a; Silverman & Zigmond, 1983). An extension of this idea is the notion of selected focus. Selected focus suggests that students with LD do not deny that they have difficulties, but selectively focus on their positive aspects rather than on their academic difficulties (Bear & Minke, 1996). Other researchers propose that students with LD discount the importance of academic success (Kistner & Osborne, 1987; Kloomok & Cosden, 1994). Although the discounting hypothesis would explain why the low academic achievement of students with LD does not appear to influence their overall self-concept, there is little empirical support for the idea that students with LD discount the importance of doing well in school (Clever, Bear, & Juvonen, 1992; Kloomok & Cosden, 1994).

In sum, compared to non-LD students, students with LD appear to have similar global self-perceptions but less positive academic self-perceptions. Whether the social self-perception of students with LD is on par with that of their non-LD classmates is less clear. Further research needs to consider the possible effects of comorbidity in areas such as depression on the self-perceptions of students with LD.

## Factors Affecting Self-Concept and Its Measurement

*Age.* Self-perceptions among most individuals tend to become more differentiated and refined with age. Generally, students' self-perceptions become less positive over time and then stabilize (Marsh, 1989; Marsh, Byrne, & Shavelson, 1988; Ruble, 1983). A longitudinal, prospective study provides initial evidence that the general and domain-specific self-perceptions of students with LD follow the same developmental trends as for other youngsters (Vaughn et al., 1992). In a study that examined the global and domain-specific self-perceptions of students both with and without LD over a 5-year period (from kindergarten through fourth grade), neither the global nor the domain-specific self-perceptions of students with LD differed from those of the non-LD group over time.

Age differences in the self-perception of students with LD were further illustrated in studies conducted by LaGreca and Stone (1990) and Bursuck (1989). LaGreca and Stone (1990) reported lower self-perceptions of social acceptance and global self-worth for both low achievers and students with LD who were fourth and fifth graders; however, Bursuck (1989) did not find lower self-perceptions for students with LD in second, third, and fourth grades.

From a developmental standpoint, we have very limited knowledge of the self-concept of students with LD. Research reported in the second half of this chapter is among the first to examine how the self-perceptions of students with LD change over the course of childhood and adolescence. Careful longitudinal research is needed to elucidate within-individual variation from a developmental perspective, to identify factors that relate to changes in self-perception over time, and to better understand variables for students with LD that influence social functioning over time (e.g., Bruck, 1986, 1987).

*Concordance Among Raters.* Students' self-perceptions have been assessed by means of both self-report and ratings provided by other individuals (e.g., teachers and parents). Concordance between raters, then, refers to the extent to which different people's ratings of a student's self-concept are congruent. Concordance between self-ratings and others' ratings has been studied with regard to the global self-concept of students with LD. Coleman (1984) found that mothers of children with LD rate their children's global self-concepts lower than their children rate themselves. In a study examining students with LD and low-achieving nondisabled students (Grolnick & Ryan, 1990), teachers rated the students with LD as having lower overall self-concepts than the low achievers, although the two groups of students did not differ in their self-ratings of global self-concept. In another study, teachers' ratings of students with LD, non-LD students, and high-achieving students indicated that teachers perceived students with LD to have significantly lower self-perceptions than average- and high-achieving students; and teachers also perceived high-achieving students as having significantly higher self-perceptions than average-achieving students have (Montgomery, 1994). The correlations between teacher and student ratings of self-concept were only modest; overall, compared with students' self-perceptions, teachers underrated the self-perceptions of students with LD. Findings by both Forman (1987) and Kloomok and Cosden (1994) also revealed contrasts between students' ratings of their self-perceptions of academic performance and teachers' ratings (or grades) in the academic area.

Reasons for the low concordance between self-ratings and the ratings of others are not entirely clear. As discussed in the beginning of this chapter, self-perceptions are largely a reflection of self-satisfaction with how one has met one's own aspirations. When parents and teachers rate children's self-perceptions, their ratings are likely to be influenced by their own aspirations for these children.

Ratings of children's self-perceptions by different adults (e.g., parents and teachers) may also be discordant. Different adults may have contact with a child in different settings (e.g., home vs. school) and have little or no information about the behavior and perceptions of the child in other settings. Keogh and colleagues (Keogh, Juvonen, & Bernheimer, 1989), who found low concordance between parent and teacher ratings of children's behavior, remarked that "it is uncertain whether discrepancies in ratings reflected real differences in children's behaviors at home and at school or whether they were a function of adults' perceptions" (p. 229). Students with LD may, indeed, behave very differently at home and in the community—where academic demands are low—than they do in the classroom, leading to different inferences about their self-perceptions. Even if context were not a factor, judgments of another person's perceptions of his or her own abilities or accomplishments are, at best, difficult to make and of uncertain reliability.

*Self-Perception of Disability.* A number of researchers have investigated the relationship between students' self-perception of their learning disability, reasoning that students who have a better understanding of the factors related to their learning disability will demonstrate more positive indexes of social development and self-concept. In Heyman's (1990) initial study of the relationship between students' perceptions of the severity of their learning disability and their self-concept, students who perceived their disability as less severe demonstrated more positive self-concepts. This suggests that how students interpret their disability and their perception of the extent to which the disability affects their lives influence their overall self-concept.

Rothman and Cosden (1995) found that students with LD vary in their perceptions of the influence of their learning disability on their functioning. They found that students who perceive that their disability is not particularly limiting and who view it as nonstigmatizing also have less serious achievement problems and have higher self-perceptions of their ability and academic competence. Because the study was correlational in design, it is not possible to determine if higher academic performance leads to perceptions of less stigmatization by the learning disability or if students who perceive their learning disability as less stigmatizing are motivated and encouraged to work harder. As Rothman and Cosden (1995) stated, "The findings parallel the views of Wright (1960, 1983), who indicated that high self-esteem among individuals with physical disabilities is often associated with the ability to accept the disability as a circumscribed handicap that does not impede positive development in other areas of life" (p. 211).

## Identification and Placement

The potential effects of the labeling and identification process on the self-concept of students have been of critical concern for many years. A common theme is that special education has a negative impact on the self-concept of students (Smith & Nagle, 1995). Some argue that the label itself is detrimental and triggers a self-fulfilling prophecy (Brophy & Good, 1970; Good, 1982) whereby students perceive themselves negatively because they are categorized as learning disabled.

However, there is no empirical evidence that the label "learning disabled" results in lowered self-concept on the part of students. In fact, the evidence that does exist suggests that few if any negative effects ensue from being identified as learning disabled. Vaughn et al. (1992) followed a cohort of students from kindergarten through fourth grade. They assessed the self-perceptions of these students each year. Students who were identified as having learning disabilities at the end of second grade were compared with matched students from the sample who were not so identified and who represented a range of achievement levels. Results indicated that the self-perception of students with LD did not differ significantly from that of students representing other achievement groups before or after identification, suggesting that the labeling process itself did not result in negative self-perceptions. In a second, related study, the self-concept of adults who were placed as students in special education settings was compared with that of adults who did not receive special education services. No differences between the groups were evident on their self-concept scores (Lewandowski & Arcangelo, 1994), suggesting no long-term effects on self-concept of identification and special education services.

## Educational Setting

In the field of special education, the setting where students are educated has been the subject of ongoing debate. There is considerable concern that students who are identified as learning disabled and provided special education services outside of the general education classroom are at risk for poor social relationships, low self-concept, and other negative outcomes. The low acceptance by peers of students with LD has been a persistent problem, and there is concern that the pull-out service delivery model contributes to their lack of membership in the classroom community as well as their overall low social status (Taylor, Asher, & Williams, 1987) and more negative self-concept. Biklen and Zollers (1986), in describing pull-out programs for students with LD, stated, "There are the negative effects of segregation, namely, stigma, stereotyping, discrimination, and alienation" (p. 582).

According to social comparison theory (Festinger, 1954), individuals compare themselves to others in their setting when there are no other standards available. Of significance is the comparison group one selects for self-appraisal. For example, minorities, women, and individuals with physical disabilities often compare themselves to others within their group rather than to members of the more dominant group (Crocker & Major, 1989). Thus, applying social comparison theory to students' self-perceptions, one would expect that students with LD in more segregated settings might compare themselves with students in those settings and thus have more positive self-perceptions. Some research suggests that this may be the case, as students with LD who were placed in special education classes exhibited greater gains in self-perception than did those in regular education classes (Battle & Blowers, 1982). However, more recent research suggests that educational setting may not have such critical impact on students' academic self-concept. Students with LD who were placed full-time in general education classrooms were found to fare about the same socially as did students with LD who were provided part-time support in resource rooms (Vaughn, Elbaum, & Schumm, 1996). Furthermore, Renick and Harter (1988, 1989) revealed that, when asked which group they compared themselves to when rating their self-perceptions, 80% of children with LD in resource room settings compared themselves to average-achieving peers rather than selecting other students with LD. Results of a recent study that addressed directly the issue of comparison group and self-perception revealed that the students whom students with LD selected as a comparison group did not influence their self-perceptions (Smith & Nagle, 1995).

Findings concerning the global self-perceptions of students with LD in general education classrooms are equivocal. When students with LD were placed in general education classrooms, their global self-concept was lower than that of their classmates who were receiving special services in some studies (Carroll, Friedrich, & Hund, 1984; Rogers & Saklofske, 1985), and on par with that of their classmates in other studies (Bear, Juvonen, & McInerney, 1993). In a recent study examining the social functioning of students with LD in general education classrooms (Vaughn et al., 1996), teachers who were interviewed throughout the school year indicated that they thought the self-concept of students with LD in their classes had improved significantly from fall to spring. Teachers felt that this outcome was a primary strength of the program. A comment representative of many others was: "Most of the students want to do what the other students are doing. They feel good about themselves because they are here all day doing the same work. I know it has improved their self-concept." Yet the data obtained from students revealed that the self-concept scores of students with LD did not change at all from the beginning to the end of the school year. Although the data do not support a conclusive interpretation of this finding, our interpretation is that the teachers who participated in this program devoted extensive time and energy to teaching in a model that they were certain was "better than a resource pull-out model" and that their investment pulled them in the direction of perceiving that students felt better about themselves as a result of the program.

Thus, the evidence overall suggests that whereas the academic self-perception of students with LD is likely to be lower than that of non-LD classmates across settings, global self-perceptions are often similar to those of non-LD students (e.g., Bear et al., 1993; Kistner & Osborne, 1987; Vaughn, Elbaum, Schumm, & Hughes, 1998). With regard to the assessment of changes in self-perceptions over time, we must acknowledge that the measurement of improvement in self-esteem is difficult, and that the measures used may not adequately assess changes that occur in individual students' self-perceptions.

There are also unresolved issues about the way in which general education classrooms are structured, the composition of the classrooms, and the long-term effects of including students with LD in general education settings that need to be better understood (Keogh, 1994). For example, in a recent study (Vaughn et al., 1998, two types of inclusion programs for students with LD were compared. In one setting, equal numbers of students with and without LD (about 15 each for a total of 30 students per classroom) were taught by two full-time classroom teachers. In a second setting, the number of students with LD per classroom ranged from four to seven, and the special education teacher co-taught with the regular education teacher for about 90 minutes a day. Students with LD fared better in the second setting where there were fewer students with LD in the classroom, demonstrating higher levels of peer acceptance and friendship quality than did LD students in the other setting. In the setting with fewer students with LD per classroom, gains occurred not only for students with LD but for other students in the class as well. Further research is needed to explicate how a smaller number of students with LD in a class contributes to improved social outcomes for all students.

We are also uncertain as to the effects on measures of students' self-concept of (a) references to different settings in self-concept instruments, and (b) the setting in which a self-concept measure is administered. Thus, students with learning problems who are asked about their self-perceptions in school settings may have more negative responses than when queried about their self-perceptions at home or other settings where they are more successful. Because students with LD are by definition low-achievers, it may be inaccurate to generalize findings regarding self-perception obtained in school settings to other settings. Hence, this issue needs to be further considered in future research.

*Grouping.*     The effects of grouping practices on students' self-concept have received considerable attention, particularly in the area of reading (Barr & Dreeban, 1991). When students are placed in homogeneous (same-ability) reading groups, the groups tend to remain relatively stable; consequently, students have little opportunity to move out of their reading group even if they evidence progress, and their restricted contact with peers ultimately influences their friendship choices (Hallinan & Sorenson, 1985). Until the last decade, most teachers taught reading through organized, same-ability reading groups. For a variety of reasons, including concerns that ability groups result in negative self-perceptions for students in the lower groups, teachers have been urged to use heterogeneous (mixed-ability) grouping for reading (Good & Brophy, 1994).

Schumm and colleagues (Schumm, Vaughn, & Elbaum, 1996) asked teachers to rate their perceptions of the effects of various grouping formats for reading on the overall self-concept of students, because they were interested in the extent to which teachers' perceptions of social outcomes for students would influence the grouping formats they used. For four out of the five achievement groups delineated (gifted, high-achieving, average-achieving, and LD), there were no statistically significant differences in teachers' perceptions of the impact on students' self-esteem of the teachers' use of same-ability versus mixed-ability groups. The one exception was with regard to low-achieving students, whom teachers saw as benefiting more (with regard to self-concept), from mixed-ability reading groups than from same-ability groups.

Teachers' perceptions of the impact of pull-out programs for reading on the self-concept of students were also assessed (Schumm et al., 1996). For both students who are gifted and students with LD, teachers perceived that pull-out programs were preferable to whole-class instruction for improving students' self-concept. Furthermore, teachers perceived that removing students who are gifted and students with LD from the general education classroom for part of the school day improves their self-concept.

*Differentiated Instruction.*     A 1-year examination of resource room teachers' grouping and differentiated instruction and materials revealed findings similar to those for general education teachers. Although the range of students' reading abilities was three to four grade levels during the same reading period, students typically read from the same book and were provided the same materials. Like their general education colleagues, the special education teachers provided primarily whole-class instruction for reading, used the same reading materials for all students, and provided little differentiated instruction or systematic monitoring of student progress.

These findings relate to self-concept in that many teachers in these studies indicated that they perceived or were taught in their undergraduate teacher preparation programs that differentiated instruction and materials could be harmful to students' self-concept (Schumm, Moody, & Vaughn, 1997; Schumm et al., 1996). One teacher's comment captured the feelings of many teachers: "I think that when kids have different books and materials the other kids can see who is doing what and they know who the smart kids are. I just don't think it's good for them. Their self-concept is already in the pits and this just doesn't help." Teachers also indicated that they did not like to group students for reading for this same reason. "I don't put them off in different groups because I feel that if you exclude kids, especially our kids—and when I say 'our' I mean the exceptional kids—it kind of makes them say, 'Oh.' They already know who is the smart group, who is the medium group, and who is the lower group.... So I just try to stay away from groups."

Interestingly, there does not seem to be much empirical evidence on the effects of grouping and the use of differentiated materials on students' self-perceptions. Even if the use of certain practices were found to have an effect on students' self-concept, one would have to weigh this result against the benefits of such practices in terms of improving students' academic performance. One finding about self-concept is that students who have real successes and accomplishments have improved self-concept (e.g., Canfield & Wells, 1994). Thus, students who are severely behind their peers in reading may, in the short run, feel better about their reading ability when given the same reading book as their classmates. However, if they do not improve their reading skills, they will have little basis for positive self-perceptions of their reading ability in the long run.

## Implications

The application of a multidimensional perspective on self-concept has yielded our most complete understanding thus far of the self-concept of students with LD. There is converging evidence that whereas the academic self-concept of students with LD is lower than that of their non-LD peers, students with LD are similar to their classmates with respect to perceptions of global self-worth. In the social domain, a consideration of additional factors such as comorbidity (e.g., depression) may help to better explicate the conflicting findings of extant research.

We also need to better understand the long-range implications of negative or positive self-concept. How do students who hold low perceptions of their global self-worth over several years fare in the long run? Are they less motivated, less successful, less able to maintain jobs than are students who have more positive self-perceptions over time? The outcomes for low self-perception, particularly by domain, need to be better understood. Also, studies need to address the extent to which subgroups of students with LD can be identified based on measures of social competence, and the extent to which subgroup may predict later social functioning. To further illustrate, the social profiles of some students with LD resemble the higher social functioning and peer acceptance profiles of students identified as average-to-high achievers (Haager & Vaughn, 1997; Vaughn & Hogan, 1994).

Furthermore, recent research suggests that, at least for boys, an examination of the components of social competence at any single point in time does not provide a good indicator of a student's social competence at future points in time (Vaughn & Hogan, 1994). Thus, studies that provide social markers for youngsters over time are critical to the goal of capturing a more thorough understanding of students' social functioning.

Finally, there is considerable need to develop more refined measures of self-perception. Self-perception scales that measure a range of domains and that are normed on students with and without LD are needed. Measures that provide appropriate open-ended interview questions are also needed to better understand and interpret the research on self-perceptions.

## FRIENDSHIPS

Children's relationships with their peers have long been considered to play an important role in development. The aspect of children's peer relationships that has received the greatest amount of attention in the literature is peer acceptance, also referred to as popularity or social status. Peer acceptance has typically been measured by sociometric instruments that ask children in a classroom to rate how much they like (or would like to play with) each of their classmates, and name the three classmates they like best and the three they like least. Peer acceptance has been a key area of study in that rejection by classmates has been demonstrated to be associated with numerous indexes of maladjustment in adolescence and adulthood (Coie, Lochman, Terry, & Hyman, 1992; Kupersmidt, Coie, & Dodge, 1990; Ollendick, Weist, Borden, & Greene, 1992).

### Peer Acceptance

With regard to students with disabilities, research indicates that these students are less popular, less well accepted, and more often rejected by peers than are classmates without disabilities (Asher & Taylor, 1981; Gresham, 1982; Sabornie, 1985; Sale & Carey, 1995; Stone & La Greca, 1990; Vaughn et al., 1993, 1996). Taken together, these findings suggest that a disproportionately high number of students with disabilities are likely to face significant challenges in the social domain in addition to facing the academic challenges related to their primary disability. At the same time, it has been noted that not all students with disabilities are poorly accepted by their peers. For example, Kistner and Gatlin (1989) found that 40% of students with LD in third- through fifth-grade classrooms were classified as popular or average with regard to social status.

Thus, students with disabilities as well as nondisabled students vary considerably with regard to peer acceptance. Moreover, peer acceptance does not relate in a highly reliable and consistent way to concurrent indexes of social adjustment such as self-concept. One explanation for this variability is that peer acceptance—particularly as it is operationalized in classroom sociometric approaches—taps only one aspect of children's social relations with their peers. An equally important but underinvestigated aspect of children's peer relationships is that of children's friendships. Various researchers have underscored that having friends and being well accepted by classmates are distinct aspects of children's social functioning (cf. Bukowski & Hoza, 1989; Furman & Robbins, 1985). In essence, peer acceptance is a measure of how well a child fits into a particular social group, from the perspective of the other group members. In contrast, measures of the number and quality characteristics of a child's friendships reveal the child's functioning in specific self-chosen dyads, most often from the point of view of the child, and most often with regard to the child's receipt, rather than provision, of the social affordances associated with friendships (e.g., attachment and affection, enhancement of self-worth, companionship, guidance, opportunities for nurturance; see, for discussion, Bukowski & Hoza, 1989; Furman & Buhrmester, 1985; Sullivan, 1953).

Peer Acceptance and Friendships

There is now empirical evidence to support the idea that friendships and peer acceptance are nonoverlapping phenomena, and that friendships make a unique and important contribution to children's social adjustment. For example, Vandell and Hembree (1994) found that 45% of rejected children had at least one mutual friend. Parker and Asher (1993) found that peer status and friendship were not redundant factors and contributed additively to children's feelings of loneliness. Furthermore, friendless children who are low in popularity evidence lower general self-worth and cognitive self-competence than friended children (Hoza, 1989). In studies controlling for social acceptance, friended as compared to friendless children scored higher on a measure of self-concept (Mannarino, 1978) and higher on measures of cognitive, social, and physical perceived competence and general self-worth (Bukowski & Newcomb, 1987). Bukowski and Hoza (1989) reported that, in previous research they conducted, general self-worth was found to be more strongly predicted by friendship measures than by popularity measures, whereas popularity measures were more strongly related to self-perceived competence measures.

It has also been suggested that friendships may moderate the effects of peer acceptance on other indexes of children's social functioning. For example, Juvonen and Bear (1992) and Bear et al. (1993) provided evidence that when children with LD have at least one friend they are likely to have favorable views of their social acceptance. Such a finding supports the idea that having even one friend—an individual who holds the child in special regard, who chooses the child over other children for companionship, support, and/or intimacy—constitutes *prima facie* evidence of the child's worth. Moreover, as suggested by George and Hartmann (1996), "A close friendship may help prevent future problems by not only attenuating the negative concomitants of peer rejection but also by fostering the development of both interpersonal and intrapersonal competencies" (p. 2302).

## Research on Children's Friendships

Recent research has examined many aspects of children's friendships, including the prevalence of reciprocal friendships among children of different social status (e.g., Parker & Asher, 1993), children's conceptions of friendships (e.g., Furman & Bierman, 1984), and the relationship between children's friendships and other measures of social functioning (e.g., Keefe & Berndt, 1996). Because it is beyond the scope of this chapter to review this extensive literature, the interested reader is referred to recent work by Newcomb and Bagwell (1995) and Bukowski, Newcomb, and Hartup (1996).

With regard to the study of friendships, Bukowski and Hoza (1989) distinguished three hierarchical levels, or aspects, of friendship relations that may be examined. These are the presence or absence of a friendship relationship, the number (extensivity) of friendships, and the quality of these friendships, typically captured as ratings of different dimensions of the relationship or different social provisions (e.g., companionship, emotional support).

With regard to the presence or absence of friendships, the literature reviewed by Newcomb and Bagwell (1995) suggests that children without a mutual friend are less well adjusted and are more negatively perceived by both themselves and others than are children who do have mutual friends. However, the direction of causality remains to be demonstrated by longitudinal research designs.

With regard to number of friends, Vandell and Hembree (1994) examined whether friendship amongst third graders is a better predictor of adjustment when measured dichotomously (presence/absence of at least one mutual friendship) or continuously (number of friendships). The number of mutual friendships contributed significantly to children's adjustment on all measures (academic performance, teacher-reported socioemotional adjustment, self-concept), and was a better predictor of adjustment than was friendship presence/absence. Thus, the authors concluded, "It did not appear that the benefits of having a single friend were equal to the benefits of having more friends" (p. 474). One of the limitations they recognized was that no measures of friendship quality were obtained. "Additional aspects of children's adjustment might be explained if measures are taken of how satisfied the children are with their friendships or how much support they derive from their friendships" (p. 475).

Friendship quality has been investigated by means of open-ended questions during interviews (Berndt, Hawkins, & Hoyle, 1986; Berndt & Perry, 1986), by having children evaluate certain features of their friendships on a rating scale in interviews (Berndt et al., 1986; Berndt & Perry, 1986) or on questionnaires (Bukowski & Hoza, 1989; Furman & Buhrmester, 1985). Although many variations exist on the number and definition of the posited dimensions of friendships (see Furman, 1996), it is generally acknowledged that friendships have both positive and negative dimensions. Whereas the negative dimensions have to do largely with conflict, the positive dimensions embrace such aspects of friendships as companionship (enjoyment of shared activity, time spent together), emotional support (enhancement of self-worth, confidence building), and intimacy (closeness, self-disclosure). Overall friendship quality (collapsing across ratings of different dimensions) is of interest in that it contributes to social outcomes in ways that are not captured by the extensivity aspect of friendships. For example, Bukowski and Hoza (1989) reported that "the results of a stepwise, hierarchical, multiple regression procedure indicated that, after the effects of friendship mutuality and extensivity [number] had been taken into account, friendship quality measures [i.e., measures of interpersonal support and closeness] added significantly to the prediction of the subjects' feelings of general self-worth, and, to a smaller extent, social competence" (p. 37). Moreover, the various dimensions of friendship may relate differently to different measures of social adjustment. Thus, measures of perceived support from friends may relate more strongly to self-concept than measures of companionship or frequency of contact with friends.

Finally, some clear developmental patterns emerge from this literature. With regard to friendship conceptions, younger children typically characterize friendships as primarily relating to shared activities. Although common activities are also important in later childhood and adolescence, intimacy takes on more importance. In the words of Bukowski and Hoza (1989): "One would expect that popularity and friendship variables would show different relative associations with measures of adjustment for children of different ages. According to this proposal, one would expect the correlation between popularity and the self-concept to peak during the school-age years, whereas the correlation between friendship and the self-concept would be expected to increase as children enter early adolescence" (p. 41).

## Issues in Research on the Friendships of Students With Learning Disabilities

Given the direct relationship of friendships to social adjustment as well as the function of friendship as a moderator of low peer acceptance by classmates, friendships are likely to make a critical difference in social outcomes for students with disabilities. To investigate the relationships between friendships and social outcomes for these children, we need to go beyond reciprocal nominations among classmates and begin to examine these students' friendships from the "insider's" perspective (Bukowski, Hoza, & Boivin, 1994; Furman & Buhrmester, 1985; Wenz-Gross & Siperstein, 1997). Although students with disabilities (and students classified as rejected or neglected) may not receive as many best-liked nominations from classmates as other students, suggesting that they have fewer close friendships with classmates, this does not preclude them from having close friendships outside the classroom. Nor does it preclude them from considering classroom peers to be friends unilaterally, obtaining many important friendship provisions from these relations, and being relatively satisfied with them. Thus, measures of reciprocal friendship nominations within a classroom may severely underestimate both the actual friendships and perceived friendship quality of a large number of children.

These considerations are beginning to be addressed in the burgeoning literature on children's friendships (see Bukowski et al., 1996). One critical issue has to do with what "counts" as a friendship. That is, is it necessary to have objective evidence of mutuality, for example, that provided by reciprocal nominations, or should we accept children's unilateral identification of a relationship as a friendship? Second, what effect does limiting the universe of nominees (e.g., to students in a single classroom) have on our view of students' friendships? Although it has been argued that the restriction of nominations to students in the same classroom should not differentially affect students with disabilities, we have reason to believe that it does; that is, that the procedure is particularly likely to underestimate the friendships of students with disabilities.

One reason for the differential impact of the restriction on students with disabilities has to do with the relative salience of their disability in the classroom as compared to other social contexts. Mild learning or behavior problems may be much more apparent, and have far greater consequences, in the classroom than outside of it; indeed, outside the classroom, where activities do not revolve around narrowly defined academic tasks and where a wider range of physical and interactive behaviors is admissible, for all intents and purposes these students may not be disabled (cf. the finding by Siperstein, Bopp, & Bak, 1978, that the more popular students with LD received many nominations for "best athlete"). Thus, we suspect that students with disabilities may actually be more likely to establish and maintain friendships outside of the classroom. This is analogous to George and Hartmann's (1996) similar remark that "Given unpopular children's low social status and negative reputations in their school peer groups (Hymel, Wagner, & Butler, 1990), they may search other contexts for more positive affiliations" (p. 2303).

Moreover, research indicates that similarity is a factor in children's friendships (Berndt, 1982; Epstein, 1989; Kandel, 1978). The literature reviewed by Newcomb and Bagwell (1995) indicates that friends appear to evidence more similarity with one another than do nonfriends. Farmer, Pearl, and Van Acker (1996) described how students sort themselves into "social networks of peer clusters that tend to be composed of students who are similar to each other on salient social features" (p. 241). These authors cited evidence from studies by Kandel (1978) and Kindermann (1993) indicating that students tend to affiliate with peers who share their orientation or motivation toward schoolwork.

Farmer and Hollowell (1994) found that girls, but not boys, who were affiliated tended to be similar on peer assessments for "good at schoolwork." Thus, to the extent that students with disabilities represent a minority in most classrooms, they are likely to find fewer students similar to themselves along several classroom-relevant dimensions.

Recent research that has attempted to overcome the practical difficulties inherent in extending friendship nominations beyond the classroom suggests that peer nominations that are limited to classmates do not give an accurate view of children's friendships. George and Hartmann (1996) studied the friendship networks of unpopular, average and popular students in grades 5 and 6 using a procedure that allowed students to nominate up to 15 friends, without contextual restrictions. All the children in the study (N = 227) named at least one good friend (unilateral friend). Unpopular children were less likely than popular children to have at least one reciprocal friend, but the vast majority—77%—did in fact have at least one reciprocal friend. Of interest as well, the research showed that unpopular children's unilateral friendship networks included fewer same-age friends, a greater number of younger friends, and more friends located outside of school (but within the same school district).

## Friendships of Students With LD

Few studies have directly addressed the friendships of students with disabilities. With regard to the presence or absence of friendships, Juvonen and Bear (1992), studying the social adjustment of children with and without learning disabilities in integrated classrooms, found that 67% of students with LD had at least one reciprocal positive nomination, compared to 78% of students without LD. Vaughn et al. (1996) also examined the functioning of students with LD in an inclusion setting and found that, at the beginning of the academic year, a smaller percentage of students with LD had at least one reciprocal friendship than did low-achieving (LA) or average-to-high achieving (AHA) students (26% vs. 71% and 63%, respectively). In spring, the percentages of students with at least one mutual friendship were 53 (LD), 58 (LA), and 72 (AHA), revealing that students with LD had made significant gains in this regard. Data from a second study by Vaughn et al. (in press) show a similar pattern of increase in the percentage of students with LD who had at least one mutual friend (from 42% in fall to 67% in spring). These findings suggest that the measurement of students' friendships at a single point in time may fail to capture the changing nature of their relationships with peers.

With regard to friendship quality, Wenz-Gross and Siperstein (1997) used Berndt and Perry's (1986) Friendship Interview to examine the friendship quality of 106 mildly disabled and nondisabled students in fourth to sixth grades. They found no difference between mildly disabled and nondisabled students in the negative features of friendship, but significant differences in four out of five positive features (intimacy, loyalty, enhancement of self-esteem, and contact). This result, they suggested, may explain another finding of the study, namely that students with LD turn to peers less often for social support, especially emotional support and companionship.

Recent research we have conducted addresses several important questions about the friendships of students with LD. The main purpose of this research was to obtain a broad, cross-sectional view of elementary, middle school, and high school students' perceptions of the positive dimensions of their friendships. We wished to examine whether students with LD differed from students without disabilities with regard to (a) their overall perceptions of friendship quality and (b) their perceptions of different dimensions of their friendships. We also wished to investigate the relationship between children's perceptions of their friendships and their self-esteem.

We obtained children's perceptions of their friendships with a 17-item questionnaire based on the Friendship Interview developed by Berndt and Perry (1986). The items were selected from those tapping five positive dimensions of friendships (play/association, prosocial behavior, intimacy, loyalty, and attachment and self-esteem enhancement). Students' unilateral nominations were accepted as friendships, even though there are limitations to this procedure (cf. Furman, 1996), as discussed earlier. In addition, students were asked to complete a Friends List, listing (by first name only) up to six individuals they considered to be "best friends," and, for each one, to indicate the person's gender and whether they knew the person from school and/or from outside of school. Students were told that if they did not have a best friend, they could leave the lines blank. Self-esteem was assessed by means of the School and Intellectual Status subscale of the Piers-Harris Children's Self-Concept Scale (Piers, 1984). This subscale, too, included 17 items.

The Friendship Survey, Friends List, and self-concept measure were administered in the spring of the academic year to over 4,000 students, including over 900 students with LD, attending 69 schools throughout the state of Florida. The schools were in large, urban school districts as well as small, rural districts.

With regard to number of friendships, students with LD listed slightly fewer best friends than did nondisabled students. Across all grade levels, the percentages of students who listed no best friends were 2% for students without disabilities and 4% for students with LD. Approximately 67% of students with LD listed six or more friends, compared to 77% of nondisabled students.

With regard to the context of friendships, a substantial percentage of the self-identified best friends of both nondisabled students and students with LD were individuals these students knew from outside of school. Across all grade levels, the percentages were 29% for nondisabled students and 32% for students with LD. These percentages are virtually identical to those reported by George and Hartmann (1996; 71% of children's unilateral friendships were from the same school; it is not known whether the participants in this study included students with LD).

With regard to overall friendship quality, perceived quality at the elementary level was only slightly higher for nondisabled students than for students with LD. For nondisabled students, perceived friendship was higher in middle school than in elementary school and higher yet in high school; in contrast, quality for students with LD was approximately the same at all levels of schooling. These data suggest a growing gap between the perceived friendship quality of students with and without LD.

The picture is more nuanced if dimensions of friendship quality are considered separately. To investigate this, students' responses to the Friendship Survey were submitted to a principal components analysis so as to discern how the items clustered empirically. Following varimax rotation, three factors emerged: the first, comprising seven items, represented support for self-esteem; the second factor, comprising four items, represented companionship; and the third, comprising six items, represented the dimension of intimacy. Factor scores representing each of the factors were then analyzed to reveal differences associated with disability status as well as developmental patterns.

Students with LD reported lower levels of support for self-esteem than did students without disabilities. However, the same developmental pattern was evidenced for the two groups of students: perceived support for self-esteem was lower in middle school than in elementary school, but did not differ significantly between middle school and high school.

Overall, students with and without LD did not differ with regard to perceived levels of companionship. For nondisabled students, perceived companionship was higher in middle school than in elementary school, but did not differ between middle school and high school. For students with LD, perceived companionship was similar in elementary and middle schools, but higher in high school.

Perceived intimacy was higher for nondisabled students than for students with LD at all levels of schooling. For both groups of students, perceived intimacy was higher in middle school than in elementary school and was higher still in high school, a finding in line with previous research on children's friendships (Buhrmester & Furman, 1987; Sullivan, 1953).

With regard to self-esteem, students with and without LD evidenced similar developmental patterns. Self-esteem for elementary students was higher than for middle school students, but middle and high school students did not differ significantly from one another. At all school levels, the self-esteem of students with LD was lower than that of students without disabilities. These findings corroborate findings of previous research, as reported in the first part of this chapter.

Overall, these data suggest some important similarities between students with and without LD. Notably, students with and without LD report similar levels of companionship. On the surface, this finding might seem surprising, given the research indicating that students with LD are more often rejected by their peers. However, previous research indicates that even unpopular students often have reciprocal friends in school, and our research indicates that students with LD (as well as nondisabled students) have many friendships outside of school. Thus, students with LD do not appear to be at a disadvantage in terms of the companionship provisions of friendships.

Also of interest, the developmental patterns in dimensions of friendship are similar for students with and without disabilities, and replicate some findings of previous research cited earlier. For example, assuming that longitudinal studies replicate the findings of this cross-sectional research, it would appear that for both groups of students, perceived support for self-esteem decreases from elementary to middle school, whereas perceived intimacy increases.

Differences are significant and persistent, however. Our research replicates findings of much previous research that the academic self-esteem of students with LD is lower than that of students without disabilities. However, other domains of self-esteem may not be so affected. In fact, as noted in the first part of this chapter, much research suggests that global self-esteem is similar for students with and without LD. Of interest, however, is the link between academic self-esteem and perceived support from friends as captured by the factor score for this dimension. For nondisabled students, correlations between these scores at the elementary, middle school and high school levels were .29 ($p <$ .0001), .21 ($p < .0001$), and .10 (ns), respectively; analogous correlations for students with LD were .35, .26, and .24 ($p < .0001$ in all cases). We note that the middle school correlations for both nondisabled students and students with LD are higher than the correlations between positive features of friendships and perceived scholastic competence on the Harter scale reported for early adolescents by Keefe and Berndt (1996). Our data provide further evidence that having supportive friendships is related to higher self-esteem, not only in the social domain but in the academic domain as well. Moreover, although directionality cannot be inferred from these correlations, the data suggest that whereas the academic self-concept of nondisabled students becomes independent of supportive friendships in later adolescence, the academic self-concept of students with LD continues to bear a relation to perceived support from peers throughout these children's school careers.

## Implications

Given these findings, how can the lower perceived support from friends reported by students with LD be reconciled with the finding, reported earlier in this chapter, of no differences between students with and without LD with regard to global self-concept? One explanation may be that friends are not the sole—or perhaps, even the most important—source of enhancement of self-worth for students. Furman and Buhrmester (1985) examined the support that early adolescents perceived that they received from a variety of sources: mother, father, grandparent, older and younger siblings, best friend, and teacher. The same type of support could come from more than one source. With regard to enhancement of worth, the authors expected that parents would be the most likely sources, followed by teachers. As expected, mothers and fathers were given the highest ratings. But contrary to expectations, teachers received the *lowest* ratings, and scores for grandparents, friends, and siblings fell in between. Thus, at least insofar as children's self-esteem is concerned, it cannot be assumed that intuitions about whose support counts the most are correct.

In conclusion, friendships represent an important aspect of the social functioning of students with LD. Whereas peer status conveys the evaluation of a larger network, friendship conveys that children are valued and selected by a specific peer who is reciprocally valued (Vandell & Hembree, 1994). Future research may explicate the impact that both unilateral and reciprocal friendships have on the development and social functioning of students with exceptionalities. Examining reciprocal friendships alone is likely to underestimate the number and quality of the friendships that students with exceptionalities experience, particularly if reciprocal friendships are studied solely in the classroom context. More research is needed on students' friendships and on the relationship of perceived friendship quality to concomitant and later indexes of social adjustment, such as self-concept.

## REFERENCES

Achenbach, T., & Zigler, E. (1963). Social competence and self-image disparity in psychiatric and nonpsychiatric patients. *Journal of Abnormal and Social Psychology, 67,* 197–205.

Asher, S. R., & Taylor, A. R. (1981). Social outcomes of mainstreaming: Sociometric assessment and beyond. *Exceptional Education Quarterly, 1,* 13–30.

Barr, R., & Dreeban, R. (1991). Grouping students for reading instruction. In R. Barr, M. Kamil, P. Mosenthal, & P. D. Pearson (Eds.), *Handbook of reading research* (Vol. 2, pp. 885–910). New York: Longman.

Battle, J., & Blowers, T. (1982). A longitudinal comparative study of the self-esteem of students in regular and special education classes. *Journal of Learning Disabilities, 15*(2), 100–102.

Bear, G. G., Juvonen, J., & McInerney, F. (1993). Self-perceptions and peer relations of boys with and boys without learning disabilities in an integrated setting: A longitudinal study. *Learning Disability Quarterly, 16,* 127–136.

Bear, G. G., & Minke, K. M. (1996). Positive bias in maintenance of self-worth among children with LD. *Learning Disability Quarterly, 19,* 23–32.

Berndt, T. J. (1982). The features and effects of friendship in early adolescence. *Child Development, 53,* 1447–1460.

Berndt, T. J., Hawkins, J. A., & Hoyle, S. G. (1986). Changes in friendship during a school year: Effects on children's and adolescents' impressions of friendship and sharing with friends. *Child Development, 57,* 1284–1297.

Berndt, T., & Perry, T. B. (1986). Children's perceptions of friendships as supportive relationships. *Developmental Psychology, 22,* 640–648.

Biklen, D., & Zollers, N. (1986). The focus of advocacy in the LD field. *Journal of Learning Disabilities, 19*(10), 579–586.

Brophy, J., & Good, T. L. (1970). Teachers' communication of differential expectations for children's classroom performance: Some behavioral data. *Journal of Educational Psychology, 20,* 941–952.

Bruck, M. (1986). Social and emotional adjustments of learning disabled children: A review of the issues. In S. J. Ceci (Ed.), *Handbook of cognitive, social, and neuropsychological aspects of learning disabilities.* Hillsdale, NJ: Lawrence Erlbaum Associates.

Bruck, M. (1987). The adult outcomes of children with learning disabilities. *Annals of Dyslexia, 37,* 252–263.

Buhrmester, D., & Furman, W. (1987). The development of companionship and intimacy. *Child Development, 58,* 1101–1113.

Bukowski, W., & Hoza, B. (1989). Popularity and friendship: Issues in theory, measurement, and outcome. In T. J. Berndt & G. W. Ladd (Eds.), *Peer relationships in child development* (pp. 15–45). New York: Wiley.

Bukowski, W., Boivin, M., & Hoza, B. (1994). Measuring friendship quality during pre- and early adolescence: The development and psychometric properties of the Friendship Qualities Scale. *Journal of Social and Personal Relationships, 11,* 471–484.

Bukowski, W. M., & Newcomb, A. F. (1987, April). *Friendship quality and the "self" during adolescence.* Paper presented at the biennial meeting of the Society for Research in Child Development, Baltimore, MD.

Bukowski, W., Newcomb, A., & Hartup, W. (1996). Friendship and its significance in childhood and adolescence: Introduction and comment. In W. Bukowski, A. Newcomb, & W. Hartup (Eds.), *The company they keep* (pp. 1–15). New York: Cambridge University Press.

Bursuck, W. (1989). A comparison of students with learning disabilities to low achieving and higher achieving students on three dimensions of social competence. *Journal of Learning Disabilities, 22* (3), 188–194.

Canfield, J., & Wells, H. C. (1994). *100 ways to enhance self-concept in the classroom.* Boston: Allyn & Bacon.

Carroll, J. L., Friedrich, D., & Hund, J. (1984). Academic self-concept and teachers' perceptions of normal, mentally retarded, and learning disabled elementary students. *Psychology in the Schools, 21,* 343–348.

Chapman, J. W. (1988a). Cognitive-motivational characteristics and academic achievement of learning disabled children: A longitudinal study. *Journal of Educational Psychology, 80,* 357–365.

Chapman, J. W. (1988b). Learning disabled children's self-concepts. *Review of Educational Research, 58,* 347–371.

Cielesz, A. J. (1983). Self-concept of mainstreamed learning disabled children in junior high and middle school. *Dissertation Abstracts International, 44*(2–A), 456–457.

Clever, A., Bear, G. G., & Juvonen, J. (1992). Discrepancies between competence and importance in self-perceptions of children in integrated classrooms. *Journal of Special Education, 26,* 125–138.

Coie, J. D., Lochman, J. E., Terry, R., & Hyman, C. (1992). Predicting early adolescent disorder from childhood aggression and peer rejection. *Journal of Consulting and Clinical Psychology, 60,* 783–792.

Colangelo, N., Kelley, K. R., & Schrepfer, R. M. (1987). A comparison of gifted, general, and special learning needs students on academic and social self-concept. *Journal of Counseling and Development, 66*(2), 73–77.

Coleman, J. M. (1984). Mothers' predictions of the self-concept of their normal or learning-disabled children. *Journal of Learning Disabilities, 17,* 214–217.

Cooley, C. H. (1902). *Human nature and the social order.* New York: Scribner's.

Cooley, E. J., & Ayers, R. R. (1988). Self-concept and success-failure attributions of nonhandicapped students and students with learning disabilities. *Journal of Learning Disabilities, 21*(3), 174–178.

Crocker, J., & Major, B. (1989). Social stigma and self-esteem: The self-protective properties of stigma. *Psychological Review, 96*, 608–630.

Epstein, J. L. (1989). The selection of friends: Changes across the grades and in different school environments. In T. J. Berndt & G. W. Ladd (Eds.), *Peer relationships in child development* (pp. 158–187). New York: Wiley.

Farmer, T. W., & Hollowell, J. H. (1994). Social networks in mainstream classrooms: Social affiliations and behavioral characteristics of students with emotional and behavioral disorders. *Journal of Emotional and Behavioral Disorders, 2*(2), 143–155, 163.

Farmer, T. W., Pearl, R., & Van Acker, R. M. (1996). Expanding the social skills deficit framework: A developmental synthesis perspective, classroom social networks, and implications for the social growth of students with disabilities. *The Journal of Special Education, 30*(3), 232–256.

Festinger, L. (1954). A theory of social comparison processes. *Human Relations, 7*, 117-140.

Forman, E. A. (1987). Peer relationships of learning disabled children: A contextualist perspective. *Learning Disabilities Research, 2*(2), 80–90.

Forman, E. A. (1988). The effects of social support and school placement on the self-concept of LD students. *Learning Disability Quarterly, 11*, 115–124.

Furman, W. (1996). The measurement of friendship perceptions: Conceptual and methodological issues. In W. Bukowski, A. Newcomb, & W. Hartup (Eds.), *The company they keep* (pp. 41–65). New York: Cambridge University Press.

Furman, W., & Bierman, K. L. (1984). Children's conceptions of friendship: A multimethod study of developmental changes. *Developmental Psychology, 20*, 925–933.

Furman, W., & Buhrmester, D. (1985). Children's perceptions of the personal relationships in their social networks. *Developmental Psychology, 21*, 1016–1022.

Furman, W., & Robbins, P. (1985). What's the point? Issues in the selection of treatment objectives. In B. Schneider, K. Rubin, & J. Leddingham (Eds.), *Children's relations: Issues in assessment and intervention* (pp. 41–54). New York: Springer-Verlag.

George, T. P., & Hartmann, D. P. (1996). Friendship networks of unpopular, average, and popular children. *Child Development, 67*, 2301–2316.

Good, T. L. (1982). How teachers' expectations affect results. *American Education, 18*(10), 25–32.

Good, T. L., & Brophy, J. E. (1994). *Looking in classrooms* (6th ed.). New York: HarperCollins.

Gresham, F. M. (1982). Misguided mainstreaming: The case for social skills training with handicapped children. *Exceptional Children, 48*, 422–433.

Grolnick, W. S., & Ryan, R. M. (1990). Self-perceptions, motivation, and adjustment in children with learning disabilities: A multiple group comparison. *Journal of Learning Disabilities, 23*, 177–184.

Haager, D., & Vaughn, S. (1995). Parent, teacher, peer, and self-reports of the social competence of students with learning disabilities. *Journal of Learning Disabilities, 28*(4), 205-215.

Haager, D., & Vaughn, S. (1997). Assessment of social competence in students with learning disabilities. In D. Chard, E. J. Kameenui, & J. W. Lloyd (Eds.), *Issues in educating students with learning disabilities* (pp. 129–152). Hillsdale, NJ: Lawrence Erlbaum Associates.

Hagborg, W. J. (1996). Self-concept and middle school students with learning disabilities: A comparison of scholastic competence subgroups. *Learning Disability Quarterly, 19,* 117–126.

Hallinan, M. T., & Sorenson, A. B. (1985). Ability grouping and student friendships. *American Educational Research Journal, 22*(4), 485–499.

Harter, S. (1985). *Manual for the self-perception profile for children.* Denver, CO: University of Denver.

Harter, S., & Pike, R. (1984). The pictorial scale of perceived competence and social acceptance for young children. *Child Development, 55,* 1969–1982.

Heath, N. L., & Wiener, J. (1996). Depression and nonacademic self-perceptions in children with and without learning disabilities. *Learning Disability Quarterly, 19,* 34–44.

Heyman, W. B. (1990). The self-perception of a learning disability and its relationship to academic self-concept and self-esteem. *Journal of Learning Disabilities, 23*(8), 472–475.

Hiebert, B., Wong, B., & Hunter, M. (1982). Affective influences on learning disabled adolescents. *Learning Disability Quarterly, 5,* 334–343.

Hildreth, B. L. (1987). An investigation of the self-concept and anxiety of learning disabled students. *Dissertation Abstracts International, 48*(5–A), 1169.

Hoza, B. (1989). *Development and validation of a method for classifying children's social status based on two types of measures: Popularity and chumship.* Unpublished doctoral dissertation, University of Maine.

Hymel, S., Wagner, E., & Butler, E. (1990). Reputational bias: View from the peer group. In S. R. Asher & J. D. Coie (Eds.), *Peer rejection in childhood* (pp. 156–188). Cambridge, England: Cambridge University Press.

James, W. (1963). *Psychology.* New York: Fawcett. (Original work published 1892)

Juvonen, J., & Bear, G. (1992). Social adjustment of children with and without learning disabilities in integrated classrooms. *Journal of Educational Psychology, 84,* 322–330.

Kandel, D. B. (1978). Similarity in real-life adolescent friendship pairs. *Journal of Personality and Social Psychology, 36,* 306–312.

Kane, J. F. (1979). A comparison of learning disabled children with learning disabled adolescents relative to non-learning disabled peers in terms of selected achievement, affective and behavioral variables. *Dissertation Abstracts International, 197–A,* 1140.

Keefe, K., & Berndt, T. (1996). Relations of friendship quality to self-esteem in early adolescence. *Journal of Early Adolescence, 16,* 110–129.

Keogh, B. K. (1994). What the special education research agenda should look like in the year 2000. *Learning Disabilities Research and Practice, 9*(2), 62–69.

Keogh, B. K., Juvonen, J., & Bernheimer, L. P. (1989). Assessing children's competence: Mothers' and teachers' ratings of competent behavior. *Psychological Assessment: A Journal of Consulting and Clinical Psychology, 1*(3), 224–229.

Kifer, E. (1975). Relationship between academic achievement and personality characteristics: A quasi-longitudinal study. *American Educational Research Journal, 12,* 191–210.

Kindermann, T. A. (1993). Natural peer groups as contexts for individual development: The case of children's motivation in school. *Developmental Psychology, 29,* 970–977.

Kistner, J. A., & Gatlin, D. (1989). Correlates of peer rejection among children with learning disabilities. *Learning Disability Quarterly, 12,* 133–140.

Kistner, J. A., Haskett, M., White, K., & Robbins, R. (1987). Perceived competence and self-worth of LD and normally achieving students. *Learning Disability Quarterly, 10,* 37–44.

Kistner, J. A., & Osborne, M. (1987). A longitudinal study of learning disabled children's self-evaluations. *Learning Disability Quarterly, 12,* 133–140.

Kloomok, S., & Cosden, M. (1994). Self-concept in children with learning disabilities: The relationship between global self-concept, academic "discounting," nonacademic self-concept, and perceived social support. *Learning Disability Quarterly, 17,* 140–153.

Kupersmidt, J. B., Coie, J. D., & Dodge, K. A. (1990). The role of poor peer relationships in the developmental disorder. In S. R. Asher & J. D. Coie (Eds.), *Peer rejection in childhood* (pp. 274–308). Cambridge, England: Cambridge University Press.

LaGreca, A. M., & Stone, W. L. (1990). Children with learning disabilities: The role of achievement in their social, personal and behavioral functioning. In H. L. Swanson & B. Keogh (Eds.), *Learning disabilities: Theoretical and research issues* (pp. 333–352). Hillsdale, NJ: Lawrence Erlbaum Associates.

Leahy, R. L. (Ed.). (1985). *The development of the self.* Orlando, FL: Academic.

Lewandowski, L., & Arcangelo, K. (1994). The social adjustment and self-concept of adults with learning disabilities. *Journal of Learning Disabilities, 27*(9), 598–605.

Mannarino, A. P. (1978). The interactional process in preadolescent friendships. *Psychiatry, 41,* 308–312.

Marsh, H. W. (1988). *The Self Description Questionnaire (SDQ) II: A theoretical and empirical basis for the measurement of multiple dimensions of preadolescent self-concept: A test manual and research monograph.* San Antonio, TX: Psychological Corporation.

Marsh, H. W. (1989). Age and sex effects in multiple dimensions of self-concept: Preadolescence to early adulthood. *Journal of Educational Psychology, 81,* 417–430.

Marsh, H. W., Byrne, B. M., & Shavelson, R. J. (1988). A multifaceted academic self-concept: Its hierarchical structure and its relations to academic achievement. *Journal of Educational Psychology, 80,* 366–380.

Montgomery, M. S. (1994). Self-concept and children with learning disabilities: Observer-child concordance across six context-dependent domains. *Journal of Learning Disabilities, 27*(4), 254–262.

Newcomb, A. F., & Bagwell, C. L. (1995). Children's friendship relations: A meta-analytic review. *Psychological Bulletin, 117,* 306–347.

Ollendick, T. I I., Weist, M. D., Borden, M. C., & Greene, R. W. (1992). Sociometric status and academic, behavioral, and psychological adjustment: A five-year longitudinal study. *Journal of Consulting and Clinical Psychology, 60,* 80–87.

Parker, J. G., & Asher, S. R. (1993). Friendships and friendship quality in middle childhood: Links with peer group acceptance and feelings of loneliness and social dissatisfaction. *Developmental Psychology, 29,* 611–621.

Pickar, D. B., & Tori, C. D. (1986). The learning disabled adolescent: Eriksonian psychosocial development, self-concept, and delinquent behavior. *Journal of Youth and Adolescence, 15*(5), 429–440.

Piers, E. V. (1984). *Piers-Harris Children's Self-Concept Scale: Revised manual 1984.* Los Angeles: Western Psychological Services.

Priel, B., & Leshem, T. (1990). Self-perception of first- and second-grade children with learning disabilities. *Journal of Learning Disabilities, 23*(10), 637–642.

Renick, M. J., & Harter, S. (1988). *Manual for the self-perception profile for learning disabled students.* Denver, CO: University of Denver.

Renick, M. J., & Harter, S. (1989). Impact of social comparisons on the developing self-perceptions of learning disabled students. *Journal of Educational Psychology, 81,* 631-638.

Rogers, H., & Saklofske, D. H. (1985). Self-concepts, locus of control and performance expectations of learning disabled children. *Journal of Learning Disabilities, 18,* 273–278.

Rosenberg, B. S., & Gaier, E. L. (1977). The self-concept of the adolescent with learning disabilities. *Adolescence, 48,* 489–498.

Rothman, H. R., & Cosden, M. (1995). The relationship between self-perception of a learning disability and achievement, self-concept, and social support. *Learning Disability Quarterly, 18*(3), 203–212.

Ruble, D. N. (1983). The development of social comparison processes and their role in achievement-related self-socialization. In E. T. Higgings, W. W. Hartup, & D. N. Ruble (Eds.), *Social cognition and social development: A sociocultural perspective* (pp. 1–15). New York: Cambridge University Press.

Sabornie, E. J. (1985). Social mainstreaming of handicapped students: Facing an unpleasant reality. *Remedial and Special Education, 6*(2), 12–16.

Sale, P., & Carey, D. M. (1995). The sociometric status of students with disabilities in a full-inclusion school. *Exceptional Children, 62,* 6–19.

Schumm, J. S., Moody, S. W., & Vaughn, S. (1997). *Grouping for reading instruction: General education teachers' perceptions and practices.* Manuscript in preparation.

Schumm, J. S., Vaughn, S., & Elbaum, B. E. (1996). Teachers' perceptions of grouping practices for reading instruction. In D. J. Leu, C. K. Kinzer, & K. A. Hinchman (Eds.), *Literacies for the 21st century: Research and practice* (pp. 543–551). Chicago: The National Reading Conference.

Shavelson, R. J., Hubner, J. J., & Stanton, G. C. (1976). Self-concept: Validation of construct interpretations. *Review of Educational Research, 46,* 407–441.

Silverman, R., & Zigmond, N. (1983). Self-concept in learning disabled adolescents. *Journal of Learning Disabilities, 16,* 478–482.

Siperstein, G. N., Bopp, M. J., & Bak, J. J. (1978). Social status of learning disabled children. *Journal of Learning Disabilities, 11,* 49–53.

Smith, D. S., & Nagle, R. J. (1995). Self-perceptions and social comparisons among children with LD. *Journal of Learning Disabilities, 28*(6), 264–371.

Stone, W. L., & La Greca, A. M. (1990). The social status of children with learning disabilities: A reexamination. *Journal of Learning Disabilities, 23,* 32–37.

Sullivan, H. S. (1953). *The interpersonal theory of psychiatry.* New York: Norton.

Taylor, A., Asher, S., & Williams, G. (1987). The social adaptation of mainstreamed mildly retarded children. *Child Development, 58,* 1321–1334.

Vandell, D., & Hembree, S. (1994). Peer social status and friendship: Independent contributors to children's social and academic adjustment. *Merrill-Palmer Quarterly, 40,* 461–477.

Vaughn, S., Elbaum, B. E., & Schumm, J. S. (1996). The effects of inclusion on the social functioning of students with learning disabilities. *Journal of Learning Disabilities, 29*(6), 598–608.

Vaughn, S., Elbaum, B., Schumm, J. S., & Hughes, M. T. (1998). Social outcomes for students with and without learning disabilities in inclusive classrooms. *Journal of Learning Disabilities, 31*(5), 428–436.

Vaughn, S., Haager, D., Hogan, A., & Kouzekanani, K. (1992). Self-concept and peer acceptance in students with learning disabilities: A four- to five-year prospective study. *Journal of Educational Psychology, 84,* 43–50.

Vaughn, S., & Hogan, A. (1990). Social competence and learning disabilities: A prospective study. In H. L. Swanson & B. Keogh (Eds.), *Learning disabilities: Theoretical and research issues* (pp. 175–191). Hillsdale, NJ: Lawrence Erlbaum Associates.

Vaughn, S., & Hogan, A. (1994). Social competence of students with LD over time: A within-individual examination. *Journal of Learning Disabilities, 27*(5), 292–303.

Vaughn, S., McIntosh, R., Schumm, J. S., Haager, D., & Callwood, D. (1993). Social status and peer acceptance revisited. *Learning Disabilities Research and Practice, 8*(2), 82–88.

Wenz-Gross, M., & Siperstein, G. (1997). Importance of social support in the adjustment of children with learning problems. *Exceptional Children, 63,* 183–193.

Winne, P., Woodlands, M. J., & Wong, B. Y. L. (1982). Comparability of self-concept among learning disabled, normal, and gifted students. *Journal of Learning Disabilities, 15,* 470–475.

Wright, B. A. (1960). *Physical disability: A psychological approach.* New York: Harper & Row.

Wright, B. A. (1983). *Physical disability: A psychological approach* (2nd ed.). New York: Harper & Row.

# PART II

## Diagnosis, Classification, and Intervention

# 6 — Utility of Current Diagnostic Categories for Research and Practice

**Donald L. MacMillan**
*University of California, Riverside*

**Deborah L. Speece**
*University of Maryland*

One need only examine the *Annual Reports to Congress* to document that year after year an increasing number of children are being served in our public schools as learning disabled (LD). Between 1976–77 and 1992–93 the number of children served as LD nationwide increased by 198%; whereas, during the same period, there was a corresponding *decrease* of 41% for children with mental retardation and 15.5% for children with speech and language impairments (U.S. Department of Education, 1994). Commenting on the magnitude of the increase in prevalence of children with LD, MacMillan, Gresham, Siperstein, and Bocian (1996b) wrote: "Were these epidemic-like figures interpreted by the Center for Disease Control one might reasonably expect to find a quarantine imposed on the public schools of America" (p. 169).

Explanations for this epidemic-like increase in identification rate have varied. Some (e.g., Hallahan, 1992) reasoned that the increase in detection rates of children with LD is due to "real increases" attributable to the maturing of LD as a field and increased sensitivity to recognizing children with LD, coupled with social and cultural changes that have put the development of children's central nervous systems more at risk for damage (e.g., prenatal substance abuse, increased stress in the home). A competing hypothesis, however, is that the category of LD is being used by the public schools as a nonspecific category that subsumes many children who fail to meet state criteria for eligibility. Support for this argument was found in several recent articles (Gottlieb, Alter, Gottlieb, & Wishner, 1994; MacMillan, Gresham, & Bocian, in press; MacMillan et al., 1996b). Regardless of the explanation, the population of school-identified LD students is extremely heterogeneous and only vaguely resembles the population described in authoritative definitions of LD and school education code criteria.

In this chapter we examine the identification of mild mental retardation (MMR) and learning disabilities (LD) from the perspectives of research and school practice. Our focus is primarily LD, using lessons from the field of MR to frame the issues on the widening gap between how LD is defined in the research literature and legislative codes and how LD is operationally defined in school practices. We believe this analysis is central to the issue of how research evidence is going to impact school practices; that is, the external validity of research evidence for children receiving services as students with LD in the schools. In our efforts to examine this linkage we discuss the possible need to revisit the interpretation of aptitude measures as a basis for "expected achievement" and the utility of certain "exclusionary criteria" (namely, mental retardation and cultural differences) given the changes in the nature of the children being identified as LD in the schools. Children presenting in the schools with absolute low achievement clearly present problems to general education, and how and under what state-sanctioned disability category such children will be assisted is debatable. One thing about this group of children vis-a-vis other disability categories (e.g., blind, deaf) is that MMR and LD are judgmental categories (Bateman, 1992; Reschly, 1997) that can only be understood in terms of contextual factors. At the present time, they are not, in our opinion, distinct clinical entities amenable to reliable detection employing diagnostic instruments. (Note: Others will strongly disagree with this position). An understanding of the "conflicting paradigms" used to guide school practice and research on "LD" children are explored in an attempt to clarify some of the disagreements that exist within the field. Finally, we draw implications from our analysis for subsequent research and efforts to maximize the extent to which research evidence can inform educational practices with low achieving students.

## AUTHORITATIVE DEFINITIONS AND EDUCATION CODES: THE ROLE OF IQ

Crafted by committees consisting of nationally visible academicians and clinicians, definitions of mental retardation and LD are widely cited, if not universally accepted. In the field of mental retardation, the American Association on Mental Retardation (AAMR) has published a number of authoritative definitions (see MacMillan & Reschly, 1996). In the field of LD, authoritative definitions have been prepared by the National Advisory Committee on Handicapped Children (1968) and the National Joint Committee for Learning Disabilities (Hammill, Leigh, McNutt, & Larsen, 1981), with revisions suggested by the Interagency Committee (Kavanagh & Truss, 1988).

All definitions of mental retardation provided by the AAMR since 1959 have specified "subaverage general intellectual functioning" as a defining feature. Definitions of LD indirectly address intelligence in the *exclusionary components*, naming children "who have learning problems which are primarily the result of visual, hearing, or motor handicaps, of mental retardation, or emotional disturbance, or of environmental, cultural, or economic disadvantage" (U.S. Office of Education, 1977, p. 65,083). In addition, LD is recognized as *unexpected underachievement* (Keogh, 1994), whereas mental retardation has been characterized as *expected underachievement* (MacMillan, 1993). Although one can derive an "expected" level of achievement from any number of bases (e.g., age, grade), the most commonly used basis for predicting expected level of achievement has been IQ. Hence, IQ has been central to definitions of mental retardation. Indirectly, IQ is important to LD in the way it defines one group excluded from LD eligibility—cases of mental retardation—and as it serves to operationalize a discrepancy.

A similar situation exists as we move from authoritative definitions to state education codes. The definitions and criteria for establishing eligibility of children in state-sanctioned disability categories of mental retardation and LD vary somewhat from state to state. Nevertheless, published analyses of state education code definitions and criteria for MR and LD reveal some rather common elements across a majority of states (Frankenberger & Fronzaglio, 1991; Frankenberger & Harper, 1987; Mercer, Hughes, & Mercer, 1985; Mercer, Jordan, Allsopp, & Mercer, 1996; Utley, Lowitzer, & Baumeister, 1987). One review reported that 81% of the states specified an IQ cutoff score (scores ranged from 69 to 84) for definitions and criteria for mental retardation. In the case of LD, the exclusionary clauses specified in the authoritative definitions were reflected in state codes, with 98% of the states excluding from LD eligibility children with mental retardation and children whose learning problems were due to environmental disadvantage. Consistent with the view of LD as unexpected underachievement, some 98% of the states included a discrepancy in the definition or criteria.

Many children in our public schools, then, who exhibit *severe and persistent low achievement* appear to be "covered" by the definitions and the state education codes referenced. That is, a child with very low reading achievement and with an IQ below the extant cutoff score for mental retardation qualifies for special education via the MR route. Other children with very low reading achievement and an IQ above the cutoff score for mental retardation *and* high enough to meet the requisite discrepancy in his or her state will qualify for special education via the LD route. A third group, however, exists that has received attention in recent research and might be described as exhibiting very low reading achievement, scoring above the IQ cutoff score for mental retardation, but whose IQ and measured reading achievement fail to meet the requisite discrepancy. We refer to these children as *nondiscrepant low achievers* and discuss them subsequently. This group is not eligible for special education services by virtue of qualifying as either MR or LD.

It should be noted that the definitions of LD that continue to be cited are quite dated, whereas the definitions of mental retardation, although revised periodically (Grossman, 1973, 1977, 1983; Luckasson, 1992), are in fact modeled after the Heber (1959, 1961) definition. Authoritative definitions of both conditions fail to adequately consider contextual factors that play a major role in increasing or decreasing the possibility that a given child will be "detected" as MMR or LD. The most recent AAMR definition (Luckasson, 1992) was criticized along these lines recently (Gresham, MacMillan, & Siperstein, 1995; MacMillan, Gresham, & Siperstein, 1993, 1995). The key to understanding such contextual factors probably resides in understanding the referral process, social class and modal achievement level of students served in schools, and teacher tolerance (e.g., Bahr, Fuchs, Stecker, & Fuchs, 1991; Gerber & Semmel, 1984; Gottlieb et al., 1994; Keogh & Speece, 1996). Let us turn our attention to the changing demographics in terms of who is classified as LD.

## CHANGING DEMOGRAPHICS OF LD

One of the major criticisms of classes for MMR in the late 1960s was the fact that they contained disproportionately high numbers of ethnic minority children. Conversely, at that time LD was viewed as the province of middle-class European Americans. One spokesperson (Johnson, 1969) for the minority perspective cast the issue as follows: When a Black child is doing poorly it is because he or she is stupid, whereas the White child doing poorly has a specific learning disability. In the infancy of the LD field, the condition was believed to be neurologically based and, as noted previously, excluded children whose learning problems were due to cultural differences. As such, LD avoided in those early years the concerns expressed regarding overrepresentation of minority group children.

However, things have changed over the years. It has been noted for some time that the decline in the MMR category was explained, in part, by an "MMR-for-LD shift" (Ortiz & Yates, 1983)—a shift thought by some to involve minority children particularly (Chinn & Hughes, 1987). In the southwestern United States, the increase in the LD identification was described by one author as follows: "It does not take much imagination to infer that there is at least the possibility that when it is no longer socially desirable to place black students in educable mentally retarded classes, it became convenient to place them in the newly provided [learning disabilities] category" (Tucker, 1980, pp. 103-104). Recent evidence published on school identification of children as mentally retarded and learning disabled (MacMillan et al., 1996b, in press) provides further support for this perspective.

Data provided by the Office of Civil Rights and the U.S. Department of Education also document the increased rate at which children from ethnic minority backgrounds have been identified as MMR and LD. Table 6.1 displays the percentages of three ethnic groups classified as MMR and LD at three different points in time: 1978, 1986, and 1990. Although the percentage of African American children identified as MMR has declined over this period of years, one can see that the rate is disproportionately high. However, for children identified as LD, the percentage for all three ethnic groups is comparable at the three time intervals. What has changed over time is the fact that there has been an increase in the percentage of children *for all three ethnic groups* — doubling over a twelve year period for all three groups. These rates of identification are not broken down by social class within ethnic groups. However, it is clear that if

### TABLE 6.1
#### Percentages of White, Black, and Hispanic Students Classified as MMR and LD

| | Disability Category | | |
| Year/Ethnic Group | MMR | LD | MR + LD |
| --- | --- | --- | --- |
| 1978 | | | |
| White | 1.07% | 2.32% | 3.69% |
| Black | 3.46 | 2.23 | 5.69 |
| Hispanic | 0.98 | 2.58 | 3.56 |
| 1986 | | | |
| White | 0.87 | 4.29 | 5.16 |
| Black | 2.30 | 4.43 | 6.73 |
| Hispanic | 0.56 | 4.31 | 4.87 |
| 1990 | | | |
| White | 0.81 | 4.97 | 5.78 |
| Black | 2.10 | 4.95 | 7.05 |
| Hispanic | 0.65 | 4.68 | 5.33 |

Note. Based on a paper presented by Reschly (1997). 1978 data are from Finn (1982, pp. 324–330). 1986 data are from Reschly & Wilson (1990) and the 1990 data are from U.S. Department of Education (1994, pp. 198, 201, 202).

ethnicity is an issue for the MMR category, it is also being considered an issue for the LD category. Twice as many African American children are classified as LD as they are MMR, and over four times the number of European American and Latino children are designated as LD than as MMR. Because a greater proportion of African American and Latino children live in poverty than do European American children, the impact of cultural differences on classification requires elaboration.

For example, in a report on LD labeling practices in a large urban district in the northeast, Gottlieb and his colleagues (Gottlieb et al., 1994) described findings from an ongoing series of studies that further document the changing demographics among LD students. Their findings should alert the LD field to the need to reassess the stance on "exclusion for reasons of cultural disadvantage" when considering inner-city children. Descriptive data provided revealed that of students receiving special education, more than 90% received some form of public assistance, and 95% are members of a minority group. Between 10% and 25% of the students in special education live at home with both parents. Among children identified as LD, 19% were foreign born and 44% came from households where English was *not* the primary language spoken by the parents. As the authors noted, many of these children do not meet the specified criteria for LD, *yet these are the kinds of children served as LD in urban settings.*

Gottlieb et al. (1994) also addressed the issue of excluding children whose learning problems are due to mental retardation. For a sample of LD students drawn in 1992, the IQ scores achieved by the children are indeed revealing. The mean IQ for the urban LD sample was 81.4 (SD = 13.9), whereas the mean IQ for a suburban sample of LD children was 102.8 (SD = 13.4)—a difference of approximately one and one-half standard deviations! For the urban LD sample, 16.6% had IQs less than 70, whereas only 25.7% had IQs above 90. In their abstract, Gottleib et al. (1994) wrote: "Data we have collected over a 10-year period indicate that today's child with learning disabilities functions very similarly to the way students with educable mental retardation performed 25 years ago" (p. 453).

The first author of this chapter (MacMillan) has been involved in an investigation of students referred by regular class teachers for prereferral intervention. Soon after referral for prereferral services, these students were administered a battery of assessment tests (IQ, individual achievement) and teachers completed ratings of the child on social skills, problem behaviors, and academic skills. These children were then monitored to determine how the schools dealt with them and how they were categorized as eligible for special education, if indeed the schools did formally evaluate them. Findings from this project have been disseminated in professional journals (Gresham, MacMillan, & Bocian, 1997; Lopez, Forness, MacMillan, Bocian, & Gresham, 1996; MacMillan et al. in press, 1996b; MacMillan, Gresham, Lopez, & Bocian, 1996a). Findings revealed very low-level adherence by the schools to the state education code criteria in classifying students. Using research diagnostic criteria, the project identified 43 children with Full-Scale IQs on the WISC-III below 75. Of the 43, the schools ultimately reached decisions on 35 cases (four had moved and eight were still "pending"). Only six children with Full-Scale IQs less than 75 were classified as mentally retarded, whereas 19 children were classified as LD, six others were found ineligible for special education, and four were classified as Speech and Language Impaired (MacMillan et al., 1996b). A total of 61 children referred for prereferral intervention were ultimately classified as LD by the schools. Less than half (n = 29) of those 61 children classified as LD by the schools met the research diagnostic criteria (modeled after the state education code criteria; average intelligence and a standard score discrepancy of 22 points between aptitude and achievement), whereas 7 students who met the research diagnostic criteria (and had been referred by their regular class teachers) were *not* identified as LD (mean IQ for this group was 109.43). Comparisons of this "False Negative" group with the students whom the schools did identify as LD revealed several reliable differences on IQ, problem behaviors, teacher ratings of academic competence, and social skills, with the False Negative group scoring higher or being perceived by teachers more favorably than were the school-identified LD children.

Similar findings were reported by Shaywitz, Shaywitz, Fletcher, and Escobar (1990), even though their sampling strategy was quite different. Based on an epidemiological sample comprising 84.3% European American children, only 45% of school-identified (SI) children with LD met research-identified (RI) criteria (IQ > 79; 22-point discrepancy). Reliable differences were found between the two groups on teachers' ratings of problem behavior favoring the RI children; that is, the RI group was perceived to exhibit fewer behavior problems. IQ and achievement differences were not tested, but descriptive data suggested that the RI group had higher intelligence and math scores, but were comparable on reading achievement.

From a different perspective, Shepard, Smith, and Vojir (1983) found that in a representative sample of 800 children classified as LD by the schools, only 30% met the IQ-achievement discrepancy criterion and only 43% of the cases reflected either discrepancy criteria or clinical signs of LD. Thirty percent of the cases were assigned more properly to low achievement, second language learners, or environmental concerns (e.g., attends many schools, excessive absences). Thus, since 1978 when PL 94-142 was to be fully implemented, there has been consistent evidence that between 52% to 70% of children identified by the schools as LD do not meet the standards as conceptualized in federal and state definitions of the disability category. Given the different sampling strategies used by the research groups over different time periods, these are startling figures.

Several observations about how the schools sort students with severe and persistent achievement problems into the LD category seem in order. First, LD in the schools is a nonspecific category of children with *absolute* low achievement relative to school peers. At present, school practices do not appear to consider aptitude and achievement simultaneously as the definitions and education codes suggest they should. Cases where the low achievement is consistent and inconsistent with "expected" levels of achievement are not differentiated. The "False Negative" group of children in the MacMillan et al. (in press) study were characterized by higher mean IQs, resulting in achievement levels that although discrepant were apparently "acceptable" by the schools in terms of absolute level. Second, the classification of "mental retardation" apparently is viewed as pessimistic in its prognosis, and LD appears to be a more acceptable diagnosis. As a consequence, the schools have evolved a practice of certifying most students with absolute low achievement as LD, *regardless* of whether the IQ is below the cutoff for mental retardation or whether the achievement qualifies as discrepant from an expected level. Qualification of children as eligible for special education services under the mental retardation and serious emotional disturbance criteria appears to be reserved for only the most apparent and dramatic cases. Finally, the schools do adhere to the requirement of administering instruments and scales required for certification of children as eligible under the various state-sanctioned disability categories. Hence, individual intelligence tests, achievement tests, adaptive behavior scales, and processing tests are administered; however, this is done more to conform to requirements than to secure data on which a differential diagnosis is to be made. As one teacher described it, "They are more concerned with 'what to do' than with 'what kind of kid this is'" (MacMillan et al., 1996b, p. 170).

## THE ROLE OF IQ IN CLASSIFYING MINORITY STUDENTS

The controversy surrounding intelligence tests and the use to which they are put in educational decision making has been with us for most of this century (Cronbach, 1975). The controversy was fueled when the overrepresentation of certain minority children in programs for MMR were attributed to: (a) the unfairness inherent in the tests for African American and Latino children, and (b) the importance placed on IQ in placement decisions, described by Judge Peckham in *Larry P.* as "primary and determinative" (Elliott, 1987; Reschly, 1988). In the previous section we showed how increasingly (i.e., from 1978 to 1986 to 1990) greater percentages of African American and Latino children are being identified as LD. Over the course of these years there has been some "correction" in the degree of overrepresentation of African American children as MMR, and the percentages of African American and Latino children being identified as LD do not reflect overrepresentation because similar percentages of children from the ethnic groups are identified. Nevertheless, there has been an *increase* in the percentage of children within each ethnic group being classified as LD by schools; for example, by 1990, 4.68% of Latino children and 4.95% of African American students were classified as LD.

As defined by the schools, LD is no longer a predominantly middle-class European American phenomenon. We also cited the review by Mercer et al. (1996), which reported that 98% of the states require a discrepancy in either the definition or criteria for LD. For a very high percentage of those requiring a discrepancy, the "discrepancy" is calculated using IQ as the basis for expected level of achievement. Hence, the challenges to the meaning of IQ for ethnic minority children that were raised in the context of MMR are very germane to the discussion of LD (MacMillan, 1989). Whether an IQ test is employed to determine that an African American child exhibits "subaverage general intellectual functioning" or to establish a level of expected reading achievement, allegations of unfairness of that IQ score for that particular child are equally relevant. In fact, in the case of Latino children, particularly when accompanied by limited English proficiency, the use of a Verbal IQ or a Full Scale IQ to estimate aptitude appears unwarranted.

Considerable attention has been devoted to the performance of Latino children on standardized tests of intelligence (McShane & Cook, 1985). An examination of more than 70 empirical studies concerning the performance of Latino children on the Wechsler scales led McShane and Cook to several conclusions. First, they found an average discrepancy of approximately 10 to 15 points on the WISC and WISC-R with the Verbal IQ (VIQ) being lower. Moreover, Latino samples achieved Full Scale IQs (FSIQ) lower than the standardization sample on a consistent basis. Professional opinion clearly favors the practice of interpreting scores other than FSIQ in estimating the aptitude of several groups of children, including Latinos and Native American Indians. In this regard, Kaufman (1994) wrote the following:

> It is quite clear that Verbal IQs or other indexes of verbal ability—although they may be meaningful for understanding children better—do not reflect their intellectual potential. When the WISC-III is deemed an appropriate instrument for use with a bilingual-bicultural child based on federal, state, and local guidelines, *the examiner is advised not to interpret the Full Scale IQ* [italics added]. (p. 161)

Evidence bearing on the consequences of employing Performance IQ (PIQ) was provided by Reschly and Jipson (1976), who examined the prevalence of mental retardation using IQ cutoff scores (i.e., mental retardation was defined on the basis of IQ alone). They reported that the use of FSIQ resulted in the overrepresentation of Latino children qualifying as mentally retarded. However, if the PIQ scores were used to estimate aptitude, the prevalence rate for Latino children was proportionate to the enrollment of Latino children in the general school population. Commenting on the use of PIQ, McShane and Cook (1985) wrote: "In fact, when Performance IQ is used for decision making on an IQ criterion alone, the number of Latino children identified as mentally retarded approximates that expected by application of the normal curve" (p. 777).

MacMillan, Gresham, and Bocian (1998) reported on a sample referred by regular class teachers for prereferral intervention. All subjects were administered the WISC-III and WRAT-R by project personnel as part of a larger battery. Although VIQ-PIQ differences within European American and African American samples did not differ notably, the difference was significant for Latino students—they scored approximately 9 points higher on the PIQ. Moreover, Latino students scored significantly lower than European American students on both the FSIQ and VIQ; however, on the PIQ scale, Latino subjects did not differ significantly from European American students.

When the consequences of these differing IQ scales, by ethnic group for special education eligibility were examined, results indicated that Latino students would be most dramatically impacted by the use of PIQ instead of FSIQ as the estimate of a child's aptitude. The percentage of cases in each ethnic group that would be classified differently (e.g., MR under one and ineligible under the other; ineligible under one to LD) using PIQ instead of FSIQ were as follows: European American—23.6%, African American—14.3%, and Latino—45.3%. There was also a dramatic reduction in the number of Latino students eligible as mentally retarded if PIQ were used. Using FSIQ, 35.8% of the Latino students qualified as MR, whereas only 15.1% qualified using PIQ. However, there was a corresponding increase in the rate that would be eligible as LD—15 additional children (out of 53 cases). That is, use of FSIQ resulted in

30.2% of the Latino children having the 22-point discrepancy, whereas 58.5% would qualify if the PIQ were used to estimate aptitude.

The foregoing attests to the frailty of the system, with a child's eligibility dependent on the decision regarding which scale should be employed. If the FSIQ is used a child is mentally retarded, but if the PIQ is used he or she is ineligible. In several cases, a child was eligible as mentally retarded using FSIQ and became eligible as LD using the PIQ! We do not claim to know which is the "right" rate, but rather introduce these findings to illustrate the complexity (and uncertainty) involved when sociocultural factors are implicated in the performance of children on scales central to defining these high-incidence disabilities such as MMR and LD. They are certainly not inconsequential for the child in question and, as shown earlier, an increasing number of Latino children are being classified as LD.

## CONFLICTING PARADIGMS

We have established that children identified by the schools as learning disabled frequently do not meet federal or state criteria for the condition. This general conclusion, in and of itself, is not news. However, the sheer magnitude of the problem (i.e., 52% to 70%) is rarely noted and deserves discussion. Plausible explanations can be offered, and many have empirical backing: absolute low achievement, social undesirability of the MMR label, and the need to reduce the number of problem behaviors in general education classrooms. We find it instructive to consider the referral process in schools and to map the underlying theoretical paradigms that, although implicit, may shed light on the phenomenon of LD identification in the schools and why there is little match with either authoritative or research definitions.

It appears that the process of teacher referral, prereferral intervention, testing, and eligibility decision operate under different theoretical assumptions. Both teacher referral and prereferral intervention reflect a behavioral orientation: The child is not meeting classroom norms from the teacher's perspective, and the application of an intervention may increase the desired behavior. That is, the intervention will result in a level of performance comparable to that of classroom peers or the teacher's personal standard. This behavioral orientation is captured in the writings on "teachers as imperfect tests" (Gerber & Semmel, 1984; Gresham et al., 1997; Gresham, Reschly, & Carey, 1987). What requires emphasis is that unless a child is referred by his or her regular class teacher, he or she is not at risk for school identification as MMR or LD. If the increase in desired behavior anticipated to result from the prereferral intervention is not obtained, testing for eligibility ensues.

There is a shift in orientation from behavioral to a cognitive perspective in that the testing effort is devoted to within-child factors of intelligence, achievement, and language. Although some examiners may include classroom observations and possibly teacher ratings, we find that this is not the norm (Wilson & Reschly, 1996). Instead, the putative purpose is confirming or disconfirming a discrepancy between intelligence and one of the seven academic areas specified by law. Additionally, the norm group changes from the child's classroom peers to a nationally representative sample. There are good reasons to invoke this switch, including examination of normal variation and use of nonbiased assessment, but the context of the problem changes dramatically from a specific classroom with all of its complexities to a national normative perspective on individual differences, devoid of intervening or moderating variables.

At this point a multidisciplinary meeting is held to discuss the evidence, and we suggest the guiding paradigm becomes sociocultural. That is, evidence is considered that is not limited to the individual testing data (e.g., teacher reports of classroom behavior, perceptions regarding need for assistance, evidence indicating interference from exclusionary criteria) and that comes from spheres of influence beyond the child and classroom (e.g., parental involvement, resources available, school district policy, ethnicity of the child). MacMillan (1995) provided summary comments from school placement teams on 12 children who met research-defined LD or MR criteria but were not identified by the schools as eligible for special education services, despite the availability of the research testing results. Reasons for nonidentification reflected parental support and involvement, lack of available services, adequate classroom progress, and the impact of severe behavioral problems and second language learning on test results. Similarly, Shepard (1983) found that larger school districts had higher validity of LD classification that possibly was due to availability of alternative services such as Title I and ESL programs, as well as close scrutiny by state officials due to the sheer number of children identified in those larger districts. Thus, forces beyond the child appear to exert influence on the committee's decisions.

The process of identification is one of shifting sands, in that the fundamental assumptions change at every step. The questions asked by the multidisciplinary, school-based committee are not "Does the child meet the letter of the definition of the disability category?" but rather "Does this child need help?" and "How can we provide it?" Shepard (1983) noted that "specialists would be more willing to make tough decisions about whether a child was really LD if rejecting the label was not tantamount to denying help" (p. 8). If one can accept the proposition that the committee's goal is to create the best possible situation for the child given limited resources, then the overidentification of LD and underidentification of MMR is entirely consistent with that goal. The process of school identification is a relative, not absolute, phenomenon that seems to befuddle academicians but is wholly logical from a practitioner's viewpoint (Speece & Harry, 1997).

The conflicting paradigms evident within the schools are mirrored in current emphases in federal agencies concerned with LD. On the one hand, the National Institutes of Health (NIH) recently established the Learning Disabilities, Cognitive, and Social Development Branch. Based on the nature of past LD research funded by NIH (Lyon, 1995), we anticipate future projects will retain the "within-child" definitional focus that we have characterized as more consistent with a cognitive paradigm than either a behavioral or sociocultural paradigm. On the other hand, the Office of Special Education Programs (OSEP) proposed dropping the requirement of placement in a specific disability category in favor of a generic category defined as "a child who has a physical or mental impairment and who by reason thereof requires special education" (OSEP, 1995, as cited in Coutinho, 1995, p. 665). Coutinho noted that OSEP intends for the definition to be "instructionally relevant" and supportive of "access to education—rather than special education per se" (p. 665).

At this writing, the inevitable policy and advocacy battles over the OSEP proposal have yet to conclude. What we find fascinating is the OSEP shift from, in the case of LD, a cognitive perspective to one that may eventually be viewed as behavioral (i.e., instructionally relevant). More specifically, the OSEP proposal appears more in tune with the reality faced by practitioners. Because "the devil is in the details" and there are precious few details in the OSEP proposal (Coutinho, 1995), it is difficult to predict whether the OSEP proposal will result in major changes in school classification practices or business as usual.

The sequence previously described is significant to children who are identified as LD by the schools. We submit that the behavioral perspective is applied first (during referral), followed by the cognitive paradigm (during assessment), which is in turn followed by the sociocultural (during committee deliberations), resulting in the qualifying of some children as LD. The ultimate group of children identified does not reflect a pristine application of any one of these paradigms. The practice of assessing children with potential LD to select only those that the school identifies as meeting criteria from a cognitive perspective will not yield *all* cases in the schools meeting criteria, because there is no assurance that the behavioral perspective employed during referral would yield all discrepant cases. Similarly, the ultimate group of children identified cannot be assumed to capture *all* children encountering learning problems. Even if we assume that the application of the behavioral perspective yielded all such cases, the application of the cognitive perspective excludes those poor learners who do not meet psychometric criteria. Moreover, the subsequent application of the sociocultural paradigm excludes yet other cases who have achievement difficulties but whose performance is considered due to factors outside the child. Appreciation of the process as it presents threats to internal and external validity of research on LD deserves much more careful examination than has been provided to date. For better or for worse, the schools are serving a group that does not resemble LD research samples regardless of whether researchers screen and identify children in unselected populations or apply more stringent criteria to school-identified children. The failure to consider the False Negative group is especially problematic in the latter scenario.

## IS DISCREPANCY DEAD?

The evolution of aptitude-achievement discrepancy as a marker for learning disabilities was based on rational arguments as opposed to scientific knowledge (Berk, 1984), with roots in the early medical interest in the condition (Doris, 1993). With few exceptions (e.g., Ysseldyke, Algozzine, Shinn, & McGue,

1982), the validity of discrepancy in differentiating a group of children with unique learning needs from nondiscrepant low achievers (LA) was not challenged in the research literature. The emphasis centered on how to reliably measure a discrepancy rather than its meaning (Fletcher & Morris, 1986; Shepard, 1983).

Several studies published within the last few years addressed the validity of discrepancy. Kavale, Fuchs, and Scruggs (1994) reanalyzed the Ysseldyke et al. (1982) data, contending that uncritical acceptance of the conclusions drawn by Ysseldyke et al. led many to conclude that LD could not be distinguished from LA. Kavale et al. (1994) found that both the original data and their reanalysis supported reliable differentiation between the two groups, and concluded that "LD students are the lowest of the low and probably represent students with qualitatively different needs" (p. 76).

These data are based on a school-identified sample that, given the issues raised thus far in this chapter, limit the generalizability of the findings. This problem was solved by Shaywitz, Fletcher, Holahan, and Shaywitz (1992), who compared discrepant and LA children who were members of a representative sample of children. Discrepancy was defined by a regression method (> 1.5 standard deviations from predicted achievement), with LA defined as reading at or below the 25th percentile and IQ at or above 80. Differences favoring the LA group were evident at second grade (reading, behavior, teacher ratings of math skill) but not at fifth grade. Variables favoring the discrepant subjects included intelligence, mother's education, and reading progress from second to fifth grade. There were no differences between the groups on second grade math, or fifth-grade reading or math.

In a more comprehensive approach to the problem, Fletcher et al. (1994) compared the performance of children defined by a variety of discrepancy formula to LA children defined as in the Shaywitz et al. (1992) study. Results for comparisons between regression-defined LD and LA showed virtually no differences between the groups on an assessment battery that included cognitive, language, and academic measures. Using a less stringent definition of regression-based discrepancy (> 1.0 standard deviation from predicted achievement) and a definition of LA that required IQ to be 90 or below, Stanovich and Siegel (1994) found differences in favor of the discrepant group on 9 of 25 cognitive and language measures, 1 difference favoring the LA group, and no differences on the remaining 15 variables. Interestingly, there were only 6 differences in favor of the younger, normally achieving group compared to a combined discrepant-LA group, and these differences accounted for less than 10% of the variance.

The authors of all three studies concluded that there are virtually no differences between discrepant and LA children, although we find only Fletcher et al. (1994) convincing on this point given the data. To accept any of the findings, one must accept a definition of low achievement as a standard score of 90 or below (i.e., the 25th percentile), which may be viewed as liberal. A more conservative view of low achievement (e.g., 80 or below) would reduce the discrepant-LA overlap cited by Shaywitz et al. (1992) and Fletcher et al.

(1994) from 80% to approximately 40% to 50%. This degree of overlap may still be regarded as substantial, but would not lead to the conclusion that discrepant and LA children are the same group. To their credit, Fletcher et al. acknowledged this issue and noted that the effect of a lower cut-score is not clear. Their preference would be to treat both types of children as reading disabled, a conclusion that seems to coincide with school practice, albeit at lower levels of intelligence and achievement.

The validity of discrepancy versus LA should also be tested in regard to response to treatment (Stanovich, 1991; Torgesen, 1989). Although it would seem reasonable to expect discrepant children with higher intelligence to respond more favorably to intervention, this hypothesis has yet to be tested. The most pertinent data to this issue also involves reading disability. Although there is a substantial correlation between intelligence and phonological awareness (Wagner, Torgesen, Laughon, Simmons, & Rashotte, 1993), intelligence does not emerge as a causal influence on reading performance whereas phonological awareness does (Wagner, Torgesen, & Rashotte, 1994). Intervention studies with young children with reading difficulties suggest intelligence is not a significant predictor of reading growth (Hatcher, Hulme, & Ellis, 1994; Torgesen & Davis, 1996). On the other hand, Fuchs, Fuchs, Mathes, and Simmons (1997) found that although classroom-based reading intervention had strong, positive effects for both school-identified children with LD and low-performing children, 20% of the children with LD who received the intervention performed more poorly than did children with LD in the *control* condition. Response to treatment seems to us to be a comparison more critical than individual differences for both definition and school practice. Before burying the aptitude-achievement discrepancy, data on intervention effects will be needed.

Several other discrepancy candidates were nominated to take the place of IQ-achievement markers. Within reading disability, Stanovich (1991) suggested listening comprehension instead of IQ. Zigmond (1993) suggested comparison of learning rates within academic areas (e.g., reading vs. math) to operationalize intraindividual discrepancy. Fuchs (1995) offered a double discrepancy within an academic area that would reflect both absolute performance and rate of learning compared to classmates. All three suggestions drop IQ from the equation and focus on achievement to some extent, and assume that the construct of discrepancy is valid. From this perspective, discrepancy is not dead, but rather awaits careful consideration of alternative methods.

## IMPLICATIONS AND FUTURE DIRECTIONS

The science and practice of learning disabilities appear to be headed in two different directions. Schools serve children as LD who exhibit extremely low achievement and do not necessarily meet IQ-achievement discrepancy standards. Researchers may use sample selection procedures that bear no resemblance to the children served by the schools, or depend on school-identified samples that vary in unknown ways. In either case, the results of research studies employing either approach to sampling have limited external validity for practitioners. Whether or not this is a problem depends on one's perspective.

If medical researchers studied disease the way we study learning disabilities, chaos would result. That is, if patients in clinical trials bore no resemblance to patients in hospitals and clinics, practicing physicians would rely on their own amalgam of lessons learned from trial and error. Research findings from the clinical trials would not inform the practice of medicine. Casualties might skyrocket, much like the identification rates have for LD in the schools. However, what medicine has that the LD field lacks are criteria to promote communication between science and practice. The science of LD is coming to grips with this issue with respect to reading, but this work is limited with respect to both age of children and type of disability. Progress in understanding early reading failure is not trivial, and may serve as an important building block to understanding learning problems in other aspects of oral and written language.

It may be, then, that research and practice must diverge, at least for the time being. Without a coherent definition and criteria that are valid for the condition, it will be impossible to progress. However, studying the condition in the absence of context makes little sense to us. For example, for the first time in more than a decade, annual deaths due to AIDS have decreased (Center for Disease Control and Prevention, 1997). This did not occur only because of more sophisticated methods of detection. Rather, it occurred in conjunction with emphasis on the context in which the disease was contracted and spread. Similarly, learning disabilities does not occur in a vacuum. Research that focuses on varying cut-points for IQ and achievement to the exclusion of context will not serve the field well.

Perhaps more problematic than where to draw the line for low achievement and intelligence is the lack of a developmental perspective on learning disabilities (Keogh, 1993). A developmental perspective includes not only chronological age but also the person-environment interaction with the attendant concepts of risk and protective factors and how the child changes over time. Longitudinal research in learning disabilities is a scarce commodity, and is devoted primarily to individual differences (e.g., Francis, Shaywitz, Stuebing, Shaywitz, & Fletcher, 1994; McKinney & Speece, 1986). Even less is known about the contextual influences on the expression of learning disabilities (Keogh & Speece, 1996). Although LD is "intrinsic to the individual, *presumed* to be due to central nervous system dysfunction" (Hammill et al., 1981, pp. 339–340), acceptance of this hypothesis does not negate the powerful role of environmental features in either the amelioration or exacerbation of a learning disability. The bias in the scientific study of LD toward intrinsic explanations of the disorder has led to virtual ignorance of the contextual factors that either coexist with or are causal to learning disabilities (Speece, 1993).

Lyon (1996) reasoned that this state of affairs is most logically due to the absence of a theoretical base that specifies ecological variables as candidates for study. In the context of schools and classrooms, this is a fair criticism. The identification of subtle differences that accumulate in the various settings and interactions between teachers and children is a daunting task. The complexity of classrooms generally lead researchers to study a corner of the ecological landscape, and assembling the various pieces into a coherent whole is unfinished business (Speece & Molloy, 1994). There is a wealth of evidence on classroom contexts, but little of it is devoted to understanding the emergence of learning disabilities. For example, teachers' beliefs about their own efficacy with problem learners (Zigmond, McCall, & George, 1990, cited in Zigmond, 1993) and general educational instructional arrangements (Cooper & Speece, 1990) are associated with school referral for special education. We would argue that findings such as these may lead to an understanding of how an "intrinsic" disability becomes an educational handicap in certain contexts, and would shed some light on the "false negative" LD category identified by researchers.

Given the evidence, we join other colleagues (Gresham & Witt, 1997) who called for a halt to the practice of IQ testing for LD eligibility in the schools until a valid classification practice is identified by research. School personnel go through the motions of adhering to authoritative definitions (i.e., determining discrepancy with published intelligence and achievement measures), but often either ignore these data or administer a variety of aptitude and achievement scales in a "search for a discrepancy," despite the enormous cost incurred in collecting these data. In contrast to Gresham and Witt (in press), we make this recommendation not because discrepancy has proven invalid or that intelligence tests have no bearing on the condition—*these issues remain to be resolved*. Rather, we make the recommendation to emphasize that learning disabilities definitions are hypotheses, not facts, and require appropriate scientific analysis. We do not dispute that some children have enormous difficulty with school learning or that there is a condition legitimately called learning disabilities. However, to continue to engage in eligibility testing as currently construed strikes us as an enormous waste of time and talent. In the debate over IQ, defenders of the test pointed to the utility for purposes of classification but conceded that IQ scores had little, if any, utility for prescribing treatment given the omnibus nature of the tests. We have presented evidence herein that shows that the schools are not using the scores for purposes of classifying the children differentially as MR and LD. In fact, in many instances they make classification decisions contraindicated by the IQ evidence. If IQ is not being used by the schools for purposes of classification and it has limited instructional validity, we find little to recommend requiring it in order to qualify children as eligible for special education services.

We make this recommendation mindful of Keogh's (1987) view that "definition has meaning only when tied to purpose. Because there are multiple purposes in the LD field, there will continue to be multiple definitions" (p. 97). Although there is truth in this assertion, we maintain that acceptance of multiple definitions impedes policy, research, and practice. The field has long recognized the folly of studying children who are school-identified as LD to understand the condition (Keogh, 1987; Keogh & MacMillan, 1983), yet the practice continues despite the accumulation of logic and evidence against this practice, some of which is cited in this chapter. Similarly, to study a group of children identified by research criteria that bears no resemblance to the children being identified in school as LD results in findings that cannot possibly inform practitioners about the population of LD they serve.

The implications for future research and practice may be disconcerting for some. It has been noted that public schools are not in the business of providing pristine samples for researchers (Keogh & MacMillan, 1983; MacMillan, Meyers, & Morrison, 1980; Morrison, MacMillan, & Kavale, 1985). If researchers require intelligence scores to identify samples or as one of the scales crucial to their study, then researchers should collect those data. This will increase research costs but it may also increase the precision of research, because investigators will need to carefully consider issues in sample selection and may result in a common scale being used on all subjects and provide *current* (as opposed to "IQ scores secured within the past 3 years") data on intellectual functioning. For example, those interested in instructional methods may not require intelligence scores, because the focus is on increasing achievement. However, research questions concerning possible differences between discrepant and non-discrepant low achievers would demand attention to IQ in sample selection. Just as the accumulation of scientific evidence on the importance of phonemic awareness has begun to impact practice, we are confident that similar scientific advances in the definition of LD will influence school practice.

Practitioners will need to decide how to appropriate services. Freedom from the shackles of the cognitive perspective on identification demands accountability. At present it would seem most reasonable to continue with a behavioral perspective: if a child is not reading, change tactics and monitor progress. An alternative approach reflecting this behavioral perspective was offered by Fuchs (1995) and appears to have much promise for both identifying children with academic problems and examining resistance to treatment as a basis for intensifying treatments. In the meantime, we would encourage research to address the benefits of differentiating among those children who do exhibit severe and persistent underachievement but differ with respect to aptitude, to determine developmental trajectories over time given the same treatment. However, to truly benefit children in school, such research, must break out of its "cognitive straightjacket" and capture the multivariate influences of contextual, motivational, and emotional factors, as well as sociocultural influences, that all contribute to the phenotype of a child with learning disabilities.

## ACKNOWLEDGMENTS

The present work was supported, in part, by grants No. H023C20002 and H023C30103 from the U.S. Department of Education. Opinions expressed herein are those of the authors alone, and should not be interpreted to have agency endorsement.

## REFERENCES

Bahr, M. W., Fuchs, D., Stecker, P. M., & Fuchs, L. S. (1991). Are teachers' perceptions of difficult-to-teach students racially biased? *School Psychology Review, 20*, 599–608.

Bateman, B. (1992). Learning disabilities: A changing landscape. *Journal of Learning Disabilities, 25*, 29–36.

Berk, R. A. (1984). *Screening and diagnosis of children with learning disabilities.* Springfield, IL: Charles C. Thomas.

Center for Disease Control and Prevention. (1997). Update: Trends in AIDS incidence, deaths, and prevalence—United States, 1996. *Morbidity and Mortality Weekly Report, 46*(8), 165–173.

Chinn, P. C., & Hughes, S. (1987). Representation of minority students in special education classes. *Remedial and Special Education, 8*(4), 41–46.

Cooper, D. H., & Speece, D. L. (1990). Maintaining at-risk children in regular education settings: The initial effects of individual differences and classroom environments. *Exceptional Children, 57*, 117–126.

Coutinho, M. J. (1995). Who will be learning disabled after the reauthorization of IDEA? Two very distinct perspectives. *Journal of Learning Disabilities, 28*, 664–668.

Cronbach, L. J. (1975). Five decades of public controversy over mental testing. *American Psychologist, 30*, 1–14.

Doris, J. L. (1993). Defining learning disabilities: A history of the search for consensus. In G. R. Lyon, D. B. Gray, J. F. Kavanagh, & N. A. Krasnegor (Eds.), *Better understanding learning disabilities: New views from research and their implications for education and public policies* (pp. 97–115). Baltimore: Brookes.

Elliott, R. (1987). *Litigating intelligence.* Dover, MA: Auburn House.

Finn, J. D. (1982). Patterns in special education as revealed by the OCR survey. In K. A. Heller, W. Holtzman, & S. Messick (Eds.), *Placing children in special education: A strategy for equity* (pp. 322–381). Washington, DC: National Academy Press.

Fletcher, J. M. Shaywitz, S. E., Shankweiler, D. P., Katz, L., Liberman, I. Y, Stuebing, K. K., Francis, D. J., Fowler, A. E., & Shaywitz, B. A. (1994). Cognitive profiles of reading disability: Comparisons of discrepancy and low achievement definitions. *Journal of Educational Psychology, 86*, 6–23.

Fletcher, J. M., & Morris, R. D. (1986). Classification of disabled learners: Beyond exclusionary definitions. In S. J. Ceci (Ed.), *Handbook of cognitive, social, and neuropsychological reports of learning disabilities* (pp. 55–80). Hillsdale, NJ: Lawrence Erlbaum Associates.

Francis, D. J., Shaywitz, S. E., Stuebing, K. K., Shaywitz, B. A., & Fletcher, J. M. (1994). Measurement of change: Assessing behavior over time and within a developmental context. In G. R. Lyon (Ed.), *Frames of reference for the assessment of learning disabilities* (pp. 29–58). Baltimore: Brookes.

Frankenberger, W., & Fronzaglio, K. (1991). States' definitions and procedures for identifying children with mental retardation: Comparison over nine years. *Mental Retardation, 29*, 315–321.

Frankenberger, W., & Harper, J. (1987). States' criteria and procedures for identifying learning disabled children: A comparison of 1981/82 and 1985/86 guidelines. *Journal of Learning Disabilities, 20*, 118–121.

Fuchs, D., Fuchs, L. S., Mathes, P. G., & Simmons, D. C. (1997). Peer-assisted learning strategies: Makes classrooms more responsive to diversity. *American Educational Research Journal, 34*, 174–206.

Fuchs, L. S. (1995, May). *Incorporating curriculum-based measurement into the eligibility decision-making process: A focus on treatment validity and student growth.* Paper presented at the Workshop on IQ Testing and Educational Decision Making, National Research Council, National Academy of Sciences, Washington, DC.

Gerber, M., & Semmel, M. (1984). Teacher as imperfect test: Reconceptualizing the referral process. *Educational Psychologist, 19*, 137–146.

Gottlieb, J., Alter, M., Gottlieb, B. W., & Wishner, J. (1994). Special education in urban America: It's not justifiable for many. *The Journal of Special Education, 27*, 453–465.

Gresham, F. M., MacMillan, D. L., & Bocian, K. M. (1997). Teachers as "tests": Differential validity of teacher judgments in identifying students at-risk for learning difficulties. *School Psychology Review, 26*, 47–60.

Gresham, F. M., MacMillan, D. L., & Siperstein, G. (1995). Critical analysis of the 1992 AAMR definition: Implications for school psychology. *School Psychology Review, 10*, 1–19.

Gresham, F. M., Reschly, D. J., & Carey, M. (1987). Teachers as "tests": Classification accuracy and concurrent validation in the identification of learning disabled children. *School Psychology Review, 16*, 543–563.

Gresham, F. M., & Witt, J. C. (1997). Utility of intelligence tests for treatment planning, classification, and placement decisions: Recent empirical findings and future directions. *School Psychology Quarterly, 12*, 249–267.

Grossman, H. J., (Ed.). (1973). *Manual on terminology and classification in mental retardation.* Washington, DC: American Association on Mental Deficiency, Special Publication Series No. 2.

Grossman, H. J. (Ed.). (1977). *Manual on terminology and classification* (Rev. ed.). Washington, DC: American Association on Mental Deficiency.

Grossman, H. J., (Ed.). (1983). *Classification in mental retardation* (3rd rev.). Washington, DC: American Association on Mental Deficiency.

Hallahan, D. P. (1992). Some thoughts on why the prevalence of learning disabilities has increased. *Journal of Learning Disabilities, 25*(8), 523–528.

Hammill, D. D., Leigh, J. E., McNutt, G., & Larsen, S. C. (1981). A new definition of learning disabilities. *Learning Disabilities Quarterly, 4*, 336–342.

Hatcher, P. J., Hulme, C., & Ellis, A. W. (1994). Ameliorating early reading failure by integrating the teaching of reading and phonological skills: The phonological linkage hypothesis. *Child Development, 65*, 41–57.

Heber, R. (1959). A manual on terminology and classification in mental retardation. *American Journal of Mental Deficiency, 56* (Monograph supplement, rev.).

Heber, R. (1961). Modifications in the manual on terminology and classification in mental retardation. *American Journal of Mental Deficiency, 65*, 499–500.

Johnson, J. L. (1969). Special education and the inner city: A challenge for the future or another means for cooling the mark out? *Journal of Special Education, 3,* 241–251.

Kaufman, A. S. (1994). *Intelligence testing with the WISC-III.* New York: Wiley-Interscience.

Kavale, K. A., Fuchs, D., & Scruggs, T. E. (1994). Setting the record straight on learning disability and low achievement: Implications for policy making. *Learning Disabilities Research and Practice, 9,* 70–77.

Kavanagh, J. F., & Truss, T. J., Jr. (Eds.). (1988). *Learning disabilities: Proceedings of the national conference* (pp. 79–163). Parkton, MD: York.

Keogh, B. K. (1987). A shared attribute model of learning disabilities. In S. Vaughn & C. S. Bos (Eds.), *Research in learning disabilities: Issues and future directions* (pp. 3–18). Boston: College Hill.

Keogh, B. K. (1993). Linking purpose and practice: Social-political and developmental perspectives. In G. R. Lyon, D. B. Gray, J. F. Kavanaugh, & N. A. Krasnegor (Eds.), *Better understanding learning disabilities: New views from research and their implications for education and public policies* (pp. 311–323). Baltimore: Brookes.

Keogh, B. K. (1994). A matrix of decision points in the measurement of learning disabilities. In G. R. Lyon (Ed.), *Frames of reference for the assessment of learning disabilities.* (pp. 15–26). Baltimore: Brookes.

Keogh, B. K., & MacMillan, D. L. (1983). The logic of sample selection: Who represents what? *Exceptional Education Quarterly, 4*(3), 84–96.

Keogh, B. K., & Speece, D. L. (1996). Learning disabilities within the context of schooling. In D. L. Speece & B. K. Keogh (Eds.), *Research on classroom ecologies: Implications for inclusion of children with learning disabilities* (pp. 1–14). Mahwah, NJ: Lawrence Erlbaum Associates.

Lopez, M. F., Forness, S. R., MacMillan, D. L., Bocian, K. M., & Gresham, F. M. (1996). Children with attention deficit hyperactivity disorder and emotional or behavioral disorders in primary grades: Inappropriate placement in the learning disability category. *Education and Treatment of Children, 19,* 272–285.

Luckasson, R. (Ed.), (1992). *Mental retardation: Definition, classification, and systems of support.* Washington, DC: American Association on Mental Retardation.

Lyon, G. R. (1995). Research initiatives in learning disabilities: Contributions from scientists supported by the National Institute of Child Health and Human Development. *Journal of Child Neurology, 10,* 5120–5126.

Lyon, G. R. (1996). Methodological issues and strategies for assessing developmental change and evaluating response to intervention. In D. L. Speece & B. K. Keogh (Eds.), *Research on classroom ecologies: Implications for inclusion of children with learning disabilities* (pp. 213–227). Mahwah, NJ: Lawrence Erlbaum Associates.

MacMillan, D. L. (1989). Equality, excellence, and the mentally retarded populations: 1970–1989. *Psychology in Mental Retardation and Developmental Disabilities, 15*(2), 1, 3–10.

MacMillan, D. L. (1993). Development of operational definitions in mental retardation: Similarities and differences with the field of learning disabilities. In G. R.

Lyon, D. B. Gray, J. F. Kavanagh, N. A. Krasnegor (Eds.), *Better understanding learning disabilities* . (pp. 117–152). Baltimore: Brookes.

MacMillan, D. L. (1995, January). *The role of IQ in establishing eligibility and placing children in special education.* Invited paper presented at Workshop on "IQ Testing and Educational Decisionmaking" for the Board on Testing and Assessment, National Research Council, National Academy of Sciences, La Jolla, CA.

MacMillan, D. L., Gresham, F. M., & Bocian, K. M. (1997). Curing mental retardation and causing learning disabilities: Consequences of using various WISC-III IQs to estimate aptitude of Hispanic Students. *Journal of Psychoeducational Assessment, 16,* 36–54.

MacMillan, D. L., Gresham, F. M., & Bocian, K. M. (in press). Discrepancy between definitions of learning disabilities and what schools use: An empirical investigation. *Journal of Learning Disabilities.*

MacMillan, D. L., Gresham, F. M., Lopez, M. F., & Bocian, K. (1996a). Comparison of students nominated for pre-referral interventions by ethnicity and gender. *The Journal of Special Education, 30,* 133–151.

MacMillan, D. L., Gresham, F. M., & Siperstein, G. N. (1993). Conceptual and psychometric concerns about the 1992 AAMR definition of mental retardation. *American Journal on Mental Retardation, 98*(3), 325–335.

MacMillan, D. L., Gresham, F. M., & Siperstein, G. N. (1995). Heightened concerns over the 1992 AAMR definition. *American Journal on Mental Retardation, 100,* 87–97.

MacMillan, D. L., Gresham, F. M., Siperstein, G. N., & Bocian, K. M. (1996b). The labyrinth of I. D. E. A.: School decisions on referred students with subaverage general intelligence. *American Journal on Mental Retardation, 101,* 161–174.

MacMillan, D. L., Meyers, C. E., & Morrison, G. M. (1980). System-identification of mildly mentally retarded children: Implications for interpreting and conducting research. *American Journal of Mental Deficiency, 85,* 108–115.

McKinney, J. D., & Speece, D. L. (1986). Academic consequences of longitudinal stability of behavioral subtypes of learning disabled children. *Journal of Educational Psychology, 78,* 365–372.

MacMillan, D. L., & Reschly, D. J. (1996). Issues of definition and classification. In W. MacLean (Ed.), *Ellis' handbook of mental deficiency: Psychological theory and research* (3rd ed., pp. 47–74). Hillsdale, NJ : Lawrence Erlbaum Associates.

McShane, D., & Cook, V. J. (1985). Transcultural intellectual assessment: Performance by Hispanics on the Wechsler scales. In B. Wolman (Ed.), *Handbook of intelligence* (pp. 737–785). New York: Wiley.

Mercer, C. D., Hughes, C., & Mercer, A. R. (1985). Learning disabilities definitions used by state education departments. *Learning Disability Quarterly, 8,* 45–55.

Mercer, C. D., Jordan, L., Allsopp, D. H., & Mercer, A. R. (1996). Learning disabilities definitions and criteria used by state education departments. *Learning Disability Quarterly, 19,* 217–232

Morrison, G. M., MacMillan, D. L., & Kavale, K. (1985). System identification of learning disabled children: Implications for research sampling. *Learning Disability Quarterly, 8,* 2–10.

National Advisory Committee on Handicapped Children. (1968). *Special education for handicapped children: First annual report.* Washington, DC: US Department of Health, Education, and Welfare.

Ortiz, A., & Yates, J. R. (1983). Incidence of exceptionality among Hispanics: Implications for manpower planning. *National Association of Bilingual Education Journal, 7*(3), 41–53.

Reschly, D. J. (1988). Minority mild mental retardation overrepresentation: Legal issues, research findings, and reform trends. In M. C. Wang, M. C. Reynolds, & H. J. Walberg (Eds.), *Handbook of special education: Research and practice.*(Vol. 2, pp. 23–41). New York: Pergamon.

Reschly, D. J. (1997). *Disproportionate minority representation in general and special education programs: Patterns, Issues, and Alternatives.* Des Moines, IA: Mountain Plains Regional Resource Center.

Reschly, D. J., & Jipson, F. J. (1976). Ethnicity, geographic locale, age, sex, and urban-rural residence as variables in the prevalence of mild retardation. *American Journal of Mental Deficiency, 81,* 154–161.

Reschly, D. J., & Wilson, M. S. (1990). Cognitive processing vs. traditional intelligence: Diagnostic utility, intervention implications, and treatment validity. *School Psychology Review, 19,* 443–458.

Shaywitz, B. A., Fletcher, J. M., Holahan, J. M., & Shaywitz, S. E. (1992). Discrepancy compared to low achievement definitions of reading disability: Results from the Connecticut longitudinal study. *Journal of Learning Disabilities, 25,* 639–648.

Shaywitz, S. E., Shaywitz, B., Fletcher, J. M., & Escobar, M. D. (1990). Prevalence of reading disability in boys and girls: Results from the Connecticut Longitudinal Study. *Journal of the American Medical Association, 264,* 998–1002.

Shepard, L. (1983, Fall). The role of measurement in educational policy: Lessons from the identification of learning disabilities. *Educational Measurement: Issues and Practices,* 4–8.

Shepard, L. A., Smith, M. L., & Vojir, C. P. (1983). Characteristics of pupils identified as learning disabled. *American Educational Research Journal, 20,* 309–331.

Speece, D. L. (1993). Broadening the scope of classification research: Conceptual and ecological perspectives. In G. R. Lyon, D. B. Gray, J. F. Kavanaugh, & N. A. Krasnegor (Eds.), *Better understanding learning disabilities: New views from research and their implications for education and public policies* (pp. 57–72). Baltimore, MD: Brookes.

Speece, D. L., & Harry, B. (1997). Classification for children. In J. Lloyd, E. Kameenui, & D. Chard (Eds.), *Issues in educating students with disabilities* (pp. 63–72). Mahwah, NJ: Lawrence Erlbaum Associates.

Speece, D. L., & Molloy, D. E. (1994, April). *Classroom ecologies, problem learners, and school success: How far have we come?* Paper presented at the Annual Meeting of the American Education Research Association, New Orleans, LA.

Stanovich, K. (1991). Discrepancy definition of reading disability. Has intelligence led us astray? *Reading Research Quarterly, 26,* 7–29.

Stanovich, K. E., & Siegel, L. S. (1994) Phenotypic performance profile of children with reading disabilities: A regression-based test of the phonological-core variable-difference model. *Journal of Educational Psychology, 86,* 24–53.

Torgesen, J. K. (1989). Why IQ is relevant to the definition of learning disabilities. *Journal of Learning Disabilities, 22*, 484–486.

Torgensen, J. K., & Davis, C. (1996). Individual difference variables that predict response to training in phonological awareness. *Journal of Experimental Child Psychology, 63*, 1–21.

Tucker, J. A. (1980). Ethnic proportions in classes for learning disabled: Issues in nonbiased assessment. *Journal of Special Education, 14*, 93–105.

U. S. Department of Education. (1994). *Sixteenth annual report to Congress on the implementation of the Individuals with Disabilities Education Act.* Washington, DC: Author.

U. S. Office of Education. (1977). Assistance to states for education for handicapped children: Procedures for evaluating specific learning disabilities. *Federal Register, 42*, 65082–65085.

Utley, C., Lowitzer, A., & Baumeister, A. (1987). A comparison of the AAMD's definitions, eligibility criteria, and classification schemes with state department of education guidelines. *Education and Training in Mental Retardation*, 35–43.

Wagner, R. K., Torgesen, J. K., Laughon, N. P., Simmons, K., & Rashotte, C. A. (1993). Development of young readers' phonological processing abilities. *Journal of Educational Psychology, 85*, 83–103.

Wagner, R. K., Torgesen, J. K., & Rashotte, C. A. (1994). Development of reading-related phonological processing abilities: New evidence of bidirectional causality from a latent variable longitudinal study. *Developmental Psychology, 30*, 73-87.

Wilson, M. & Reschly, D. J. (1996). Assessment in school psychology training and practice. *School Psychology Review, 25*, 9–23.

Ysseldyke, J., Algozzine, B., Shinn, M., & McGue, K. (1982). Similarities and differences between low achievers and students classified as learning disabled. *The Journal of Special Education, 16*, 73–85.

Zigmond, N. (1993). Learning disabilities from an educational perspective. In G. R. Lyon, D. B. Gray, J. F. Kavanaugh, & N. A. Krasnegor (Eds.) *Better understanding learning disabilities: New views from research and their implications for education and public policies* (pp. 251–272). Baltimore: Brookes.

# 7 🐛 Identifying Children at Risk for Antisocial Behavior: The Case for Comorbidity

**Steven R. Forness**
*University of California, Los Angeles*

**Kenneth A. Kavale**
*University of Iowa*

**Hill M. Walker**
*University of Oregon*

Schools not only have a unique role in the initial detection of young children at risk for antisocial behavior, but also a unique ability to marshal resources to address these problems in a coordinated fashion. In this effort, they can address many of the risk factors that, if left unattended, lead to a host of unfortunate outcomes, including later violence and criminal behavior (Patterson, Reid, & Dishion, 1992; Reid, 1993; Walker & Bullis, 1996; Walker & Sylvester, 1991). Schools, however, can only play this role effectively if their actions are more broadly coordinated with other agencies in the community, including mental health and social welfare services among others. Schools can and probably should serve as lead agency within an interagency effort (Dryfoos, 1990). This leadership will require dramatic changes in the ways that schools have traditionally dealt with this student population, their attitudes toward antisocial behavior, and the necessary identification and reallocation of resources. To date, the effective role of schools in developing solutions to the problems of antisocial behavior, interpersonal conflict, and violence has been largely unrealized. Educators, like the larger society, have unfortunately tended to respond to these problems reactively and after the fact, with punishing alternatives.

The purpose of this chapter is to describe a more complete conceptualization of antisocial behavior in the context of schooling. Although this chapter is

**135**

not about intervention per se, its purpose is to discuss critical factors of identification and diagnosis that bear heavily on the type of intervention that might be required for children with antisocial behavior. School personnel tend to apply simple solutions to complex student behavior problems and then express understandable disappointment when these attempts tend not to work as expected. They often blame other factors for unsatisfactory outcomes (e.g., the child's home life, poor motivation for change, or lack of parent support). The failure, however, to achieve effective outcomes is frequently due to a poor match between the presenting problem (or incomplete identification of the problem) and the intervention selected (or a failure to treat the problem comprehensively) throughout the intervention process. Rarely are the necessary resources, time, and expertise employed to thoroughly identify and then address the problem.

Moreover, there is a natural tendency to attempt to eliminate the immediate presenting behavior(s) rather than to focus on more significant sources of the problem. Thus, indirect intervention approaches, (e.g., counseling, insight-based therapies, social skills training, improving self-esteem) are often used to solve intractable student behavior problems that require more direct forms of intervention (Eysenck, 1994; Mayer, 1995; Shamise, 1981). Referral of the problem student for counseling consistently ranks as *the* most popular intervention option among teachers, primarily because responsibility for change is placed on the student. Such indirect approaches are rarely adequate or sufficient, either because these students tend to be unmotivated to engage in these therapies or because other sources of their problem are being ignored (Dryfoos, 1990; Forness, Kavale, King, & Kasari, 1994; Kavale, Forness, & Duncan 1996).

When such indirect intervention approaches fail, school personnel often resort to punitive measures or exclude students from the school setting. Exclusion, suspension, expulsion, verbal reprimands, or detention are common reactive responses. Although the consequences of punishment provide an immediate short-term reprieve from the problem, positive long-term change in behavior is not achieved. In fact, punishment-based interventions for students with serious antisocial or violent behavior usually result in an *increase* in the problem behavior (Mayer & Sulzer-Azaroff, 1990). The intractability and severity of antisocial behavior problems are seldom matched to appropriate interventions. Intervention responses to students with severe problem behaviors tend to be developed and implemented by individual teachers rather than by an interdisciplinary team of staff members with expertise in mental health, social welfare, or related areas. Prevention strategies and interventions appropriate for students who are at risk for academic and social failure should address and systematically take into account a more comprehensive view of antisocial behavior. As we show in this chapter, a majority of students who display at-risk and antisocial forms of behavior may have underlying disorders that require much more complex treatment. Left untreated, children become deficient in many critically important behavioral competencies and are ultimately rejected by teachers and peers (Walker, Colvin, & Ramsey, 1995). Some even band together and form deviant and/or disruptive peer groups that wreak havoc and often get involved with the law (Patterson et al., 1992; Reid, 1993). The work of Dodge and his colleagues has provided important insights into the developmental trajectories and peer relations problems of antisocial children and youth (see Dodge, 1985; Dodge, Coie, & Brakke, 1982).

Children with antisocial behavior are often above minimally acceptable classroom limits in terms of maladaptive forms of behavior, and well below classroom expectations in relation to critical adaptive competencies. Thus, a risk and protective factors approach in this context could reduce or eliminate the student's likelihood of engaging in unacceptable maladaptive behaviors (risk factors) and develop or increase the student's frequency of displaying the adaptive competencies (protective factors). It should be noted that some school systems are responding proactively by creating learning and opportunity centers, establishing schools within a school, and investing in programs designed to keep at-risk students in school. Unfortunately, our approaches for coping with such children often neglect the possibility that, in some cases, other conditions or disorders may underlie antisocial behavior. As noted earlier, by pushing these students out of the school system or otherwise disengaging them from schooling, we are merely turning them loose on communities and displacing the problem to another sector of our society.

Our thesis in this chapter is that antisocial behavior may sometimes be a symptom of beginning or prodromal psychiatric disorders. These emotional or behavioral disorders are often not detected until after the child has been subjected to coercive or punitive school interventions or other programs that focus only on surface symptoms and not on comprehensive programs designed to address mental health issues (Forness, Kavale, MacMillan, Asarnow, & Duncan, 1996). We therefore begin by discussing conduct disorder, a diagnosis that is somewhat synonymous with antisocial behavior or social maladjustment and that is used by both school and mental health professionals to denote children with persistent antisocial behavior. We then discuss how other diagnoses are often comorbid with conduct disorder, and how common such "complex" conduct disorders actually are. We end with additional research on the overlap of these disorders and implications for treatment and intervention.

## ANTISOCIAL BEHAVIOR AND ITS CORRELATES

Antisocial behavior is often equated with conduct disorder in child psychiatric or mental health practice. Terminology here is often confusing, because some terms are used primarily in school settings and others are used primarily in hospital or clinic settings. Terms tend to lose their meaning somewhat in translation from one setting to the next (Forness, 1992a, 1992b). *Antisocial behavior* or *social maladjustment* are terms used, primarily in school settings, to denote behavior that usually involves consistent disregard for societal norms or rules and usually connotes a pattern of aggressive or dishonest behavior. Antisocial behavior or social maladjustment do not necessarily have precise definitions nor diagnostic criteria for their use.

Conduct disorder and its variant, oppositional defiant disorder, are rather common psychiatric diagnoses. Although *conduct disorder* is a term often used by school professionals for children with intractable antisocial behavior, as a psychiatric diagnosis, it is characterized by a repetitive or persistent pattern of behavior violating basic rights of others or major age-appropriate social norms or rules (American Psychiatric Association [APA], 1994). Symptoms involve a wide range of aggressive (bullying, initiating fights, using a weapon), destructive (destroying property, fire setting), dishonest (lying, stealing), or noncompliant (running away from home or school) behaviors. Only three such symptoms from a list of more than a dozen are displayed in mild forms of the disorder. Those cases with more symptoms are considered moderate, and the disorder is considered severe when many symptoms occur beyond those required for a threshold diagnosis. Oppositional defiant disorder is a related psychiatric diagnosis with symptoms of negative, hostile, or defiant behavior that are more mild and directed primarily toward adults. Its symptoms generally emerge earlier than do those of conduct disorder, and tend to lead (but not invariably so) to the emergence of conduct disorder (Lahey, Loeber, Quay, Frick, & Grimm, 1992). Although the two diagnoses (conduct disorder, oppositional defiant disorder) are made separately, for the sake of simplicity the term, *conduct disorders* will be used to designate both in this chapter. It is very important to note that none of the designations cited previously are necessarily synonymous with the term *antisocial personality disorder* which is a psychiatric diagnosis denoting a ruthless, often aggressive, personality synonymous with sociopathic or criminal behavior—a diagnosis usually reserved only for adults (APA, 1994).

In the context of antisocial behavior, conduct disorders represent a significant diagnosis for at least two reasons. First, it is among the most stable and enduring of all psychiatric diagnoses and is one of the most common disorders seen in mental health practice, with a prevalence of 4% to 10% among children and adolescents (Kazdin, 1987; Offord & Bennett, 1994). Second, the diagnosis of conduct disorders is often automatically excluded from eligibility for special education or related services in the public schools (Forness, Kavale & Lopez, 1993). The reason for this exclusion is that schools currently mandate services for children or youth with any emotional or behavioral disorders only under the category of serious emotional disturbance (SED; Forness & Knitzer, 1992). Note that the term *serious emotional disturbance*, is expected to be changed in federal law to *emotional disturbance*, as a result of the 1997 reauthorization of IDEA. However, in this chapter we continue to use the term, SED, because federal changes will not officially occur until late in 1998, and state terminology changes may not occur until much later. Federal regulations, however, continue to stipulate that pupils may not be served in this category if their problems are considered merely social maladjustment and not a serious emotional disorder. Because social maladjustment is not further defined in law, the psychiatric diagnosis of conduct disorders (or sometimes even the term *conduct disorders*, used by school professionals without precise diagnostic criteria being applied) is frequently used as the operational definition of social maladjustment. School professionals thus regard symptoms of this diagnosis as potential cause for denying eligibility for special education or related services (Weinberg & Weinberg, 1990). A recent history of Supreme Court decisions also have made it more difficult to suspend or expel any pupil once he or she has been identified as eligible for special education, thus further discouraging schools from using the SED category to identify any child with conduct disorders (Yell, 1989).

Our contention in this chapter is that conduct disorders do not always represent social maladjustment (which is usually defined as a willful disregard for societal norms or the rights of others), as advocates of exclusion have contended (Kelly, 1990; Slenkovich, 1992). Such views mistakenly tend to cast behavior of children with conduct disorders as wholly volitional and resulting solely from inconsistent discipline in home or school environments (Weinberg & Weinberg, 1990). Instances such as these—in which a single set of variables is responsible for conduct disorders—may indeed be rare, and "complex" disorders may tend to be the norm, particularly in instances when children fail to respond to the usual interventions in the regular classroom (Hinshaw, 1992). Complex conduct disorders are those in which another psychiatric disorder is comorbid, or co-occurs, with overt conduct disorders. There are significant implications inherent in the distinction between simple and complex conduct disorders in that prevention and treatment may be quite different in each case (Achenbach, 1990/1991; Forness et al., 1993).

Early identification of other possible psychiatric diagnoses underlying conduct disorders and treatment with mental health, psychopharmacologic, or related therapies, in tandem with school interventions, may lead to a much better prognosis. Viewing the disorder as a simple matter requiring only behavioral approaches or corrective discipline seems less likely to be effective in the long term. Teachers, however, often view not paying attention and disrupting the classroom or other school activities as a simple conduct problem or antisocial behavior that requires disciplinary action. It is true that not paying attention or disrupting activities or lessons are indeed broad-based categories of observable classroom behavior that appear not only to distinguish referred from nonreferred pupils, but also predict ultimate need for special education or related services in later school years (Forness, 1983; Walker & Severson, 1990). Such behaviors also correlate inversely with classroom achievement, teacher rating scales of appropriate behavior, and other indicators used to screen for at-risk behavior. Although teachers or other school professionals are generally trained to identify and manage problems of inattention and disruption in the classroom, they are nonetheless seldom prepared systematically to view these problems as incipient symptoms of other disorders (Knitzer, Steinberg, & Fleisch, 1990). If a "disorder" is suspected, it is often initially perceived within the conduct disorders spectrum, a possibility that is increasingly confirmed as routine classroom management or school disciplinary procedures fail to reduce the inattentive or disruptive behavior.

It is plausible that these two broad-based behaviors (inattention and disruption) may be misconstrued in a significant number of cases, and that classroom expression of these behaviors over time might be symptomatic of other underlying psychiatric disorders in either their premorbid or comorbid state. Examination of selected diagnostic symptoms and phenomenology of attention deficit disorders (Cantwell, 1996; Werry, Reeves, & Elkind, 1987), mood disorders (Fleming & Offord, 1990; Kovacs, 1996), anxiety disorders (Bernstein & Borchardt, 1991; Bernstein, Borchardt, & Perwien, 1996; Messer & Beidel, 1994), or even schizophrenic disorders (Green, Padron-Gayol, Hardesty, & Bassiri, 1992; Russell, Bott, & Sammons, 1989; Volkmar, 1996) reveals the distinct possibility of overlap and confusion with symptoms normally associated with conduct disorders. Such behaviors may, however, be symptomatic of other psychiatric disorders, including conduct disorders. In *conduct disorders*, not paying attention often results from lack of interest or motivation in academics or prosocial activities commonly associated with this disorder, whereas disruptive behavior could result from any of a long list of symptoms of the disorder itself, as noted above. In *attention deficit disorders*, inattention is a key symptom, whereas disruptive behavior could result from other key symptoms of impulsivity or hyperactivity. In *mood disorders*, such as depression or dysthymia, inattention could derive from diminished ability to concentrate that is characteristic of children or adolescents with these disorders, whereas disruptive behavior may derive from irritability, a key symptom of mood disorders in children and youth. In *anxiety disorders*, inattention might be due to excessive apprehension or preoccupation with events that have no functional basis in reality, whereas disruptive behavior could derive from restlessness, tension, or even compulsions to engage repetitively in certain acts. In *schizophrenic disorders*, inattention could result from thought disturbances or even hallucinations, whereas disruptive behavior could occur as a result of agitation commonly associated with these disorders.

Although such a brief review of psychiatric syndromes cannot do justice to the full range of symptoms of these or other possible disorders in child and adolescent psychiatry, it does depict the opportunity for considerable misperception on the part of school professionals when confronted with such behaviors. Even when inattention or disruption do not respond to these professionals' standard disciplinary efforts, the impression may continue that some form of conduct disorders alone exists. They may thus fail to consider alternatives for intervention other than standard behavioral or social skills approaches. As implied in the list of major psychiatric disorders cited previously, alternatives might well include identification, treatment, or referral of other psychiatric disorders that may undergird what seemed at first glance to be simple conduct disorders or antisocial behavior.

## THE EXTENT OF COMORBIDITY
## IN ANTISOCIAL BEHAVIOR

If antisocial behavior or conduct disorders is indeed driven, in at least some cases, by underlying psychiatric disorders, what is the extent of this problem? The answer to this depends on existing evidence of co-occurrence between conduct disorders and other psychiatric disorders. There are relatively few good recent studies specifically related to comorbidity of conduct disorders in school settings, although a number of studies have been done on school-age children or youth in juvenile justice or child welfare systems (Bullis & Walker, 1996; Hunt, 1993). Another way to approach this problem, therefore, is to consider premorbid or comorbid expression of conduct disorders in children or youth diagnosed with other psychiatric disorders. Table 7.1 provides such data on the psychiatric disorders presented earlier. These data were derived not only from reviews on each disorder previously cited, but also from several pertinent longitudinal studies on childhood psychiatric disorders (Biederman et al., 1996; Bird, Gould, & Staghenzza, 1993; Jensen, Hoagwood, & Petti, 1996; McGee, Feeham, Williams, & Anderson, 1992; Offord et al., 1992; Rutter, 1989; Shaffer et al., 1996; Silver et al., 1992; Taylor, Chadwick, Hepinstall, & Danckaerts, 1996).

It should be noted that data in Table 7.1 represent very conservative estimates of prevalence and comorbidity of each of these disorders, and that the range of findings in epidemiologic research on child mental health varies considerably from study to study (Brandenburg, Friedman, & Silver, 1990; Jensen et al., 1996). Conservative estimates were used both for the sake of consistency across disorders and for more relevance to school situations in which only more severe levels of disorder tend to be referred. Estimates were also limited to childhood and early adolescence, because most school referrals are made by that point (Duncan, Forness, & Hartsough, 1995). Finally, it should be noted that attention deficit disorders and mood disorders have been studied widely, whereas the data on anxiety disorders and schizophrenic disorders in children or early adolescence are more limited. Given these limitations, more conservative estimates of premorbidity and comorbidity were selected. The estimated prevalence of each disorder is depicted in Table 7.1 along with estimated percentage of children or young adolescents with premorbid or comorbid conduct disorders. The combined cases provide an estimate of prevalence for complex conduct disorders. Note that the sum of these combined disorders (2.3%) in the general population would seem to account for well more than half of the likewise conservative prevalence estimate of conduct disorders itself, which is around 4% of the general population.

There is a possibility that this figure may slightly overestimate the prevalence of complex conduct disorders in that the four psychiatric disorders themselves sometimes overlap as well (Zoccolillo, 1992). There are, however, other disorders that may account for at least some of the remaining 40% to 50%. Research on learning disability subtypes suggests that some types of children with learning disabilities may be at risk for certain emotional or behavioral disorders (Forness, 1990b; San Miguel, Forness, & Kavale, 1996). These not only include conduct disorders but also other disorders that commonly co-occur with conduct disorders, thus suggesting that undetected learning disabilities may further complicate the picture of conduct disorders. There is likewise high probability that physical and/or sexual abuse are also implicated, in that signs of post-traumatic stress resemble symptoms of conduct disorder (Ciccetti &

### TABLE 7.1
**Pre- or Comorbidity of Conduct Disorders With Other Early
Onset Psychiatric Disorders**

| Disorder | Approximate Prevalence | Pre- or Comorbidity | Combined Prevalence |
|---|---|---|---|
| Attention deficit disorders | 3% | 50% | 1.5% |
| Mood disorders | 2 | 30 | 0.6 |
| Anxiety disorders | 1 | 20 | 0.2 |
| Schizophrenic disorders | 0.1 | 30 | 0.03 |

*Note.* Adapted from data in Forness, Kavale, King, and Kasari (1994).

Toth, 1995; Finkelhor & Berliner, 1995; Walker, Bonner, & Kaufman, 1988). The diagnosis of posttraumatic stress disorders, often applied to these instances, encompasses a range of such symptoms (American Psychiatric Association, 1994). A variety of other disorders—such as fetal alcohol syndrome, fragile X syndrome, and traumatic brain injury—are also recognized to produce symptoms of conduct disorders (Forness & Kavale, 1994). There is thus a possibility that the percentage of conduct disorders that may be "uncomplicated" could therefore be relatively small. In fact, a recent longitudinal study of 812 children with SED suggests that nearly two thirds of children had a primary diagnosis of conduct disorder, and that two thirds of these had another comorbid psychiatric diagnosis (Greenbaum et al., 1996).

## CONSEQUENCES OF IGNORING COMORBIDITY

It may be informative to examine a few selective studies in regard to the comorbidity issue and the fact that ignoring underlying conditions may be very counterproductive in dealing with antisocial behavior. For example, Duncan et al. (1995) examined 85 youngsters placed in special day-treatment classrooms in two California counties. The two counties were widely recognized for their exemplary comprehensive systems of care. Retrospective analysis of records from various agencies and parent interviews suggested that several years passed before a severe emotional or behavioral disorder was recognized as such, very possibly because most children had either premorbid or comorbid conduct or oppositional defiant disorders. These masked the symptoms of more serious psychiatric disorders that were not instantly recognized by school or related professionals. In this sample, most parents or guardians appeared to know that something was seriously amiss in their child's social or emotional development by his or her preschool years; and a professional, such as a family physician, identified the problem at the beginning of kindergarten, on the average. Data on mean age of these children at each subsequent state of intervention are summarized in Table 7.2 by diagnosis.

As noted in Table 7.2, the child initially received intervention at a mean age of 6.4 years, mainly an isolated treatment such as therapy or referral for child abuse. Identification for special education did not occur until 7.8 years, and then was mainly for learning disability (LD) in 53% of the cases. Appropriate placement in an SED program did not occur until the mean age of the child was 10.4 years. About 15% of this sample had a primary psychiatric diagnosis of conduct or oppositional defiant disorder, and about 25% more were diagnosed as ADHD (attention deficit hyperactivity disorder). These disruptive be-

## TABLE 7.2

**Mean Age of First Intervention, Special Education Identification, and First SED Placement of Children With Emotional or Behavioral Disorders**

| Diagnosis | N | First Intervention | Special Education Identification[a] | First SED Placement |
|---|---|---|---|---|
| Conduct or oppositional disorders | 14 | 5.4 | 7.8 | 10.3 |
| Attention deficit hyperactivity disorder | 21 | 5.0 | 6.6 | 9.4 |
| Depressive or other mood disorders | 31 | 8.6 | 9.5 | 11.5 |
| Schizophrenic or other disorders | 8 | 5.4 | 7.9 | 11.9 |
| Posttraumatic stress disorder | 11 | 5.0 | 6.3 | 8.3 |
| Total or mean | 85 | 6.4 | 7.8 | 10.4 |

*Note.* Adapted from data in Duncan, Forness, and Hartsough (1995).

[a]Eligibility for total sample at this point was 53% for LD, 31% for SED, and 16% for other special education categories.

havior disorders also tended to be a secondary diagnosis in a substantial number of children who had psychiatric diagnoses such as depression, schizophrenia, or posttraumatic stress disorder resulting from sustained physical or sexual abuse.

The possibility of children in this sample being initially excluded from SED services because of their perceived antisocial behavior thus may have been a serious barrier to appropriate identification in well more than half this sample. Children with depression or dysthymia were among the last to be identified, possibly due to potential masking of their diagnosis by comorbidity with antisocial behavior (Biederman, Farone, Mick, & Lelone, 1995). The salient findings of Duncan et al. (1995) were that 4 or more years passed until appropriate recognition of the problem, and that initial school intervention, when it came, was usually for problems other than emotional or behavioral disorders. That initial intervention appeared mistakenly to focus only on school learning problems or on superficial behavioral problems suggests that both accurate recognition and appropriate intervention for underlying psychiatric disorders were needlessly delayed. We speculate as well that this resistance to initial treatment is similar in concept to that hypothesized by Fuchs and Fuchs (1995) for children who do not respond to enhanced instructional strategies that ignore the possibility of undetected learning disabilities.

The potential for disregarding the significance of emotional or behavioral disorders was also confirmed in a subsequent study of 150 children in Grades 2 and 4 who were referred to student study teams (Lopez, Forness, MacMillan, Bocian, & Gresham, 1996). In this study, research diagnostic criteria were used to identify children with ADHD, emotional or behavioral disorders (EBD), and other disabilities such as mental retardation and learning disabilities. School personnel were not aware of the test results from which these diagnostic criteria were derived. At the end of the study, all 150 children were tracked to determine if they had been placed in special education, were not found eligible for special education, were still being considered by the study teams, or had moved out of district. Summary data on children with ADHD (28.6% of the sample) and EBD (8%) are presented in Table 7.3, along with data on the remaining children in the study. Note that about 37% of the ADHD and 50% of the EBD children had been placed in learning disability programs, but that only about 2% of the ADHD and none of the EBD children were apparently considered appropriate for SED programs. In fact only 1 child of the total 55 children with ADHD and EBD who might reasonably be expected to receive SED services actually ended up doing so. That the remaining 54 children who might be expected to profit from SED services were placed in classrooms not ostensibly designed for intervention or treatment of emotional or behavioral problems is a matter of grave concern.

A similar study of 204 children referred to student study teams in another school district focused on referring complaints by regular classroom teachers (Del'Homme, Kasari, Forness, & Bagley, 1996). In this study, referrals were categorized by academic, behavioral, or combined problems (both academic and behavioral). Only about one quarter of the 204 children were referred pri-

## TABLE 7.3

**Special Education Identification of Children Meeting Research Diagnostic Criteria for Attention Deficit Hyperactivity Disorder (ADHD) and Emotional or Behavioral Disorders (EBD)**

| Research ADHD | SED | LD | Other Education Categories | Not Identified[a] | Total |
|---|---|---|---|---|---|
| ADHD | 1 | 16 | 44 | 22 | 43 |
| EBD | 0 | 6 | 1 | 5 | 12 |
| Other[b] | 0 | 38 | 5 | 52 | 95 |
| Total | 1 | 60 | 10 | 79 | 150 |

*Note.* Adapted from data in Lopez, Forness, MacMillan, Bocian, and Gresham (1996).

[a]Includes children who were not found eligible ($N = 41$), whose eligibility had not been determined by the close of the study ($N = 25$), or who had moved out of district ($N = 13$).

[b]Includes children with mental retardation, learning disabilities, or other children who did not score above clinical cutoff points for a disability on research diagnostic criteria.

marily for behavioral problems or for behavioral problems with some minor academic difficulties, with another fifth of the sample having behavioral problems and academic problems in relatively equal measure. The rate of subsequent referral to special education for the entire sample was 45%, but the proportion of children with primary behavioral problems was significantly lower, suggesting that potential emotional or behavioral disorders were underidentified in this study as well. This appeared due either to masking of these disorders by antisocial behavior or conduct problems, or to a focus on academic issues rather than on potential emotional or behavioral disorders.

Finally, the relative lack of importance placed on intervention for serious internalizing disorders by school personnel is illustrated in a study of 111 children with depression or dysthymia seen in a psychiatric outpatient clinic (Forness, 1988; Forness et al., 1993). Dysthymia is a variant of depression involving less intense symptoms over a longer period of time. Although these children were initially referred to the clinic because of school problems, they were subsequently diagnosed with depression or dysthymia in the clinic. They seldom received special education, however, *after* they returned to school.

Diagnoses of depression or dysthymia were made by advanced child psychiatry residents under the supervision of a faculty team, and were based both on psychiatric diagnostic criteria and on severity of global impairment. Three subgroups were identified. The first had severe impairment but no other comorbid conditions. The second group was similar, but also had a comorbid conduct or oppositional defiant disorder. The last group was similar to the sec-

## TABLE 7.4

### Special Education Identification by Diagnostic Subgroup of Children With Depression or Dysthymia Discharged From a Psychiatric Clinic

| Diagnosis | N | Number Identified for Special Education (%) |
|---|---|---|
| Depression or dysthymia (no other diagnosis) | 47 | 10 (21%) |
| Depression or dysthymia (with conduct or related disorders) | 38 | 17 (45) |
| Depression or dysthymia (with learning disabilities) | 26 | 22 (85) |
| Total | 111 | 49 (44) |

*Note.* Adapted from data in Forness (1988) and Forness, Kavale, and Lopez (1993).

ond, but had a comorbid learning disability as well. Data on the number in each group and on the rate of subsequent identification for special education on discharge are presented in Table 7.4. Note that children with depression or dysthymia but without conduct disorders or learning disabilities were found eligible for special education at relatively low rates, even after the results of clinic diagnoses were available to school professionals. As in studies discussed previously, comorbid learning problems were more likely to be the deciding factor in identification for special services. Antisocial behavior or conduct disorders were usually the chief complaint for referral to the psychiatric clinic, but it took a comprehensive mental health workup to identify the underlying internalizing disorder that the psychiatric team considered to be the *primary* diagnosis. School professionals seemed reluctant to identify children with these internalizing disorders for any special education services unless they also had a learning disorder. It may well be that school professionals consider it impossible for both externalizing and internalizing disorders to coexist in the same child. Achenbach (1990/1991) demonstrated that such coexistence is indeed quite common in referred populations, and data from the previously cited studies tend to confirm this phenomenon.

## IMPLICATIONS FOR DETECTION AND INTERVENTION

Complex conduct disorders are likely to be viewed very differently in terms of school identification and intervention, at least compared with more traditional concepts of antisocial behavior or conduct disorders. Intervention for most types of antisocial behavior or conduct disorders is currently likely to involve behavioral or social skills approaches, disciplinary procedures, or referrals to juvenile justice. For complex conduct disorders, on the other hand, prereferral intervention, eligibility for special education, referral for psychiatric or other mental health services, psychopharmacological treatment, and therapeutic family approaches might more profitably be brought to bear as a means of addressing possible disorders underlying conduct disorder symptomatology. Evidence has also begun to appear that even specific classroom or curricular approaches may have very different outcomes for children with different types of emotional or behavioral disorders (Dolan et al., 1993). Assessment for other possible disorders in the earliest stages of antisocial behavior may thus be well advised, and there are a number of standardized instruments or other systematic procedures that can be used by school professionals to identify specific psychiatric diagnoses during initial evaluation of any child or youth with inattention or disruptive behavior (Forness, 1990a; Kauffman, 1997).

Assessments to detect comorbid conditions are seldom routinely used in school settings, however. This is especially true when initial impressions or presenting problems suggest that only antisocial behavior or simple conduct disorders are involved. Such evaluations need not be extensive, and effective screening instruments that require relatively modest effort on the part of school professionals have begun to appear. Among the most promising is the Systematic Screening for Behavioral Disorders (SSBD; Walker et al., 1988; Walker & Severson, 1990), designed specifically for schoolwide screening. This is a multistage system in which the teacher first identifies from his or her class list those pupils with either externalizing or internalizing behavioral patterns. In the second stage, the teacher subsequently rates only the top-ranked children in each group on brief rating scales of adaptive and maladaptive behaviors and on a critical events index. Any children meeting clinical cutoff points on these scales pass into a third or confirmatory stage, involving brief observations in the classroom and on the playground by another school professional. A downward extension of the same multistage system, the Early Screening Project (or ESP), was recently published for use in preschool or day-care settings (Walker, Severson, & Feil, 1995). Another system incorporating multiple components was designed by Achenbach and McConaughy (1987; McConaughy & Achenbach, 1989). This system involves a comprehensive series of diagnostic instruments involving both parent and teacher checklists with accompanying profiles of various disorders, self-report profiles for selected older children, and a direct classroom or group activity observation. Checklists are available for children as young as 2 or 3 years of age.

A variety of other rating instruments are available for single or multiple disorders, especially those that are often comorbid with conduct disorders (e.g., attention deficit disorders or depression; Niebuhr & Smith, 1990). These instruments can be used singly or in combination to identify specific emotional or behavioral disorders in children referred by parents or teachers. Although definitive diagnoses may not always be possible given the expertise or professional experience of most school personnel, such instruments may at least suggest the need for more specific diagnostic workups, either by school professionals who specialize in this area or in collaboration with mental health professionals.

An important component missing from most of those instruments, however, is evaluation of the significance of scores or items in a multicultural setting. In this regard, McIntyre (1994) developed a system in which items or subscales can be contrasted with standards for behavior in a variety of cultural contexts, thus helping to ensure that validity of clinical judgments can be maintained during identification and treatment. The issue of gender bias in referral also cannot be overlooked. Recent studies suggest underreferral of girls despite a variety of serious emotional or behavioral disorders (Caseau, Luchasson, & Kroth 1994; Green, Clopton, & Pope 1996; Keogh & Bernheimer, 1998).

The advantage of both the SSBD and ESP, however, is that they were designed for wide-scale, school-based screening; are characterized by considerable economy of effort; and have exceptionally good reliability and validity (Walker et al., 1988). Use of all or part of these systems in Head Start settings has been especially effective (Del'Homme, Sinclair, & Kasari, 1994; Sinclair, 1993; Sinclair, Del'Homme, & Gonzalez, 1993). Although not a formal part of the SSBD or ESP systems, a formal archival records search (School Archival Records Search, or SARS) is also available with indexes for at-risk behavior that can be helpful in determining whether functional impairments warrant more definitive diagnosis (Walker, Block-Pedego, Todis, & Severson, 1991). As noted previously, both systems have adaptive as well as maladaptive scales, thus identifying both protective factors and risk factors (Coie et al., 1993).

A final advantage is that, at any gate or stage during identification, intervention by school or related agencies can occur. Although discussion of the full range of intervention options in mental health is beyond the scope of this chapter, the reader is referred to Forness et al. (1996), Nelson (1996); Nelson and Pearson (1991); Duchnowski and Kutash (1996); or Walker (1994) for further description. It should be noted that such programs are incremental and initiated as early as possible in the sequence of developmental psychopathology. They also involve extensive interagency collaboration and case management, a hallmark of any effective intervention program. These treatments can also supplement a range of effective interventions available for less complex antisocial behavior (Walker et al., 1996).

## CONCLUSION

Such assessments may indeed yield findings completely negative for any evidence of disturbance other than conduct disorders. The extra effort involved in ruling out other disorders may nonetheless prove worthwhile. To persist in intervention narrowly directed at only conduct disorders symptomatology may be much more inefficient in the long run. Although discussion of appropriate interventions is beyond the scope of this chapter, a few illustrations of the perils of not considering treatment implications of complex conduct disorders may be useful.

Cognitive behavioral strategies, for example, appear not to have a very substantial impact on conduct disorder symptoms such as aggression yet do seem effective in managing symptoms of impulsivity in ADHD (Robinson, Brownell, Smith, & Miller, in press). Other cognitive behavioral strategies are the hallmark of psychosocial treatment programs to manage symptoms of depression or dysthymia (Maag & Forness, 1991). To treat only symptoms of conduct disorders with standard behavioral or social skill strategies might well prove both less effective and less efficient for children with complex conduct disorders, in whom ADHD or depressive diagnoses are present. More significant is the possibility of psychopharmacologic treatment. Although there is no widely accepted psychotropic medication to treat conduct disorders per se, the range and effectiveness of medications for symptoms of ADHD, depression, and related diagnoses have increased substantially in recent years (Forness, Sweeney, & Toy, 1996; Sweeney, Forness, Kavale, & Levitt, 1997). Not to recognize the possibility of psychiatric diagnoses underlying conduct disorders substantially limits the probability of effective psychopharmacologic treatment.

Although we have questioned the placement of children with primary emotional or behavioral disorders in learning disability classrooms, there is more widespread acceptance that undetected learning disabilities may well be the genesis of at least some conduct disorders (Coie, Underwood, & Lochman, 1991; Hinshaw, 1992). Coie and Kriehbel (1984), in fact, demonstrated that academic tutoring may be more effective than social skills training in some children with conduct disorders. It thus seems clear that ignoring the possibility of comorbidity in antisocial behavior may severely limit treatment options only to those interventions normally used for conduct disorders, which may prove too narrow to be effective in complex conduct disorders.

It is important to note, however, that there are dangers inherent in overextending the notion of complex conduct disorders, just as there have been problems in not recognizing that conduct disorders can be complex. For example, use of underlying diagnoses to excuse one's actions has been too readily used to excuse behavior that intrudes on rights of others or seized on as a primary reason for one's own failings (Wilson, 1993). Nonetheless, recognition that in many instances conduct disorders may be based on a complex set of underlying conditions rather than simply on a failure of will or poor parenting may allow more appropriate programs and interventions for these children in a significant number of cases.

## REFERENCES

Achenbach, T. M. (1990/1991). "Comorbidity" in child and adolescent psychiatry: Categorical and quantitative perspective. *Journal of Child and Adolescent Psychopharmacology, 1,* 271–278.

Achenbach, T. M., & McConaughy, S. H. (1987). *Empirically based assessment of child and adolescent psychopathology: Practical application.* Newbury Park, CA: Sage.

American Psychiatric Association. (1994). *Diagnostic and statistical manual of mental disorders* (4th ed.). Washington, DC: Author.

Bernstein, G. A., & Borchardt, C. M. (1991). Anxiety disorders of childhood and adolescence: A critical review. *Journal of American Academy of Child and Adolescent Psychiatry, 30*, 519–532.

Bernstein, G. A., Borchardt, C. M., & Perwien, A. R. (1996). Anxiety disorders in children and adolescents: A review of the last 10 years. *Journal of American Academy of Child and Adolescent Psychiatry, 35*, 1110–1119.

Biederman, J., Faraone, S., Mick, E., & Lelone, E. (1995). Psychiatric comorbidity among referred juveniles with major depression: Fact or artifact? *Journal of the American Academy of Child and Adolescent Psychiatry, 34*, 579–590.

Biederman, J., Faraone, S. V., Milberger, S., Jetton, J. G., Chen, L., Mick, E., Greene, R. W., & Russell, R. L. (1996). Is childhood oppositional defiant disorder a precursor to adolescent conduct disorder: Findings from a four-year follow-up study of children with ADHD. *Journal of American Academy of Child and Adolescent Psychiatry, 35*, 1193–1204.

Bird, H. R., Gould, M. S., & Staghenzza, B. M. (1993). Patterns of diagnostic comorbidity in a community sample of children aged 9 through 16 years. *Journal of American Academy of Child and Adolescent Psychiatry, 32*, 361–368.

Brandenburg, N. A., Friedman, R. M., & Silver, S. E. (1990). The epidemiology of childhood psychiatric disorders: Recent prevalence findings and methodologic issues. *Journal of American Academy of Child and Adolescent Psychiatry, 29*, 76–83.

Bullis, M., & Walker, H. M. (1996). Characteristics and causal factors of troubled youth. In M. N. Nelson, R. B. Rutherford, & B. I. Wolford (Eds.), *Comprehensive and collaborative systems that work for troubled youth: A national agenda* (pp. 15–28). Richmond, KY: National Juvenile Detention Association.

Cantwell, D. P. (1996). Attention deficit disorder: A review of the past 10 years. *Journal of American Academy of Child and Adolescent Psychiatry, 35*, 978–987.

Caseau, D. L., Luchasson, R., & Kroth, R. L. (1994). Special education services for girls with serious emotional disturbance: A case of gender bias? *Behavioral Disorders, 20*, 51–60.

Cicchetti, D., & Toth, S. L. (1995). A developmental psychopathology perspective on child abuse and neglect. *Journal of American Academy of Child and Adolescent Psychiatry, 34*, 541–565.

Coie, J. D., & Kriehbel, T. (1984). Effects of academic tutoring on the social status of low-achieving, socially rejected children. *Child Development, 55*, 1465–1478.

Coie, J. D., Underwood, M., & Lochman, J. E. (1991). Programmatic interventions with aggressive children in the school setting. In D. Pepler & K. Rubin (Eds.), *The development and treatment of childhood aggression* (pp. 389–407). Hillsdale, NJ: Lawrence Erlbaum Associates.

Coie, J. D., Watt, N. F., West, S. G., Hawkins, J. D., Asarnow, J. R., Markman, J. J., Ramey, S. L., Shire, M. B., & Long, B. (1993). The science of prevention: A conceptual framework and some directions for a national research program *American Psychologist, 4*, 1013–1022.

Del'Homme, M., Kasari, C., Forness, S. R., & Bagley, R. (1996). Prereferral intervention and children at risk for emotional or behavioral disorders. *Education and Treatment of Children, 19*, 272–285.

Del'Homme, M., Sinclair, E., & Kasari, C. (1994). Preschool children with behavioral problems: Observation in instructional and free play contexts. *Behavioral Disorders, 19*, 221–232.

Dodge, K. (1985). A social information processing model of social competence in children. In M. Perlmutter (Ed.), *Minnesota symposium in child psychology* (pp. 41–60). Hillsdale, NJ: Lawrence Erlbaum Associates.

Dodge, K., Coie, J., & Brakke, N. (1982). Behavioral patterns of socially rejected and neglected adolescents: The roles of social approach and aggression. *Journal of Abnormal Child Psychology, 10*, 389–410.

Dolan, L. J., Kellam, S. G., Brown, C. H., Werthamer-Larson, L., Rebok, G. W., Mayer, L. S., Landoltt, J. J., Turkkan, J. S., Ford, C., & Wheeler, L. (1993). The short-term impact of two classroom-based preventive interventions on aggressive and shy behaviors and poor achievement. *Journal of Applied Developmental Psychology, 14*, 317–345.

Dryfoos, J. (1990). *Adolescents at risk.* New York: Oxford University Press.

Duchnowski, A. J., & Kutash, K. (1996). A mental health perspective. In C. M. Nelson, R. B. Rutherford, Jr., & B. I. Wolford (Eds.), *Developing comprehensive systems for troubled youth: A national agenda* (pp. 90–110). Richmond, KY: National Juvenile Detention Association.

Duncan, B. B., Forness, S. R., & Hartsough, C. (1995). Students identified as seriously emotionally disturbed in day treatment classrooms: Cognitive, psychiatric and special education characteristics. *Behavioral Disorders, 20*, 238–252.

Eyesenck, H. (1994). The outcome problem in psychotherapy: What have we learned? *Behavior Research and Therapy, 22*, 477–495.

Finkelhor, D., & Berliner, L. (1995). Research on the treatment of sexually abused children: A review and recommendations. *Journal of American Academy on Child and Adolescent Psychiatry, 34*, 1408–1423.

Fleming, J. E., & Offord, D. R. (1990). Epidemiology of childhood depressive disorders: A critical review. *Journal of American Academy of Child and Adolescent Psychiatry, 29*, 571–580.

Forness, S. R. (1983). *Classroom observation: A procedures manual for gathering research or clinical data in ongoing classroom situations.* Culver City, CA: Bradley.

Forness, S. R. (1988). School characteristics of children and adolescents with depression. *Monographs in Behavioral Disorders, 10*, 177–203.

Forness, S. R. (1990a). Resolving the definitional diagnostic issues of serious emotional disturbance in the schools. In S. Braaten & G. Wrobel (Eds.), *Perspectives on the diagnosis and treatment of students with emotional/behavioral disorders* (pp. 1–15). Minneapolis, MN: Council for Children With Behavioral Disorders.

Forness, S. R. (1990b). A subtyping in learning disabilities: Introduction to the issues. In H. L. Swanson & B. Keogh (Eds.), *Learning disabilities: Theoretical and research issues* (pp. 195–200). Hillsdale, NJ: Lawrence Erlbaum Associates.

Forness, S. R. (1992a). Broadening the cultural-organizational perspective in exclusion of youth with social maladjustment. *Remedial and Special Education, 13*, 55–59.

Forness, S. R. (1992b). Legalism versus professionalism in diagnosing SED in the public schools. *School Psychology Review, 21*, 29–34.

Forness, S. R., & Kavale, K. A. (1994). The Balkanization of special education: Proliferation of categories for new behavioral disorders. *Education and Treatment of Children, 17*, 215–217.

Forness, S. R., Kavale, K. A., King, B. H., & Kasari, C. (1994). Simple versus complex conduct disorders: Identification and phenomenology. *Behavioral Disorders, 19*, 306–312.

Forness, S. R., Kavale, K. A., & Lopez, M. (1993). Conduct disorders in school: Special education eligibility and co-morbidity. *Journal of Emotional and Behavioral Disorders, 1*, 101–108.

Forness, S. R., Kavale, K. A., MacMillan, D. L., Asarnow, J. R., & Duncan, B. B. (1996). Early detection and prevention of emotional or behavioral disorders: Developmental aspects of systems of care. *Behavioral Disorders, 21*, 226–240.

Forness, S. R., & Knitzer, J. (1992). A new proposed definition and terminology to replace "serious emotional disturbance" in the Individuals with Disabilities Education Act. *School Psychology Review, 21*, 12–20.

Forness, S. R., Sweeney, D. P., & Toy, K. (1996). Psychopharmacologic medication: What teachers need to know. *Beyond Behavior, 7*(2), 4–11.

Fuchs, L. S., & Fuchs, D. N. (1995, May). *Treatment validity: A unifying concept for reconceptualizing the identification of learning disabilities.* Paper presented at Workshop on IQ Testing and Educational Decision Making, National Research Council, National Academy of Sciences, Washington, DC.

Green, M. T., Clopton, J. R., & Pope, A. W. (1996). Understanding gender differences in referral of children to mental health services. *Journal of Emotional and Behavioral Disorders, 4*, 182–190.

Green, W. H., Padron-Gayol, M., Hardesty, A. S., & Bassiri, M. (1992). Schizophrenia with childhood onset: A phenomenological study of 38 cases. *Journal of American Academy of Child and Adolescent Psychiatry, 31*, 968–976.

Greenbaum, P. E., Dedrick, R. F., Friedman, R. M., Kutash, K., Brown, E. C., Lardieri, S. P., & Pugh, A. M. (1996). National adolescent and child treatment study (NACTS): Outcomes for children with serious emotional and behavioral disturbance. *Journal of Emotional and Behavioral Disorders, 4*, 130–146.

Hinshaw, S. (1992). Externalizing behavior problems and academic underachievement in childhood and adolescence: Causal relationships and underlying mechanisms. *Psychological Bulletin, 111*, 127–155.

Hunt, R. D. (1993). Neurobiological patterns of aggression. *Journal of Emotional and Behavioral Problems, 2*, 14–19.

Jensen, P. S., Hoagwood, K., & Petti, T. (1996). Outcomes of mental health care for children and adolescents: II. Literature review and application of comprehensive mode. *Journal of American Academy of Child and Adolescent Psychiatry, 35*, 1064–1077.

Kauffman, J. M. (1997). *Characteristics of emotional and behavioral disorders of children and youth* (sixth ed.) Upper Sadde River, NJ: Prentice-Hall.

Kavale, K. A., Forness, S. R., & Duncan, B. B. (1996). Defining emotional or behavioral disorders: Divergence and convergence. In T. Scruggs & M. Mastropieri (Eds.), *Advances in learning and behavioral disabilities*, (Vol. 10, pp. 1–45). Greenwich, CT: JAI.

Kazdin, A. E. (1987). *Conduct disorders in childhood and adolescence.* Newbury Park, CA: Sage.

Kelly, E. J. (1990). *The differential test of conduct and emotional problems*. Aurora, CO: Slosson.

Keogh, B. K., & Bernheimer, L. P. (1998). Concordance between parents and teachers perceptions of behavior problems of children with developmental delays. *Journal of Emotional and Behavior Disorders, 6*, 33–41.

Knitzer, J., Steinberg, Z., & Fleisch, B. (1990). *At the schoolhouse door: An examination of programs and policies for children with behavioral and emotional problems*. New York: Bank Street College of Education.

Kovacs, M. (1996). Presentation and course of major depressive disorder during childhood and later years of the life span. *Journal of American Academy of Child and Adolescent Psychiatry, 35*, 705–715.

Lahey, B. B., Loeber, R., Quay, H. C., Frick, P. J., & Grimm, J. (1992). Oppositional defiant and conduct disorders: Issues to be resolved for DSM IV. *Journal of American Academy of Child and Adolescent Psychiatry, 31*, 539–546.

Lopez, M., Forness, S. R., MacMillan, D. L., Bocian, K., & Gresham, F. M. (1996). Children with attention deficit hyperactivity disorder and emotional or behavioral disorders in the primary grades: Inappropriate placement in the learning disability category. *Education and Treatment of Children, 19*, 286–299.

Maag, J. W., & Forness, S. R. (1991). Depression in children and adolescents: Identification, assessment and treatment. *Focus on Exceptional Children, 24*(1), 1–19.

Mayer, G. R. (1995). Preventing antisocial behavior in the schools. *Journal of Applied Behavioral Analysis, 28*, 467–478.

Mayer, G. R., & Sulzer-Azaroff, B. (1990). Interventions for vandalism. In G. Stoner, M. R. Shinn, & H. M. Walker (Eds.), *Interventions for achievement and behavior problems* (pp. 559–580). Washington, DC: National Association of School Psychologists.

McConaughy, S. H., & Achenbach, T. M. (1989). *Practical guide for the child behavior checklist and related materials*. Burlington, VT: University Associates in Psychiatry.

McGee, R., Feeham, M., William, S., & Anderson, J. (1992). DSM III disorders from age 11 to age 15 years. *Journal of American Academy of Child and Adolescent Psychiatry, 31*, 50–59.

McIntyre, T. (1994). *McIntyre assessment of culture: An instrument for evaluating the influence of culture on behavior and learning*. Columbia, MO: Hawthorn Educational Services.

Messer, S. C., & Beidel, D. C. (1994). Psychosocial correlates of childhood anxiety disorders. *Journal of American Academy of Child and Adolescent Psychiatry, 33*, 975–983.

Nelson, C. M., & Pearson, C. A. (1991). *Integrating services for children and youth with emotional/behavioral disorders*. Reston, VA: The Council for Exceptional Children.

Nelson, J. R. (1996). Designing schools to meet the needs of students who exhibit disruptive behavior. *Journal of Emotional and Behavioral Disorders, 4*, 147–161.

Niebuhr, V. N., & Smith, K. E. (1990). Simple tests to assess behavior problems. *Contemporary Pediatrics, 12*, 118–138.

Offord, D. R., & Bennett, K. J. (1994). Conduct disorder: Long-term outcomes and intervention effectiveness. *Journal of American Academy on Child and Adolescent Psychiatry, 33*, 1069–1078.

Offord, D. R., Boyle, M. H., Racine, Y. A., Fleming, J. E., Cadman, D. T., Blum, H. M., Byrne, C., Links, P. S., Lipman, E. L., MacMillan, H. L., Grant, N. R., Sanford, M. N., Szatmari, P., Thomas, H., & Woodward, C. A. (1992). Outcome, prognosis, and risk in a longitudinal follow-up study. *Journal of American Academy of Child and Adolescent Psychiatry, 31*, 916–923.

Patterson, G. R., Reid, J. B., & Dishion, T. J. (1992). *Antisocial boys.* Eugene, OR: Castalia.

Reid, J. (1993). Prevention of conduct disorder before and after school entry: Relating interventions to developmental findings. *Development and Psychopathology, 5*, 243–262.

Robinson, T. R., Brownell, M. T., Smith, S. W., & Miller, M. D. (in press). Cognitive-behavior modification of hyperactivity/impulsivity and aggression: A meta-analysis. *Journal of Educational Psychology.*

Russell, A. T., Bott, L., & Sammons, C. (1989). The phenomenolgy of schizophrenia occurring in childhood. *Journal of American Academy of Child and Adolescent Psychiatry, 28*, 399–407.

Rutter, M. (1989). Isle of Wight revisited: Twenty-five years of child psychiatric epidemiology. *Journal of American Academy of Child and Adolescent Psychiatry, 28*, 633–653.

San Miguel, S. K., Forness, S. R., & Kavale, K. A. (1996). Social skill deficits and learning disabilities: The psychiatric comorbidity hypothesis. *Learning Disability Quarterly, 19*, 252–261.

Shaffer, D., Fisher, P., Dulcan, M. D., Davies, M., Piacentini, J., Schwab-Stone, M. D., Laheh, B. B., Bourdon, K., Jensen, P. S., Bird, H. R., Canino, G., & Regier, D. A. (1996). The NIMH diagnostic interview schedule for children version 2. 3 (DISC-2. 3): Description, acceptability prevalence rates, and performance in the MECA study. *Journal of American Academy on Child and Adolescent Psychiatry, 35*, 865–877.

Shamise, S. (1981). Antisocial adolescents: Our treatments do not work—where do we go from here? *Canadian Journal of Psychiatry, 26*, 357–364.

Silver, S. E., Duchnowski, A. J., Kutash, K., Friedman, R. M., Eisen, M., Prange, M. E., Brandenburg, N. A., & Greenbaum, P. E. (1992). A comparison of children with serious emotional disturbance served in residential and school settings. *Journal of Child and Family Studies, 1*, 43–59.

Sinclair, E. (1993). Early identification of preschoolers with special needs in head start. *Topics in Early Childhood Special Education, 13*, 12–18.

Sinclair, E., Del'Homme, M., & Gonzalez, M. (1993). Systematic screening for preschool behavioral disorders. *Behavioral Disorders, 18*, 177–188.

Slenkovich, J. (1992). Can the language "social maladjustment" in the SED definition be ignored? The final words. *School Psychology Review, 21*, 43–45.

Sweeney, D. P., Forness, S. R., Kavale, K. A., & Levitt, J. G. (1997). An update on psychopharmacologic medication: What teachers, clinicians and parents need to know. *Intervention in School and Clinic, 33* (1), 4–21.

Taylor, E., Chadwick, O., Hepinstall, E., & Danckaerts, M. (1996). Hyperactivity and conduct problems as risk factors for adolescent development. *Journal of American Academy on Child and Adolescent Psychiatry, 35*, 1213–1226.

Volkmar, F. R. (1996). Childhood and adolescent psychosis: A review of the past 10 years. *Journal of American Academy on Child and Adolescent Psychiatry, 35,* 843–851.

Walker, C. E., Bonner, B. L., & Kaufman, K. L. (1988). *The physically and sexually abused child.* New York: Pergamon.

Walker, H. M. (1994). *Violence prevention and school safety.* Washington, DC: National Council on Disabilities.

Walker, H. M., Block-Pedego, A., Todis, B., & Severson, H. (1991). *School archival records search.* Longmont, CO: Sopris West.

Walker, H. M., & Bullis, M. (1996). Comprehensive services model for troubled youth. In C. M. Nelson, R. B. Rutherford, Jr., & B. I. Wolford, (Eds.), *Developing comprehensive systems for troubled youth* (pp. 122–148). Richmond, KY: National Juvenile Detention Association.

Walker, H. M., Colvin, G., & Ramsey, E. (1995). *Antisocial behavior in schools: Strategies and best practices.* Pacific Grove, CA: Brooks/Cole.

Walker, H. M., Horner, R. H., Sugai, G., Bullis, M., Sprague, J. R., Bricker, D. & Kaufman, M. (1996). Integrated approaches to preventing antisocial behavior patterns among school-age children and youth. *Journal of Emotional and Behavioral Disorders, 4,* 194–209.

Walker, H. M., & Severson, H. H. (1990). *Systematic screening for behavioral disorders.* Longmont, CO: Sopris West.

Walker, H. M., Severson, H. H., & Feil, E. (1995). *The early screening project.* Longmont, CO: Sopris West.

Walker, H. M., Severson, H. W., Stiller, B., Williams, G., Haring, N. G., Shinn, M. R., & Todis, B. (1988). Systematic screening of pupils in the elementary age range at risk for behavior disorders: Development and trial testing. *Remedial and Special Education, 9*(1), 8–19.

Walker, H. M., & Sylvester, R. (1991). Where is school along the path to prison? *Educational Leadership, 49,* 14–16.

Weinberg, L., & Weinberg, C. (1990). Seriously emotionally disturbed or socially maladjusted? A critique of interpretations. *Behavioral Disorders, 15,* 149–158

Werry, J. S., Reeves, J. C., & Elkind, G. S. (1987). Attention deficit, conduct, oppositional, and anxiety disorders in children: 1. A review of research on differentiating characteristics. *Journal of American Academy of Child and Adolescent Psychiatry, 26,* 133–143.

Wilson, J. Q. (1993). *The moral sense.* New York: Free Press.

Yell, M. L. (1989). Honig vs. Doe: The suspension and expulsion of handicapped students. *Exceptional Children, 56,* 60–69.

Zoccolillo, M. (1992). Co-occurrence of conduct disorders and its adult outcomes with depressive and anxiety disorders: A review. *Journal of American Academy of Child and Adolescent Psychiatry, 31,* 547–556.

# 8 ❧ Reading Disabilities

**Joseph K. Torgesen**
*Florida State University*

In seeking to honor Barbara Keogh's contributions to the study of children with learning disabilities, two themes that permeate her work were used as a framework for this chapter. First, I discuss our current understanding of reading disabilities from a general developmental perspective. Second, I try to draw attention to a few of the most interesting and important questions that currently confront the field. Over the past 2 decades, our general faith in a scientific approach to the study of learning disabilities has born considerable fruit. During that time, Keogh's voice (Keogh, 1993, 1994; Keogh & MacMillan, 1983) has been both strong and consistent in urging us to frame our questions about learning disabilities from a developmental perspective and answer them using the methods of science.

One of Keogh's major contributions has been to help us think about ways to deal with the problem of heterogeneity among children and adults who are categorized as "learning disabled." In fact, the very title of this chapter represents one solution to this problem. Because of the variety of learning disabilities manifested by children and adults, it is not possible to make coherent theoretical or empirical statements about the class as a whole (Keogh, Major-Kingsley, Omori-Gordon, & Reid, 1982; Torgesen, 1993), but rather we should narrow our focus to specific types of learning disabilities. Hence, this chapter focuses on disabilities in learning to read, rather than the larger category of learning disabilities in general.

However, even "reading disabilities" is too broad a term to encompass in a single theoretical treatment. Although it is universally acknowledged that the essence of good reading involves comprehension of written material, there are two broad types of skill that contribute to good reading comprehension. One set of skills is required in identifying words on the printed page, whereas another set of skills and knowledge is required in constructing the overall meaning of the text. The former types of skill are typically referred to as *word identification*, or *word decoding* skills, whereas the latter are referred to as *comprehension skills*. It is now widely accepted that efficient word identification skills are critically necessary for good reading comprehension (Gough, 1996). However, they are obviously not sufficient by themselves. One's ability to comprehend text depends on a very complex array of knowledge and skill. At the very least, it is affected by the size of one's vocabulary, the amount of one's general knowledge about the world, one's knowledge about grammar and organizing principles in text, one's ability to select and apply appropriate cognitive strategies (such as rereading, summarizing, prereading, and asking questions) to enhance comprehension, and one's interest in and motivation to understand the material being read (Beck, Perfetti, & McKeown, 1982; Bisanz & Vass, 1981; Borkowski, Weyhing, & Carr, l988; Brown & Palincsar, 1987).

One fact that has been clearly established over the last 2 decades of research on children with reading disabilities is that the most common form of this disorder has its primary impact on limiting children's ability to acquire accurate and fluent word identification skills (Morrison, 1987; Stanovich, 1988). Particularly for children whose general intelligence is within normal limits, it is their difficulty in reading words accurately that is the primary stumbling block to good reading comprehension. Accordingly, this chapter focuses on the majority of children with reading problems who experience difficulties acquiring the accurate and fluent word identification skills that have been shown to be so necessary to good reading comprehension.

## A DEVELOPMENTAL FRAMEWORK FOR UNDERSTANDING READING DISABILITIES

In order to place the most common learning difficulties of children with reading disabilities within a developmental perspective, it is helpful to understand what children need to learn when they begin reading instruction in kindergarten or first grade. Fortunately, the last 2 decades have produced a great deal of new knowledge about reading acquisition processes (Adams, 1990), so that we can describe with some confidence the learning challenges in this area.

### Initial Learning Challenges

The most important challenge that children face when they enter school and begin learning to read is to understand how the oral language they have learned to use with great facility is represented in print (Beck & Juel, 1995). This brings them face to face with the alphabet, and the alphabetic principle. English is an alphabetic language, meaning that words are represented in print roughly at the level of phonemes. A phoneme is the smallest unit of sound in a word that makes a difference to its identity. Thus, the word *cat* has three phonemes—/k/, /a/, /t/—and by changing the initial phoneme, we could make the words *fat*, *bat*, or *hat*. Altering the middle phoneme could produce *cut* or *cot*, and changing the last phoneme could make *cab*, *can*, or *cap*.

In English, the alphabetic principle presents two important learning challenges to children. First, individual phonemes are not readily apparent as individual entities in normal speech. When we say the word *cat*, the phonemes overlap with one another (they are coarticulated), so that we hear a single

burst of sound rather than three separate sounds. Coarticulating the phonemes in words (i.e., starting to pronounce the second phoneme, /r/, in the
word *from* while we are still saying the first phoneme, /f/) makes speech fluent, but it also makes it hard for many children to become aware of phonemes as individual segments of sound within words. Second, English is not
a perfectly alphabetic language. There is not always a regular one-to-one
correspondence between letters and phonemes, such that some single phonemes are represented by more than one letter (e.g. *ch, sh, wh, ai,* or *oi*), or a
single letter, (e.g., *x*) can stand for more than one phoneme. Furthermore,
sometimes the phoneme represented by a letter is modified by other letters in
a word (e.g., *mat* vs. *mate, bit* vs. *bight, note* vs. *notion*), or pronunciation of
parts of some words may not follow any regular letter-phoneme correspondence pattern, such as in *yacht* or *choir.*

The most obvious question arising from this brief discussion of the difficulties inherent in understanding the alphabetic principle and using
grapheme-phoneme correspondences as an aid to reading words (for more
extensive discussions of this issue, see Goodman, 1986; Smith, 1977; Venezky,
1970) is whether it is really necessary for children to understand the principle
and master its use in learning to read. Based on a massive amount of data acquired over the last 2 decades about the nature of skilled reading and reading
acquisition processes, the answer to this question is very strongly in the affirmative.

The evidence in support of this assertion is presented thoroughly in several
recent reviews (Ehri, 1998; Share & Stanovich, 1995), and space limitations
permit only a broad outline of the arguments here. These arguments start with
two important facts about the nature of word identification processes in skilled
readers. The first of these facts is that skilled readers fixate, or look directly at,
almost every word in text as they read (Rayner & Pollatsek, 1989). Skilled readers are able to process text rapidly, not because they only selectively sample
words and letters as they construct their meaning, but because they read the
individual words so rapidly and with so little effort. Skilled readers process
words as *orthographic units* (Ehri, 1998). The orthography of a language refers to the way it is represented visually. Hence, when researchers indicate that
words are processed as orthographic units, they are implying that they are recognized on the basis of an integrated visual representation.

A key piece of knowledge here, and the second important fact about text
processing in skilled readers, is that the mental representations used to identify
words as whole units (orthographic representations) include information
about all the letters in words (for reviews, see Just & Carpenter, 1987,
Patterson & Coltheart, 1987). Because many words are differentiated from
one another by only one or two letters, a global (or gestalt) image of a word is
not sufficient to help recognize it reliably. Instead, the memory image used in
reading words by sight must include information about all, or almost all, the
letters in a word's spelling. Even when reading very rapidly, the good reader
extracts information about all the letters in a word as part of the recognition
process.

Adams (1991), summarized these facts about word recognition processes in skilled readers this way:

> It has been proven beyond any shade of doubt that skillful readers process virtually each and every word and letter of text as they read. This is extremely counter-intuitive. For sure, skillful readers neither look nor feel as if that's what they do. But that's because they do it so quickly and effortlessly. Almost automatically; with almost no conscious attention whatsoever, skillful readers recognize words by drawing on deep and ready knowledge of spellings and their connections to speech and meaning. (p. 207)

If the key to becoming a skilled reader is to acquire a large vocabulary of words that can be recognized fluently and accurately by sight, then the next question we must consider is how these orthographic representations are normally acquired.

## Processes Involved in the Normal Growth of Word Reading Skill

Share and his colleagues (Share, 1995; Share & Jorm, 1987; Share & Stanovich, 1995) have presented a compelling case for the role of *phonemic reading skills* in the development of fully specified (complete) orthographic representations of words. Phonemic reading skills involve using information about letter-sound correspondences to completely or partially "sound out" words in text. In Share's model, as well as in Ehri's (1998) discussions of the growth of orthographic reading skills, emergent skills in phonemic decoding provide the basis for acquiring accurate orthographic representations of words beginning very early in the learning process.

A central tenet of Share and Stanovich's (1995) argument involves the importance of "reading through" each word phonemically as it is first being acquired. If children use phonemic cues to derive an approximate pronunciation for a word in text, and combine this approximate pronunciation with contextual cues to identify the fully correct pronunciation, the prior attention to individual letters that is involved in phonemic decoding familiarizes the child with the word's spelling.

Ehri (1998) suggested that orthographic representations are built from an "amalgamation" or linking of the phonemic segments in a word with graphemic units in the word's spelling. For example, acquiring orthographic knowledge about words involves such things as learning that the middle vowel sound in *kite* is represented by a single letter (signaled by the final *e*), the same middle vowel sound in *night* is represented by three letters, whereas the same vowel sound in *pie* is represented by two letters. A great deal of orthographic knowledge is word specific: It is knowledge about the particular ways that the phonemes in a given word are represented in its spelling. As children's increasingly developed phonemic reading skills lead to more detailed analysis of the internal structure of words in print, they begin to acquire increasingly explicit and more fully specified orthographic representations. An orthographic representation is fully specified when it contains information about all the letters in the word's spelling.

Thus, for a word to be added to a child's orthographic reading vocabulary, its *exactly* correct pronunciation must be associated several times with its *exactly* correct spelling. It is important to note here that children encounter far too many new words in the later stages of elementary school for all the words to be directly taught by teachers. For example, Nagy and Herman (1987) reported analyses suggesting that the average fifth grader encounters about 10,000 new words during the year! For a word to be added to a child's orthographic reading vocabulary, it must be encountered and pronounced correctly several times. Unless a child has the phonemic skills to ensure that word reading is relatively accurate (guessing from context alone produces too many errors; Gough, 1983), it is extremely difficult to acquire enough fully specified orthographic representations to support fluent and accurate reading.

A final argument for the importance of phonemic reading skills comes from a consideration of the wide range of frequencies of words in text. Although children gradually come to read more and more words orthographically, because there are so many words in children's vocabularies that occur relatively infrequently in print, the period in which orthographic representations are being formed extends far past the early elementary school years.

For example, Carroll, Davies, and Richman (1971) sampled 5,088,721 words from school texts in Grades 3 through 8, and counted the number of times each word occurred. Of the 86,741 different words that occurred in the text, the most frequent word was *the*, which occurred 73,000 times in *every* million words the 100th most frequent word was *know* (1,000 in a million), the 1,000[th] most frequent was *pass* (86 in a million), and the 5,000[th] most frequent was *vibrate* (10 in a million). There were many supposedly "common" words that children are expected to know—such as *crayon, fiction, sweater, pebble, horrible, and disappointment*—which occurred fewer than 10 times in the amount of reading an individual child could normally be expected to do in a year! Given the low frequency with which so many words appear, it is apparent that, if these words are to be read accurately, phonemic reading skills need to be in good working order.

The problem of low-frequency words is compounded by the fact that the information conveyed by a word in a passage varies inversely with its frequency (Finn, 1977–1978). Less-frequent words are usually more important to the meaning of a passage than are words that occur more frequently. Furthermore, it is precisely these less-frequent words that are the most difficult to guess from context. Gough (1983) showed that trying to guess a less frequent content word's identity on the basis of context alone will produce an error almost 90% of the time. Thus, in order to accurately identify many infrequent words that are critical to the meaning of text (and thus to acquire the practice necessary for forming orthographic representations), it is essential for children, even in late elementary school, to have strong phonemic reading skills they can use to supplement their orthographic and context-based word identification skills.

Concluding Caveat

Can a child become a good reader without acquiring strong phonetic reading skills? Campbell and Butterworth (1985) reported the case of a female college student who was discovered when a class she was attending was asked to spell a set of nonwords. She was almost completely unable to do this, and when they tested her further by asking her to read unfamiliar words, she showed a very low level of phonemic reading ability. However, her word reading skills and passage comprehension were average for the college class she was attending. In describing her history, she indicated that she had experienced a great deal of difficulty learning to read during the elementary years, but had persevered and realized that she would just have to "memorize all the words." Further testing showed that her verbal IQ was substantially above average, and she also had very strong visual memory skills. Thus, under some circumstances, it may be possible to become a relatively good reader with very poor phonetic reading skills. However, the vast preponderance of evidence suggests that this is highly unlikely in the absence of special conditions such as those pertaining to this case study (Gough, 1996).

## THE CRITICAL PROBLEM IN READING DISABILITIES

In fact, the most salient academic difficulty experienced by children with reading disabilities involves learning to understand and apply the alphabetic principle in translating between written and oral language (Bruck, 1990; Castles & Coltheart, 1993; Rack, Snowling, & Olson, 1992; Stanovich & Siegel, 1994). Children with this particular learning disability have trouble with the very first learning challenge described earlier. It is especially difficult for them to become aware of the individual phonemes in the words of their oral language, and thus they have a difficult time understanding the way that print represents speech. They also have difficulties learning correspondences between individual letters and the sounds (phonemes) they represent, and they have special problems in applying letter-sound knowledge in "sounding out" novel words. Given the important role that phonemic processes play in supporting normal reading growth, it is not surprising that children with this type of reading disability also find it very difficult to develop the fluent and accurate orthographic reading skills that are critical to good reading comprehension.

The Nature of the Underlying Cognitive Processing Disability

There is now a very strong consensus that the problems that children experience in acquiring phonetic reading skills are caused by variation among children "in the phonological component of their natural capacity for language"(Liberman, Shankweiler, & Liberman, 1989, p. 1). Most speech scientists believe that the human brain is specifically adapted for processing various kinds of linguistic information (Bohannon & Warren-Leubecker, 1989). One set of linguistic processing abilities allows us to interpret the complex array of phonological information in speech without actually being aware of the individual phonemes themselves. Children with word-level reading disabilities have a subtle dysfunction of the phonological processing module that does not necessarily affect their ability to speak or to understand speech, but does interfere with their ability to take advantage of the alphabetic principle in reading. Share and Stanovich (1995) summarized the evidence this way:

> There is virtually unassailable evidence that poor readers, as a group, are impaired in a very wide range of basic cognitive tasks in the phonological domain. This applies both to reading disabled children with discrepancies from IQ and to those without such discrepancies. These deficits are consistently found to be domain-specific, longitudinally predictive, and not primarily attributable to non-phonological factors such as general intelligence, semantic, or visual processing. (p. 9)

Although the phonological processing difficulties of children with reading disabilities have been demonstrated on a wide range of tasks, the two types of task that consistently show the strongest relationship to the development of word reading skills are those that assess phonological awareness and rapid automatic naming. Tasks assessing phonological awareness require children to notice, think about, or manipulate the individual sounds in orally presented words (e.g., "What word begins with the same first sound as *cat—mit, car,* or *sit?*" or "What word do you get if you blend together the sounds /k/-/a/-/t/?"). Measures of rapid automatic naming require children to name, as rapidly as possible, series of up to 50 visually presented familiar items like colors, objects, digits, or letters. On these tasks, a small set of items (six different colors or digits) are randomly arranged in rows on a card.

In their original thinking about reading disabilities, Liberman, and her colleagues began by asking the question, "What is required of the child in reading a language but not in speaking or listening to it?" (Liberman, et al., 1989, p. 4). Their answer was that the child must master the alphabetic principle: "This entails an awareness of the internal phonological structure of words of the language, an awareness that must be more explicit than is ever demanded in the ordinary course of listening and responding to speech. If this is so, it should follow that beginning learners with a weakness in phonological awareness would be at risk" (p. 5).

Empirical research on this hypothesis has, indeed, amply verified that children who experience difficulties acquiring phonemic reading skills are, as a group, substantially impaired in their performance on tasks that assess awareness of the phonological structure of words using oral language tasks (Bowey, Cain, & Ryan, 1992; Fletcher et al., 1994; Stanovich & Siegel, 1994; Wagner, Torgesen, & Rashotte, 1994).

Beginning with the seminal work of Denckla (Denckla & Rudel, 1976), slow performance on measures of rapid automatic naming has also been shown to be characteristic of older children with severe word-level reading disabilities and longitudinally predictive of which children are at risk to develop these difficulties (Wagner, et al., 1997; Wolf, 1991). As an illustration of the impact of deficient phonological awareness and rapid naming ability on the growth of word reading skills, Fig. 8.1 presents data from our longitudinal project (Wagner et al., 1994; 1997) on the reading growth of children selected at the beginning of first grade to be in the bottom 20% of a randomly selected sample of 200 children in either phonological awareness, rapid naming ability, or both. The solid line represents average growth of all children who fell above the 20% on both abilities. Phonological awareness was assessed by three tasks that asked children either to blend sounds together or to identify individual sounds in words presented orally. Rapid automatic naming skill was assessed by two tasks that required children to name as rapidly as possible a series of 36 digits or letters that were printed on a card.

Children who began first grade below the 20th percentile of the sample in these abilities had obvious difficulties acquiring both phonemic reading skills and a strong sight-word reading vocabulary. In this study, our measure of phonemic reading skills was the Word Attack subtest from the Woodcock Reading Mastery Test-Revised (Woodcock, 1987), and the measure of sight-word growth was the Word Identification subtest from the same test. The numbers at the right of the graphs represent average reading grade level of each group at the end of fifth grade. Children whose phonological awareness fell below the 20th percentile at the beginning of first grade, for example, achieved an average grade level score on the Word Attack subtest of 2.3 at the end of fifth grade. Children who were in the bottom 20th percentile on *both* phonological awareness and rapid naming ability ended up almost 4 years behind in phonemic reading skills at the end of fifth grade, and experienced a similar decrement in performance on the Word Identification subtest.

## Double or Single Deficit?

The major controversy within the theory of phonologically based reading disabilities at present concerns the question of whether rapid automatic naming tasks belong within the family of phonological measures, or whether they measure different skills that influence aspects of reading growth other than the initial attainment of accuracy in using phonemic reading strategies. For example, Bowers and Wolf and their colleagues (Bowers, Golden, Kennedy, & Young, 1994; Bowers & Wolf, 1993a; Wolf, 1991) argued against viewing rapid automatic naming tasks as primarily phonological in nature, and instead emphasized the visual and speed components of these tasks. They proposed that rapid naming tasks assess the operation of a "precise timing mechanism" that is important in the formation of orthographic codes for words. They hypothesized, "that slow letter (or digit) naming speed may signal disruption of the automatic processes which support induction of orthographic patterns, which, in turn, result in quick word recognition" (Bowers & Wolf, 1993a, p. 70).

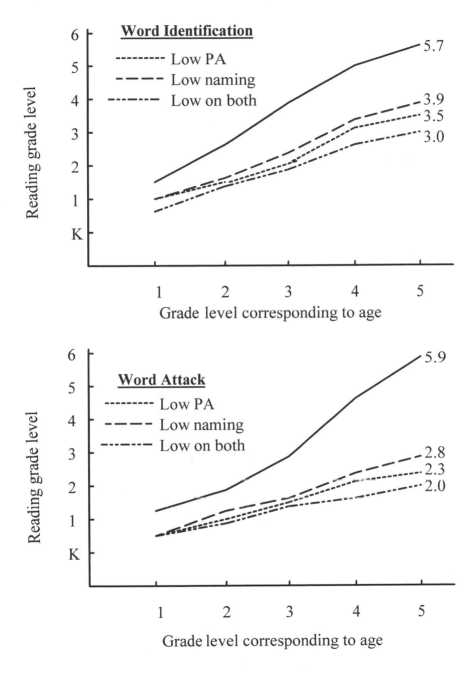

FIG. 8.1. Growth in word reading skills from first to fifth grade in children selected to be low in phonological awareness and rapid naming ability at the beginning of first grade.

**165**

The controversy about the nature and role of individual differences in rapid automatic naming ability in causing reading difficulties stems from questions about the sufficiency of poor phonetic reading skills as an explanation of problems establishing orthographic representations and moving into fluent reading. In fact, Bowers and Wolf (1993b) proposed a "double deficit hypothesis" in which problems in phonological abilities (primarily assessed by difficulties performing phonological awareness tasks) interfere with acquisition of phonemic reading strategies; and deficiencies in a "precise timing mechanism" (assessed by rapid automatic naming tasks) cause special difficulties acquiring orthographic representations and reading fluency. It is beyond the scope of this chapter to detail the evidence on either side of this controversy (see Bowers et al., 1994; Bowers & Wolf, 1993b; Torgesen & Burgess, 1998; Torgesen, Wagner, Rashotte, Burgess, & Hecht, 1997, for a more complete discussion of this issue).

However, if Bowers and Wolf are correct, combinations of deficiencies in phonological ability and rapid naming skill would produce three different patterns of reading disability: (a) children with only a phonological deficiency who might show initial delays in word reading accuracy, but then, with proper instruction and practice, eventually become accurate and fluent readers; (b) children with only rapid naming problems who might show no delays in early acquisition of accurate phonemic reading strategies but would be limited in growth of fluent reading skills; and, (c) children with both kinds of difficulties who would remain more severely impaired in reading than would children in either of the other two groups. Although there can be little doubt that these different patterns of word reading growth do exist (Spear-Swerling & Sternberg, 1994), it is still open to question whether they result from a single family of cognitive limitations (phonological disability as assessed by both phonological awareness and rapid naming tasks) and are produced by different patterns of instruction, practice, and motivation; or whether they reflect the operation of two different intrinsic cognitive limitations.

## Summary, Stipulations, and Remaining Questions

The thing we know with greatest certainty about word level reading disabilities is that problems in processing the phonological features of language cause difficulties learning to use phonemic reading skills as an aid to the identification of words in text. From theory and data about normal reading development, we can infer that these initial and chronic difficulties with phonemic reading processes interfere with the development of fluent orthographic reading skill. What remains controversial at present is whether another type of deficit, less specifically phonological and more related to the timing of mental processes in general, provides an additional interference with the development of orthographic representations in some children.

Two other facts about both phonemic and orthographic reading difficulties are also well established from current research. The first fact is that these disabilities exist within the continuum of normal reading skill variation, and do not constitute identifiably separate or unique distributions of reading skill (Shaywitz, Escobar, Shaywitz, Fletcher, & Makuch, 1992). In other words, it is apparent that "talent" for processing phonological information exists on a continuum from completely normal (or even hypernormal) to severely impaired. It is the children and adults who occupy the lower end of the normal distribution of phonological "talent" that are identified by schools and clinics as reading disabled.

The second fact that is clear from research conducted over the past 2 decades is that phonologically based reading disabilities can be transmitted genetically. There is now evidence to suggest that approximately 50% of the variation in phonological abilities underlying word reading difficulties is transmitted genetically (Gayan, Datta, Castles, & Olson, 1997; Olson, Forsberg, & Wise, 1994). Phonologically based reading disabilities co-occur more often in twins than in siblings, and the concordance rate in monozygotic twins is much higher than in dizygotic twins (DeFries, Fulker, & LaBuda, 1987).

If a child has a genetically based weakness in phonological processing ability, does this imply that these skills cannot be improved through appropriate instruction and training? Not if we take as evidence the voluminous literature (Levin, Benton, & Grossman, 1982) showing that cognitive dysfunction caused by verifiable, overt brain damage can be improved by specific instructional activities. In fact, we are beginning to acquire strong evidence that the right kind of instructional intervention, offered with sufficient intensity, can have a very substantial impact on the reading growth of children with even the severest phonological processing disabilities, given that their general intelligence levels fall within broadly normal limits.

## INTERVENTIONS FOR CHILDREN WITH WORD LEVEL READING DISABILITIES

If the goal of preventive and remedial instruction for children with reading disabilities is to help them acquire reading skills similar to those of their nondisabled peers, then there are several very clear implications for instructional practice from current knowledge about normal reading growth and reading disabilities. The content of reading instruction should seek to:

1. *Stimulate the Growth of Phonological Awareness as the Basis for Understanding and Applying the Alphabetic Principle in Decoding Novel Words.* This principle is based on evidence that individual differences in phonological awareness are causally related to the acquisition of phonemic reading skills, and children with poor phonemic decoding skills are consistently weak in phonological awareness.

2. *Foster the Early Growth of Phonemic Reading Skills as the Basis for Early Independence in Word Identification and Gradual Development of Fully Specified Orthographic Representations.* This principle is based on knowledge that the path to accurate and fluent visually based word reading ability goes through the early development and utilization of phonemic reading strategies. This may be the most controversial principle, because this involves teaching to the weakness of children with reading disabilities rather than to their strengths. Previous research and clinical evidence has also shown that it is very difficult for these children to acquire functional phonemic reading skills (Lovett, Warren-Chapin, Ransby, & Borden, 1990; Lyon, 1985; Snowling & Hulme, 1989). Nevertheless, given the importance of phonemic reading skills in most scientific accounts of reading growth (Adams, 1990; Ehri, 1998, Share & Stanovich, 1995), it seems essential to address this issue if children with word level reading disabilities are to become functional, adaptive, and independent readers.

3. *Build Accurate and Fluent Print-Based, Visually-Driven, Word Identification Skills.* This principle requires that instruction address the question of helping children with reading disabilities utilize their phonetic reading skills, and other word identification strategies, to build a rich orthographic reading vocabulary. For example, we know that phonological reading skills provide necessary but not entirely sufficient support for the development of good orthographic reading ability. That is, a child may be able to identify words accurately by using phonological/analytic strategies, but if these skills are not applied in extensive exposure to print, the development of a rich orthographic reading vocabulary will not take place (Cunningham & Stanovich, 1991; Stanovich & West, 1989). It may also be helpful to explicitly teach children how to use context to constrain their search for correct pronunciations of words in print (Tunmer & Chapman, 1995) and to explicitly teach them how to identify and search for "chunks" within words that are larger than single grapheme-phoneme units (Gaskins, Ehri, Cress, O'Hara, & Donnelly, 1996; Henry & Redding, 1996).

4. *Assist Children With Dyslexia to Apply Their Fluent and Accurate Word Reading Skills to Comprehend the Meaning of Print.* Although children whose general verbal abilities are adequately developed already possess most of the knowledge and skill required to construct the meaning of print, they still may need some special help to enhance their reading comprehension. For example, if the acquisition of their word reading skills has been slow, and most of their reading instruction has focused on word identification skills, they may lag behind their normally developing peers in understanding and utilizing a range of reading strategies that can enhance print comprehension, or repair it if it breaks down (Brown, Palincsar, & Purcell, 1986).

Examples of Relatively Successful Interventions

Although research on interventions for children with reading disabilities has a very long and rich history (Clark & Uhry, 1995), I focus here on three studies that have been conducted within the context of the knowledge about reading and reading disabilities that I have already discussed. All three of these studies investigated preventive interventions with children just beginning to learn to read, and they all focused on children with specific difficulties in processing phonological information.

In the first study (Brown & Felton, 1990; Felton 1993), children were selected for participation on the basis of delays in the development of phonological processing skills in kindergarten. Children who fell below the 16th percentile of the sample in these abilities were randomly assigned to receive instruction that emphasized either early acquisition of phonetic reading skills or meaning-based strategies for word identification. The instruction took place in groups of eight, and it was led by specially trained teachers who provided essentially all of the reading instruction the children received in first and second grades.

At the end of second grade, children in the group that emphasized phonetic reading strategies were generally stronger on all reading measures, although the reliability, or statistical significance, of these differences was mixed. In a later reanalysis of the data from this study using children with the most severe phonological disabilities, Felton (1993) presented evidence that children in the phonics-emphasis condition were able to perform significantly better than children in the meaning-based condition on the most difficult reading tasks that involved reading polysyllabic real words and nonwords. The overall pattern of results from this study suggests that the code-oriented instruction had a substantial positive effect on both the phonemic and the real-word reading abilities of children at risk for the development of phonologically based reading disorders.

Two other aspects of the data from Brown and Felton (1990) are very important. First, the average phonemic reading skills of children in the phonics-oriented instruction group were very close to those of normal readers at the end of second grade. However, approximately one fourth of the group was at least a year behind in the development of phonemic reading skill at this point. Because children in this group were originally drawn from the bottom 16% of all children in terms of their phonological abilities, and the intervention was relatively unsuccessful with one fourth of them, we can project that the intervention described in this study would be insufficient to prevent reading problems in about 4% of all children in elementary school.

Vellutino and his colleagues (1996) reported results from a very successful early intervention effort in which children who were experiencing severe difficulties acquiring word-level reading skills in first grade received individual tutoring during the second semester. The tutoring was administered for 30 minutes per day over the course of the semester, and it emphasized instruction in word-level reading strategies. This study was not designed to compare instructional methods, but rather to determine what percentage of the population would prove resistant to well-designed early intervention. The children came from a middle- to upper-middle-class suburban setting, and the average intelligence of even the lowest performing groups was slightly above average. Children from the bottom 15% in reading ability who had either verbal or performance IQ above 90 were included in the study.

At the end of first grade, about 16% of the intervention sample remained seriously impaired in basic word reading skills (below the 15th percentile), which represented about 1.5% of the total first-grade population. If children who were found to remain moderately impaired in reading (between 15th and 30th percentiles) were added to this group, a total of 3% of the population could be said to suffer continuing reading problems after 1 semester of high-quality tutorial reading instruction. Even after an additional semester of tutoring in second grade, the 1.5% of children in the very bottom group remained seriously impaired in their word level reading skills.

We (Torgesen, Wagner, & Rashotte, 1997) recently also completed a prevention study in which children were selected in kindergarten because of extremely poor performance (bottom 12%) on measures of prereading knowledge and phonological awareness. Only children whose estimated general verbal intelligence was above 75 were included in the sample. The 180 children selected for the study were randomly assigned to four instructional conditions: (a) phonological awareness training at an oral/motor level plus synthetic phonics instruction (PASP); (b) implicit phonological awareness training plus phonics instruction embedded within real-word reading and spelling activities (EP); (c) a regular classroom support group receiving individual instruction to support the goals of the regular classroom reading program (RCS); and (d) a no-treatment control group. The RCS group received individual tutoring in the activities and skills taught in the regular classroom reading program, and primarily served as a control for the added intensity of individual instruction.

Children in each instructional condition were provided with 80 minutes of individual supplemental instruction in reading each week during the 2 1/2 year intervention period. Two of these 20-minute instructional sessions were led by certified teachers, and two of the sessions were led by instructional aides who followed the teacher's instructions to reinforce what the children learned in the previous teacher-led session. Over the course of the study, the children received a total of about 88 hours of supplemental instruction (47 hours from teachers, and 41 hours from aides).

The primary instructional contrast between the two experimental/instructional conditions (PASP and EP) involved the degree of explicitness of instruction in phonological awareness and phonetic reading skills as well as the extent of focused practice on these skills. The most alphabetically explicit approach, which we have labeled Phonological Awareness Plus Synthetic Phonics (PASP), was based almost exclusively on the Auditory Discrimination in Depth method developed by Lindamood and Lindamood (1984).

In Table 8.1, scores on the Word Attack, Word Identification, and Passage Comprehension subtests from the Woodcock Reading Mastery Test–Revised (Woodcock, 1987) tests are presented in age-based standard score units (mean = 100, SD = 15), so that we can estimate the extent to which the reading skills of children in each group approached normal levels for children their age. The data in this table represent the performance of all children who remained in the study at the end of the instructional period. Most of the children were finishing second grade, although a total of about 26% of the children from the total sample were retained in either kindergarten or first grade, and so were finishing first grade. Rates of retention differed across instructional condition, with children in the PASP group showing the smallest rate (9%), and rates for the EP, RCS, and no-treatment groups being 25%, 30%, and 41%, respectively.

Overall group differences were statistically significant only for the Word Attack and Word Identification standard scores. Follow-up contrasts showed that the PASP group was significantly stronger than all other groups on the Word Attack test, but the only reliable difference on Word Identification was between the PASP group and the no-treatment control. Although overall differences were not statistically reliable for the Passage Comprehension subtest, the PASP group once again performed significantly better than did the no-treatment group.

One of the most important things to notice in Table 8.1 is that children in the PASP group attained a standard score of 99.4 on the Word Attack subtest, and a score of 98.2 on the Word Identification measure. These scores are right at average levels for children their age. We were also able to estimate an age-based standard score for experimental measures of word and nonword reading fluency because of the availability of local norms for these tests. For the nonword efficiency measure the average standard score of children in the PASP group was 102.6, and for the word efficiency measure, it was 96.2. These data suggest that the context-free phonemic reading skills and word

## TABLE 8.1
### Reading Scores for All Groups at the End of Second Grade

| Measure | Group | | | | | | | |
| --- | --- | --- | --- | --- | --- | --- | --- | --- |
| | Control (N = 32) | | RCS (N = 37) | | PAS (N = 33) | | EP (N = 36) | |
| | M | SD | M | SD | M | SD | M | SD |
| Word Attack | 81.6 | 17.1 | 86.7 | 19.4 | 99.4 | 16.8 | 86.7 | 13.1 |
| Word Identification | 86.3 | 17.8 | 92.0 | 15.5 | 98.2 | 17.9 | 92.1 | 14.5 |
| Passage Comprehension | 85.2 | 15.7 | 86.4 | 14.8 | 91.7 | 14.5 | 87.4 | 15.6 |

reading skills of children in the PASP group were the same as those of "average" children in terms of both accuracy and fluency. It should be noted that the comprehension standard score for children in the PASP condition was almost exactly equivalent to the average verbal IQ (91) for the group. It is likely that this comprehension score is limited by the children's general language comprehension ability and does not reflect the influence of poor word reading skills, as is commonly the case with children who have phonologically based reading disabilities.

Although the phonemic reading skills of children in the PASP condition approached average levels for the group as a whole, there was considerable variability in response to instruction within the group. Within this condition, 24% of the children remained more than one standard deviation below normal in these skills at the end of training. This means that the PASP treatment, as delivered in this study, was relatively ineffective in "normalizing" the phonemic reading skills of approximately 2.9% of children in the total population from which our treatment sample (bottom 12%) was selected.

## Summary of Early Intervention Results

These three studies, and others that could be cited (Foorman, et al., 1998; Olson, Wise, Johnson, & Ring, 1997; Torgesen, Wagner, Rashotte, Alexander, & Conway, 1997), support two very firm conclusions about interventions for children with phonologically based reading disabilities. First, it is clearly possible to bring the average phonemic reading skills of children falling beneath the 15th percentile in phonological abilities into the average range by the end of second grade, if appropriate instruction is delivered with sufficient intensity. Second, instructional methods that are most effective in accomplishing this goal contain relatively more explicit and systematic instruction in phonological awareness and phonemic reading strategies than do less effective methods. Two of the prevention studies discussed here utilized one-on-one tutorial methods, whereas the other study employed instructional groups consisting of eight children. However, children in the latter study received many more total hours of instruction within their groups than did the children in the studies employing tutorial methods.

Another way in which these three prevention studies differed from one another is in the range of sociocultural and economic differences among the children who were taught. The study reported by Vellutino and colleagues (1996) included only suburban children from middle- to upper-middle-class homes, whereas children in the other two studies were drawn from much more diverse family/economic environments. In their analysis of child characteristics that predicted response to intervention, Torgesen, Wagner, and Rashotte (1997) reported that socioeconomic status, along with entering levels of phonological ability and classroom teacher ratings of behavior, was consistently related to rate of reading growth in the intervention conditions. Socioeconomic status was estimated from parental occupation and education levels. This sociocultural/family background difference among samples might help to explain the slightly different percentages of children who remained poor readers in the three studies, because differences in home environment indexed by socioeconomic status do constitute an additional risk factor for early difficulties learning to read (Bowey, 1995; Warren-Leubecker & Carter, 1988).

Although the conclusions that can be drawn from these studies are important, they represent only a beginning in the development of a systematic, scientifically established knowledge base about instructional strategies for children with reading disabilities. What is not clear from these studies (or from any available research) is that phonologically more explicit instructional programs lead to reliably better orthographically based reading skills or stronger reading comprehension in children with phonologically based reading disabilities than do methods that are less explicit phonologically but devote more time to providing opportunities to read, write, and practice comprehension of connected text. Given that the ultimate impact of strong phonemic reading skills on reading growth can only be assessed over a considerable period of time, extensive follow-up of children from both preventive and remedial interventions will be required in order to determine the ultimate value of phonologically explicit instructional programs for reading disabled children.

Another reason for careful follow-up of children from these prevention studies is to determine whether they are able to maintain a normal rate of reading growth without further intervention. These data are ultimately important in determining whether any of the instructional conditions studied thus far is adequate to the task of "preventing" reading disabilities, and they assume particular importance in light of reported (Shanahan & Barr, 1995) failures of many children who have gone through the widely popular Reading Recovery program to maintain normal rates of reading growth through elementary school.

Another point that should not be neglected is that a significant percentage of children have remained poor readers even within the best instructional conditions examined so far. Therefore, we still do not know about the conditions that need to be in place for children with the most severe phonological disabilities (bottom 1% to 4%), who have broadly normal general intelligence, to acquire adequate early reading skills. In a remedial study we are currently conducting (Torgesen et al., 1997), we are beginning to find evidence that the number of children who remain poor phonemic readers after the intervention is related to both the explicitness and the intensity of the instructional program. This, of course, makes good sense if we accept the idea that children with serious reading disabilities require both more explicit and more intense instruction than do other children in order to acquire good reading skills. It also suggests that, if we are to seriously address the question of instruction for our most seriously disabled students, both those who fund research and those who conduct it will need to provide for the expense and effort required to examine more complex and intensive interventions.

Other Important Remaining Issues

The two most important remaining issues in the study of reading disabilities involve the validity of current widespread diagnostic practices and the viability of early identification procedures. Actually, questions about the diagnostic validity of widely used discrepancy-based definitions of reading disabilities have been quite firmly resolved by research, but the answers from science have yet to be implemented in practice.

Traditional practices that defined reading disabilities in terms of a discrepancy between general intelligence and reading level made the assumption that *specific* reading disability (reading ability discrepant from intelligence) has a different etiology, involves different cognitive impairments, requires a different kind of intervention, and has a different prognosis than do the reading difficulties of children whose poor reading skills are consistent with their level of general intelligence. There are now at least three kinds of evidence against this assumption.

First, early reports (Rutter & Yule, 1975) that reading disabilities were distributed bi-modally (implying that there were two different underlying populations of poor readers) have not been replicated in more recent, well designed epidemiological investigations (Shaywitz et al., 1992; Silva, McGee, & Williams, 1985; Stevenson, 1988). Second, well-controlled investigations of the cognitive profiles of discrepant and nondiscrepant poor readers indicate that they do not differ in the cognitive abilities most related to word-level reading difficulties (Fletcher et al., 1994; Stanovich & Siegel, 1994). Third, discrepant and nondiscrepant groups show a similar rate of growth in word-level reading skill, both during early elementary school (Foorman, Francis, & Fletcher, 1995) and into early adolescence (Francis, Shaywitz, Stuebing, Shaywitz, & Fletcher, 1995).

Stanovich and Siegel (1994) summed up the evidence about the validity of discrepancy-based definitions of specific reading disabilities in the following way:

> Neither the phenotypic nor the genotypic indicators of poor reading are correlated in a reliable way with IQ discrepancy. If there is a special group of children with reading disabilities who are behaviorally, cognitively, genetically, or neurologically different, it is becoming increasingly unlikely that they can be easily identified by using IQ discrepancy as a proxy for the genetic and neurological differences themselves. Thus, the basic assumption that underlies decades of classification in research and educational practice regarding reading disabilities is becoming increasingly untenable. (p. 48)

Movement away from discrepancy-based definitions of reading disability toward more inclusive definitions is bound to raise many difficult issues in practice (e.g., how to serve the expanded number of children with genuine disabilities in reading). However, it should also materially assist in the movement toward early identification and treatment of children at risk for reading failure. The possibility of providing special assistance to children before they establish a significant track record of failure in reading raises questions about our current ability to identify which children are most in need of preventive interventions.

If the goal is to identify children at risk for reading failure before formal reading instruction begins, we are still some distance away from being able to do this with a high degree of precision. For example, there have been a number of recent attempts to use measures of early phonological awareness given either in kindergarten or at the beginning of first grade (Catts, 1996). With the exception of two studies (Hurford et al., 1993, 1994) that measured phonological and early reading skills at the beginning of first grade, however, these studies have universally had high numbers of false positives (children who are predicted to be poor readers but turn out to be good readers), with rates ranging from 23% to 69%.

Using data from our own longitudinal study of phonological processes and reading, we (Torgesen, Burgess, & Rashotte, 1996) used a combination of three measures (phonological awareness, rapid naming ability, and letter-name knowledge) to predict which children would fall in the bottom 10% in word reading ability by the beginning of second grade. When we attempted to identify only 10% of the children as "at risk," our overall identification accuracy was 91%, with a false positive rate of only 5%, but a false negative rate (children who were not identified as at risk, but who ended in the bottom 10%) of 48%. This false negative rate means that approximately half the children who eventually ended up in the bottom 10% of readers were missed in the kindergarten prediction. However, if we allowed our prediction equation to identify 20% of the kindergarten children as "at risk", the false positive rate escalated to approximately 14%, but the false negative rate was reduced to 8%. These rates suggest that if schools were able to provide preventive interventions for 20% of kindergarten children, only about 1 in 10 children destined to fall in the bottom 10% of readers by second grade would be missed in that early screening.

Given what we now know about the nature of reading disabilities, and reading skill acquisition in general, it seems that diagnostic issues and early identification procedures will only be a small part of a real, school- and family-based solution for children with reading disabilities. As we continue to add to the scientific knowledge base in this area, we must also face important challenges in the area of teacher and parent training (Moats, 1995). Additionally, as the science of reading disabilities matures we must find more effective ways to bring science into the classroom. In few other areas is the gap between what we know how to do and what is actually being done so large. Closing this gap is clearly one of our greatest challenges for the immediate future.

## ACKNOWLEDGMENTS

The research reported in this chapter was supported by grant numbers HD23340 and HD30988 from the National Institute of Child Health and Human Development, and by grants from the National Center for Learning Disabilities and the Donald D. Hammill Foundation.

## REFERENCES

Adams, M. J. (1990). *Beginning to read: Thinking and learning about print.* Cambridge, MA: MIT Press.

Adams, M. J. (1991). A talk with Marilyn Adams. *Language Arts, 68,* 206–212.

Beck, I. L., & Juel, C. (1995). The role of decoding in learning to read. *American Educator, 19,* 8–20.

Beck, I. L., Perfetti, C. A., & McKeown, M. G. (1982). Effects of long-term vocabulary instruction on lexical access and reading comprehension. *Journal of Educational Psychology, 74,* 506–521.

Bisanz, G. L., & Vass, J. F. (1981). Sources of knowledge in reading comprehension: cognitive development and expertise in a content domain. In A. Lesgold & C. Perfetti (Eds.), *Interactive processes in reading (pp. 123–123-147).* Hillsdale, NJ: Lawrence Erlbaum Associates.

Bohannon, J. N., & Warren-Leubecker, A. (1989). Theoretical approaches to language acquisition. In J. B. Gleason (Ed.), *The development of language* (2nd ed., pp. 152-181).) Columbus, OH: Merrill.

Borkowski, J. G., Weyhing, R. S., & Carr, M. (1988). Effects of attributional retraining on strategy-based reading comprehension in learning-disabled students. *Journal of Educational Psychology, 80,* 46–53.

Bowers, P., Golden, J., Kennedy, A., & Young, A. (1994) Limits upon orthographic knowledge due to processes indexed by naming speed. In V. W. Berninger (Ed.) *The varieties of orthographic knowledge I: Theoretical and developmental issues, (*pp. 173–218). Dordrecht, The Netherlands: Kluwer.

Bowers, P. G., & Wolf, M. (1993a). Theoretical links between naming speed, precise timing mechanisms and orthographic skill in dyslexia. *Reading and Writing: An Interdisciplinary Journal, 5,* 69–85.

Bowers, P. G. & Wolf, M. (1993b, March). *A double-deficit hypothesis for developmental reading disorders.* Paper presented to meetings of the Society for Research in Child Development, New Orleans.

Bowey, J. A. (1995). Socioeconomic Status differences in preschool phonological sensitivity and first-grade reading achievement. *Journal of Educational Psychology, 87,* 476–487.

Bowey, J. A., Cain, M. T., & Ryan, S. M. (1992). A reading-level design study of phonological skills underlying fourth-grade children's word reading difficulties. *Child Development, 63,* 999–1011.

Brown, A. L., & Palincsar, A. S. (1987). Reciprocal teaching of comprehension strategies: a natural history of one program for enhancing learning. In L. Borkowski & L. D. Day(Eds.), *Intelligence and exceptionality: New directions for theory, assessment, and instructional practices* (pp. 81–132). Norwood, NJ: Ablex.

Brown, A. L., Palincsar, A. S., & Purcell, L. (1986). Poor readers: Teach, don't label. In U. Neisser (Ed.) *The school achievement of minority children: New perspectives* (pp. 105–143). Hillsdale, NJ: Lawrence Erlbaum Associates.

Brown, I. S., & Felton, R. H. (1990). Effects of instruction on beginning reading skills in children at risk for reading disability. *Reading and Writing: An Interdisciplinary Journal, 2,* 223–241.

Bruck, M. (1990). Word-recognition skills of adults with childhood diagnoses of dyslexia. *Developmental Psychology, 26,* 439–454.

Campbell, R., & Butterworth, B. (1985). Phonological dyslexia and dysgraphia in a highly literate subject: A developmental case with associated deficits of phonemic processing and awareness. *The Quarterly Journal of Experimental Psychology, 37,* 435–475.

Carroll, J. B., Davies, P., & Richman, B. (1971). *Word frequency book.* Boston: Houghton Mifflin.

Castles, A., & Coltheart, M. (1993). Varieties of developmental dyslexia. *Cognition, 47,* 149–180.

Catts, H. (1996, March). Phonological awareness: A key to detection. Paper presented at the conference The Spectrum of Developmental Disabilities XVIII: Dyslexia. Johns Hopkins Medical Institutions, Baltimore, MD.

Clark, D. B. & Uhry, C. (1995). *Dyslexia: Theory and practice of remedial instruction.* Parkton, MD: York.

Cunningham, A. E., & Stanovich, K. E. (1991). Tracking the unique effects of print exposure in children: Associations with vocabulary, general knowledge, and spelling. *Journal of Educational Psychology, 83,* 264–274.

DeFries, J. C., Fulker, D. W., & LaBuda, M. C. (1987). Evidence for a genetic aetiology in reading disability of twins. *Nature, 329,* 537–539.

Denckla, M. B., & Rudel, R. (1976). Rapid automatized naming (R. A. N.): dyslexia differentiated from other learning disabilities. *Neuropsychologia, 14,* 471–479.

Ehri, L. C. (1998). Grapheme-phoneme knowledge is essential for learning to read words in English. In J. Metsala & L. Ehri (Eds.). *Word recognition in beginning reading.* (pp. 3–40). Hillsdale, NJ: Lawrence Erlbaum Associates.

Felton, R. H. (1993). Effects of instruction on the decoding skills of children with phonological-processing problems. *Journal of Learning Disabilities, 26,* 583–589.

Finn, P. J. (1977–1978). Word frequency, information theory, and cloze performance: A transfer feature theory of processing in reading. *Reading Research Quarterly, 23,* 510–537.

Fletcher, J. M., Shaywitz, S. E., Shankweiler, D. P., Katz, L., Liberman, I. Y., Stuebing, K. K., Francis, D. J., Fowler, A. E., & Shaywitz, B. A. (1994). Cognitive profiles of reading disability: Comparisons of discrepancy and low achievement definitions. *Journal of Educational Psychology, 86,* 6–23.

Foorman, B. R., Francis, D. J., & Fletcher, J. M. (1995, March). Growth of phonological processing skills in beginning reading: The lag versus deficit model revisited. Paper presented at the Society for Research on Child Development, Indianapolis, IN, March 31, 1995.

Foorman, B. R., Francis, D. J., Fletcher, J. M., Schatschneider, C., Mehta, P., & Beeler, T. (1998). The role of instruction in learning to read: Preventing reading failure in at-risk children. *Journal of Educational Psychology, 90,* 37–55.

Francis, D. J., Shaywitz, S. E., Stuebing, K. K., Shaywitz, B. A., & Fletcher, J. M. (1995, March). *Developmental lag versus deficit models of reading disability: A longitudinal, individual growth curves analysis.* Paper presented at the Society for Research in Child Development, Indianapolis, IN.

Gaskins, I. W., Ehri, L. C., Cress, C., O'Hara, C., & Donnelly, K. (1996). Procedures for word learning: Making discoveries about words. *The Reading Teacher, 50,* 312–327.

Gayan, J., Datta, H. E., Castles, A., & Olson, R. K. (1997, March). *The etiology of group deficits in word decoding across levels of phonological decoding and orthographic coding.* Paper presented at the Society for the Scientific Study of Reading, Chicago.

Goodman, K. (1986). *What's whole in whole language?* Portsmouth, NH: Heinemann.

Gough, P. B. (1983) Context, form and interaction. In K. Raynor (Ed.), *Eye movements in reading* (pp. 97-118) New York: Academic.

Gough, P. B. (1996). How children learn to read and why they fail. *Annals of Dyslexia, 46,* 3–20.

Henry, M. K. & Redding, N. C. (1996). *Patterns for success in reading and spelling: A multisensory approach to teaching phonics and word analysis.* Austin, TX: PRO-ED.

Hurford, D. P., Darrow, L. J., Edwards, T. L., Howerton, C. J., Mote, C. R., Schauf, J. D., & Coffey, P. (1993). An examination of phonemic processing abilities in children during their first-grade year. *Journal of Learning Disabilities, 26,* 167–177.

Hurford, D. P., Johnston, M., Nepote, P., Hampton, S., Moore, S., Neal, J., Mueller, A., McGeorge, K., Huff, L., Awad, A., Tatro, C., Juliano, C., & Huffman, D. (1994). Early identification and remediation of phonological-processing deficits in first-grade children at risk for reading disabilities. *Journal of Learning Disabilities, 27,* 647–659.

Just, M. A., & Carpenter, P. A. (1987). *The psychology of reading and language comprehension.* Boston: Allyn & Bacon.

Keogh, B. K. (1993). Linking purpose and practice: Social-political and developmental perspectives on classification. In G. R. Lyon, D. B. Gray, J. F. Kavanagh, & N. A. Krasnegor (Eds.), *Better understanding learning disabilities: New views from research and their implications for education and public policies* (pp. 311–323). Baltimore, MD: Paul H. Brookes.

Keogh, B. K. (1994). A matrix of decision points in the measurement of learning disabilities. In G. R. Lyon (Ed.), *Frames of reference for the assessment of learning disability* (pp. 15–26). Baltimore, MD: Brookes Publishing.

Keogh, B. K., & MacMillan, D. L. (1983). The logic of sample selection: Who represents what? *Exceptional Educational Quarterly, 4,* 84–96.

Keogh, B. K., Major-Kingsley, S., Omori-Gordon, H., Reid, H. P. (1982). *A system of marker variables for the field of learning disabilities.* Syracuse, NY: Alexander R. Luria Research Monograph Series, Syracuse University Press.

Levin, H. S., Benton, A. L., & Grossman, R. G. (1982*). Neurobehavioral consequences of closed head injury.* New York: Oxford University Press.

Liberman, I. Y., Shankweiler, D. P., & Liberman, A. M. (1989). The alphabetic principle and learning to read. In D. P. Shankweiler & I. Y. Liberman (Eds.), *Phonology and reading disability: Solving the reading puzzle* (pp. 1–33). Ann Arbor: University of Michigan Press.

Lindamood, C. H., & Lindamood, P. C. (1984). *Auditory discrimination in depth.* Austin, TX: PRO-ED.

Lovett, M. W., Warren-Chaplin, P. M., Ransby, M. J., & Borden, S. L. (1990). Training the word recognition skills of reading disabled children: Treatment and transfer effects. *Journal of Educational Psychology, 82,* 769–780.

Lyon, G. R. (1985). Identification and remediation of learning disability subtypes: Preliminary findings. *Learning Disabilities Focus, 1,* 21–35.

Moats, L. C. (1995). The missing foundation in teacher education. *American Educator, 19,* 9–51.

Morrison, F. J. (1987). The nature of reading disability: Toward an integrative framework. In S. Ceci (Ed.), *Handbook of cognitive, social, and neuropsychological aspects of learning disabilities* (pp. 33–63). Hillsdale, NJ: Lawence Erlbaum Associates.

Nagy, W. E., & Herman, P. A. (1987). Breadth and depth of vocabulary knowledge: Implications for acquisition and instruction. In M. McKeown & M. Curtis (Eds.*), The nature of vocabulary acquisition* (pp. 19–35). Hillsdale, NJ: Lawrence Erlbaum Associates.

Olson, R., Forsberg, H., & Wise, B. (1994). Genes, environment, and the development of orthographic skills. In V. W. Berninger (Ed.), *The varieties of orthographic knowledge I: Theoretical and developmental issues* (pp. 27–71).

Olson, R. K., Wise, B., Johnson, M., & Ring, J. (1997). The etiology and remediation of phonologically based word recognition and spelling disabilities: Are phonological deficits the "hole" story? In B. Blachman (Ed.), *Foundations of reading acquisition,* (pp. 305–326) Mahwah, NJ: Lawrence Erlbaum Associates.

Patterson, K. E., & Coltheart, V. (1987). Phonological processes in reading: A tutorial review. In M. Coltheart (Ed.) *Attention and performance, Vol. 12: The psychology of reading* (pp. 421–447). Hillsdale, NJ: Lawrence Erlbaum Associates.

Rack, J. P. Snowling, M. J., & Olson, R. K. (1992). The nonword reading deficit in developmental dyslexia: A review. *Reading Research Quarterly, 27,* 29–53.

Rayner, K. & Pollatsek, A. (1989). *The psychology of reading.* Englewood Cliffs, NJ: Prentice Hall.

Rutter, M., & Yule, W. (1975). The concept of specific reading retardation. *Journal of Child Psychology and Psychiatry, 16,* 181–197.

Shanahan, T. & Barr, R. (1995). Reading recovery: An independent evaluation of the effects of an early instructional intervention for at-risk learners. *Reading Research Quarterly, 30,* 958–996.

Share, D. L., (1995). Phonological recoding and self-teaching: Sine qua non of reading acquisition. *Cognition, 55,* 151–218.

Share, D. L. & Jorm, A. F. (1987). Segmental analysis: Co-requisite to reading, vital for self-teaching, requiring phonological memory. *European Bulletin of Cognitive Psychology, 7,* 509–513.

Share, D. L., & Stanovich, K. E. (1995). Cognitive processes in early reading development: A model of acquisition and individual differences. *Issues in Education: Contributions from Educational Psychology, 1,* 1-57.

Shaywitz, S. E., Escobar, M. D., Shaywitz, B. A., Fletcher, J. M., & Makuch, R. (1992). Evidence that dyslexia may represent the lower tail of a normal distribution of reading ability. *The New England Journal of Medicine, 326,* 145–150.

Silva, P. A., McGee, R., & Williams, S. (1985). Some characteristics of nine-year-old boys with general reading backwardness or specific reading retardation. *Journal of Child Psychology and Psychiatry, 20,* 407–421.

Smith, F. (1977) Making sense of reading and of reading instruction. *Harvard Educational Review, 47,* 386–395,

Snowling, M., & Hulme, C. (1989). A longitudinal case study of developmental phonological dyslexia. *Cognitive Neuropsychology, 6,* 379-401.

Spear-Swerling, L., & Sternberg, R. J. (1994). The road not taken: An integrative theoretical model of reading disability. *Journal of Learning Disabilities, 27,* 91–103.

Stanovich, K. E. (1988). Explaining the differences between the dyslexic and the garden-variety poor reader: The phonological-core variable-difference model. *Journal of Learning Disabilities, 21,* 590–604.

Stanovich, K. E., & Siegel, L. S. (1994). The phenotypic performance profile of reading-disabled children: A regression-based test of the phonological-core variable-difference model. *Journal of Educational Psychology, 86,* 24–53.

Stanovich, K. E., & West, R. F. (1989). Exposure to print and orthographic processing. *Reading Research Quarterly, 24,* 402-433.

Stevenson, J. (1988). Which aspects of reading disability show a "hump" in their distribution? *Applied Cognitive Psychology, 2,* 77–85.

Torgesen, J. K. (1993). Variations on theory in learning disabilities. In R. Lyon, D. Gray, N Krasnegor, & J. Kavenagh (Eds.), *Better understanding learning disabilities: Perspectives on classification, identification, and assessment and their implications for education and policy.* (pp. 153–170) Baltimore: Brookes Publishing.

Torgesen, J. K., & Burgess, S. R. (1998). Consistency of reading-related phonological processes throughout early childhood: Evidence from longitudinal correlational and instructional studies. In J. Metsala & L. Ehri (Eds.), *Word recognition in beginning literacy.* (pp. 168–188). Mahwah, NJ: Lawrence Erlbaum Associates.

Torgesen, J. K., Burgess, S., & Rashotte, C. A. (1996, April). Predicting phonologically based reading disabilities: What is gained by waiting a year? Paper presented at the annual meetings of the *Society for the Scientific Study of Reading,* New York.

Torgesen, J. K., Wagner, R. K., & Rashotte, C. A. (1997, April). *Prevention of reading disabilities: individual and group differences in response to treatment.* Paper presented at Society for the Scientific Study of Reading, Chicago.

Torgesen, J. K., Wagner, R. K., Rashotte, C. A., Alexander, A. W., & Conway, T. (1997). Preventive and remedial interventions for children with severe reading disabilities. *Learning Disabilities: An Interdisciplinary Journal., 8,* 51–62.

Torgesen, J. K., Wagner, R. K., Rashotte, C. A., Burgess, S. R., & Hecht, S. A. (1997). The contributions of phonological awareness and rapid automatic naming ability to the growth of word reading skills in second to fifth grade children. *Scientific Studies of Reading, 1,* 161–185.

Tunmer, W. E., & Chapman, J. W. (1995). Context use in early reading development: Premature exclusion of a source of individual differences? *Issues in Education, 1,* 97–100.

Vellutino, F. R., Scanlon, D. M., Sipay, E. R., Small, S. G., Pratt, A., Chen, R., & Denckla, M. B. (1996). Cognitive profiles of difficult-to-remediate and readily remediated poor readers: Early intervention as a vehicle for distinguishing between cognitive and experiential deficits as basic causes of specific reading disability. *Journal of Educational Psychology, 88,* 601–638.

Venezky, R. L. (1970). *The structure of English orthography.* The Hague, Netherlands: Mouton.

Wagner, R. K., Torgesen, J. K., & Rashotte, C. A. (1994). The development of reading-related phonological processing abilities: New evidence of bi-directional causality from a latent variable longitudinal study. *Developmental Psychology, 30,* 73–87.

Wagner, R. K., Torgesen, J. K., Rashotte, C. A., Hecht, S. A., Barker, T. A., Burgess, S. R., Donahue, J., & Garon, T. (1997). Changing causal relations between phonological processing abilities and word-level reading as children develop from beginning to fluent readings: A five-year longitudinal study. *Developmental Psychology, 33,* 468–479.

Warren-Leubecker, A., & Carter, B. W. (1988). Reading and growth in metalinguistic awareness: Relations to socioeconomic status and reading readiness skills. *Child Development, 59,* 738–742.

Wolf, M. (1991). Naming speed and reading: The contribution of the cognitive neurosciences. *Reading Research Quarterly, 26,* 123–141.

Woodcock, R. W. (1987). *Woodcock Reading Mastery Tests-Revised.* Circle Pines, MN: American Guidance Service.

# 9 🦐 Metacognition in Writing

**Bernice Y. L. Wong**
*Simon Fraser University*

The theoretical construct of metacognition originated from the observation that young children could readily learn a mnemonic strategy to enhance recall of objects, but showed little maintenance of it. To explain these findings, Flavell (1976) developed the construct of metacognition, which contains two aspects: awareness and self-regulation. *Awareness* refers to knowledge of one's cognitive strengths and weaknesses, and *self-regulation* refers to coordinating one's awareness with appropriate action. Subsequently, Brown (1980) applied the construct of metacognition to reading. She considered metacognitive skills to characterize thinking skills that occur generally in academic learning settings and that include reading and studying.

Metacognition in reading became a very fertile topic in research between the late 1970s and 1980s. In this research, younger and poor readers were found to have misconceptions about the purpose of reading: They considered it to be decoding accuracy instead of meaning construction. They were less able to match appropriate reading strategies with appropriate materials, and less flexible in allocating attention in reading (e.g., reading a textbook more attentively in preparation for a test, and reading a magazine less attentively). Moreover, poor readers do not self-monitor their own state of reading comprehension. Fortunately, poor readers' metacognitive skills in reading can be enhanced through suitable interventions. Baker and Brown (1984a, 1984b) provided excellent summaries of the research in metacognition in reading.

In contrast to reading, there is nascent interest in metacognition in writing, which refers to awareness of the purpose and process of writing and self-regulation of writing. *Awareness of the writing process* refers to an individual's awareness of clarity, organization, and evocation of interest in readers, among other audience needs. Awareness of these higher-order processes is distinguishable from lower-order processes such as the mechanics of spelling, punctuation, and neatness of handwriting. Additionally, *awareness of the writing process of writing* refers to understanding that writing involves three recursive subprocesses of planning, sentence generation, and revision. *Self-regulation in writing* refers to individuals regulating their cognitive processes in writing, their knowledge of writing, and the differential demands of different genres.

Good adult writers are aware of the social, communicative purpose of writing, and of audience needs. They are also aware of the cognitive processes of planning, sentence generating, and revising in writing. They regulate efficiently the distribution of their cognitive resources as they juggle the simultaneous demands of the subprocesses of writing (Flower & Hayes, 1980; Hayes & Flower, 1980). For example, they allocate attention to word choice, to clarity in writing, and to generation of interest in the reader. Simultaneously, they hold at bay attention to spelling errors, which they redress at the end of writing when they begin the revising and editing process. Moreover, good adult writers personify the recursive nature of the subprocesses in writing. They may revise their writing plans during the act of writing when they realize that initial ideas may be irrelevant, or they may add ideas that they now realize are highly relevant. Similarly, they may revise a sentence in the middle of writing it rather than wait until they complete the writing. Indeed, through internal dialogues, good adult writers serve as both writer and critic to their own ideas and writings. The writer generates ideas and text; the critic listens, reads, evaluates, and indicates where revisions are in order (Murray, 1982). Thus, good writers highlight the complex interweavings of metacognitive awareness and self-regulation in writing.

This chapter has two purposes: to trace children's development of the awareness of the purpose and process of writing and self-regulation in writing, and to examine research on the impact of instruction on children's development in metacognition of writing. The organization of the chapter parallels the two components in the definition of metacognition: awareness and self-regulation. Thus, the chapter begins with an examination of the research on the awareness of the writing purpose and process in writing in children and adolescents. Next examined is research on the impact of instruction on students' awareness aspects of metacognition. A summary of the research on the self-regulation aspects of writing follows. The chapter concludes with suggestions for future research.

## CHILDREN'S AWARENESS OF WRITING PURPOSE IN PRIMARY GRADES

### Are Children Aware of the Social Communicative Purpose of Writing?

The answer to this question appears to be in the affirmative. Shook, Marrion, and Ollila (1989) interviewed 108 children in Grades 1 and 2 about their conceptions of writing. They found that the young children enjoyed writing. The children wrote chiefly about animals, as well as notes and stories to their friends. Also, they preferred to write at home than at school. For this the authors proffered two plausible explanations: At home, the child's writing was modeled or helped by parents; and the parents probably accepted the child's writing unconditionally, so that the child did not anticipate typical criticism on spelling or other feedback about problems with mechanics. The children also stated observing their mothers to do the most writing.

More specifically, 94% of the children considered writing to be enjoyable, something they did at home. Fifty-seven percent of them preferred writing at home instead of at school. Sixty-eight percent stated that they wrote for a person other than teacher, such as parents, grandparents, siblings, and friends. Only 5% indicated neatness in handwriting to be a priority in whereas, while 12% stated that they needed to improve neatness in their handwriting.

That children in Grades 1 and 2 enjoyed writing stories about animals or notes to be read by persons other than the teacher suggests that they understood the social communicative purpose in writing, and derived their enjoyment of writing from that social communicative aspect (Shook et al., 1989). But the finding that children preferred to write at home rather than at school hints at what children in early grades may perceive as constraints to their writing, namely teachers' emphasis on neat handwriting and correct spelling, an emphasis not held by parents, grandparents, siblings or friends who were invited to read the children's writings at home.

## AWARENESS OF THE WRITING PROCESS IN YOUNG CHILDREN

Although aware of purposes and variations in quality of writing, initially children are more concerned with the "secretarial" aspects of writing, such as spelling and neatness of handwriting (Isaacson, 1992). With development, however, their awareness of processes contributing to good writing becomes more balanced as they come to embrace the importance of higher-order cognitive aspects of writing such as choice of words, ideas, and organization.

Wray (1994) described a study that investigated children's thinking about writing. The 475 participants consisted of four age groups of children ranging from 7 years to 11 years of age. The study examined the writing attributes that were named by the children in their writing responses "as the most important aspects of writing in their classes" (Wray, 1994, p. 46). Students' responses were categorized as either "secretarial" or "composition." Secretarial responses included spelling, neatness, length, punctuation, tools, and layout. Composition responses included words, ideas, structure, characters, and style (Wray, 1994)

Developmental variations in children's awareness of important aspects of writing were evident (Wray, 1994). Focusing first on total scores, across the four age groups the distribution of percentages in children's mention of secretarial attributes of writing ranged from a high of 79% (7 to 8 years old) to a low of 50% (10 to 11 years old). Thus, there was a progressive decline in children's concern with secretarial aspects of writing as they grew older. The oldest group showed a marked decline in their perception of the importance of the lower-order mechanical aspects of writing. Of the six subtypes of secretarial features of writing, concerns with spelling and neatness of handwriting ranked highest in percentage scores in the four groups. Again, there was a steady decline in such concerns as children matured.

Regarding composition, the reverse pattern was evident. Sixteen percent of the youngest children mentioned these elements, whereas 47% of the oldest identified composition elements. These data indicate a developmental increase in children's awareness of the importance of composition features from age 7 to 11.

Several studies have been conducted with older children (Englert, Raphael, Fear, & Anderson, 1988; Graham, Schwartz, & MacArthur, 1993; Wong, Wong, & Blenkinsop, 1989). Of interest and importance is the convergent nature of the data from these studies. They point to the consistent finding that normally achieving students in Grades 4 and 5, and Grades 7 through 10 appear to be well on track in developing awareness and knowledge of the writing process. They focus on function rather than form of writing, and command sufficient knowledge of procedural aspects of writing. In contrast, students with learning disabilities (LD) focus on form rather than function of the writing process. In particular, they put priority on mechanical aspects of writing such as spelling and neatness of handwriting. In sum, the data from these three studies consistently underscore the possession of more mature and articulate awareness and knowledge of the writing process and related aspects of metacognition in writing in normally achieving students.

Graham et al. (1993) and Wong et al. (1989) compared normally achieving students (NA) and students with learning disabilities (LD) on the following criteria: awareness of what good writing is about, and awareness of how writers write (the cognitive processes and strategies activated in the process of writing). In specific, Graham et al. interviewed students individually from grades 4, 5, 7, and 8. They found that students with LD in Grades 7 and 8 emphasized form over function in their conceptions of good writing. Their notion of a good paper was one devoid of spelling errors. In contrast, NA students in the same grades emphasized function over form in their conceptions of good writing. Sample responses illustrate the differential conceptions of good writing between NA students and students with LD. A typical NA student response to the question of "What is good writing?" was: "Have a beginning, middle, and end...has descriptive words and detail." A typical response to the same question from a student with LD was: "Spelling every word right." A similar contrast was found between NA and LD students' responses to the question of "What do good writers do?" Again, sample responses illustrate the differences between NA students and students with LD in their awareness of the cognitive processes deployed in writing. A typical response from NA students was: "Think of very creative ideas." A typical response from students with LD was: "Check their spelling."

Ninety-two percent of NA students gave responses that focused on function of writing, compared to 8% of responses that focused on form of writing. In contrast, 58% of students with LD focused on function, and 31% focused on form of writing. By middle school, normally achieving students showed impressive development in awareness of higher-order cognitive and metacognitive aspects of writing. Those with LD were still more focused on lower-order mechanical aspects of writing.

In response to the question, "What do good writers do?" fourth- and fifth-grade students with LD in Graham et al.'s study showed an equal focus on the form and function of writing: 43% gave responses focused on form, and 46% of the responses focused on function. In contrast, 31% of the NA students from the same grades focused on form, and 58% focused on the function of writing. These data suggest that, like older students with LD, younger students with LD in Grades 4 and 5 showed slower development in awareness of higher-order cognitive processes in writing.

Wong et al. (1989) found that similar to younger NA students, in Grade 6, students with LD in Grades 8 and 11 used a very primitive writing strategy as revealed in their answers to the question of "How do you write?" To these students with LD, writing meant putting down whatever ideas that came to mind. Knowledge-telling and knowledge-transformation are two vastly different approaches to writing that have been described by Scardamalia and Bereiter (1987). Knowledge-telling occurs most noticeably in the writing of novice writers, who simply activate their prior knowledge from which they transfer retrieved knowledge or ideas onto paper without modification. Knowledge-transformation, in contrast, requires the writer to actively modify, elaborate, clarify, and seek relationships in existent knowledge and ideas during the writing process. Through such modification and elaboration of knowledge and ideas, the writer gains new understanding and insight. Thus, in knowledge-transformation, the writer changes his or her structure of knowledge. Knowledge-transformation is more frequently used by skilled writers (Scardamalia & Bereiter, 1987).

Wong et al. (1989) concluded that the adolescents with LD in Grades 8 and 11 in their study showed less mature and coherent conceptions/awareness of the writing process, of their own cognitive processes as they engaged in writing, and the reasons for an individual's difficulties in writing. In contrast, normally achieving adolescents in Grade 8 appeared to be well on track in developing mature conceptions of the writing process, purpose of writing, and awareness of audience. The metacognitive development in writing of normally achieving sixth graders appears to be somewhere between the normally achieving adolescents and those with LD.

The findings of Wong et al. (1989) support prior research by Englert et al. (1988) on metacognition and knowledge of text structure in normally achieving and LD fourth and fifth graders. Englert et al. found children with LD to have less mature and coherent conceptions of the writing process and deficient knowledge of text structure. Wong et al.'s findings also corroborate those by Graham et al. (1993). Unraveling the causes of such developmental differences may lead to valuable instructional implications for students with LD on this score.

## STUDENTS' AWARENESS OF THE PROCESS
## OF REVISION

### Are Children Aware of Variations in the Quality of Writing?

For students to be aware of the need to revise (a key element in the writing process), they must identify or detect unsatisfactory parts of their writings. In turn, such detection requires application of internal criteria to gauge critically the quality of their own writings. McCormick, Busching, and Potter (1992) conducted a 2-year longitudinal study in which they examined the evaluative criteria that were applied to stories by high and low achievers, and how they changed across the 2 years. The children's task was to rank order the top three out of four of their own written stories. Subsequently, they were asked to rank order four experimenter-generated stories that varied on two dimensions: interest and craft.

The researchers found that children had a wide pool of evaluative criteria of good writing. Moreover, they used their evaluative knowledge selectively; only calling forth what the specific text appeared to elicit from them. On further examination of their data, McCormick et al. found interesting differential patterns of evaluation among high and low achievers. First, although both high and low achievers used evaluative criteria relevant to the text (e.g., how interesting the story is), high achievers used them more frequently than did low achievers. Second, low achievers used more immature evaluative criteria of good writing. Third, high achievers were able to merge personal (subjective) with more objective views in their evaluations. In contrast, low achievers tended to fixate more on personal perspectives. Fourth, high achievers were able to articulate specific positive attributes of stories that they liked, the aesthetic aspects of them. In contrast, low achievers had difficulty articulating the positive or aesthetic qualities of stories, and groped with the right words to express themselves. In contrast, they had no difficulty verbalizing negative attributes of the stories.

The most instructive finding from the second year of McCormick et al.'s study came from the low achievers when the children entered sixth grade. As fifth graders, they were found to use more immature evaluative criteria than did the high achievers. In the sixth grade, low achievers showed a marked reduction in use of immature criteria. Hence, McCormick et al. considered low achievers to demonstrate significant developmental gains in their use of evaluative criteria for good writing.

In contrast, McCormick et al. observed that high-achieving students had regressed. In specific, they had decreased in the use of the evaluative criterion of author's ability to interest readers, and increased in the use of textual clarity in evaluating good writing. (McCormick et al. considered the former to be a more mature evaluative criterion of good writing.) The researchers rightly conjectured that this finding reflected differential instructional emphases given in the sixth-grade class. The sixth grade teacher emphasized basic writing and, perhaps, functions of writing. The fifth grade teacher, in contrast, had emphasized a wide range of forms and writing purposes.

McCormick et al.'s (1992) 2-year longitudinal study of fifth graders shed needed light on children's development of internal evaluative criteria for good writing. The data indicated that children use multiple criteria in evaluating a piece of writing. More important, they do not appear to apply rigidly preset lists of evaluative criteria, they simply respond to the salient presence (e.g., interestingness) or the absence (e.g., making sense/clarity) of particular features in the individual story. These data call for caution in both researchers and teachers when assessing children's knowledge of evaluative criteria regarding good writing. They must not assume too readily that absence of use of a particular evaluative criterion in a child equates unequivocally his or her lack of knowledge. The data also indicated progressive development of low achievers to move away from using evaluative criteria that were irrelevant to the text. Finally, the data indicated the inadvertent negative impact of instruction on the use of evaluative criteria among high achievers, as well as the value of good instruction to low-achieving students.

## Do Children Have Knowledge of the Revision Process?

MacArthur, Graham, and Schwartz (1991) posed two questions to 26 students with LD in Grades 7 and 8. The first question was: "Teachers often ask students to change their papers to make them better. If you were asked to change your paper to make it better or improve it, what kinds of changes would you make?" (MacArthur et al., 1991, p. 63). The second question asked students for specific suggestions on revising a paper supposedly written by another student. In fact, the paper was prepared by MacArthur et al. and contained eight sentences on Abraham Lincoln as well as specific errors in spelling, punctuation, capitalization, and grammar. Moreover, the paper was poor in content and organization. It begged for a more forceful beginning and conclusion, more detail, improved ordering of content, and deletion of a trivial observation.

In response to the first question, MacArthur et al. found that 76% of the students referred to correcting mechanical errors. In specific, 60% focused on spelling, 32% on capitalization, 40% on punctuation, 28% on neatness of handwriting, and 8% on grammar. However, there were some students (28%) who focused on more substantive changes involving content. (Substantive changes or revisions refer to changes in meaning.) Four students recommended the addition of content, and two the addition of a title. However, no student suggested changes in organization, deletion, sentence structure, or the starting and ending of the paper. Sixty-eight percent of the students gave responses that were too vague for scoring.

The situation improved in the students' responses to the second question when they were given an actual piece of writing to critique. Here, 76% of the students gave substantive suggestions. However, 68% still focused on suggestions of mechanical corrections. On scrutiny of the substantive responses, MacArthur et al. found that adding content or information was the chief subcategory in those responses. Some examples were: "Talk more about how Lincoln freed the slaves " and "Give more details, like what he did to become President, why he became President, and the date " (MacArthur et al., 1991, p. 69).

Interestingly, students' suggestions of mechanics did not correlate with revision measures in MacArthur et al.'s study, in which students were also asked to write and revise one story and one opinion essay. However, the number of substantive suggestions made by students did correlate with the number of substantive revisions in students' own writings.

In sum, the findings in MacArthur et al. (1991) suggest that middle-school students with LD mainly view revision as a process of detecting and correcting mechanical errors in writing. Thus, in revision, they search for and focus on errors in spelling, punctuation, and grammar. Their awareness, conception, and knowledge of revision needs broadening to encompass additional and more important dimensions, such as clarity and good development of ideas, and content organization.

Middle school students with LD, however, were more able to make substantive suggestions for revision in a paper written by another person than they were for themselves. Nevertheless, even here, they were only able to make one kind of recommendation—namely, adding more details. This information underscores the need to cultivate awareness and knowledge of the process of revision.


## IMPACT OF INSTRUCTION


Purpose and Process Goals. Can Students' Metacognition in Writing Be Enhanced?

The answer appears to be a tentative "yes " based on informal reports from teachers (Atwell, 1988; D'Ambrosio, 1988) and indirect effects of writing intervention research (Wong et al., 1994) (Wong, Butler, Ficzere, & Kuperis, 1996; 1997).

Using the writing process approach, D'Ambrosio (1989) described how he taught his second-grade pupils to write and enjoy writing. In daily 20 to 30 minute writing sessions, D'Ambrosio had his class write about personal experiences they deemed important and/or interesting. He met with them before, during, and after writing. In these conferences, D'Ambrosio emphasized the importance of focusing on developing their ideas and downplaying mechanical aspects of spelling and neatness of handwriting. Initially in the academic year, the children relied on meeting with D'Ambrosio for feedback on their writing plans and writings. Soon after, through reading aloud their writings in class, they learned to seek out one another for conferences in addition to meeting with their teacher. In peer conferences, the students mimicked the teacher's questions and style. They also frankly informed their classmates of what they liked and disliked about their writings, with suggestions for revisions of the less popular parts.

The children were able to publish what they wrote after suitable revisions in which they focused first on clarity and necessary elaboration of ideas. Next, they attended to revisions on mechanical aspects of their writings such as spelling. Through his dedicated application of the writing process instructional approach in his classroom, D'Ambrosio's second graders all became involved and interested in writing by the end of the academic year. However, he had the typical range of individual differences in desire to write among his students. He began the year with a few who were highly enthusiastic and responsive to his writing session and an equal number of reluctant writers. D'Ambrosio never coerced the latter to write; he waited them out with patience and constant encouragement, and tried to elicit their responsiveness to writing by getting them to focus and elaborate on personally interesting experiences.

The most striking aspect of this study is D'Ambrosio's success in getting his second graders to understand the importance and necessity of revision. In specific, he made them realize the purposes of revisions: making one's ideas clearer and making one's writing more interesting. Through repeated emphasis in individual conferences with each pupil, he underscored the importance of paying primary attention to higher-order cognitive aspects of writing, and secondary attention to mechanical aspects of writing.

Turning to the impact of the writing process approach of instruction in junior high school, Atwell (1988) reported an interesting and instructive case study of a female eighth grader with LD. Diagnosed with language disabilities, severe auditory short-term memory problems, and organizational problems, Laura had been given what appears to be mainly drill work on things such as sentence structure. Atwell took Laura into her eighth-grade English class and involved her in writing.

Initially, Laura wrote short letters to Atwell in which she relayed her enjoyment in reading the stories that were accessible to her in Atwell's classroom. Through Atwell's patient encouragement and help in choosing writing topics, Laura began to write. Atwell's case study traced how Laura's writing blossomed while receiving collaborative help in idea generation, writing, and revising from peers and the teacher. At the end of the school year, this initially shy adolescent with low sense of self-efficacy initiated an innovative interview project with the teacher and worked doggedly on the revisions three times before it was published. Subsequently, she wrote her first free-verse poem to express her thoughts and feelings over the tragedy of the NASA shuttle disaster, focusing her theme on teacher-astronaut Christa McAuliffe. Laura ended the year by winning second prize from a local Rotary Club on a letter to then Russian Prime Minister Mikhail Gorbachev. The theme of the letter was to promote peace and understanding between the United States and Russia.

Laura felt elated by the opportunity to write on topics chosen by herself, rather than being limited by topics on which every student must write. She was stimulated by class readings, including stories and poems. These reading sources generated ideas for her written work, as well as exposed her to different genres of writing. In specific, the most important benefits Laura obtained from her year with Atwell appeared to involve learning to use writing to "shape and control " her emotions over both her grandmother's and Christa McAuliffe's deaths, and dealing with mechanical writing problems in the context of her writings.

These studies by D'Ambrosio and Atwell demonstrate that instruction can increase substantially students' awareness of the centrality of the communicative purpose of writing, and the higher-order cognitive aspects of writing that subsumes awareness of audience. However, there does not seem to be any investigations into students' metacognitive awareness of such consequences of the writing process approach in writing instruction. Perhaps one reason is the difficulty in getting students, particularly children, to articulate their explicit awareness of their thoughts about themselves as writers and the cognitive processes in which they engage as they write. Indeed, problems in assessing metacognition are well recognized (Garner, 1987).

In a 3 year longitudinal study of writing intervention, Wong et al. (1994, 1996, 1997) effectively taught low-achieving (LA) and learning-disabled (LD) adolescents three genre-specific strategies in the context of the more general writing process of planning, sentence generating, and revising. One genre-specific strategy was taught per year: reportive essays the first (e.g., "The best birthday present I ever received"); opinion essays the second (e.g., "Should high school students have a dress code in school?"); and compare and contrast essays (e.g., "Compare Toronto to Vancouver"). Students learned to write the target essays to the satisfaction of the instructors. However, LA and LD adolescents did not evidence gains in metacognition in writing until the third year. Qualitative data indicated that they improved in their awareness of the importance of planning, organization, and clarity in their writing only in the last year of training. In specific, out of 16 students, 13 (seven adolescents with LD, six LA adolescents) evidenced changes in their answers on the metacognitive questionnaire from pre-test to posttest. However, three (two adolescents with LD, one LA adolescent) evidenced few changes in their pre and posttest answers.

This increase in awareness ranged from knowing to use planning in their writing, to seeing the training procedures as a usable approach to writing, to understanding the importance of gaining readers' interest. Sample answers to the question "How do you write?" from adolescents with LD illustrate such post-training awareness: "I make a plan, think of ideas, then just write," "Make a plan and a rough copy on the computer, then do clarity, and COPS and then put your changes in and print out your good copy," and "I write with words which are expressive, words that jump out and grab people to make them interested in what you're writing." At pretest, LA and LD adolescents typically were mute on this question.

Students also moved from fixating on mechanics to content knowledge as elements of good writing. Although they still embraced the importance of mechanics, students appeared to realize that planning and organizing ideas was also important for becoming a good writer. Sample responses that illustrate this point include (from LD adolescents): "They have to pick a topic that they're really interested in and they should know a little bit about it," "You have to know a lot of vocabulary words. How to word it, putting it into sentences. How to plan and organize it," and "How to organize ideas." Pretest answers included: "You have to know how to write proper sentences and be able to think of ideas; how to spell" and "Spelling, punctuation."

Finally, students appeared to gain awareness of the importance of clarity in writing. LD adolescents' posttest answers to the question of what they need to learn to be a better writer included: "Making it (writing) make sense" and "Getting others to understand what I say—clarity." Some LD and LA students mentioned that adding specific examples increases clarity of writing.

Although 13 out of 16 of the trainees demonstrated improvements in metacognition in writing, Wong et al. (1997) maintained that such improvement was nascent and fragile. They based their opinion on the results of students' lack of change in their answers from pretest to posttest to the question: "Why do you think some adolescents have trouble writing stories/essays?" Students' responses fell into two categories. One was motivational explanations, such as that adolescents lack interest in writing, they would rather pursue their own interests, or they do not feel it is worthwhile to invest effort in writing. The other category of explanations was deficient knowledge: Adolescents haven't learned how to write, and they do not know about mechanics in writing. Even students who had shown nascent awareness of their own writing process, and who at posttest could better analyze their extant needs in writing improvement, could not apply their new insights to explain writing problems in other adolescents.

## Enhancing Self-Regulation Goals

As Wray (1994) aptly pointed out, awareness of the writing process or one's cognitive processes in writing enables the individual "to bring into conscious control" those very processes. Essentially, such conscious control enables us to distribute more effectively our cognitive resources, and to harness them more efficiently. Moreover, it can lead to better management of our own cognitive weaknesses in writing. For example, students say to us, "I'm the pits when it comes to spelling!" or "I've got great ideas for writing any paper, but I'm lousy at organizing my ideas!" When students verbalize such awareness, we can give them proper help or guidance immediately. With the first example, we can tell the student to first put his or her resources on higher-order cognitive goals in writing such as clarity, securing audience' interest, and organization. When these writing goals are met, then the student can attend to lower-order mechanical concerns in writing, such as spelling. With the second type of student, we can help him or her work on organizing his or her ideas so that they flow logically and coherently in the paragraphs.

Thus, students' awareness of the writing process and their own cognitive processes in writing must be yoked with self-regulation to good effect; namely, the generation of a quality piece of writing. Self-regulation assumes importance as we realize the need for students to stay focused in their writing, and to complete the necessary revisions at both higher-order and lower-order cognitive levels. To date, there is no research on children's development of self-regulation in writing. However, there is ample instructional research on self-regulation in writing.

For close to 2 decades now, Graham and Harris have engaged in programmatic intervention research in writing involving intermediate students with LD. To guide their intervention research, they developed the model of Self-Regulated Strategy Development (SRSD; Graham & Harris, 1994; Harris & Graham, 1992). Although the development of their model has been shaped by three theoretical sources—the roles of declarative and procedural knowledge, metacognition, and self-regulation in the development of autonomous learners—the cornerstone of their model is self-regulation (Graham & Harris, 1996). In their various interventions, Graham and Harris provide students with LD instruction in the writing process in tandem with strategy instruction. The strategies taught are carefully matched to the instructional needs of the target students. They comprise four broad categories: (a) strategies designed to teach students with LD to regulate subprocesses in writing (planning, sentence generating, and revising); for example, how to set goals in writing so as to make a good writing plan, how to better organize ideas derived from brainstorming before proceeding to write about them; (b) strategies to teach students with LD to regulate procedural applications of the writing process and/or self-monitoring use of a writing strategy for a particular genre—for example, an opinion essay; (c) strategies to self-monitor one's academic engagement, or self-monitor one's writing output (quantity); and (d) strategies to cue students to provide self-reinforcement—for example, "I've worked hard at my writing," "I have generated good ideas for writing."

These strategies are put in the form of self-questions. The intervention researcher first models the self-questions in the target strategy for the students with LD, ensuring that they understand the rationale for the entire strategy as well as each step in the strategy. Trainees watch the demonstration of strategy use and the beneficial results of strategy application. Subsequently, in the context of guided practice, an individual trainee verbalizes strategy steps in applying the strategy. As each trainee progresses in mastery of strategy use, the student demonstrates parallel mastery of the strategy steps. Over time, the student proceeds from verbalization to subvocalization of those steps until finally, with complete internalization of the steps, the student ceases to subvocalize them.

## CONCLUSIONS

This chapter focused on students' development in metacognition in writing. Although the empirical base is presently meager, it does afford useful information on several fronts. First, by Grade 8 normally achieving students have well-developed awareness of the purpose in writing and the writing process.

Prompted by questions to turn inward, they are able to reflect on their own cognitive processes when engaged in writing. More important, they were found to place more emphasis on higher cognitive processes in writing, such as planning, and being aware of the need to interest the audience in their writing. Normally achieving sixth graders appear to be progressing in the same direction as the eighth graders. However, the same cannot be said of students with learning disabilities. They lag behind their normally achieving peers. They appear to have, at best, rudimentary and inarticulate ideas about the writing process. Moreover, they are exclusively concerned with lower-order cognitive processes in writing, such as the mechanics of spelling, punctuation, and neatness of handwriting.

The extant empirical picture of normally achieving students calls for longitudinal research that enables understanding on students' spontaneous development of metacognition in writing, including (but not restricted) to awareness of: (a) the purpose/conception of writing, (b) the writing process, (c) the need to focus on higher-order cognitive processes of writing, (d) audience, and (e) self-regulation in writing. Understanding normal developmental processes may provide instructional clues for how to promote metacognition in writing among children and adolescents. And why should such promotion matter? To quote Wray (1994), we want to promote awareness of the writing process in children and adolescents so that we can enable them "to bring into conscious control " the cognitive processes involved in writing. To underscore the importance of promoting awareness of what writing is about and the writing process among students, I need only to resort to the plight of students with learning disabilities.

To our utmost amazement and concern, children and adolescents with LD unanimously view a good piece of writing to be one devoid of spelling errors (Graham, Harris, MacArthur, & Schwartz, 1998; Wong et al., 1997). This misconception costs them enormously in their writing and revising. In specific, their cognitive resources for writing are exclusively consumed in attempts to spell each word correctly to the extent that their sentence generation is impeded. In revising, following the misguided evaluative criterion that good writing is equivalent to having no spelling errors, these students look to revise only spelling errors. The preceding suggests that we should inculcate in all students the awareness of the purpose of writing, which is to communicate our thoughts, ideas, and feelings. A proper conception of writing guides students to deploy and distribute their cognitive resources on higher-order cognitive processes (e.g., to focus on expressing their communicative intent clearly and sufficiently), and to attend to lower-order mechanical processes (spelling, grammar) in due time at the editing stage of writing. Similarly, inculcating awareness of the writing process enables students to understand the various subprocesses of writing, and, more important, the subprocesss' nonlinear and recursive nature.

Additionally, we need to research the role of instruction on students' development of metacognition in writing. In specific, we need more formal research on the kinds of instructional approaches that would foster students' development of metacognition in writing. One instructional approach that merits study is the writing process instructional approach, because there is reason to think that students' awareness of what writing is about and the writing process itself may be best fostered in classrooms in which teachers enact the following: establish routines in writing for the students, create safe environments for peer feedback and teacher's own feedback to students' writings, set clear standards in good writing and enable students to reach them, allow student autonomy in choosing writing topics and genres, and insure authenticity of writing tasks (Graham & Harris, 1997; Wong, 1998). These were the very conditions present in the classrooms of D'Ambrosio (1988) and Atwell (1988), and we have seen the positive effects on their students' love of writing, motivation to write and revise, and readiness to share their writings with peers. Thus, I propose that we conduct more formal experimental as well as naturalistic observational studies in classrooms, to capture the developmental course and trajectory in metacognition in writing in students.

Parallel to research on normally achieving students, we need to research the causes underlying the delay of learning-disabled students in developing proper understanding and awareness of the purpose of writing and the writing process. Research here would guide us to appropriate courses of remediation.

Two other remaining areas merit consideration for research. One is direct attempts at inculcating awareness of the writing process among students in middle and senior high school. These attempts would include teacher-scaffolded discussions and reflections among students of their cognitive processes in writing, and their perceived strengths and weaknesses in writing, their thoughts and feelings toward their completed stories and essays. These discussions and reflections could be at the individual, dyadic level or in small groups. The purpose is to enable students to turn inward and articulate, for example, their realization of the impact of the knowledge of writing processes on their own writings (e.g., their incorporation of planning in their writings); and their awareness of their own improvements in writing. Second, direct intervention in students' awareness and self-regulation in writing appears to merit future research (Graham & Harris, 1997). The justification in choosing the grade level of students for this research lies in their capacity for better articulating their thoughts than can younger children.

As mentioned earlier, the empirical base on the topic of metacognition in writing is small, but there is nascent interest in it. More important, the current zeitgeist in cognitive psychology and instructional psychology indicates a marked interest in self-regulated learning in general, and a budding interest in the role of self-regulation in writing in particular, as evident in Zimmerman and Risemberg's (1997) social cognitive theory of writing. Their theory focuses on and accentuates the role of self-regulation. Interests in these research trends may well spread to and incorporate future research endeavors in metacognition in writing.

## REFERENCES

Atwell, N. (1988). A special writer at work. In T. Newkirk & N. Atwell (Eds.), *Understanding writing: Ways of observing, learning, and teaching* (pp. 114–129). Portsmouth, NH: Heinmann.

Baker, L., & Brown, A. L. (1984a). Metacognitive skills in reading. In D. P. Pearson (Ed.), *Handbook on research in reading* (pp. 353–394). New York: Longman.

Baker, L., & Brown, A. L. (1984b). Cognitive monitoring in reading. In J. Flood (Ed.), *Understanding reading comprehension* (pp. 21–44). Newark, DE: International Reading Association.

Brown, A. L. (1980). Metacognitive development and reading. In R. J. Spiro, B. Bruce, & W. F. Brewer (Eds.), *Theoretical issues in reading comprehension* (pp. 453–481). Hillsdale, NJ: Lawrence Erlbaum Associates.

D'Ambrosio, V. (1988). Second graders can so write. In T. Newkirk & N. Atwell (Eds.), *Understanding writing: Ways of observing, learning, and teaching* (pp. 52–61). Portsmouth, NH: Heinmann.

Englert, C. S., Raphael, T. E., Fear, K. L., & Anderson, L. M. (1988). Students' metacognitive knowledge about how to write informational text. *Learning Disability Quarterly, 11*(1), 18–46.

Flavell, J. H. (1976). Metacognitive aspects of problem solving. In L. B. Resnick (Ed.), *The nature of intelligence* (pp. 231–235). Hillsdale, NJ: Lawrence Erlbaum Associates.

Flower, L. S., & Hayes, J. R. (1980). The dynamics of composing: Making plans and juggling constraints. In L. W. Gregg & E. R. Steinberg (Eds.), *Cognitive processes in writing* (pp. 31–50). Hillsdale, NJ: Lawrence Erlbaum Associates.

Garner, R. (1987). *Metacognition and reading comprehension.* Norwood, NJ: Ablex.

Graham, S., & Harris, K. R. (1994). The role of self-regulation in the writing process. In D. Schunk & B. Zimmerman (Eds.), *Self-regulation of learning and performance: Issues and educational applications* (pp. 203–228). Hillsdale, NJ: Lawrence Erlbaum Associates.

Graham, S., & Harris, K. R. (1996). Self-regulation and strategy instruction for students who find writing and learning challenging. In C. M. Levy & S. Ransdell (Eds.), *The science of writing: Theories, methods, individual differences, and applications* (pp. 347–360). Mahwah, NJ: Lawrence Erlbaum Associates.

Graham, S., & Harris, K. R. (1997). Self-regulation and writing: Where do we go from here? *Contemporary Educational Psychology, 22*, 102–114.

Graham, S., Harris, K. R., MacArthur, C., & Schwartz, S. (1998). Writing instruction. In B. Y. L. Wong (Ed.), *Learning about learning disabilities* (2nd ed., pp. 391–423). San Diego, CA: Academic.

Graham, S., Schwartz, S. S., & MacArthur, C. A. (1993). Knowledge of writing and the composing process, attitude toward writing, and self-efficacy for students with and without learning disabilities. *Journal of Learning Disabilities, 26*(4), 237–249.

Harris, K. R., & Graham, S. (1992). Self-regulated strategy development: A part of the writing process. In M. Pressley, K. R. Harris, & J. Guthrie (Eds.), *Promoting academic competence and literacy in school* (pp. 277–309). New York: Academic.

Hayes, J. R., & Flower, L. S. (1980). Identifying the organization of writing processes. In L. W. Gregg & E. R. Steinberg (Eds.), *Cognitive processes in writing* (pp. 3–30). Hillsdale, NJ: Lawrence Erlbaum Associates.

Isaacson, S. L. (1992). Volleyball and other analogies: A response to Englert. *Journal of Learning Disabilities, 25*(3), 173–177.

MacArthur, C. A., Graham, S., & Schwartz, S. (1991). Knowledge of revision and revising behavior among students with learning disabilities. *Learning Disability Quarterly, 14*, 61–73.

McCormick, C. B., Busching, B. A., & Potter, E. F. (1992). Children's knowledge about writing: The development and use of evaluative criteria. In M. Pressley, K. R. Harris, & J. T. Guthrie (Eds.), *Promoting academic competence and literacy in school* (pp. 313–336). San Diego, CA: Academic.

Murray, D. M. (1982). Teaching the other self: The writer's first reader. *College Composition and Communication, 33*(2), 140–147.

Scardamalia, M., & Bereiter, C. (1987). Knowledge telling and knowledge transforming in written composition. In S. Rosenberg (Ed.), *Advances in applied psycholinguistics: Vol. 2. Reading, writing, and language learning* (pp. 142–175). Cambridge, England: Cambridge University Press.

Shook, S. E., Marrion, L. V., & Ollila, L. O. (1989). Primary children's concepts about writing. *Journal of Educational Research, 82*(3), 133–138.

Wong, B. Y. L. (1998). Reflections on future directions in writing intervention research. *Advances in Learning and Behavioral Disabilities, 12*, 127–149.

Wong, B. Y. L., Butler, D. L., Ficzere, S. A., & Kuperis, S. (1996). Teaching adolescents with learning disabilities and low achievers to plan, write, and revise opinion essays. *Journal of Learning Disabilities, 29*(2), 197–212.

Wong, B. Y. L., Butler, D. L., Ficzere, S. A., Kuperis, S. (1997). Teaching adolescents with learning disabilities and low achievers to plan, write, and revise compare-and-contrast essays. *Learning Disabilities Research and Practice, 12*(1), 2–15.

Wong, B. Y. L., Butler, D. L., Ficzere, S. A., Kuperis, S., Corden, M., & Zelmer, J. (1994). Teaching problem learners revision skills and sensitivity to audience through two instructional modes: Student-teacher versus student-student interactive dialogues. *Learning Disability Research & Practice, 9*(2), 78–90.

Wong, B. Y. L., Wong, R., & Blenkinsop, J. (1989). Cognitive and metacognitive aspects of learning-disabled adolescents' composing problems. *Learning Disability Quarterly, 12*(4), 300–322.

Wray, D. (1994). *Literacy and awareness* (pp. 41–58, 82–121). London: Hodder & Stoughton.

Zimmerman, B. J., & Risemberg, R. (1997). Becoming a self-regulated writer: A social cognitive perspective. *Contemporary Educational Psychology, 22*, 73–101.

# 10 ❧ Performance Assessment Using Complex Tasks: Implications for Children With High-Incidence Disabilities

**Lynn S. Fuchs**
**Douglas Fuchs**
*Vanderbilt University*

In the United States, the practice of assessment in the public schools often mirrors important trends in our nation's values and goals. At the beginning of the 20th century, for example, with public commitment to the principles of democracy strong, compulsory school attendance laws combined with liberal immigration policies to create precipitous increases in the size and diversity of the public school population (Hendrick & MacMillan, 1984). At the same time, however, the industrialization of America's growing cities introduced pressures for schools to produce a better-qualified labor force. The business community, therefore, issued calls for efficiency in the schooling process to promote steady student progress through the grades and to reduce dropout rates (Callahan, 1962). These goals, which competed with urban schools' increasing size and diversity, were served by and reflected in the introduction of aptitude testing in schools to track low-ability students into separate classes (Hendrick & MacMillan, 1989).

As we now approach the turn of the next century, assessment still serves as a bellwether for this country's emerging trends, values, and problems, and ironically, some of today's most pressing issues echo themes important at the turn of the last century. For example, the diversity of the nation's school population is increasing again. Currently, 8.7% of Americans are foreign born—the highest percentage since before World War II (Hodgkinson, 1995). In the past decade, the population also has become more diverse ethnically, with Latinos increasing by 65%, Asian Americans by 32%, African Americans by 16%, and

**199**

European Americans by only 8% (Hodgkinson, 1995). Additionally, the proportion of school children living below the official poverty line is increasing steadily (Stallings, 1995). At the same time, commitment to democratic principles remains strong, as reflected in the schools' initiatives to detrack classrooms (Braddock et al., 1992) and to include students with disabilities in the mainstream (Fuchs & Fuchs, 1994).

Together, an increasingly diverse school population and a commitment to serving students in democratically heterogeneous groups converge to create this fact: The average range of student performance in the typical classroom in the United States now exceeds five grade levels (Jenkins, Jewell, Leceister, Jenkins, & Troutner, 1990). This means that the typical fourth-grade general educator can expect to teach students who perform at first-, second-, third-, fourth-, fifth-, and sixth-grade levels. For even our best teachers, this represents a substantial challenge to providing an appropriate instructional environment for all students.

Concurrently, however, just as in earlier times, the changing economic environment of the 1990s has created demands for a more highly skilled labor pool that can tackle increasingly complex problems. This, in turn, has renewed pressures from the business community for educational accountability. Today, accountability is operationalized in terms of how much and what type of knowledge students acquire as a function of schooling.

How are these forces reflected in the critical assessment issues of our time? Today's economy has created demands for increased numbers of highly skilled workers who can apply knowledge in flexible ways to solve novel problems (Darling-Hammond, 1992; Mory & Salisbury, 1992). This increasing complexity in our workplace has helped shape the direction of the current education reform movement, called *standards-based reform*, which seeks to upgrade and enrich the content of our schools' curricula (Goodman, 1995). The goal is for students to learn complex problem-solving, comprehension, written expression, critical thinking, and metacognitive skills, and social cooperation within authentic contexts.

This focus on rich, complicated tasks, which reflect the requirements of the real world, has prompted some reformers to reject skills-based instructional models, where teachers provide explicit instruction on discrete skills. Instead, the reform movement has embraced constructivist approaches to learning, which emphasize the importance of children's active construction of knowledge within functional and meaningful situations (Harris & Graham, 1994). As constructivist perspectives have been introduced to classrooms, many leaders of the reform movement have fixed their attention on assessment (Archbald & Newmann, 1988; Linn, 1991; Shepard, 1989; Wiggins, 1989). As dictated by constructivism, these leaders discourage the testing of isolated skills. Instead, they call for the development of an alternative assessment model, known as *performance assessment*. In this chapter, we discuss how the use of performance assessment is likely to affect students with high-incidence disabilities.

We organize our discussion into two parts, focusing on how this shift toward more complex assessment models is producing important changes first for "internal testing" and then for "external testing." Internal tests are used to formulate day-to-day teaching decisions to increase student motivation for and involvement in learning through enhanced feedback; to inform teachers about their students' learning progress and difficulties; and to help teachers improve their responsiveness to individual students and increase the quality of the instructional programs they deliver. By contrast, external tests are created, imposed, and controlled by agencies outside a teacher's school, and are used for the purpose of accountability. Each application has potentially critical implications for how much and what students with high-incidence disabilities learn.

## ASSESSING PERFORMANCE ON MORE COMPLEX TASKS: IMPLICATIONS FOR TEACHERS' INTERNAL USE OF ASSESSMENT IN INSTRUCTIONAL PLANNING

Performance assessment provides students with real-life problem-solving situations and requires them to develop solutions that involve the application and integration of multiple skills and strategies. The goal of this new brand of assessment is to inform teachers about students' strategies and processes (rather than about isolated skill deficiencies), and to redirect teachers' instructional efforts to incorporate learning activities with greater generalizability to real-life dilemmas (Archbald & Newmann, 1988; Fuchs, 1994; Shepard, 1989; Wiggins, 1989).

As might be expected, the constructivist perspective on learning and assessment, popular today, has resulted in controversy and debate—especially about its relevance and effectiveness for students with serious learning problems. For example, an entire issue of *The Journal of Special Education* (Harris & Graham, 1994) was devoted to this controversy, and an invited symposium at the 1995 annual meeting of the American Educational Research Association debated this topic (Bransford, Goldman, & Hasselbring, 1995). On the one hand, children with high-incidence disabilities already have demonstrated a failure to profit from the unstructured, incidental learning experiences promoted by constructivism (Harris & Graham, 1994; Pearson, 1989; Symons, Woloshyn, & Pressley, 1994). On the other hand, contextualizing assessment, so that it demands the skill transfer and generalization necessary for real-life application, may be especially important for these students, who demonstrate persistent difficulties in applying the skills they learn in isolation (Anderson-Inman, Walker, & Purcell, 1984; White, 1984). The hope is that if assessment demands the generalization and application of skills, then teachers will focus their instructional effort on the requirements of that transfer and application.

Despite this lofty goal, serious questions remain about how performance assessments can be designed to enhance teachers' capacity to monitor the effects of their instruction and to improve their teaching so that learning increases for students with high-incidence disabilities. In the following section, we review some of the problems and challenges presented by performance assessment for internal testing purposes. Then, we describe the results of some early attempts to help teachers incorporate these tools into their instructional planning for learners with and without high-incidence disabilities.

## PERFORMANCE ASSESSMENTS: STRENGTHS, PROBLEMS, AND CHALLENGES

According to the U. S. Congress Office of Technology Assessment (1992), performance assessments demonstrate three key features: (a) the assessment tasks require students to construct, rather than select, responses; (b) the assessment formats create opportunities for teachers to observe student behavior on tasks reflecting real-world requirements; and (c) the scoring methods reveal patterns in students' learning and thinking in addition to the correctness of the students' answers. The major purposes of performance assessments are to direct teachers and students toward important, well-integrated learning outcomes and to enhance teachers' capacity to design superior instructional plans and effect better student learning.

Many varieties of performance assessment are described in the current literature, and a wide range of methods are implemented today in classrooms (Baker, O'Neil, & Linn, 1993). Because performance assessment is relatively new, underdeveloped, and yet to be studied systematically, practitioners are often in the undesirable position of interpreting vague design features and operationalizing those features into specific assessments on their own (Baker, 1991; Brewer, 1991; Sammons, Kobett, Heiss, & Fennell, 1992). These operationalizations take a variety of forms—some of which are closer than others in approximating performance assessment's conceptual and theoretical underpinnings (Baker et al., 1993; Fuchs, 1994).

Performance assessment, therefore, exists more as a vision of what classroom assessment methods might strive to achieve rather than as a clearly defined, readily usable assessment technology. Difficult issues in operationalizing these assessments remain. Relatedly, although rhetoric suggests performance assessment's potential contribution to instructional planning (Archbald & Newmann, 1988), research examining that contribution only is beginning to emerge. Nevertheless, in this section, we provide a *conceptual* analysis of performance assessment's potential strengths and limitations, while relying to the greatest extent possible on available empirical evidence to determine whether, and if so how, performance assessment might achieve its intended goals.

### Strengths

Performance assessment's major advantages relate to measuring skill application and integration, yielding rich analyses that correspond to instructional decisions, and serving as a communication vehicle. With respect to measuring skill application and integration, a major, distinctive advantage of performance assessment is its deliberate focus on authentic performances that require students to integrate many skills within age-appropriate, real-world situations. As with all assessment methods (Fuchs, 1994), however, tension exists between designing an assessment strategy that mirrors valued, authentic, real-world performances in a world where those values may change rapidly, and developing a measurement system that can focus teachers and learners on an appropriately sized instructional domain (i.e., a small-enough chunk for students to learn). One clear challenge for performance assessment is to resolve this dilemma: At the present time, it is unclear whether performance assessment provides teachers and diagnosticians with a small-enough chunk to preclude floors on student performance (i.e., children scoring zero, which provides little information) and to facilitate specific links to instructional strategies (we return to this point later). To resolve this dilemma, core sets of outcomes need to be identified, which avoid both unmanageably long lists of assessment domains as well as short ones with only tangential relation to truly critical outcomes (Baker, 1991).

With respect to communicating the goals of learning to teachers and students, a much-discussed advantage of performance assessment is that the assessments closely reflect the desired instructional goals. Therefore, teachers should be able to use performance assessments to direct their instruction. Moreover, to the extent that the scoring rubrics are clear, concrete, and visible to students, pupils should be able to use performance assessments to establish personal learning goals and to seek assistance in achieving those goals. Communicating clearly about what is important for teachers to teach and students to learn is a highly valued emphasis of performance assessment. Consequently, as methods are defined, we should expect to see clearly articulated goals and scoring criteria to assist teachers and students in translating the assessments into everyday learning activities.

With respect to instructional decision making, given that providing insights into students' strategies is a major tenet of performance assessment, we assume that useful diagnostic planning decisions can be formulated on the basis of the assessments. Performance assessments should permit teachers to identify the strategies students employ in addressing complicated problems. Ideally, this focus on strategies should yield rich descriptions of student performance with clear connections to specific instructional ideas. As with any assessment method, however, teachers' capacities vary considerably in the extent to which they can identify insights into students' strategic behavior and relate those descriptions to specific instructional techniques. Research suggests that teachers typically experience difficulty in both dimensions of diagnostic planning—even when the assessment method and the conceptual framework for learning are more simple than with performance assessment. With curriculum-based measurement, for example, research suggests that teachers experience difficulty in generating accurate skills profiles on the basis of assessments that incorporate multiple skills (Fuchs, Fuchs, Hamlett, &

Stecker, 1990). Because of this difficulty, we eventually moved to computerized strategies for generating reliable profiles of student competence based on curriculum-based measurement. In addition, teachers sometimes find it difficult to connect student problems with corrective instructional strategies (Fuchs, Fuchs, Hamlett, & Stecker, 1991). Because of this difficulty, curriculum-based measurement typically is used in conjunction with human or computerized instructional consultation methods. Consequently, despite performance assessment's potential for yielding rich, detailed analyses of student performance that connect to instructional methods, work is still required to identify the means by which this can be achieved.

## Problems

Despite these three important, potential strengths associated with performance assessment, major concerns exist about performance assessment's capacity to measure skill acquisition, to index growth and provide the basis for formative evaluation decisions, to produce technically viable information, and to be implemented feasibly within the constraints of ordinary classroom life. With respect to skill acquisition, when a child fails to demonstrate skill application and integration within the context of a complex, rich task, it is not possible to identify whether the failure to apply knowledge is a function of poor strategies for generalizing acquired skills, or whether the child has not mastered the skill in isolation.

Moreover, assessment methods should provide the basis for formative evaluation decisions. Unfortunately, the methods by which formative evaluation decisions might be derived are unclear: Such decisions require scoring methods that can be used to describe progress as well as procedures for designing alternate forms of relatively complex problems. Initial work suggests the potential difficulty in achieving assessment comparability when different, complex problems are involved (Baxter, Shavelson, Goldman, & Pine, 1992; Shavelson, Baxter, & Pine, 1992).

With respect to feasibility, performance assessments require large amounts of teacher time for the design and administration of assessments, and the careful scrutiny of student performances to identify accurate learning patterns and to connect those patterns to corrective teaching strategies. Therefore, constraints on teacher time need to be addressed—especially in light of increasing student caseloads in both general and special education settings (Research for Better Schools, 1988) and increasing diversity of student skills in public school settings (Jenkins et al., 1990; Stallings, 1995).

In addition, planning decisions formulated on the basis of performance assessments can lead to a complicated instructional setting, where different students need to be working on different content in different ways. It is easy to imagine, for example, how developing plans to address simultaneously the needs of 20 to 30 students can lead some teachers quickly to reject the assessment paradigm unless we address the issue of how to feasibly implement performance assessment-based plans within the constraints of everyday classroom life. With curriculum-based measurement, for example, a similar problem exists: The assessment system often leads teachers to introduce different intervention strategies for different students at different times (Fuchs, Fuchs, Hamlett, Phillips, & Bentz, 1994). Over the years, it became evident that, unless we could identify feasible ways for teachers to implement the variety of instructional decisions based on the assessment, teachers would reject the assessment method. In response to this problem within general education, we designed peer-assisted teaching methods to facilitate implementation of the instructional decisions produced via the curriculum-based measurement information (Fuchs et al., 1994). Performance assessment developers inevitably will have to face this same issue.

In terms of generating accurate, meaningful information, some have suggested that, in light of performance assessment's emphasis on embedding tests within authentic contexts, a need may exist to rethink the technical standards by which quality is judged. Linn, Baker, and Dunbar (1991) and Baker et al. (1993), for example, proposed the following set of alternative criteria for evaluating the accuracy and meaningfulness of performance assessments:

- Evidence about the intended and unintended effects of the assessments on the ways teachers and students spend their time and think about the goals of education.

- The fairness of the assessments for different populations of learners.

- The accuracy of generalizations from the specific assessment tasks to broader domains of achievement.

- The consistency of the content of the assessment with current understandings of important features of the domain of knowledge.

- The comprehensiveness of the content coverage of the assessment.

- Acceptable costs and efficiency associated with the methods.

These criteria articulate an important research program.

At the present time, unfortunately, little is known about the extent to which performance assessment systems can satisfy these or more traditional criteria (Baker et al., 1993; Elliott, 1995). Early evidence from external testing programs, however, does raise concerns. For example, a comprehensive evaluation (Hambleton et al., 1995) of Kentucky's Instructional Results Information System, which relies strongly on performance assessment, concluded that the large improvement registered on this statewide assessment program did not correspond to results on another, better developed assessment instrument; the setting of performance standards was seriously flawed; and the assessment information resulted in high rates of misclassification in the state's reward program. With respect to students with high-incidence disabilities, Fuchs et al. (1998) studied fourth graders who completed three measures representing three points on a traditional-alternative mathematics assessment continuum: a traditional, commercial multiple-choice achievement test; computation and application curriculum-based measurement (CBMs); and a performance assessment. The traditional test and CBM demonstrated the capacity to discriminate individuals with and without serious learning problems; the performance assessment did not.

These preliminary investigations, conducted within external rather than internal testing frameworks, indicate that substantial work remains to develop technically acceptable performance assessments—especially for students at the lower end of the achievement continuum. If experienced test developers, with substantial measurement expertise, have difficulty creating performance assessments that yield accurate, meaningful information, then it seems probable that classroom teachers will experience problems in developing sound assessments to match their classroom curricula. Clearly, additional work—defining performance assessment features and test-development methods—is required.

## EARLY ATTEMPTS TO HELP TEACHERS CONNECT PERFORMANCE ASSESSMENTS WITH INSTRUCTIONAL DECISIONS

In light of these potential strengths and problems, it is interesting to consider how teachers may integrate performance assessment information into their instructional decision making, especially for students with serious learning problems. In this section, we report on two data sources that begin to shed light on teachers' successes and difficulties.

Koretz, Mitchell, Barron, and Keith (1996) surveyed fifth- and eighth-grade general educators who had participated in the new performance assessments of Maryland's statewide annual testing program. As part of that program, teachers had been offered opportunities to receive staff development on using performance assessment information to enhance their instructional programming. Two thirds of the sampled teachers had attended at least one informational activity about how the performance assessments were structured; approximately two thirds had been involved in developing, piloting, or scoring tasks for these performance assessments; over half had participated in staff-development sessions about disciplinary content and instruction related to the assessments; and four fifths had attended sessions on teaching strategies.

Among this relatively well-informed sample of Maryland general educators, 55% of fifth-grade teachers and 33% of eighth-grade teachers reported focusing a great deal of effort on improving the match between the content of their instruction and the content of the assessments. Three quarters reported that they address some content more because of the assessment, whereas just over half reported that they address some content less.

Although 66% of the teachers indicated increases in the amount of time spent on teaching writing and mathematics, they also reported making up for this increased time primarily by decreasing reading instruction. This is predictable but alarming with respect to the needs of students with high-incidence disabilities and their demonstrated problems in achieving literacy: As we discuss later in this chapter, reading performance assessments tend to avoid measurement of low-level skills such as reading or decoding text. This appears to decrease the pressure on teachers to help students achieve basic literacy skills.

Moreover, teachers indicated that the performance assessments had had greatest impact on their teaching by increasing the amount of time they required students to practice testlike material, rather than by modifying how they taught or by individualizing the nature of their methods to match the strategies individual students demonstrated on these practice assessments. In fact, they attributed student improvements on these assessments primarily to students' exposure to test and preparation materials, increased familiarity with the assessment, and improved test-taking skills, rather than to true improvements in the knowledge or skills measured in the performance assessments.

Perhaps of greatest concern, however, was that when asked to report the extent to which they had increased expectations as a function of these more challenging assessments, the teachers reported that they held higher goals for less than one fifth of their special education and low-achieving students. Moreover, the eighth-grade teachers judged the higher standards reflected in these assessments to be "harmful" for 43% of their special education students.

These findings are disturbing. The once-per-year statewide testing framework, along with the limited nature of the available professional development activities, reflect less-than-optimal conditions for supporting teachers' efforts to connect a relatively new, complicated assessment structure with instructional planning. Consequently, we (see Fuchs, Fuchs, Karns, Hamlett, & Katzaroff, 1997) recently conducted a year-long investigation designed to examine eight general educators' instructional planning and student learning improved as a function of the introduction of performance assessment to the classroom. In this project, we provided teachers with ongoing support for understanding performance assessments and for integrating that assessment information into their instructional planning.

We began by involving the teachers in the creation of six alternate forms of a performance assessment at each grade level (see Fuchs et al., 1997 for development methods). Each multipage performance began with a multiparagraph narrative describing the problem situation and presenting students with tabular and graphic information for potential application in the assessment. The problem included four questions, which provided students with opportunities to apply a core set of skills deemed essential at the target grade level, to discriminate relevant from irrelevant information in the narrative, to generate information not contained in the narrative, to explain their mathematical work, and to produce written communication related to the mathematics.

Teachers administered these six performance assessments between September and April. In September, students received one 45-minute lesson on how performance assessments are structured, strategies for approaching performance assessments, and scoring methods. Following each performance assessment administration, we provided teachers with a release day, when they:

- Reviewed procedures for scoring the performance assessments and providing written feedback to students;

- Worked with fellow teachers at their grade level to achieve interscorer agreement of at least 80% on five protocols from their classrooms and to discuss their written comments back to students;

- Scored the performances of all their own students;

- Reviewed a scripted lesson for teaching their students how to interpret performance assessment feedback;

- Brainstormed in the large group about how to modify their instruction to enhance student performance on the performance assessments; and

- Completed instructional plan sheets on which they described their plans to modify instructional programs before the next performance assessment administration.

Within 2 days after this session, teachers delivered the lesson explaining to students how to interpret performance assessment feedback, and distributed the scored performance assessments.

As reported on the instructional plan sheets across the release days, teachers modified instructional programs to address the performance assessment content by teaching:

- Computational skills (cited 5 times);

- Application skills (cited 11 times);

- Word problems (cited 9 times);

- Problem-solving strategies (cited 28 times);

- Methods for labeling and showing work (cited 23 times); and

- Content aligned directly to the performance assessment activities (cited 27 times).

If we combine the last two categories, methods for labeling/showing work and directly aligned content—we see that teachers allocated much of their revised instructional activity to methods that might be considered test preparation or practice. This pattern of findings echoes those of Koretz et al. (1996).

However, we also measured student learning as a function of students' prior learning histories. We found an interaction between learning and students' prior learning histories on all three types of outcome measures we indexed: an acquisition task (a performance assessment structured in parallel fashion to the alternate forms students took in their classrooms), a near-transfer task (a performance assessment structured similarly but assessing a different set of skills), and a far-transfer task (a commercial performance assessment, The Performance Assessments for the Iowa Test of Basic Skills, which was structured differently and assessed different skills). On the acquisition and near-transfer measures, high-achieving and averaging-achieving pupils grew more than did comparable sets of students in "control" classrooms, who had the same mathematics curriculum without use of the performance assessments. In contrast to the high- and average-achieving students, the low-achieving pupils and students with high-incidence disabilities failed to demonstrate more learning than did comparable sets of control students. On the far-transfer task, only the high-achieving students demonstrated superior learning compared to their control peers.

Consequently, teachers attempted to teach the computation skills, applications skills, word problem skills, and problem-solving strategies represented on these assessments. They also provided direct practice on and exposure to similar activities during their classroom activities, where the teachers were free to mediate their learners' experiences with these performance assessment tasks. Nevertheless, students who had demonstrated persistent and serious problems in the past failed to profit. It is important also to note that our participating teachers were highly motivated and earnest in their attempts to help their students master these authentic, complex mathematical tasks (especially in light of the researchers' perspectives) for their low-performing students with and without identified disabilities. Clearly, difficult challenges remain for teachers and researchers alike to develop methods that can help practitioners capitalize on performance assessment's potential to refocus effort on teaching for skill application and generalization within complex, authentic, problem-solving contexts.

## DEMANDS FOR UNIVERSALLY CHALLENGING STANDARDS OF ACHIEVEMENT WITHIN EXTERNAL ASSESSMENT FRAMEWORKS

Much of the pressure teachers currently face to develop "internal" performance assessments for their classrooms and to teach these challenging forms of knowledge application stems from standards-based reform's requirement that all students, including those with high-incidence disabilities, participate in "externally" controlled, state and national high-stakes assessments that index students' performance on difficult standards. In fact, the 1997 Individuals with Disabilities Education Act requires students with disabilities to participate in these state and national assessments to the maximum extent possible. Additionally, over 40 states now incorporate performance assessment tasks in their statewide annual testing programs (Thurlow, 1994). In this section, we discuss how performance assessment's focus on challenging standards corresponds with the demonstrated needs of students with high-incidence disabilities. Then, we identify three related, critical assessment issues for the field of high-incidence disabilities, which are prompted by the demands of the external testing programs associated with standards-based reform.

Reform Standards' Alignment With Available Services
and Student Needs

As already discussed, despite the lofty rhetoric associated with standards-based reform's high expectations for all students, it remains unclear
whether the knowledge base currently exists to help students acquire the advanced content reflected in the reform's testing programs. This proposition,
which may be especially true for students with high-incidence disabilities, remains largely untested: Research with individuals with high-incidence disabilities has focused primarily on the acquisition of the fundamental skills
necessary to promote transitions to adult life outside of institutions of higher
education—skills that include, for example, learning to read, applying for jobs,
or developing social skills.

At best, it remains unclear whether and, if so, for which students with
high-incidence disabilities it will be possible to deliver the promise of standards-based reform. As reflected in the studies conducted by Koretz et al.
(1996) and Fuchs et al. (1997), early findings raise concern about what level of
support might be required for teachers to help students with high-incidence
disabilities achieve acceptable levels of performance on these assessments. It
seems safe to assume that, given the available knowledge base, current resources, and present levels of practice within special and general education,
large numbers of students with high-incidence disabilities will fall short of the
mark as they participate in the high-stakes external testing programs assessing
the reform movement's challenging standards.

Declaring high standards for all students, without providing educators with
access to the necessary knowledge, skills, and resources for achieving those
standards, victimizes students who fail to meet the standards (McLaughlin,
Shepard, & O'Day, 1995). This problem assumes added significance for students with high-incidence disabilities in light of the substantial body of evidence documenting how high-stakes testing programs disproportionately and
negatively have affected children at the low ends of the achievement continuum in the past (McLaughlin et al., 1995).

In addition, even if it were possible to identify methods for successfully
teaching these challenging standards to students with high-incidence disabilities, one must entertain the notion of competing educational goals—or the potential trade-offs involved in diverting instructional effort toward the reform's
standards and away from the attainment of more basic skills. This option may
in fact become attractive to school systems, because standards-based reform
rewards the achievement of complex reform standards while assuming mastery of (and thereby tending to ignore) more basic skills—such as decoding the
words on the written page. Moreover, given the availability of testing accommodations (which may permit adults to read tests to and encode responses
from students with learning disabilities), the press on school systems to help
children achieve basic reading skills may decrease. Unfortunately, the decision
to forego acquisition of basic forms of knowledge may result in serious, nega-

tive consequences for students with high-incidence disabilities after they leave school. Literacy, for example, is a fundamental requirement for satisfactory adjustment within the work world.

## Three Critical Assessment Issues Prompted by Standards-Based Reform

In light of these problems, the external performance assessment programs associated with standards-based reform prompt urgent concern about three related assessment issues for the field of high-incidence disabilities: (a) ensuring these students' meaningful participation in state and national accountability programs; (b) constructing assessment methods to determine when students with high-incidence disabilities should be exempted from the high-stakes, individual consequences associated with these external tests; and (c) determining whether external accountability programs alone, with individually tailored accountability mechanisms, are adequate to achieve better outcomes for students with high-incidence disabilities.

*Meaningful Participation in Accountability Programs.*   Before considering the high-stakes consequences associated with the participation of individuals with high-incidence disabilities in external performance assessments, it is necessary to determine the extent to which students with high-incidence disabilities currently take such tests, and what conditions are required to ensure valid measurement. With respect to current participation rates, available information suggests that students with disabilities are not included broadly in state or national testing programs. As recently as 1995-1996, when the first tests of some accommodations occurred, only 45% to 75% of students with disabilities participated in the National Assessment of Educational Progress, and statewide testing programs continue to exclude large numbers of students with disabilities (Erickson & Thurlow, 1996; Erickson, Thurlow, & Thor, 1995). In addition, even when students with disabilities are permitted to take high-stakes assessments, some states or districts exclude their scores from public reports (Thurlow, Scott, & Ysseldyke, 1995).

Low participation rates, along with questionable reporting practices, are disappointing. If schools are to consider the needs of students with disabilities deliberately and proactively in reform and improvement activities, the outcomes of students with high-incidence disabilities (who constitute the vast majority of the population of individuals with disabilities) must be represented in public accountability systems (Shriner & Thurlow, 1992; Thurlow, 1994). Only with representation in assessment databases will schools be held accountable for the learning of students with disabilities, be encouraged to establish challenging goals for students with disabilities, and be prompted to identify more effective instructional approaches for students with disabilities.

Unfortunately, before meaningful, valid participation can be accomplished, two critical assessment problems must be addressed. One relates to reporting mechanisms; the other to accommodation policies. When *reporting* mechanisms incorporate only one summary (i.e., the percentage of students reaching a high proficiency standard), it seems likely that schools will focus their efforts and resources on students just below the cutoff and will ignore students whom they consider to be far from the proficiency range (McLaughlin et al., 1995). Therefore, if standards-based reform activities are to yield potential benefits for children with high-incidence disabilities, accountability systems must incorporate additional reporting mechanisms that focus the educational system's attention on the lowest-performing children. This requires the careful design and reporting of partially mastered categories, with separate aggregation for students with high-incidence disabilities. Design of such a reporting/aggregation mechanism will require attention to difficult technical and privacy issues, so that individual students cannot be identified.

The second problem that must be addressed before meaningful participation in state and federal assessment programs can be achieved is our lack of standard methods for determining which testing *accommodations* preserve the meaningfulness of scores. Accommodations are changes in standardized assessment conditions introduced to "level the playing field" for students with disabilities by removing the construct-irrelevant variance (or barriers to performance) created by the disability. Valid accommodation policies produce scores for students with disabilities that measure the same attributes as do standard assessments in nondisabled individuals. To design accommodations that preserve the meaningfulness of scores, one must identify the nature and severity of the barriers the accommodation will offset. This depends on the individual's disability, characteristics of the assessment, conditions under which the assessment is administered, and the inferences scores are used to support.

Great variability in states' accommodation policies currently exists, with some states prohibiting the very accommodations that other states recommend. Typically, decisions for individual students with disabilities are formulated idiosyncratically (Erickson & Thurlow, 1996) with vague decision-making rules that often focus on superficial variables (Ysseldyke, Thurlow, McGrew, & Shriner, 1994). Without well-agreed on criteria for determining whether and if so which accommodations are allowed, the concern is that comparisons among schools, districts, or states with varying accommodation policies, are unfair. In response, schools, states, and districts often exclude students with disabilities from their databases.

And, unfortunately, research on the validity of scores from accommodated assessments is limited; most available data are restricted to college admissions and other postsecondary tests (Wightman, 1993; Willingham, 1988). The most pertinent, available database—generated with the 1995 National Assessment of Educational Progress accommodations field tests—suggests technical problems requiring additional study (McDonnell, McLaughlin, & Morison, 1997). Clearly, research is needed on procedures to identify fair, technically sound, valid accommodations for students with disabilities. On the one hand, disallowing fair, and valid accommodations prevent students with disabilities from demonstrating their abilities. On the other hand, overly permissive accommodation policies inflate scores and inadvertently reduce pressure on schools to increase expectations and outcomes for students with disabilities.

Nevertheless, some of the stickiest questions about the meaningfulness of accommodations occur for students with high-incidence disabilities. Questions are particularly difficult for these students for two reasons. First, this population of learners is especially heterogeneous: It is well known that school-identified students with high-incidence disabilities can be subtyped into clusters with varying underlying problems (Speece & Cooper, 1990). This makes conceptual analysis of meaningful accommodations impossible (as it might be, e.g., with students with visual disabilities). Instead, heterogeneity within the population of learners with high-incidence disabilites dictates empirical study with a strong focus on individual differences.

The second problem raising important questions for students with high-incidence disabilities is the nature of the cognitive problems experienced by these students. The most distinguishing characteristic of students with high-incidence disabilities is reading and math deficits (Kavale & Reece, 1992), whereas most high-stakes assessments directly measure or rely heavily on those very skills. Therefore, many accommodations currently used to address the disadvantages inherent in the population of individuals with high-incidence disabilities (extended time, decoding questions, encoding responses) may distort the meaning and interpretation of the scores. In essence, because the disability is intertwined with the constructs being measured, allowing accommodations may effectively exempt these students with high-incidence disabilities from demonstrating the cognitive skills that the assessments are designed to index (Phillips, 1994).

Assuming that high rates of participation in external testing programs can be achieved via the development of appropriate reporting mechanisms and standard accommodation policies, two critical challenges for the assessment community will nevertheless still remain. These additional challenges persist because of inadequte knowledge about how teachers can achieve the reform's difficult standards, and because school resources often preclude the kinds of intensive instruction required to make achievement of those standards a reality for students with high-incidence disabilities. One challenge involves the development of a defensible assessment process for determining the appropriateness of attaching individual high-stakes consequences to the participation of students with disabilities in external testing programs. The other challenge is to examine the viability of, necessity for, and requirements of supplementary, individually tailored assessment systems for guiding teachers' instructional decision making for individuals with high-incidence disabilities.

*Developing Assessments to Identify Students for Exemption From High-Stakes Individual Consequences.* To ensure representation in accountability programs and to increase the probability of reaping the benefits of reform efforts, students with disabilities must be included in state and national testing programs to the greatest extent possible. Participation and representation do not, however, dictate that the high-stake *individual* consequences associated with some of these programs, such as high school graduation, must be attached to that participation. If, in fact, the knowledge and resources for achieving those standards currently are underdeveloped, then it will be necessary to assess each individual's disability to determine when the attachment of those consequences is fair and reasonable.

Considerations that must be factored into such an assessment process include identification of the skills required for success in the targeted postschool setting, the extent to which the school system has the knowledge and resources to deliver an instructional program to realize mastery of the reform standards for that individual, and the potential trade-offs between allocating instructional time on the reform standards as opposed to other instructional focuses. Moreover, when individual consequences are deemed inappropriate for a student with a disability, alternative policies for determining high-stakes decisions, such as when to award a high school diploma or when to advance to a higher grade, must be developed to reflect equitable and legal treatment.

*Is Participation in These State Accountability Programs Adequate to Accomplish Better Outcomes?* The third critical assessment issue related to external testing on performance assessments is whether these state accountability programs are adequate to accomplish the goal of higher expectations and outcomes for students with high-incidence disabilities. On the one hand, as already discussed, it is possible that broad participation in these assessment programs activities may be necessary. On the other hand, such participation is unlikely to represent a sufficient condition for promoting high expectations for students with disabilities. This is due to the enormous gap between the level of achievement required in most performance assessments and the actual performance levels of most students with high-incidence disabilities. Research documents that such distal goals may not motivate students and teachers, and may not enhance student learning (Locke, Shaw, Saari, & Latham, 1981). Consequently, for many students with high-incidence disabilities, it may be necessary to supplement common, high-stakes assessment programs with a supplementary assessment and accountability system that provides a more proximal framework for assessing and monitoring individual student learning.

In fact, for students with high-incidence disabilities, a second approach to accountability currently does exist. That is, special education has a supplementary accountability system with the explicit purpose of increasing expectations and learning. Whereas the general education strategy involves annual (or less frequent) large-scale assessments and sets high, uniform standards without consideration of individual differences, the special education strategy requires frequent assessment and sets flexible standards that allow for individual differences. This special education perspective is codified in the Individual Education Plan (IEP) process.

Unfortunately, the IEP assessment and accountability process has been shown to operate ineffectively (National Academy of Sciences, 1997). Nevertheless, the potential for a greatly revised IEP process to increase expectations and learning already has been demonstrated. Although not currently implemented widely, researchers (Deno, 1985; Shapiro & Kratochwill, 1988) have developed systems, such as CBM, that provides reliable and valid assessment information about student learning. Research illustrates how increases in teacher and student expectations as well as student learning can be achieved when practitioners use these individually referenced assessment systems (Fuchs et al., 1991; Wesson, 1991). A revised IEP framework, built on these strong measurement systems for monitoring students' acquisition of fundamental skills, would correct many of the ills associated with current, common IEP practice. These revised systems focus on student outcomes rather than procedural inputs; they help teachers attend to broad, important, but realistic goals, rather than long lists of short-term objectives; they correspond directly with the skills necessary to promote successful postschool adjustments for students with high-incidence disabilities; and, for students with disabilities, they provide a mechanism for supplementing the broader, more distal standards-based reform assessment activities.

Clearly, however, additional research must be conducted to answer questions related to how the general and special education accountability systems operate separately and in combination. These questions include: What kinds of structures promote the potential benefits of general education accountability frameworks for students with high-incidence disabilities? Is a special education, IEP strategy still necessary when students with high-incidence disabilities participate broadly in general education accountability programs? In what ways does a revamped IEP system, with a strong focus on objective measurement of student outcomes (represented in systems such as CBM), supplement the general education perpsective? How do the general and special education accountability systems, separately and in combination, contribute to program planning and student learning? What costs are associated with revamped IEP accountability systems that incorporate a strong focus on outcomes? These questions, central to the assessment of students with high-incidence disabilities, are essential to understanding whether, and if so how, the IEP process should be maintained as part of special education practice.

Before closing, it is important to note that a key disadvantage to a supplementary, special education accountability system is that it may be viewed as a capitulation to present inequities in performance. This could represent a political liability. After all, as summarized by McLaughlin et al. (1995), the most important impetus for the performance assessment movement associated with standards-based reform is to affirm high-level performance standards for all students and to prevent the self-fulfilling consequences of setting lower expectations for previously low-achieving groups—including students with high-incidence disabilities. Political problems notwithstanding, however, providing a realistic, supplementary mechanism for addressing the specific learning requirements, acknowledging the skills necessary for successful postschool adjustments, and creating high and challenging but individualized standards for students with high-incidence disabilities seem to reflect the substantive spirit of standards-based reform. Moreover, such a supplementary system could be designed in a fair and rigorous manner so that schools are not permitted to use that system as an excuse to set low standards for students with high-incidence disabilities.

## CONCLUSIONS

Performance assessment's focus on the solution of real-life problems creates some important opportunities for the field of high-incidence disabilities. These children often master discrete skills without demonstrating the capacity to transfer those skills to situations where the application of multiple skills and strategies is required. This sort of skill acquisition, without corresponding skill application, severely restricts an individual's capacity to function flexibly and adaptably outside of school. On the one hand, internal performance assessments offer systematic opportunities for teachers to examine this type of skill application; the hope is that the resulting classroom assessment information will help teachers design more effective programs for accomplishing skill application. On the other hand, external performance assessments provide the impetus for teachers to take this teaching agenda seriously—to strive to achieve these complex standards for their students with high-incidence disabilities.

Nevertheless, as illustrated in this chapter, performance assessment also poses some formidable challenges to the field of high-incidence disabilities. It remains unknown whether schools, in light of constraints on available knowledge and resources, can deliver on the promises associated with the implementation of performance assessments. The first order of business is to design technically defensible assessments that can satisfy internal as well as external testing purposes. The second obstacle is to develop methods for helping teachers use these assessments to improve their instructional planning. The third challenge is to identify fair, clear policies that permit students with high-incidence disabilities to participate in these assessment programs in ways that do not threaten their simultaneous, and sometimes competing, need to accomplish more fundamental skills—such as achieving literacy.

As described by Steve Forman, a project officer with the National Assessment of Education Progress (NAEP) during an interview with *The Wall Street Journal* (Trost, 1992), the testing pendulum "swings back and forth .... Twenty-three years ago, NAEP was using open-ended, hands-on types of exercises ... then the pendulum swung back to multiple choice, and now it's swinging back the other way" (p. 16). To avoid another pendulum swing back toward a singular focus on traditional testing models, performance assessment developers need to define clear sets of methods, that practitioners can use profitably and efficiently for the range of learners they find in their classrooms, including individuals with high-incidence disabilities. The developers also need to document related effects empirically and carefully—using rules of evidence that can satisfy a wide range of audiences. As teachers seek to identify assessment methods that broaden and enrich their instructional programs for students with high-incidence disabilities, they must demand this type of evidence.

## REFERENCES

Anderson-Inman, L., Walker, H. M., & Purcell, J. (1984). Promoting the transfer of skills across settings: Transenvironmental programming for handicapped students in the mainstream. In W. L. Heward, T. E. Heron, D. S. Hill, & J. Trap-Porter (Eds.), *Focus on behavior analysis in education* (pp. 17–37). Columbus, OH: Merrill.

Archbald, D. A., & Newmann, F. M. (1988). *Beyond standardized testing: Assessing academic achievement in the secondary school.* Reston, VA: National Association of Secondary School Principals.

Baker, E. L. (1991, April). *Expectations and evidence for alternative assessment.* Paper presented at the annual meeting of the American Educational Research Association, Chicago.

Baker, E. L., O'Neil, H. F., & Linn, R. L. (1993). Policy and validity prospects for performance-based assessment. *American Psychologist, 48,* 1210–1218.

Baxter, G. P., Shavelson, R. J., Goldman, S. R., & Pine, J. (1992). Evaluation of procedure-based scoring for hands-on science assessment. *Journal of Educational Measurement, 29,* 1–17.

Braddock, J., II, Hawley, W., Hunt, T., Oakes, J., Slavin, R., & Wheelock, A. (1992). *Realizing our nation's diversity as an opportunity: Alternatives to sorting America's children.* Nashville, TN: Vanderbilt Institute for Public Policy Studies, Center for Education and Human Development Policy.

Bransford, J., Goldman, S. R., & Hasselbring, T. S. (1995, April). *Marrying constructivist and skills-based models: Should we and could technology help?* Symposium presented at the annual meeting of the American Educational Research Association, San Francisco.

Brewer, R. (1991, April). *Authentic assessment: The rhetoric and the reality.* Paper presented at the annual meeting of the American Educational Research Association, Chicago.

Callahan, R. E. (1962). *Education and the cult of efficiency.* Chicago: University of Chicago Press.

Darling-Hammond, L. (1992, April). *Reframing the school reform agenda: Developing capacity for school transformation.* Paper presented at the annual meeting of the American Educational Research Association, San Francisco.

Deno, S. L. (1985). Curriculum-based measurement: The emerging alternative. *Exceptional Children, 52,* 219–232.

Elliott, S. N. (1995). *Performance assessment of students' achievement: Research and practice.* Paper prepared for the Board on Testing and Assessment, National Research Council, National Academy of Sciences.

Erickson, R. N., & Thurlow, M. (1996). *State special education outcomes 1995.* Minneapolis: University of Minnesota, National Center on Educational Outcomes.

Erickson, R. N., Thurlow, M., & Thor, K. (1995). *1994 state special education outcomes.* Minneapolis: University of Minnesota, National Center on Educational Outcomes.

Fuchs, D., & Fuchs, L. S. (1994). Inclusive schools movement and the radicalization of special education reform. *Exceptional Children, 60,* 294–309.

Fuchs, L. S. (1994). *Connecting performance assessment to instruction*. Reston, VA: Council for Exceptional Children.

Fuchs, L. S., Fuchs, D., Hamlett, C. L., Phillips, N. R., & Bentz, J. (1994). Classwide curriculum-based measurement: Helping general educators meet the challenge of student diversity. *Exceptional Children, 61,* 440–451.

Fuchs, L. S., Fuchs, D., Hamlett, C. L., & Stecker, P. M. (1990). The role of skills analysis in curriculum-based measurement in math. *School Psychology Review, 19,* 6–22.

Fuchs, L. S., Fuchs, D., Hamlett, C. L., & Stecker, P. M. (1991). Effects of curriculum-based measurement and consultation on teacher planning and student achievement in mathematics operations. *American Educational Research Journal, 28,* 617–641.

Fuchs, L. S., Fuchs, D., Karns, K., Hamlett, C. L., & Katzaroff, M. (1997). *Mathematics performance in the classroom: Effects on teacher planning and student learning*. Manuscript submitted for publication.

Fuchs, L. S., Fuchs, D., Karns, K., Hamlett, C. L., Katzaroff, M., & Dutka, S. (1998). Comparisons among individual and cooperative performance assessments and other measures of mathematics competence. *Elementary School Journal, 99,* 3–22.

Goodman, J. (1995). Change without difference: School restructuring in historical perspective. *Harvard Educational Review, 65,* 1–28.

Hambleton, R. K., Jaeger, R. M., Koretz, D., Linn, R. L., Millman, J., & Phillips, S. E. (1995). *Review of the measurement quality of the Kentucky Instructional Results Information System* (Final Report). Prepared for the Office of Educational Accountability, Kentucky General Assembly, Lexington, KY.

Harris, K. R., & Graham, S. (Eds.). (1994). Implications of constructivism for students with disabilities and students at risk: Issues and directions [Special Issue]. *The Journal of Special Education, 28*(3).

Hendrick, I. G., & MacMillan, D. L. (1984, April). *The role of mental testing in shaping special classes for the retarded*. Paper presented at the annual meeting of the American Educational Research Association, New Orleans.

Hendrick, I. G., & MacMillan, D. L. (1989). Selecting children for special education in New York City: William Maxwell, Elizabeth Farrell, and the development of ungraded classes, 1900–1920. *The Journal of Special Education, 22,* 395–418.

Hodgkinson, H. L. (1995). What should we call people? Race, class, and the census for 2000. *Phi Delta Kappan, 77,* 173–179.

Jenkins, J. R., Jewell, M., Leceister, N., Jenkins, L., & Troutner, N. (1990, April). *Development of a school building model for educating handicapped and at risk students in general education classrooms*. Paper presented at the annual meeting of the American Educational Research Association, Boston.

Kavale, K. A., & Reece, J. H. (1992). The character of learning disabilities. *Learning Disability Quarterly, 15,* 74–94.

Koretz, D., Mitchell, K., Barron, S., & Keith, S. (1996). *Final report: Perceived effects of the Maryland School Performance Assessment Program*. Los Angeles: National Center for Research on Evaluation, Standards, and Student Testing (CRESST).

Linn, R. L. (1991). Dimensions of thinking: Implications for testing. In B. F. Jones & L. Idol (Eds.), *Educational values and cognitive instruction: Implications for reform* (pp. 179–208). Hillsdale, NJ: Lawrence Erlbaum Associates.

Linn, R. L., Baker, E. L., & Dunbar, S. B. (1991, November). Complex, performance-based assessment: Expectations and validation criteria. *Educational Researcher*, 15–21.

Locke, E. A., Shaw, K. N., Saari, L. M., & Latham, G. P. (1981). Goal-setting and task performance: 1969–1980. *Psychological Bulletin, 90*, 125–152.

McDonnel, L. M., McLaughlin, M. J., & Morison, P. (Eds.). (1997). *Educating one and all: Students with disabilities and standards-based reform*. Washington, DC: National Academic Press.

McLaughlin, M. W., Shepard, L. A., & O'Day, J. A. (1995). *Improving education through standard-based reform: A report of the National Academy of Education panel on standards-based reform*. Stanford, CA: The National Academy of Education.

Mory, E., & Salisbury, D. (1992, April). *School restructuring: The critical element of total system design*. Paper presented at the annual meeting of the American Educational Research Association, San Francisco.

National Academy of Sciences, Committee on Goals 2000 and the Inclusion of Students with Disabilities. (1997). *Educating one and all: Students with disabilities and standards-based reform*. Washington, DC: National Academy Press.

Pearson, D. P. (1989). Commentary: Reading the whole-language movement. *Elementary School Journal, 90*, 231–241.

Phillips, S. E. (1994). High-stakes testing accommodations: Validity versus disabled rights. *Applied Measurement in Education, 7*(2), 93–120.

Research for Better Schools. (1988). *Special education in America's cities: A descriptive study*. Philadelphia: Author.

Sammons, K. B., Kobett, B., Heiss, J., & Fennell, F. S. (1992, February). Linking instruction and assessment in the mathematics classroom. *Arithmetic Teacher*, pp. 11–15.

Shapiro, E. S., & Kratochwill, T. R. (Eds., 1988). *Behavioral assessment in schools: Conceptual foundations and practical applications*. New York: Guilford.

Shavelson, R. J., Baxter, G. P., & Pine, J. (1992). Performance assessments: Political rhetoric and measurement reality. *Educational Researcher, 21*(4), 22–27.

Shepard, L. A. (1989). Why we need better assessments. *Educational Leadership, 46*.

Shriner, J., & Thurlow, M. (1992). *State special education outcomes 1991*. Minneapolis: University of Minnesota, National Center on Educational Outcomes.

Speece, D. L., & Cooper, D. H. (1990). Ontogeny of school failure: Classification of first-grade children. *American Educational Research Journal, 27*, 119–140.

Stallings, J. A. (1995). Ensuring teaching and learning in the 21st century. *Educational Researchers, 24*(6), 4–8.

Symons, S., Woloshyn, V., & Pressley, M. (Eds.). (1994). The scientific evaluation of the whole-language approach to literacy development. *Educational Psychologist, 29*(4), 173–222.

Thurlow, M. L. (1994). *National and state perspectives on performance assessment and students with disabilities*. Reston, VA: Council for Exceptional Children.

Thurlow, M., Scott, D., & Ysseldyke, J. (1995). *A compilation of states' guidelines for including students with disabilities in assessments* (Synthesis Report No. 17). Minneapolis: University of Minnesota, National Center on Educational Outcomes.

Trost, C. (1992, November 4). Report criticizes traditional methods of math testing and offers new models. *The Wall Street Journal.*

U.S. Congress, Office of Technology Assessment. (1992, February). *Testing in American schools: Asking the right questions* (OTA-SET-519). Washington, DC: U. S. Government Printing Office. (ED 340 770)

Wesson, C. L. (1991). Curriculum-based measurement and two models of follow-up consultation. *Exceptional Children, 57*, 246–257.

White, O. R. (1984). Descriptive analysis of extant research literature concerning skill generalization and the severely/profoundly handicapped. In M. Boer (Ed.), *Investigating the problem of skill generalization: Literature review* (pp. 1–19). Seattle: University of Washington, Washington Research Organization.

Wiggins, G. (1989). A true test: Toward more authentic and equitable assessment. *Phi Delta Kappan, 70*, 703–713.

Wightman, L. F. (1993). *Test takers with disabilities: A summary of data from special administrations of the LSAT* (Research Report 93–03). Newton, PA: Law School Admission Council. Willingham, W. W. (1988). Discussion and conclusions. In W. W. Willingham, M. Ragosta, R. Bennett, H. Braun, D. Rock, & D. Powers (Eds.), *Testing handicapped people* (pp. 143–185). Boston: Allyn & Bacon.

Willingham, W. W. (1988). Discussion and conclusions. In W. W. Willingham, M. Ragosta, R. Bennett, H. Braun, D. Rock, & D. Powers (Eds.), *Testing handicapped people* (pp. 143–185). Boston: Allyn & Bacon.

Ysseldyke, J., Thurlow, M., McGrew, K. S., & Shriner, J. (1994). *Recommendations for making decisions about the participation of students with disabilities in statewide assessment programs* (Synthesis Report No. 15). Minneapolis: University of Minnesota, National Center on Educational Outcomes.

# PART III

## Policy

# 11 Confusing Each With All: A Policy Warning

**Martin J. Kaufman**
**Linda M. Lewis**
*University of Oregon*

The 1997 amendments to the Individuals With Disabilities Education Act (IDEA, PL 105-17) have dramatically altered the environment of policy in special education, and revealed policy tensions and issues that augur to muddle the continued emergence of deep re-formation of our nation's schools. Examination of these changes in the context of five policy goals underlying general and special education reform reveals a host of paradoxes and conflicting reference points, values, beliefs, and assumptions related to the sum of general and special education reforms and policy issues—with a disturbing view of the comprehensive effect. The reauthorization of IDEA provides ample evidence from a policy perspective that, utilizing a metaphor from Lester Thurow's (1997) recent book *The Future of Capitalism*, we have entered a "period of punctuated equilibrium" in federal special education policy.

This metaphor is drawn from a concept used in evolutionary biology. It refers to a disjuncture resulting from sudden change in the environment. The disappearance of the dinosaurs due to climate changes, or the movement from an agrarian to an industrial society following the invention of the steam engine, are examples of two such evolutionary disjunctures. Associated with a change of such dramatic magnitude is the uncertainty as to what will emerge. The 1997 reauthorization of IDEA produced, metaphorically, such a change in the policy environment related to educating individuals with disabilities.

For over 20 years, special education has been unique in federal education policy, defined by its focus on determining the needs and developing an individualized family service plan or educational program for each infant, toddler, child, and youth with disabilities. A distinctive feature of special education is that it is designed to meet the unique needs of an individual with disabilities, rather than to address the educational needs of a group or category of children. Federal grants to states for special education were justified and limited to sharing the excess costs associated with providing individually determined special education and related services and supports to individuals with disabil-

**223**

ities. Furthermore, federal funds were distributed to states based on the numbers of children identified and receiving special education services. This policy environment has been significantly changed by the IDEA amendments enacted in 1997.

Specifically, the amendments expand the educational scope of what is defined as a free appropriate public education (FAPE); they change the basis for calculating and distributing state formula grant awards; they broaden the use of IDEA state formula grant and discretionary grant funds; and they increase legislative prescriptiveness linking policy, administration, and professional practice. This shift in policy intention underlying expanded use of IDEA state formula grant and discretionary grant assistance is stated in Part A, Findings—Section 601 (c) (7) (A): "The Federal Government must be responsive to the growing needs of an increasingly more diverse society. A more equitable allocation of resources is essential for the Federal Government to meet its responsibility to provide an equal educational opportunity for all individuals." The 1997 amendments to IDEA have created a new policy environment which confuses the focus on *each* child needing special education with the aphorism of educating *all* children associated with educational reform.

This chapter is an effort to issue a warning about the policy intention and implementation dangers associated with the expansion of IDEA authorities from its focus on providing each individual with a disability a free appropriate public education (FAPE), to enabling federal special education funds to be used to enhance educational and health/social service system capacities to meet the needs of all. It is unclear what protections, special education programs, services, and supports will survive, become extinct, or evolve for individuals with disabilities and their families in this new policy ecology created by the 1997 amendments to IDEA.

The political consensus of stakeholders, policy influencers, and policymakers that occurred during the reauthorization of IDEA should not be construed to mean that they held common understanding or beliefs. It did represent a synchronization of multiple perspectives emphasizing the imperative to achieve sufficient agreement among legislators, general and special education administrators, professional associations, disability groups, and parent organizations to complete the more than 2-year reauthorization process. Underlying this reauthorization remain deep and significant differences related to educational policy goals (i.e., efficiency, equity, excellence, choice, and dignity) and policy intention (i.e., providing each individual with disabilities FAPE vs. building system capacity to meet the needs of all).

## DIMINISHES FREE AND APPROPRIATE PUBLIC EDUCATION

Until the recent amendments, FAPE was limited to those unique educational needs of individuals with disabilities requiring special education as delineated in a student's individualized education program (IEP). Through changes to the required content of the IEP (§614(d)), the 1997 amendments expand the scope of FAPE beyond the historical IEP focus on a student's annual goals, benchmarks, or short-term objectives related to special education, along with related and transition services. Now, through a shift in policy intention, the focus on individuals with disabilities and their unique needs for special education and related services has been expanded to encompass their participation and progress in the general education curriculum and assessment programs, where appropriate.

It might seem an advancement to expand federal special education focus on each disabled individual's special and general educational needs. After all, no one can question the desire for overall educational success for children with disabilities. The expanded policy intention underlying the change in IDEA's definition of FAPE appears to confuse meeting the special education needs of each individual with disabilities—whether in a special education placement or general education classroom—with their learning opportunities and progress in general education. The 1997 amendments to IDEA both expand the focus to include a student with disabilities' participation and progress in general education (whether receiving special education and related services or not related to this participation in general education), and authorize the use of special education funds to improve school district and building efforts to improve the learning opportunities and experiences provided to all children. The combined effect of these changes leads to a very slippery policy path.

## CHANGES IN CALCULATION AND DISTRIBUTION OF FUNDS TO STATES

The expansion of IDEA policy intention is further evidenced in the changes that were made in how federal grants to states are calculated and distributed. Previously, the size of each state's grant was based on the number of individuals with disabilities having an IEP and receiving special education and related services reported annually by states. Each annual appropriation was divided proportionately among the states based on this annual child count. As a state's annual count of children with disabilities receiving special education and related services changed, so did its relative share of the federal funds. Thus, the calculation and distribution of IDEA state formula grant assistance made an explicit connection between the number of individuals with disabilities provided special education and related services, and the amount of federal assistance distributed to a state (the purpose of that assistance being to share with states the excess costs associated with providing these services).

The 1997 amendments altered that connection ( §611 (e)). For the time being (perhaps for 1 or 2 more years, depending on Congressional appropriations), the basic formula for allocating federal funds on the basis of an annual child count will remain in place. However, once Congress appropriates $4.9 billion or more for state grants (the FY 1998 appropriation was $3.8 billion, a 22% increase over the previous year), a change in the allocation formula will take effect. At that funding level, the size of each state grant will no longer be based on the number of children with disabilities being served. Instead, at $4.9 billion and beyond, grants to states will be based on three calculations, with each state receiving : (a) an amount equal to each state's allocation in the fiscal year prior to the "trigger" year; (b) of the remaining funds, 85% to each state based on its 3 to 21 year old population as a proportion of the nation's census for this age group; and (c) the remaining 15% of the "new" funds to each state based on its 3 to 21-year-old population living in poverty as a proportion of the other states' similar-age population living in poverty.

The new federal allocation formula effectively eliminates the relationship between the excess cost of providing special education and related services to meet the unique needs of individuals with disabilities. It erases the historical rationale for the federal government providing states with financial assistance to educate individuals with disabilities. Consistent with the expanded operational definition of FAPE, the policy intention is to create regular education learning environments to enhance equal educational opportunities for all children, not just those requiring special education and related services. This shift in policy intention will result in policy actions and stakeholder policy experience (Guba, 1984), which in time will likely diminish federal funding to support the delivery of special education and related services. This policy shift reflects a change in political priorities to find resources, within deficit reduction guidelines, that can contribute and be redirected to address pressing urban and poverty issues. In this instance, the policy intention, metaphorically, is that all ships will benefit from a rising tide. That is, investment in general school reform will benefit all children in a public education system built for the masses, including individuals with disabilities. In effect, this policy shift diminishes the size of the ration of federal education assistance available to provide special education and related services.


## BROADENS THE USE OF IDEA FUNDS

### State Formula Grants

The 1997 amendments broadened the use of federal funds going to states and local education agencies for direct and support services, as well as funds awarded through competitive grants for research and development, personnel preparation, parent training, technical assistance, and other special purposes. By expanding the use of these funds, the focus of federal assistance on individuals with disabilities and their special education will be diminished.

In several ways, the 1997 amendments changed how state formula grant assistance can be used. States are now permitted to use these funds for children ages three to nine experiencing "developmental delays," as defined by the state (§602(3)(B)). Prior to 1997, this general category was limited to use for children ages three through five. This represents a potential expansion of services and use of special education resources, to primary grade children at risk for school failure, as well as to individuals with disabilities. Another example is the potential use of IDEA state formula grant funds to advance implementation of general education's school improvement plans. Comingling of IDEA resources with general education funds in such a manner may have nothing to do with the federal role of sharing the excess costs associated with providing special education and related services. Rather, these funds may be used to provide all children, including those with disabilities, improved general education learning opportunities. Another illustration of the incremental disappearance of the federal role in contributing to the excess costs of providing special education and related services is the use of IDEA state formula grant assistance to support the development and implementation of a statewide coordinated services system to improve results for all children, including children with disabilities (§611(f)(3)(G)). Again, the policy intention is to improve results for all children and families, including children with disabilities and their families who require such supports.

The danger inherent in changing the basis for distribution of IDEA state formula grant funds and for their use is the disappearance of the distinctive legislative policy which required that special education funds be used to meet the unique educational needs of each individual with disabilities. All other major federal education programs (e.g., serving low-income/low-achieving students, or limited English proficient students) support the provision of services to an explicitly defined group or category of students with no special requirement for individualization. IDEA's distinctive legislative architecture is being redesigned and replaced such that it may become indistinguishable from other equity-oriented legislation (PL 103-382, Improving America's Schools Act of 1994). If one is cynical, this shift can readily be viewed as one more step potentially leading toward support for a political agenda that would incorporate federal assistance for individuals with disabilities into a general purpose education block grant.

## Local Education Agencies (LEA) Use of Funds

Along with broadening the use of IDEA formula grant funds by state education agencies for purposes other than special education and related services, the IDEA amendments of 1997 also free up local education agencies (LEAs) to spend their IDEA dollars in new ways. When federal appropriations reach $4.1 billion for the assistance to states program—an event expected to occur as early as FY 1999 in light of recent large increases allocated to this program by Congress—school districts will be permitted to spend up to 20% of the funds they receive that exceed what they received in the previous year as if those funds were "local" funds (§613(a)(2)(C)). In other words, none of the IDEA requirements governing the expenditure of federal dollars by school districts will apply to the 20% of federal funds they receive in excess of their prior year award. School districts will be free to reduce the level of effort, or to use these funds for purposes other than serving children with disabilities.

In another change expanding the ways in which LEA can use IDEA funds, the 1997 amendments permit school districts to use some or all of their IDEA dollars to carry out a schoolwide program for disadvantaged children under Section 1114 of the Elementary and Secondary Education Act of 1965 (§ 613(a)(2)(D)). Under this new provision, for those children with disabilities served in a district's schoolwide program for educationally disadvantaged children, the LEA will be able to allocate each disabled child's share of the district's IDEA funds to support that program rather than for special education and related services directly. Finally, as a result of the 1997 amendments of the act, school districts (like their state education agency counterparts) are now permitted to use up to "five percent of the IDEA funds they receive to develop and implement a coordinated services system designed to improve results for children and families, including children with disabilities and their families" (§613(f)). Together, these policy changes governing LEA use of funds have the potential to further erode the relationship between federal funding and the provision of special education and related services to meet the unique needs of individuals with disabilities.

## Part D Discretionary Grant Funds

Since the 1960s the federal government has provided support, through competitive grants and contracts, for research and development, professional preparation, technical assistance, parent training, systems change, information services, and other activities to improve outcomes for individuals with disabilities. Part D of the act as amended continues to authorize such activities to create, maintain, and improve the quality and effectiveness of early intervention, special education, and related services for children with disabilities. The resources provided through these discretionary programs have been instrumental in the development of a national infrastructure of organizations, individuals, and agencies distributed across the country and within each state, creating a national capacity to continuously improve educational and developmental outcomes for children with disabilities.

A feature of these discretionary grant programs, a component of IDEA since 1975 (and before that in other federal special education legislation), has been that the resources they provide have been almost exclusively restricted to activities focusing on the needs of children with disabilities. These programs were intended to support the continuous improvement and advancement of the quality and effectiveness of early intervention, special education, transition, and related services, and advancement of professional preparation and practices provided to individuals with disabilities.

The 1997 amendments to IDEA have expanded how these discretionary grant funds can be used, just as they broadened the use of state formula grant funds. Amendments to the law's administrative provisions give the Secretary of Education authority to fund projects that will benefit individuals with disabilities as well as projects that address the needs of low-achieving students, under-served populations, children from low-income families, and children with limited English proficiency (§661(e)(2)(C)). Still another amendment, driven perhaps by the goals of reinventing government, frees the Secretary of

Education from the generally required practice of inviting public notice, review, and comment prior to the publication of most funding priorities for the discretionary grant programs (§661(e)(2)). Not only does the law now permit the Department of Education to use IDEA discretionary grant funds to address the needs of nondisabled children, but it also permits the Department to do so without public notice, review, or comment.

As with the state formula grant program, policy intention has shifted in the discretionary programs, which previously were legislatively designated to support the advancement and quality of special education and related services, to a new design intended to systematically enhance school improvement and educational outcomes for all children. The policy danger in permitting IDEA discretionary grant support to be used to address system capacity to meet the needs of all children is to diminish support for programs solely focused on early intervention, special education, transition, and related services to meet the unique developmental and learning needs of each individual with disabilities.

This shift in policy focus endangers the future maintenance of a national synergism between special education professionals and parents of children with disabilities to continuously advance professional practice and advocate for improving the education of individuals with disabilities. The redirection of IDEA discretionary grant support will diminish the resources necessary to maintain a national infrastructure connecting families, parent and advocate organizations, professional organizations, early intervention and special education teachers and administrators, and universities. It is this national infrastructure of stakeholders and its performance capacity that have quietly, effectively, and dramatically enhanced America's public education system to be able to make the modifications, accommodations, and adjustments needed to meet the needs of each individual with a disability.

What is in jeopardy is the federal support to sustain the national performance capacity essential to create future knowledge and practice advancements underlying the remarkable achievements of our nation's communities and schools, in developing and supporting the early intervention, special education, transition, and related service system—and in parent training and professional preparation programs. Past investments by IDEA discretionary grant programs have changed not only the education of children with disabilities, but also their lives. These Part D discretionary competitive grant programs have focused on meeting the needs of each infant, toddler, child, and youth with a disability, and their families. As well, these grants have been significant in providing the essential resources to create the knowledge, prepare professional personnel, induce system change, and support training and advocacy that have transformed parents' hopes for their children with disabilities into tomorrow's realistic expectations.

Broadening the use of IDEA funds represents the first serious legislative policy shift that has the potential to serve as the impetus for separating the administration of state formula grant programs from its management of discretionary programs. The 1997 amendments make more likely the success of future efforts, which have failed in previous congressional sessions, to reassign administrative responsibility for discretionary programs under the auspices of the Office of Special Education Programs within the U.S. Department of Education (OSEP) to the Department of Education's Office of Educational Research and Improvement (OERI). Such an organizational separation of IDEA programs jeopardizes the unique synergism and leveraging power of the linkages between federal state formula grant and discretionary competitive grant programs. Federal legislation and leadership that fosters and enables the creation and strength of this national infrastructure (i.e., local, state, and federal) linking policy leaders, service providers, and university professionals, along with parent and professional organizations, has been and will continue to be the unique strength producing the extraordinary advancements in meeting the unique developmental and educational needs of individuals with disabilities. It is this national "community of practice" and its linked infrastructure that contributed to the National Academy of Education's (1991) citing the administration of IDEA's research and demonstration programs as exemplary and recommending that they serve as a model for all federal education programs.

The underlying explanation of how this punctuated policy equilibrium emerged in the policy shifts reflected in the 1997 amendments to IDEA requires understanding the beliefs, values, and policy goals of the stakeholders influencing the IDEA reauthorization process. The reauthorization of IDEA occurred in the context of the Executive Branch's efforts to foster educational reform, the recent amendments to the Elementary and Secondary Education Act (PL 103-382, Improving America's Schools Act of 1994), and recent Congressional legislative actions to design federal legislation to support reform of our nation's public education system. Consensus emerged from these initiatives focusing on the need for systemic change to reduce policy fragmentation to create an education system focused on meeting the needs of all children to achieve raised academic standards.

The reauthorization of IDEA resulted in legislative compromises associated with resolving contradictory policy goals of efficiency, equity, excellence, choice, and human dignity. The resolution of these contradictions is all the more difficult in the context of a public education system that provides rationed services. Thus, the question is who should receive what type and amount of rationed services, and who should make such decisions and how they should be made. Historically, the past 30-plus years have focused on policy goals of efficiency and equity. Educational reform has brought to the foreground the policy goal of excellence and choice, whereas the advances in meeting the educational needs of individuals with disability have added a policy goal of human dignity.

The 1997 amendments to IDEA occurred in part because general educators, special educators, and parents of children with disabilities were supportive of creating an inclusive education system (Davis, 1992; Gartner & Lipsky, 1987; National Association of State Boards of Education, 1992). However, the policy goals of stakeholder advocates for general and special education systemic reform and inclusive education were not necessarily in synchronization. *All* became an aphorism that for general educators was associated with systemic reform based on the contradictory goals of efficiency and excellence; whereas, for parents of children with disabilities and many special educators *all* was a synonym for *each*, and support for policy goals focused on equity, choice, and dignity. Thus, the political consensus reached reflected a belief that the 1997 amendments to IDEA represented the best compromise that could be reached among stakeholders, and that having the act reauthorized was of primary importance. Furthermore, the compromises were incremental and could be revisited in future Congressional oversight and reauthorization hearings.

## TOP-DOWN LINKING OF POLICY, ADMINISTRATION, AND PRACTICE

Underlying many of the IDEA Amendments of 1997 is a top-down, or forward-mapping assumption, which presumes a tight linkage among policy, administration, and professional practice. In contrast, a bottom-up or backward mapping assumption for establishing policy intention is based on a presumption that policy, administration, and professional practice are loosely coupled (Elmore, 1979). General education reform and IDEA increasingly either presume or expect a tight hierarchical linkage among the federal, state, and local agencies.

In spite of its inability to complete the reauthorization of IDEA, the 104th Congress appropriated for FY 1997 the largest increase in Part B state formula grant assistance since the enactment of PL94-142 in FY 1975. This $785 million increase represented a one third increase in the level of federal Part B state formula grant assistance. In fact, between FY 1996 and FY 1998 Congress increased Part B state formula grant assistance by $1.5 billion, or 64%. This also represented a windfall increase for state education agencies (SEAs) which receive 25% of these funds (5% for administration, and 20% for their discretion to use for direct and support services). Thus, in this same 3-year period (FY 1996 to FY 1998), SEAs received an additional $369 million, or 64%, increase to add to their administrative capacity and to fund SEA established priorities. In comparison, Congressional funding for IDEA discretionary competitive grant programs during this same 3-year period increased by $34 million, or 13.9%. This is the equivalent of designing a superb automobile (state formula grants) and leaving it parked at a curb where it can be seen, but not providing any funds for a driver or fuel (e.g., knowledge creation, professional preparation, parent training) to take it to future destinations.

Concurrently, the Executive Branch (i.e., U.S. Department of Education, Office of Special Education Programs) recommended to Congress that a new discretionary assistance program for state education agencies—State Program Improvement Grants for Children With Disabilities—be added to the act. This action was taken in spite of the fact that in FY 1998 states already received 94.2% of all IDEA federal assistance. The policy intention of this new top-down-oriented program is to provide state education agencies and "their" designated partners discretionary grant awards to reform and improve their systems for providing "educational, early intervention, and transitional services, including their systems for professional development, technical assistance, and dissemination of knowledge about best practices, to improve results for children with disabilities" (§651(b)).

IDEA, Part D, Subpart 1—State Program Improvement Grants for Children With Disabilities (§655 (a)(1)) authorizes the Secretary of Education to make an award to each state education agency whose application the Secretary has selected for funding. In addition, the act provides the Secretary, at his or her discretion, the authority to make inflationary adjustments to these discretionary awards (§655(b)). The awards to states will range from $500,000 to $2 million for each state, including the District of Columbia and the Commonwealth of Puerto Rico, and not less than $80,000 for outlying areas. Thus, if on average each state education agency were to receive a $1 million state program improvement grant, a minimum of $52 million plus awards to outlying areas would be requested to fund this section of the Act. This would amount to approximately 20% of all discretionary competitive grant funds.

Funded at $35.2 million in FY 1998, support for the state program improvement grants leaves $244 million for the remaining Part D national initiative programs that represent a bottom-up orientation to improving educational practice and outcomes. At the FY 1998 level, only 5 cents of each IDEA dollar is allocated to these-bottom up initiatives. If, as it seems likely, Congress appropriates more funds in the next few years to state program improvement grants, the relative IDEA investment in bottom-up solutions will decrease even further, unless Congress also increases support for the other Part D programs.

The top-down policy presumption of tight linkages among federal policy, state and local administration, and professional practice is evidenced in Part D (§653(c)), titled "Improvement Strategies." For example, (§653(c)(3)(D)(vi)) states that "the State will enhance the ability of teachers and others to use strategies, such as behavioral interventions, to address the conduct of children with disabilities that impedes the learning of children with disabilities and others." A similar example suggesting the existence of a tight linkage among policy, administration, and professional practice is "the State will, ... when appropriate, adopt promising practices, materials, and technology" (§653(c)(3)(D)(vii)). Such statutory language represents a belief that policymakers should, through legislation, guide professional practice.

This top-down orientation to policy is also evidenced in Part B (§614(d)), Individualized Education Programs. The amendments expand policy intentions from statements of student needs and objectives to prescriptions for professional practice. For example, in Section 614(d)(3)(B) it states that "the IEP Team shall—(i) in the case of a child whose behavior impedes his or her learning or that of others, consider, when appropriate, strategies, including *positive behavioral interventions, strategies, and supports* (italics added) to address that behavior." As with the earlier-cited example, Congress demonstrated its belief in the tight linkage between legislation and professional practice by directing attention to specific interventions.

Such top-down prescriptiveness and assumed linkage among federal policy intention, state and local administration, and professional practice reaches its zenith in Section 614(d)(3)(C). This section, titled "Requirement With Respect to Regular Education Teacher," provides the following:

> The regular education teacher of the child, as a member of the IEP Team, shall, to the extent appropriate, participate in the development of the IEP of the child, including the determination of appropriate positive behavioral interventions and strategies and the determination of supplementary aids and services, program modifications, and support for school personnel. (§ 614(d)(3)(C))

In this instance, federal legislators are directing local IEP teams, specifically the expectations for what regular teachers should contribute to an IEP meeting. It is not difficult to interpret such top-down policy intentions as confusing the need for broad federal legislative policy direction for all students with the bottom-up professional expertise and parent perspectives required by the IEP process to determine the needs of each individual child with disabilities, current student levels of performance, development and learning objectives, evaluation criteria, and special education services and supports to be provided. Once again, the policy intention, when examined from a top-down versus bottom-up perspective, confuses *each* with *all*.

While the IDEA Amendments of 1997 contain many other changes, the policy intentions associated with these particular modifications create an unprecedented period of punctuated equilibrium. As we enter this period of implementing and experiencing the opportunities and impact of these new policy intentions, the evolutionary implications for the provision of special education and related services in the future cannot be predicted. Although no crystal ball can guide us through this disjuncture, it is imperative that we better understand not the policy symptoms described previously, but rather the underlying paradoxes, perspectives, values, and assumptions associated with special education and general education policy goals and reforms.

## A POLICY THICKET

Once again, we use a metaphor drawn from Thurow (1997) on the concept of plate tectonics. In geology, the metaphor of plate tectonics refers to the appearance of the earth's surface as static when, in fact, the continental tectonic plates are continuously shifting. This movement is invisible from the surface, resulting from the current in the earth's magma. Metaphorically, the IDEA amendments of 1997 may appear, like the surface of the earth, to have only slightly changed the policy environment. However, like the movement of tectonic plates, significant movement is occurring as five policy goals (i.e., plates) continue to move and will potentially and unpredictably change the future policy environment enveloping general and special education.

The overt behavior of a volcano does not explain what is occurring under or within it. It is similarly true that understanding the policy magma contributing to the IDEA amendments of 1997 will not be discernible from the statute or report language. The starting points, metaphorically, are the policy goals (i.e., plates) of efficiency, equity, excellence, choice, and human dignity. These are not new policy goals. It is the emphasis or weight given to these goals that change over time. Linda Darling-Hammond (1993), writing about "Reframing the School Reform Agenda," described the current federal, state, and local educational policy ecology as requiring: "A massive geological dig ... to unearth the tangled influences that created the many layers of policy that people in schools must contend with. These influences make the serious implementation of new policies difficult, even impossible, without excavation and reform of what has gone before" (p. 756).

Special education and general education policy and reforms cannot distance themselves from politics. Politics is how differing perspectives, values, and contradictions are mediated and resolved. Coming to such judgments will require democratically resolving policy goals and values related to excellence, efficiency, equity, human dignity, and choice (Kearney, 1988).

*Efficiency* has been the sine qua non of our nation's education policy. It has meant doing the best for the most students at the least cost. When this goal was found to have unintentional, differential, and negative impacts on specific categories or individual students, an *equity* policy goal focused on equal educational opportunity and access was coupled to an educational system grounded on a policy intention of efficiency. In this instance, federal categorical programs such as those targeting low-income/low-achieving students, limited English proficient students, and individuals with disabilities were established in an effort to remedy perceived inequities. Currently, a policy of high expectations and standards of academic excellence undergirds education reforms. Historically, these standards have been associated with the 50% or fewer students anticipating pursuing a postsecondary education program, not with all students, and not with those with disabilities. Both general and special education have experienced demand for educational policy and opportunities that provide for student and family choice. Advocates of choice include parents dissatisfied with their neighborhood or other public schools because they have been unresponsive to a student's needs, are low-performing schools, or are unsafe. Parents and others want vouchers, charter schools, and private school placement options as publicly supported choices. Finally, disability advocates and special education reformers have pressed for public policies that are perceived as providing human dignity, such as self- or family determined supports, and full inclusion through opportunities to participate in all academic, cultural, athletic/recreational, and extracurricular programs with nonhandicapped peers.

It is the authors' position that the tensions raised by these five policy goals are longstanding, and have been relatively intractable to professional and political resolution. Their intractability derives from the difficulty in reconciling opinions, attitudes, beliefs, and values associated with the contradictions inherent in these five policy goals. The inherent contradictions among the five policy goals create a policy thicket preventing resolution. That is why Sarason (1990) wrote about the predictable failure of educational reform; Cuban (1990) analyzed why reforms return again, again, and again; and Tyack (1991) examined from an historical perspective policy talk and institutional practice. The exchange of aphorisms by stakeholders who have competing perspectives does not clarify or contribute to resolving the confusion associated with making less intractable the contradictory policy goals: how to resolve the rationing of fixed resources to meet the educational needs of each individual with disabilities while creating system capacity to provide all students with the necessary learning opportunities to successfully clear the bar of raised academic standards.

## POLICY CONTEXT ENVELOPING IDEA REAUTHORIZATION

The 1997 amendments to IDEA significantly expanded the policy intention and, concomitantly, the boundaries of this legislation. Underlying the amendments was a policy shift from a focus on access and provision of early intervention, preschool, elementary, and secondary special education, and transition services to individuals with disabilities, to enhancing the overall systemic capacity of community agencies and general education to be more effective with a wider, more diverse range of at-risk students. In making these amendments, Congress expanded the policy space previously defined as entitlements, requirements, and protections associated with the delivery of specialized services to individuals with disabilities from birth through the age of 21. The 1997 amendments resulted from a confluence of changing professional/advocate values, general education reform, a growing recognition by parents and special educators that community and school capacities must be strengthened, and inclusive contexts created that can support and provide individuals with disabilities effective opportunities to develop and learn.

The 1997 amendments to IDEA represent resolutions rather than solutions to open-ended social-political tensions among multiple policy goals (i.e., efficiency, equity, excellence, choice, and dignity). One should not think that the judgments and political compromises resulting in the significant changes in the policy space defined by these amendments will not change over time. The resolutions reached in balancing these multiple policy goals will need to be reviewed, and will require future adjustments in response to changing external events (e.g., national defense, economy, demography, technological changes), public satisfaction with school practices and student performance, and a professional knowledge base supported by research and policy analysis.

Because of the complex, interdependent relationships which loosely couple federal, state, and local general and special education policy, differing perspectives will continue to exist. These differences are reflected in the intentions, scope, prescriptiveness, and criteria for assessing educational reforms. It is imperative that policy research and analysis contribute to achieving and maintaining the interest and attention (Downs, 1972), trust, confidence, and support of policymakers, policy influencers, and policy stakeholders for overseeing the implementation and impact of the 1997 amendments to IDEA and their interaction with other federal and state general and special education reform initiatives.

Nelson (1977), in his book *The Moon and the Ghetto,* made clear the limits of rational analysis in coming to policy judgments. He suggested that underlying values, intentions, attitudes, and beliefs ultimately influence our choices. Yankelovich (1991) in his book *Coming to Public Judgment,* offered a theory stipulating the limits of information as a basis for coming to judgments. It is evident that policy research and analyses that address both the rationale and the values enveloping policy issues, solutions, and options are needed.

The following section is meant to illustrate the values and beliefs impeding a deeper understanding of the fundamental contradictions among policy goals associated with the 1997 amendments to IDEA. The implications of these underlying values and beliefs contribute to the stakeholder gridlock and policy goal confusion associated with meeting the unique needs of each individual with a disability and improving the systemic capacity to achieve better results for all students.

## RATIONALITY AND VALUES

### Meritocracy Versus Universality

The cultural, political, and professional values and beliefs underlying the following paradoxes may make more understandable the shifting balance of IDEA policy goals, legislative directions, implementation actions, and potential stakeholder reactions. *Meritocracy* refers to the position that "the purpose of schooling in a democracy is to allow children and youth to progress and develop on the basis of their own ability and talent—meritocratically" (Astuto, Clark, Read, McGree, & Fernandez, 1993, p. 9). It should be noted that this belief in meritocracy is often couched within the context of a policy goal of efficiency (do the best for the most children at the least cost). This orientation places the primary responsibility on each individual to pull himself or herself up by the bootstraps. Immerwahr (1991), in a study for the Public Agenda entitled *Crosstalk: The Public, The Experts, and Competitiveness,* illustrated this perspective in the attitude of the public about educational reform. During 12 focus groups held across the nation, the public expressed the belief that what is needed is for students to work harder.

*Universality* refers to a belief that society has a responsibility to ensure that all students learn, develop, and succeed (Clark & Astuto, 1994; Darling-Hammond, 1993). Implicit to this orientation is a recognition that our society does not provide an even playing field for all children to begin school at the same starting line. This perspective considers education not as a maintenance function, but instead as an instrument for social transformation and social class mobility. A belief in a universal approach to schooling is consistent with a policy goal of equity, where each individual has access to and is provided with the learning opportunities, services, and supports needed to realize his or her potential and/or established standards.

These two contradictory perspectives on the purpose of schools exist in the context of a public school system that survives on rationed (i.e., fixed) resources. Thus, the balancing or weighting of policy goals such as efficiency, equity, excellence, dignity, and choice occurs in a social-economic-political arena where the amount and distribution of fixed resources for educational goals must be determined. The current political and professional debates and resolutions associated with general and special education reform legislation are creating a new policy environment. The paradox between the beliefs associated with a meritocratic or universal orientation to public education dramatically shapes leaders' and stakeholders' opinions, attitudes, and beliefs about what reforms are needed, the nature of restructuring, the desirability of inclusion, and the types of accountability appropriate for schools.

The impact of these competing orientations for schools is evidenced in two studies conducted by the Public Agenda (Farkas, 1992, 1993), clearly documenting a cultural clash in perspectives. Business executives made judgments about schools based on productivity, efficiency, and results. They felt schools were "out of touch" with the demands of the workplace, tolerated mediocrity, and reflected a bloated bureaucracy. In contrast, educators made judgments about schools based on values of fairness, giving people a second chance, empathy, and nurturance. They felt business executives did not realize the pressure on today's children and dramatic changes in families and neighborhoods.

Implicit to these perspectives are the basic values as to what rights and entitlements students and families have to services, programs, and supports. These perspectives are likely to engender significantly different degrees of trust and confidence in educational policy, administration, and practices (e.g., monitoring, dispute settlement procedures, sanctions) depending on the aptitudes, abilities, and needs of the child.

## Professionalization Versus Accountability

Two of the significant trends of school reform—decentralized decision-making and increased demands for accountability—appear to be on a collision course (Foster, 1991; Steffy, 1993). In many states and districts, schools will be empowered to make more decisions locally through school-site councils or other vehicles. At the same time, national and state trends reflect a continuing desire to hold schools more accountable for performance. It will be challenging to devise accountability systems that provide wide latitude for local decisions and still institute accountability. It will require better ways to measure or judge school (and individual student) success (Ysseldyke, Thurlow, & Geenen, 1994).

Tension reflects itself in the ongoing debate about the overemphasis on performance standards and assessment, turning organizational resources and energies to documenting failure instead of to improvement activities. Clark and Astuto's (1994) article entitled "Redirecting Reform: Challenges to Popular Assumptions About Teachers and Students" represented the perceived contradiction between accountability and professionalization. Darling-Hammond (1993) focused on this tension when she wrote:

> Policy makers shift their efforts from designing controls intended to direct the system to developing the capacity of schools and teachers to be responsible for student learning and responsive to student and community needs, interests, and concerns.... The dramatic inequalities that currently exist in American schools cannot be addressed by pretending that mandating and measuring are the same thing as improving schools. (p. 754)

The cornerstone of educational reform is to ensure that there be high academic learning expectations and performance standards for all students. Realizing the goals of educational reform creates a tension between bottom-up professionalization and top-down accountability. Children with disabilities are caught in this conundrum. They need individualized programs based on bottom-up parent and professional planning and decision making focused on each child's unique educational needs resulting from their disability. At the same time, top-down federal legislation is emphasizing participation and progress in general education curriculum and state/national assessment programs designed for all students.

## Services and Programs Versus Supports

The federal and state statutes for special education have attempted to balance the rights of students to be educated with a highly individualized, deficit/remediation or amelioration model of disability, and a general educational system that has stipulated curricula, programs, and services. The starting point in these statutes is one of determining the types of adjustments and adaptations the system must undertake in order for children with disabilities to access the educational, social, and vocational benefits available through their schools.

Historically, these adjustments and adaptations have been made by local school districts developing special education services and programs delivered along some variants of a continuum of locations. Students are screened and referred for special education, and evaluated to determine their eligibility for special education by determining whether the child has a particular category of disability. Schools then develop an IEP specifying the student's present levels of performance and how the child's disability affects his or her involvement and progress in the general curriculum; identifying and meeting the educational needs of the child that result from the disability; determining and specifying the special education and related services and supplementary aids and services to be provided to the child; stating the program modifications or supports for school personnel that will be provided for the child; and stipulating annual educational goals and short-term objectives. Using this information, and following federal- and state- established procedural requirements, school district personnel attempt to match the students needs within the parameters of established special education programs, services, and resources.

Special education has evolved as a top-down created array of programs and services to enhance the capacity of a school district to more effectively and appropriately meet the unique educational needs of children with disabilities. Historically, special education programs and services emerged as a parallel add-on constellation of programs and services to supplement the capacity of general education. Mainstreaming and integration efforts that preceded inclusion were attempts to incrementally diminish the magnitude of special education's separation from general education programs.

Initially, inclusion as a special education reform was aimed at moving students with disabilities, especially those with moderate and severe disabilities, from self-contained classrooms and schools to general education classroom placements together with the services and supports needed to achieve effective social and learning outcomes. Mainstreaming, integration, and inclusion can be conceived of as emergent, dynamic, complex, and adapting concepts (Sailor, 1992).

Inclusion is a process of meshing general and special education reform initiatives and strategies in order to achieve a unified system of public education that incorporates all children and youths as active, fully participating members of the school community. Diversity is viewed by the school community as the norm. Administrators and teachers maintain a high-quality education by ensuring meaningful curriculum, effective teaching, and necessary supports for each student (e.g., Davis, 1992; NASBE, 1992). Some perceive this latest phase as special education's "break the mold" restructuring model for general education (Ferguson, 1994; Forest & Pearpoint, 1991). On the other hand, others raise the flag of caution that such an approach to special/general education reform that is universally focused on all is contradictory to effectively meeting the unique needs of each individual with disabilities (Fuchs & Fuchs, 1994).

The architects of inclusion in part are attempting to reengineer a system that looks up from the perspective of a client/family rather than top-down from the perspective of educational, health, and social system providers. Such a system would be oriented to client/family access and continuity of supports, rather than focused primarily on system coordination to provide and match preexisting programs and services to client/family needs. It would be designed to have the capacity and procedural flexibility to provide individuals with disabilities identified supports that meet child and family needs. Ideally, inclusionists envision a universal system where all, not just individuals with disabilities and their families, are empowered to access and benefit from natural "community" and "system" supports (e.g., educational, social, health, and employment) that can be tailored to comprehensively and holistically meet their changing needs.

It is the foundational design concept of supports resulting from inclusionary architecture that has the potential for making policy less fragmented, more coherent, and universal. However, it must be proven that such a reengineered special/general education system of individually determined supports can be designed, be efficient and effective, be taken to scale, and result in improved learning and development for each individual with disabilities.

## Learning Versus Curricula

The American Constitution leaves to states the responsibility for providing public education. In so doing, historically states and local school boards, not the federal government, have been considered to be the appropriate governmental entity for establishing school curricula. (This, coupled with a dominant professional and culturally accepted belief in a progressive orientation to education, underlies much of this century's romanticist philosophy to child development and learning.) This philosophy and orientation in education has emphasized learning that supports and aligns with the natural development of children, emphasizing creativity and imagination rather than prescribed curricula aligned with performance standards.

In contrast, a growing belief underlying the emergence of the current emphasis has been a policy goal of excellence rather than a policy goal focused on equity. This value has its origins in the enlightenment beliefs of our country's founding fathers, which posited the need to implement a curriculum that focused "on cultivating an aristocracy of talent and virtue, as well as the stringent rules for moral education" (Hirsch, 1996, p. 73).

The 1997 amendments to IDEA attempt to bridge the progressive, romantic values of an education based on individualized educational programs, with the enlightenment beliefs in a coherent, general education core curriculum. Special education is the basis for tailoring learning to meet the development and needs of each individual with a disability. Concurrently, general education provides appropriate opportunities to learn for all students, including those with disabilities, consistent with making progress in a standards-based general education curriculum and participation in national and state assessment programs.

The difficulty in reconciling these two educational philosophies of learning and the divergent cultural beliefs of both educators and our society is evidenced in the recent political debates associated with national testing to achieve greater coherence related to core curriculum content goals. Such standards-based curriculum content goals present a strong centralizing force operating in potential opposition to philosophies of education that emphasize student-centered educational programs. The resolution of whether policies are going to be driven by an accountability model, curricula/teaching frameworks, or continuous student learning concepts has significant implications for the extent to which special education designed to meet the unique needs of each individual with disabilities can be made compatible with standards-based reforms designed to be inclusive of all children, including those with disabilities.

These deeply held cultural, political, and professional values and beliefs create the policy magma and context that lead to the shifting balance in policy goals, as evidenced in the 1997 amendments to IDEA. Thus, at any given time the nature and extent of synchronization among our policy makers, stakeholders, and society in our democracy will temporarily struggle to come to judgments in order to resolve these educational paradoxes and contradictory policy goals shaping general and special education reforms.

## NEED FOR POLICY RESEARCH

Metaphorically, this changed policy environment represents a punctuated equilibrium where what have been the traditional policy intentions for the use of special education funds, and the boundaries of special education programs and services, have been significantly altered. What ultimately survives and evolves as protections, systemic capacity, early intervention, special education, and transition services in this new policy environment demands rigorous and ongoing policy research. Such policy research needs to heavily rely on bottom-up analysis of administrative implementation, professional and parent experience, and student outcomes. It is essential that ongoing policy research provide the feedback necessary to contribute precision in defining the problems, not symptoms, in need of implementation solutions.

Policy research is designed to focus on relationships between variables that reflect social problems and other variables that can be manipulated by public policy (Weimer & Vining, 1992). Policy analysis is a means of synthesizing information, including research results, to produce a format for policy decisions (i.e., alternative options), and of determining future needs for policy relevant information (Williams, 1971). Policy analysis is applied, interdisciplinary, politically sensitive, and client oriented (Hogwood & Gunn, 1984). Policy research is necessary but insufficient for effecting change. Policy research is needed to ensure that the policy problems and issues identified are not symptoms or proxies of a more deeply rooted set of relationships, values, or intentions. However, policy analysis is needed to generate alternative options and evaluate and forecast the consequences and trade-offs associated with each alternative-action or no-action option.

The primary policy need is to make more coherent and effective the expanded IDEA policy space within the context of general education reforms. The policy thicket described earlier is the result of an add-on fragmented approach to resolving multiple policy goals—excellence, efficiency, equity, human dignity, and choice (Kearney, 1988). The intractability of these issues and the fragmented approach to resolving contradictory policy goals derive from a fundamental contradiction between what policy leaders and stakeholders think are the nature and type of educational entitlements to be accorded to students and their families. Some assert that student entitlements to educational planning, decision making, supports, and protections should extend to each student on an individual basis or to only some categories of students. Others contend that educational entitlements should be limited to those provided to all students. These competing perspectives raise policy issues regarding what types of supports, services, adjustments, adaptations, and alternatives are available to which students, under what conditions, and how those decisions are to be made.

In light of the reality that American public education will continue to be a rationed system, the IDEA amendments create a policy environment that redistributes federal formula grant assistance to states in order to enhance the systemic capacity of school systems to be more effective for all students at the expense of meeting the unique educational needs of each individual with a disability. Operationally, all may be nothing more than another means for strengthening the policy goal of efficiency at the cost of support for policy goals that focus on equity and dignity. The policy conundrum is how to balance, in a public education system having rationed resources, the creation of enhanced system capacity to meet the needs of all students, and continue to provide special education and related services associated with providing each student with a disability a free, appropriate public education.

As we enter this new era of a punctuated equilibrium resulting from the 1997 IDEA amendments and the shifting balance of policy goals, their implications, and impact associated with confusing *each* and *all,* it is critical that policy research and analysis serve to:

1. Increase the capacity of stakeholders, policy influencers, and policymakers to oversee and guide implementation, and future IDEA reauthorizations and related legislation to ensure that the gains that have been achieved are not lost through policy initiatives to reform and improve education for all students at the expense of legislation that assures protections, early intervention, special education, and transition services for each infant, toddler, child, and youth with disabilities.

2. Increase the bottom-up influence of the perceptions, needs, and experiences of children with disabilities, parents, and professionals as policy implementers and stakeholders in the balancing of policy goals, values, and evolution of IDEA policy intention and implementation.

3. Redefine the policy space that currently shapes the dialogue between general and special education in order to make less intractable the values, administrative barriers, and the professional practices impeding coherent policies that ensure the supports necessary to meet the unique needs of each student with disabilities and the educational goals for all students to learn and develop.

4. Identify policy designs that resolve the often competing goals of excellence, equity, efficiency, human dignity, and choice in a rationed, publicly supported education system necessary to support and strengthen classroom practices that produce positive learning results for both *each* and *all* students.

## REFERENCES

Astuto, T. A., Clark, D. L., Read, A., McGree, K., & Fernandez, L. (1993). *Challenges to dominant assumptions controlling educational reform* (Final Report to the Regional Laboratory for Educational Improvement of the Northeast and Islands). Andover, MA: Regional Laboratory for Educational Improvement of the Northeast and the Islands.

Clark, D. L., & Astuto, T. A. (1994). Redirecting reform: Challenges to popular assumptions about teachers and students. *Phi Delta Kappan, 75*(7), 513–520.

Cuban, L. (1990). Reforming again, again, and again. *Educational Researcher, 19*(1), 3–13.

Darling-Hammond, L. (1993, June). Reframing the school reform agenda: Developing capacity for school transformation. *Phi Delta Kappa, 74,* (10), 753–761.

Davis, S. (1992, October). *Report card to the nation on inclusion in education of students with mental retardation,* Dallas, TX: The Arc.

Downs, A. (1972, Summer). Up and down with ecology—the issue-attention cycle. *Public Interest, 28,* 38–50.

Elmore, R. (1979). *Complexity and control: What legislators and administrators can do about implementing policy.* Seattle: Institute of Governmental Research, University of Washington.

Farkas, S. (1992). *Educational reform: The players and the politics.* New York: Public Agenda Foundation.

Farkas, S. (1993). *Divided within, besieged without: The politics of education in four American school districts.* New York: Public Agenda Foundation.

Ferguson, D. (1994). Persons with severe developmental disabilities: "Mainstreaming" to supported community membership. In T. Husen & T. Postlethwaite (Eds.), *The international encyclopedia of education.* (Pp. 1504–1508). New York: Pergamon.

Forest, M., & Pearpoint, J. (1991). Two roads: Exclusion or inclusion? *Developmental Disabilities Bulletin, 19*(1), 1–11.

Foster, J. D. (1991). The role of accountability in Kentucky's education reform act of 1990. *Educational Leadership, 48*(5), 34–36.

Fuchs, D., & Fuchs, L. S. (1994). Inclusive schools movement and the radicalization of special education reform. *Exceptional Children, 60*(4), 294–309.

Gartner, A., & Lipsky, D. (1987). Beyond special education: Toward a quality system for all students. *Harvard Educational Review, 57,* 367–395.

Guba, E. G. (1984). The effect of definitions of policy on the nature and outcomes of policy analysis. *Educational Leadership, 42*(2), 63–70.

Hirsch, E.D., Jr. (1996). *The schools we need and why we don't have them.* New York: Doubleday.

Hogwood, B. W., & Gunn, L. A. (1984). *Policy analysis for the real world.* New York: Oxford University Press.

Immerwahr, J. (1991). *Crosstalk: The public, the experts, and competitiveness.* New York: Public Agenda Foundation.

Kearney, C. P. (1988). *Value polarities and complementarities in American education policy making: Efficiency and choice.* Paper presented at the annual meeting of the American Educational Research Association, New Orleans, LA.

National Academy of Education. (1991). *Research and the Renewal of Education*. Stanford, CA: Author.

National Association of State Boards of Education (NASBE). (1992). Winners all: A call for inclusive schools. In *Report of the NASBE Study Group on Special Education*. Alexandria, VA: Author.

Nelson, R. R. (1977). *The moon and the ghetto*. New York: Norton.

Sailor, W. (1992). Special education in the restructured school. *Remedial and Special Education, 12*(6), 8–22.

Sarason, S. (1990). *The predictable failure of educational reform*. San Francisco: Jossey-Bass.

Steffy, B. (1993). *The Kentucky education reform act: Lessons for America*. Lancaster, PA: Technomics.

Thurow, L. C. (1997). *The future of capitalism*. New York: Penguin.

Tyack, D. (1991). Public school reform: Policy talk and institutional practice. *American Journal of Education, 100*(1), 1–19.

Weimer, D. L., & Vining, A. R. (1992). *Policy analysis: Concepts and practice* (2nd ed.). Englewood Cliffs, NJ: Prentice-Hall.

Williams, W. (1971). *Social policy research and analysis*. New York: Elsevier.

Yankelovich, D. (1991). *Coming to public judgment: Making democracy work in a complex world*. Syracuse, NY: Syracuse University Press.

Ysseldyke, J., Thurlow, M., & Geenen, K. (1994). *Report on implementation of alternative methods for making educational accountability decisions for students with disabilities*. Minneapolis: National Center on Educational Outcomes, University of Minnesota College of Education.

# 12 ☙ Knowledge Versus Policy in Special Education

**James J. Gallagher**

*The University of North Carolina at Chapel Hill*

Many observers of the field of special education have become increasingly distressed at the apparent gap between what we know about children with special needs and the design of services to help them (Fullan, 1993). What we know is increasingly impressive (due in no small measure to a continuing flow of research money from the federal government), but often that new knowledge stands in stark contrast to the service delivery systems that we have devised to cope with children with special needs. This chapter attempts to highlight three major disjunctions between what we know and what we do, to discuss the reasons for them, and provide some suggestions about ways to close the gap.

It is not too surprising that social policy sometimes departs from understanding and knowledge of exceptional children and their education. There is often a time lag between new knowledge and policy implementation. In addition, some substantial translation may be necessary before the "knowledge" becomes useful, because the knowledge must fit into the context of the cultural situation. Nevertheless, we should be alert to the need to bring knowledge and policy into better alignment.

Here are three puzzles with which we are currently wrestling:

1. Although we are impressed by the range of individual differences in the children we serve, the service delivery is often a "one size fits all" model for children with special needs.

2. Although we have increasing evidence of the power of ecological conditions surrounding the children with special needs, we continue to treat the child as though the problem and the solutions lay exclusively within that child.

3. Although we trumpet our commitments to multidisciplinary efforts, we continue to prepare our specialists in narrow channels of specialties (rarely in multidisciplinary programs or settings), and design our treatments in single-disciplined chunks.

**245**

Let us see what the impact of these disjunctions have been on our ability to use the knowledge that we currently possess. It has been wisely said that science is the true revolutionary movement of the 20th century (Bronowski, 1973). It is revolutionary because new knowledge is produced on an ongoing basis that forces us to continually recast our original suppositions about the world around us. It is hard to estimate the number of beautifully constructed theories that have been shot down by some ugly facts that contradict them. Obviously, the field of special education is not immune from the consequences of these additions of new knowledge, and special educators should be ready to adapt and adjust their models, theories and practices to take into account what we know now that we did not know 30 years ago.

There are many reasons for research not to be isomorphic with policy and practice. For one thing, policies are formulated on the basis of many social and economic forces besides our knowledge of particular persons or programs. These forces influencing policy include such things as community values, past practices, cost factors, personnel shortages and needs, and so on. Each of these factors can keep us from changing in directions where our "knowledge" tells us we could go constructively, if we so desired. However, if we desire quality services for children with special needs and their families, we should be able to study such disjunctions carefully to see if more appropriate actions need to be taken.

The four questions listed in Table 12.1 cover the major policy dimensions. The question as to *who shall receive* the resources is the eligibility question, and much of our energies in special education have been devoted to developing the rules and standards for answering this question. The second question, in Table 12.1, as to *who shall* deliver the services, relates to the qualifications of the service deliverer and issues related to certification and personnel preparation are a part of this policy question.

### TABLE 12.1
#### What Is Social Policy?

Social policies are the rules and standards by which scarce public resources are allocated to almost unlimited social needs. Written social policy should provide the answer to four major questions:

1. Who shall receive the resources (services)?

2. Who shall deliver the services?

3. What is the nature of the services to be delivered?

4. What are the conditions under which the services will be delivered?

*Note.* Source: Gallagher (1994).

The nature of the services to be delivered (Question 3) addresses the *nature of the differentiated services* that we propose as needed for the child with special needs. It deals with curriculum and adaptations of the standard program, whereas the conditions under which the services will be delivered (question 4) often deals with the issue as to *where such differentiated programs will be presented* (e.g., in the regular classroom, resource room, tutorial sessions, etc.).

Special educational programs must provide answers to these four key questions as listed in Table 12.1, and those answers comprise the rules and standards by which the program is governed. Together, these answers provide the structure of special education and—make no mistake about it—these questions must be answered with the best of available knowledge if we are to have an effective program. Those who are responsible for conducting the program must know who the students are who will receive the program, who will teach the program, and so on.

The dilemma we now face is that structures designed to meet the problems as we conceptualized them in decades past may not be appropriate for our current knowledge, but it is very time consuming to modify such structures once they have been placed into the rules and standards to which we have become accustomed.

Wildavsky (1979), in his seminal book *Speaking Truth to Power*, described an inevitable progression of policy once there has been a program established for a particular subgroup of citizens.

1. There is a trend to expand the number of persons eligible for the special services.

2. The range of services available through that program also tends to expand.

3. An inevitable consequence of the first two points is that the cost of the program also increases.

We have seen many examples of those Wildavsky rules in special education. The category of learning disabilities is a prime case. Starting out as a small category of children with quite distinctive learning problems and suspected neurological problems, it has grown to the largest category in special education, with broad definitions and, of course, a dramatically increased price tag.

There have been enormous shifts of children from the category of mental retardation (down 30%) to the category of learning disabilities (up 67%) over a 10 year period (Kirk, Gallagher, & Anastasiow, 1994). Does this mean that there has been a virus causing learning disabilities sweeping the country, and that some miracle cure has been found for types of mental retardation? Much more to the point is the greater convenience and acceptability of the learning disability label to educational administrators. (See MacMillan and Speece, chap. 6, this volume, for an elaboration on this point.)

## SERVING THE FAR END OF THE DISTRIBUTION

There has not been sufficient recognition of the qualitative differences that occur at the ends of the distributions of those dimensions that define children with special needs. A relevant analogy from the physical world is that when we place water on a temperature continuum, the quantitative difference in degrees of temperature at the extremes of hot and cold results in qualitatively different states—steam and ice, respectively.

At a certain point near the end of the distribution, problems of visual acuity become qualitatively different and we refer to children who are blind (not just children who have various degrees of partial sight) or children who are deaf (not just children with increasing hearing loss). At the ends of their quantitative continuum we find a qualitative difference that requires a qualitatively different educational response. Thus, we teach youngsters with severe problems in vision the unique curricula of travel training and Braille, but we do not teach these curricula to those closer to the average, even if they are called children with special needs.

It has been insufficiently recognized that high-incidence children in the domains of mental retardation, behavioral differences, and learning disabilities also have similar qualitative problems at the ends of the distribution. The youngster with severe retardation is qualitatively different from the youngster with borderline IQ scores. The youngster with severe learning disabilities is qualitatively different from those with mild problems of learning in school. Those with a compulsive need to attack others, or who are schizophrenic or autistic certainly have educational needs that are qualitatively different from those who are closer to the average of the distribution in showing behavioral problems. Thus, one classification may not mean only one type of treatment.

Keogh and Weisner (1993) have pointed out that there are three basic purposes for attempting to classify youngsters who are having educational difficulties. One of these is to focus our *advocacy* efforts, the second is to allow for the *design of special services*, and the third is for *scientific study*. These are very different purposes and lead to very different actions, even though we often seem to pretend that the category remains the same regardless of which of the three purposes we are considering. Consider the scientific goal of trying to identify the special characteristics of "children with learning disabilities," for example. We have noted the phenomenon of investigators going into school systems and collecting a group of students who have been identified by that system as "children with learning disabilities" and then attempting to find out which special characteristics these children all have in common, a distinctly scientific question.

But this is an attempt to use a "service-designed category" for "scientific purposes," and it does not work. These "school-system-identified" subjects have probably been identified as learning disabled for the purposes of providing some special educational service, certainly not because they belong to some meaningful scientific category.

Much of the current disputes about proper models for special services in the field of learning disabilities or behavioral disorders would seem to result from one camp describing and planning for a cluster of students with the milder form of that disability, and thus capable of adapting to the regular classroom with supportive help, whereas the other camp is describing the children at the far end of the distribution and is calling for more intensive individual work or separate small group experiences for this qualitatively different group of severely dyslexic or aggressive children.

A comprehensive program of educational services would seem to call for both approaches, with each program appropriate for a particular set of students with special needs. Therefore, the call for *full inclusion*, of maintaining children with disabilities in the normal setting, seems to be quite unrealistic (Stainback & Stainback, 1992) when one thinks of individual cases at the extremes of the distributions of intellect, behavior, or learning disabilities, just as a call for a totally separate special education program of services for children with more moderate problems would seem to be an overreaction (Fuchs & Fuchs, 1994). Many of these mild problems could be cared for within a more recognizable classroom setting with a support team of specialists supporting the general education teacher.

A key question that would need to be answered before an appropriate program of services can be designed is whether the problems of children with special needs are seen as *chronic* or acute, in nature. If they are perceived as *acute* then a major infusion of services, designed to correct the momentary problem might be called for; if it is chronic then plans have to be made for continuing services throughout the school and perhaps through the lifetime of the student, with no expectation that the problem will go away even with appropriate treatment.

Chronic conditions need continuous attention, much as various physical conditions such as diabetes, asthma, or heart problems can be contained (but not cured) with maintenance doses of medication. There is no thought that just because the child has maintained him- or herself through medication from asthma attacks or diabetic comas for five years that it is now permissable to take the child off medication. One problem in special education is that we pretend that the problems are acute and can be treated in an analogous way with a dose of strong antibiotics so that the child is "cured," when in reality we most often face a chronic problem that requires continued help and assistance.

When we remove the child from special services in education, we see revealing results. Fuchs, Roberts, Fuchs, and Bowers (1996) reported on a treatment program for students with learning disabilities that seemed to result, in the first instance, with the students responding well to an intensive and directed program. However, when the students were released into the regular classroom their progress slowed markedly, and many of them had to return to special education settings. Similarly, attempts to bring special educational services into the general classroom (Zigmond et. al., 1995) have yielded only modest results, even when the resources available were impressive, far beyond that available to an ordinary school system.

For those youngsters at the far end of the distribution of mental retardation, learning disabilities, or behavioral problems, there can be no serious thought that they can be released from their special education services merely because they are "doing well." They will probably need some version of services for the time they remain in school and beyond.

Follow-up studies by Werner and Smith (1992) and Wagner et al. (1991) indicated that many of these special education students with chronic difficulties need continued special assistance as adults if they are to make a good adjustment into adulthood. It is not a matter of shaking hands at the schoolhouse door and wishing them well; a failure to follow through with adult services runs the risk of those students losing much of the gains that they made in their school programs.

Many of these high-incidence youngsters have varying degrees of difficulty in adult life. We were obviously correct in identifying this broader class of youngsters as children in "educational trouble." Although we might argue whether a child is "behaviorally disordered," or "attention deficit disordered," or a "child with learning disabilities," there is little question that this child is in educational and ecological trouble and unfortunately, there is a substantial likelihood that trouble will follow the child into adulthood.

For those youngsters at the qualitative ends of the distribution, a highly individual program seems required and should be part of the expected process, as would a treatment program characterized by intensity and length. The Individual Education Program (IEP) has received substantial criticism (see Gallagher & Desimone, 1995), but it remains a potential tool for team planning for a particular student. In this instance we would expect to find an IEP with instructional, social, and family goals together with assignments of personnel to indicate our action commitments to the child in interaction with his or her environment.

One of the educational ideas that has influenced current special education practice and is especially relevant for the student at the end of the distribution has been the *zone of proximal development,* a construct initiated by Vygotsky (1978). He believed that the best instruction should be directed to this zone of partial but incomplete knowledge, or uncertain skills mastery that the student has revealed regarding a particular concept. For example, the student may "know" various properties of water but not that it changes form and structure at extremes of temperature, or why. The student has partial knowledge of these concepts but lacks some essential element(s) that would allow full mastery of the concept being taught. Starting at the zone of proximal development is a particularly appealing concept for teachers who no longer have grade-level performance indicators as a guide to how, where, and at what level to approach the student. However, the question that teachers quite appropriately pose to psychologists and educators is, "How do I find that zone?" We need a team approach that will handle these very special students at the ends of the distribution, and perhaps even a different strategy of treatment or special education.

It would seem foolish to project these proposed changes in the teacher-pupil relationship and teacher-teacher relationship designed to help children with mild, moderate, and severe disabilities and still maintain the same antiquated structure in special education that now contains these elements. One of the elements within this special education system that would likely change would be that the department of special education would become the department of special services, and would be staffed with a variety of personnel that would provide support services on a regular basis, or on call, to the rest of the system. They would be the system's technical assistance arm.

Such a support system could be financed at a percentage rate of the regular system costs, in the range of 20% to 25% of the general system costs, and would include the existing support personnel in school psychology, nursing, and social services, as well as special education personnel. Initially, some of the funding provided to other community services (e.g., mental health for children) might be incorporated, as would be the appropriate services. Within this community services model, it appears that we would need different service delivery models for the mild and for the extreme cases.

## ECOLOGY AND ITS PLACE IN POLICY
## AND SERVICE DELIVERY

Children with mild mental retardation look qualitatively different from those with moderate and severe retardation (Baumeister, Jupstas, & Klindworth, 1990; Zigler & Hodapp, 1986). These categories of children with mild disabilities have been referred to as "high-incidence" categories. There are many more of these youngsters than of the more severely impaired youngsters at the ends of the distribution. New categories such as mild mental retardation, mild behavior disorders, and mild learning disabilities have been added to the array of students that now require some special educational adaptation.

But as we studied these high-incidence youngsters and their educational setting, it became clearer that their very condition was often partially determined, at least, by the interaction with the culture surrounding the child, and even by the quality of their previous schooling (Kauffman, 1993). These ecological conditions can be represented by the model developed by Bronfenbrenner (1989) who conceived of nested concentric circles of child, family, community, and society. The child with mild disabilities who faced the special educator was a product, not merely of his or her own inherent physical characteristics, but of family and culture as well.

In many instances, no discernible physical or neurological problem could be found in such youngsters (Keogh & Weisner, 1993). An earlier generation of children with learning disabilities were referred to as "minimal brain damaged." The "minimal" in these cases usually meant, "We think there is damage but we can't find it" (Strauss & Lehtinen, 1947). One has to increasingly wonder as to whether the categories or classifications of "mild mental retardation" or "learning disabilities" were more political creations than scientific classifications (Kauffman, 1989). We did not often consider in the 1960s and 1970s that if the environment is partially the cause, perhaps it should also be part of the treatment; that is, that interventions might rather target the conditions in the family or the neighborhood or the school.

We have increasingly observed that severe disadvantages in the socioeconomic environment did not, necessarily, create exceptional children. Many youngsters have survived the experience of poverty without traumatic consequences. However, when it became evident that there were more minority students involved in special education than their proportion in the general society (Artiles & Trent, 1994), some people saw this as a conspiracy to remove minority youngsters from the general education mainstream (Hilliard, 1992). A simpler answer is that when youngsters have a number of educationally negative conditions in family and community, there will likely be more such youngsters in educational trouble (Sameroff, 1990). Conversely, as is the case with "gifted children," when the culture and family and neighborhood factors are all positive, we would expect more youngsters from those environments to appear in the gifted range than would their proportions in the general population, and so it appears to be (Gallagher & Gallagher, 1994).

For the youngsters at the far ends of the distribution, the special educator might possibly be in a one-on-one tutorial environment where the educator could cope with the special individual needs of a youngster more directly and appropriately. But if a major proportion of the determining factors in the condition lie in the environment, shouldn't one be more interested in "cleaning up the neighborhood or counseling the family" than in tutoring a reluctant and hostile child (Keogh, Gallimore, & Weisner, 1997)?

Ecological Adaptations

Although there have been many attempts to capture the developmental cognitive patterns of the child, knowledge of the ecological background was rarely accessible to aid the planning team in designing an educational program or specific experiences, despite our current acknowledgment of how important that background is to the child's adaptation.

There are few schools that have used tools such as the Ecocultural Family Interview (Weisner & Gallimore, 1994), which focuses on discussion with family members about family life, the organization of family living, sources of family support and the parents' perceptions of short- and long-term goals for the child. Shouldn't something like the data from this instrument be available to a teacher assistance team (Chalfant & Pysh, 1989) if we hope to have a chance of doing meaningful intervention planning that would take into account the family and culture of the child (Bernheimer & Keogh, 1995)?

This school-based committee can also take into account the *protective* factors in the child's environment, positive factors that can mute or buffer some of the problems faced by the child with special needs (Rutter, 1987). If we use a version of a child-based committee for programming, then we can have a team that can draw on a variety of skills and expertise. There could be a specialist on cultural factors who can bring their family interviews into play, the regular class teacher who will point out that modifications of the curriculum have to take into account the standard curriculum that is being presented in that general education classroom (e.g., in social studies, the history and culture of our state) and the special educator who can use that information about the general curriculum goals to help the child see how he or she and his or her family fit into that history.

If the family and peer culture is considered so important to the future of the child with special needs, then what do we propose to do with that information (Gallimore, Weisner, Kauffman, & Bernheimer, 1989)? Surely we will need someone to make contact with that family on a regular basis and help them understand the school's goals, and hopefully dovetail the goals of the family for the child with the goals of the school. In the preschool areas, with the implementation of an Individual Family Service Plan (IFSP), we have seen the development of a new personnel role identified as a *service coordinator*, a person who tries to coordinate the various services provided to the child with disabilities and his or her family.

As the school becomes more and more like a community service center (Holtzman, 1997), such a service coordinator/family liaison role could probably be added to the staff, and this can provide the family-school liaison that is so desperately needed in many communities. The staff of service coordinators should also be ethnically diverse, so that a cultural match may be made between school and home, where that factor is important.

## THE NEED FOR A MULTIDISCIPLINARY SERVICE SYSTEM

In special education we have come to accept the proposition that some children have problems that far outrun the training and skills of any one professional. A child with cerebral palsy, a serious hearing problem, and severe communication difficulties can soon make any single professional humble in terms of his or her own limited knowledge and skills. A natural response to such comprehensive problems is to form teams of people, with each bringing some necessary skills and specialized knowledge to the table, so that a reasonable plan of education and treatment can be designed and activated to meet the needs of that particular child.

We have already recognized the need to involve a variety of disciplines and roles in a school-based committee that decides who is eligible to receive special services. Such discussions often merely involve entry into the special education program. We need to combine our certification of eligibility with some usable and continuing program suggestions. There should be relevant staff available to aid in the continuing program for a student. Can't a version of this school-based committee also be operational for the general instructional program as well? Chalfant and Pysh (1989) proposed *teacher assistance teams* assigned to provide the general classroom teacher with strategies to help her cope with children in educational trouble *before* referral to special education. This strategy brings a variety of professionals together to contribute suggestions on how to cope within the framework of the regular classroom.

Many children with mild disabilities are now being placed in the regular classroom under the philosophy of *inclusion* (Stainback & Stainback, 1992).

These children with mild (and sometimes moderate and severe) disabilities, are placed in a normal classroom setting where the regular class teacher has often had precious little background in coping with children with special needs and, at best, may get the help of a special educator on a limited basis. The special educator can be supportive either as a consultant or by working in the classroom with some students for relatively brief periods of time.

As we look around, we can see that group practice has been the reaction of most other professions as well. The explosion of knowledge has encouraged general practitioners in medicine, for example, to develop *team practice* as a means of more adequately meeting the diverse needs of their patients and their own inevitably limited knowledge base. In addition, they have developed elaborate referral sources to pass on patients who have very special problems and who need highly specialized treatment.

In the education profession there has been almost a denial of the inevitability of similar structural changes, also brought on by increasing knowledge. Instead of stressing specialization, they have emphasized the importance of the general classroom teacher, particularly at the elementary level. That teacher is expected to deal with the full range of pupil abilities, personalities, and motivations (e.g., inclusion) with only a passing visit from some specialists to comment and make suggestions.

Such denial of the need for team practice most likely comes from educational administrators being mindful of the limited resources that they have available to them, so that they start from a set sum of money and try to answer the question, "What can we do given these resources?" instead of saying, "What is needed to cope with the problem?"

A commitment to multidisciplinary activity means that we will have to break out of a discipline-oriented program and a discipline-oriented personnel preparation. The structure of universities themselves, featuring departments organized by professional discipline, discourages multidisciplinary activity. New structures within the university, such as centers and institutes, have had to be created to encourage more multidisciplinary activities.

Direct attempts to change this bias toward discipline-based training have had ongoing difficulties. The Office of Special Education Programs recently initiated a series of interdisciplinary personnel preparation programs designed to establish the importance and necessity of a multidisciplinary training model. Rooney (1994) reported on the fate of 10 of these multidisciplinary training programs once the federal funding was removed. Only 1 of the 10 survived, and that program was headed by a senior and respected professor. Those programs headed by nontenured staff members disappeared or were drastically changed. The power of the status quo during tight budget years has often been underestimated (Gallagher, 1997).

One potential solution to this problem for the university is to allow these multidisciplinary centers and institutes to play a larger role in personnel preparation. Their basic multidisciplinary orientation should be a model for the students who will have to work in a multidisciplinary world when they complete their preparation.

The middle school concept of teaming teachers from various disciplines and specializations representing math, science, social studies, and language arts, plus support personnel for children with special needs, merits consideration. This team is given a "family" of 100 to 125 children with which to cope (Alexander & George, 1981), and the team (including special educators) uses their collective knowledge to plan for the children. Such an approach represents a more likely solution to the inevitable limitations of an individual teacher.

How should this broad category of children with mild disabilities—but still in serious educational, social, and economic trouble—be handled? Are we special educators or social workers or mental health personnel? Or should we be a team of various disciplines that organizes professional attention to the child and the family and the community? The vision of the public schools being transformed into community service centers in the near future has been noted by a number of observers (see Comer, 1988; Holtzman, 1997). Not only would educational services be delivered through this community service center, but so would there be care for basic health needs and social service needs, combining diverse professional forces for a comprehensive approach to the difficulties that are no longer seen as embedded in an individual child, but instead as a combination of forces including child, family, and community.

Too often our discussions about desirable special education for exceptional children have involved the geography of the educational setting rather than the instructional content. We became obsessed with *where* the child would be placed—a special class, a resource room, a cluster group, inclusion, and so on—and many arguments have been presented about the relative virtues of these various geographic places to the education of exceptional children. It does not take much reflection, however, to see that these are misplaced arguments. What is more relevant is that such placements are designed to create a particular environment in which certain desirable educational practices could be applied. The real question is, "Were these opportunities taken advantage of?"

One of our unfortunate tendencies when we consider alternative futures is that we often accept the financial limitations of the present. We think about only what we can do given the current budget, because that is surely the "practical way" to approach the problem. But if we automatically eliminate any options that would raise the ante for school finance, then we may have eliminated many concepts that might bring help and condemned ourselves to a "bare bones" future that matches our past and present. If we are to continue to expand our responsibilities into the health and social service spheres, then clearly we must have a revised look at the financial support for this community service center model.

The Harvard economist Thurow (1988) once commented that it was a common misperception that there are no solutions available to deal with important social problems such as poverty and crime. There are, in fact, dozens of possible solutions. The problem is, Thurow elaborated, that none of these solutions can be carried out without creating pain and sorrow to some group who will naturally protest and create barriers to such solutions. We have consistently underestimated the power of self-interest in resisting the consideration of new policies.

Regardless of the system changes made here, we will need to attend to one of the newest interest in education: accountability. The new community support system would be expected to detail the services that they have provided, and the outcomes (the improvement brought forth) of these services. If such structural modifications as the community service center would take place, they would not happen without distress and turmoil within the various helping communities or professions. Problems of finance transfers, status, job security, and so on would be only a few of the problems with which to be coped, so we would not expect such changes to take place tomorrow, or the day after tomorrow. But we should have some vision of what the desirable future would be, so that we know where we are headed.

The price of receiving increased resources is a clear commitment to desirable and measurable outcomes. Special education has not often had to face the question as to whether the methods and procedures that we have introduced are making a meaningful difference in the development of the child with special needs, or in their eventual adult adjustment. In earlier years, just the willingness to work with children with disabilities was taken as sufficient indication of our worthiness, but no more. Accountability can be looked on as the "spinach of education," something that is good for you but that you may personally dislike (Gallagher, 1997). We never enjoy having our current practices challenged, yet we rarely improve without such challenges.

Such accountability has increasingly been tied to instructional objectives. Instead of relying on broad-scale achievement tests, we have increasingly turned to performance assessment (Wiggins, 1991). Such assessment includes tasks that require the application of knowledge to specific problems rather than the simple absorption of knowledge. This approach to accountability represents a unique challenge for special education, because generalization or transfer of knowledge has often proven to be a particular challenge for children with special needs. But how else can we prove the worth of our efforts? If our student cannot display, in some format, a product that might report on, for example, how the various immigrant populations have changed the character and culture of our home state, then has that student really learned what we have desired him or her to know about the history of the community? We can certainly anticipate a more thorough commitment to performance assessment and authentic assessment in special education in the immediate future, and our differentiated curriculum should reflect that expectation.

Those struggling with educational policy, trying to make it come closer to our essential knowledge base, can appreciate the old story of the farmer who, when approached by a salesperson trying to sell him on a new approach to farming said, "Heck, I'm not farming near as well as I know how now." So we can say, "We are not educating students with special needs near as well as we know how now." The three propositions presented in this chapter—the children at the extreme of the distribution, the need to take into account ecological forces on the child, and the reluctance to adopt a multidisciplinary approach—are cases in point. But we have demonstrated from place to place and time to time that we do know how to cope with these issues, and to do so with excellent programs. It may be up to our professional associations, our parents' groups, and other advocates to push policymakers in the desired and desirable directions, so that our current rules and standards more clearly align with what we know how to do.

Someone has certainly applied the ancient Chinese curse "May you live in interesting times" to special educators. The status quo no longer seems to be a viable option, and so we must look toward change, recognizing how painful and difficult it is to modify how we do things (Fullan, 1993). If we do not have some beginning vision of our desired future, we may well be condemned to skitter from crisis to crisis, trying to use inadequate or inappropriate resources to patch an increasingly leaky boat. The reader may not like the particular vision as sketched in this chapter, but what is the vision that you prefer?

# REFERENCES

Alexander, W., & George, P. (1981). *The exemplary middle school.* New York: Holt, Rinehart, & Winston.

Artiles, A., & Trent. S. (1994). Over-representation of minority students in special education: A continuing debate. *Journal of Special Education, 27*, 410–437.

Baumeister, A., Jupstas, F., & Klindworth, L. (1990). New morbidity: Implications for prevention of children's disabilities. *Exceptionality, 1*, 1–16.

Bernheimer, L. P., & Keogh, B. K. (1995). Weaving interventions into the fabric of everyday life: An approach to family assessment. *Topics in Early Childhood Special Education, 15*, 415–433.

Bronfenbrenner, U. (1989). Ecological systems theory. *Annals of Child Development, 6*, 187–249.

Bronowski, J. (1973). *The Ascent of Man.* Boston: Little, Brown.

Chalfant, J., & Pysh, M. (1989). Teacher assistance teams: Five descriptive studies on 96 teams. *Remedial and Special Education, 10*(6), 49–58.

Comer, T. (1988). Educating poor minority children. *Scientific American, 254*, 42–48.

Fuchs, D., & Fuchs, L. (1994). Inclusive schools movement and the radicalization of special education reform. *Exceptional Children, 60* (4), 294–309.

Fuchs, D., Roberts, P., Fuchs, L., & Bowers, J. (1996). Reintegrating students with learning disabilities into the mainstream: A two year study. *Learning Disabilities: Research and Practice, 11*(4), 214–229.

Fullan, M. (1993). *Change forces: Probing the depths of educational reform.* Bristol, PA: Falmer.

Gallagher, J. (1997, March). *Accountability: The spinach of education.* Address at the North Carolina Association for Gifted Children Meetings, Winston Salem, North Carolina.

Gallagher, J., & Desimone, L. (1995). Lessons learned from implementations of the IEP: Applications to the IFSP. *Topics in Early Childhood Special Education, 15*(3), 353–378.

Gallagher, J., & Gallagher, S. (1994). *Teaching the gifted child* (4th ed.). Newton, MA: Allyn & Bacon.

Gallimore, R., Weisner, T. S., Kauffman, S., & Bernheimer, L. P. (1989). The social construction of ecocultural niches: Family accommodation of developmentally delayed children. *American Journal of Mental Retardation, 94*, 216–220.

Hilliard, A. (1992). The pitfalls and promises of special education practice. *Exceptional Children, 59*(2), 168–172.

Holtzman, W. (1997). Community psychology and full service schools in different cultures. *American Psychologist, 52*(4), 381–389.

Kauffman, J. (1989). The regular education initiative as Reagan-Bush education policy: A trickle down theory of education of the "hard-to-teach." *Journal of Special Education, 23*, 256–278.

Kauffman, J. (1993). How we might achieve the radical reform of special education. *Exceptional Children, 60*(1), 6–16.

Keogh, B., Gallimore, R., & Weisner, T. (1997). A sociocultural perspective on learning and learning disabilities. *Learning Disabilities Research and Practice, 12*(2), 107–113.

Keogh, B., & Weisner, T. (1993). An ecocultural perspective on risk and protective factors in children's development: Implications for learning disabilities. *Learning Disabilities Research and Practice, 8*(1), 3–10.

Kirk, S., Gallagher, J., & Anastasiow, N. J. (1994). *Educating exceptional children* (7th ed.). Boston: Houghton Mifflin.

Rooney, R. (1994). *Implementation of interdisciplinary personnel preparation for early intervention.* Unpublished doctoral dissertation. University of North Carolina at Chapel Hill.

Rutter, M. (1987). Psychosocial resilience and protective mechanisms. *American Journal of Orthopsychiatry, 57*, 316–331.

Sameroff, A. (1990). Neo-environmental perspectives on developmental theory. In R Hodapp, J. Burack, & E. Zigler (Eds.), *Issues in the developmental approach to mental retardation.* New York: Cambridge University Press.

Stainback, S., & Stainback, W. (1992). *Curriculum considerations on inclusive classrooms.* Baltimore, MD: Brookes.

Strauss, A., & Lehtinen, L. (1947). *Psychopathology of the brain-injured child.* New York: Grune & Strattan.

Thurow, L. (1988). *Zero sum games.* Cambridge, MA: Harvard University Press.

Vygotsky, L. (1978). *Mind in society: The development of higher psychological processes.* Cambridge, MA: Harvard University Press.

Wagner, M., Newman, L., D'Amico, R., Jay, E., Butler-Nalen, P., Marker, C., & Cox, R. (1991). *Youth with disabilities: How are they doing?* Menlo Park, CA: SRI International.

Weisner, T., & Gallimore, R. (1994). Ecocultural studies of families adapting to childhood developmental delays: Unique features, defining differences, and applied implications. In M. Leskinen (Ed.), *Family in focus: New perspectives on early childhood special education* (pp. 11-25). Jyvaskyla, Finland: University of Jyvaskyla.

Werner, E. E., & Smith, R. S. (1992). *Overcoming the odds: High risk children from birth to adulthood.* Ithaca, NY: Cornell University Press.

Wiggins, G. (1991, February). Standards not standardization: Evoking quality student work. *Educational Leadership*, pp. 18–25.

Wildavsky, A. (1979). *Speaking truth to power: The art and craft of policy analysis.* Boston: Little, Brown.

Zigler, E., & Hodapp, R. M. (1986). *Understanding mental retardation.* New York: Cambridge University Press.

Zigmond, N., Jenkins, J., Fuchs, L., Deno, S., Fuchs, D., Baker, J., Jenkins, L., & Couthino, M. (1995). Special education in restructured schools: Findings from three multi-year studies. *Phi Delta Kappan, 76*, 531–540.

# 13 ⚬Programmatic Research in Learning Disabilities

**G. Reid Lyon**
*The National Institute of Child Health and Human Development (NICHD),*
*The National Institutes of Health*

## THE FORGING OF NICHD RESEARCH POLICIES AND DIRECTIONS IN LEARNING DISABILITIES

Our understanding of learning disabilities (LD) has been limited due to a number of factors, some scientific, some social and political (Keogh, 1983, 1986, 1987a, 1987b, 1993, 1994, 1996; Keogh & MacMillan, 1983; Keogh, Major-Kingsley, Omori-Gordon, & Reid, 1982; Speece & Keogh, 1996). On the scientific side, precise definitions of LD have been difficult to frame, because professionals in the field represent many disciplines, each with their own vocabularies, diagnostic assumptions, theories, and treatment considerations. In addition, the ambiguity inherent in extant definitions of LD leaves the diagnostic and identification process open for wide interpretation and misinterpretation. Imprecise diagnostic decision-making criteria allow some children to be identified as having learning disabilities when they do not, whereas others with LD are overlooked.

For instance, Keogh and her colleagues (Keogh et al., 1982) pointed out over 15 years ago that children with LD may differ radically from one another across identification and programmatic variables depending on the setting or state from which the sample is collected. Because many research studies have been done with children identified as LD according to these varying and ambiguous criteria (i.e., "school-identified subjects"), our knowledge of LD has reflected ambiguity as well. Samples of LD children selected for study frequently vary widely among themselves in terms of relevant characteristics (e.g., IQ, age, socioeconomic status) that are typically unaccounted for in the interpretation of the data. Such unaccounted-for variability in sample characteristics may prohibit the reliability and generalizability of scientific findings.

What's needed is "a classification system or taxonomy of LD that takes into account and orders the diversity of conditions subsumed under this rubric. This will require both conceptual and empirical approaches and will necessarily cut across disciplinary and professional perspectives" (Keogh, 1987b, p. 12).

Also, many studies of LD have ignored developmental factors (Keogh, 1994, 1996). This is because most studies have been conducted at only one point in time and may not have accounted for developmental differences within a sample, even when they existed. A developmental perspective is required for this research because "patterns of growth and change may vary widely among subgroups of learning-disabled children. Understanding how the many personal and social contributions to development and to the expressions of LD interact and transact over time requires commitment to longitudinal, developmental research designs" (Keogh, 1987b, p. 12). Because of the developmental nature of the learning process, it would be expected that disabilities in learning could be expressed in different ways at different age levels, thus pointing to the need for developmental, longitudinal studies of different types of LD. In addition, because LD co-occurs with other types of difficulties in the social, emotional, and attentional domains, longitudinal efforts should take into account the range of difficulties (comorbidities) manifested by each child. Such studies might shed light on whether differential assessment, classification, early intervention, or remediation might be required, depending on the type of LD, the multiple manifestations of the LD, and the developmental status of the individual.

With respect to social and political influences on the development of the field of LD, advocacy has not only been critical in the recognition of LD as a handicapping condition, but is also critical in bringing attention and support to the needs of many pupils with LD (Keogh, 1987b, 1993). In ensuring that the role of advocacy is recognized in research and educational policy, we must recognize that different definitions and classification systems will be necessary for research purposes, for the provision of services, and for advocacy. To capitalize on the gains won through advocacy, however, we must do more to link research to practice. To accomplish this essential linking, "The interactive links between LD conditions and intervention and treatment approaches must be identified and tested. We have often intervened on faith, and sometimes this has been enough. Too often, however, our successes, as well as our failures, have occurred for unknown reasons." (Keogh, 1987b, p. 12).

Through the work of Keogh and others (Fletcher, 1985; Fletcher & Morris, 1986; Satz & Morris, 1981), it became clear that if learning disabilities were to be understood, it was necessary to move research in LD to a higher scientific plane: In 1987, Keogh put in writing a vision that she had shared with me and my predecessors at the National Institute of Child Health and Human Development (NICHD) since the mid-1970s:

> The time seems right for this field of study to become part of a larger scientific tradition. This would involve improved and more rigorous scientific research methods, as well as improved and more rigorous thinking.

We have evolved from an applied need and a pragmatic perspective. We face many serious and pressing "real world" problems. Yet, we are not likely to understand the many expressions of LD unless we make the topic a legitimate focus of scientific study. This means, in part, that we support and encourage research that does not necessarily have immediate practical payoff...classification must be tied to purpose ... and one purpose is to understand the conditions of LD. Understanding learning disabilities will require a continued tolerance of ambiguity, along with a commitment to theoretical as well as applied research. (Keogh, 1987b, p. 12)

To reach this higher scientific plane about which Keogh taught and wrote, it was essential that research strategies be designed and implemented that could circumvent the seemingly insurmountable definitional problems that had plagued the field since its inception. A program of longitudinal research would also have to be developed that could account for the various expressions of LD that may emerge at different points during the life span. Within the context of this challenge, the NICHD research program in learning disabilities began to take shape in 1983 and has now developed into a research network composed of 18 research sites (Fig. 13.1). In 1985, the Interagency Committee on Learning Disabilities, under policy directives established by the Health Research Extension Act (PL 99-158), designated the NICHD as the lead scientific agency to:

Develop a classification system that more clearly defines and diagnoses learning disabilities, conduct disorders, and attention deficit disorders, and their interrelationships. Such information is prerequisite to the delineation of homogeneous subgroups and the delineation of more precise and reliable strategies for treatment, remediation, and prevention that will increase the effectiveness of both research and therapy. (Kavanagh & Truss, 1988, p. 1)

Within this context, the NICHD proceeded to plan the development of requests for research applications (RFAs) to construct valid definitions of LD, determine the developmental course of each type of LD specified in public law (PL 94-142; IDEA), identify the prevalence of each type of LD, identify the etiologies for each type of LD, and understand which teaching approaches have the most success for children with LD. In the planning process, it was essential that NICHD be informed by the best thinking and scholarship available with respect to the development of a valid definition for LD, and the development of a classification system that could account for different types of learning disabilities, at different developmental stages, as well as the distinctions and interrelationships between learning disabilities and other types of learning disorders.

An overview of the NICHD Research Program in Learning Disabilities and selected findings that have been obtained through these research efforts are discussed next.

# NICHD LD and Reading Research Network

☐ Learning Disability Research Center
▲ Dyslexia Program Project
○ NICHD Treatment / Intervention Project
● Collaborating Research Site

University of
Washington LDRC
Berninger

Boy's Town
Smith

Syracuse U.
Blachman

Tufts Rx
Wolf

Toronto Rx
Lovett

SUNY-Albany
Vellutino

Children's Hospital/
Harvard LDRC
Waber

Beth Israel Dyslexia
Galaburda

Yale LDRC
Shaywitz

Haskins Labs
Fowler

UC Irvine
Filipek

Yale Dyslexia
Shaywitz

Johns Hopkins LDRC
Denckla

D.C. / Houston Rx
Foorman / Moats

Colorado LDRC
DeFries

U. Houston Rx
Foorman

Bowman Gray Dyslexia
Wood

Yale Methodology
Fletcher

Georgia State Rx
Morris

Florida State Rx
Torgesen

U. Florida Rx
Alexander

FIG. 13.1.   Locations of multidisciplinary and longitudinal research programs in learning disabilities supported by the NICHD. Dashed lines (- - -) depict collaborating research sites for the Yale, Johns Hopkins and University of Colorado LDRCs. Shading has been applied to enhance visual clarity and to depict regions of the U.S.

## The NICHD Research Program in Learning Disabilities

Until 1985, the study of learning disabilities had not been effectively coordinated (see Lyon, 1995a, for review). Much of our research-based thinking about LD was based on information obtained from ambiguously defined school-identified samples of children. Frequently, these studies were not informed by a longitudinal, developmental perspective. Why has the lack of a longitudinal, developmental perspective in learning disabilities research been of such concern, and how can longitudinal investigations better inform our thinking? Studies that compare children achieving normally with children with LD on one or more dependent variables of interest at only one point in time ignore the developmental nature of learning and change. "Single-shot" studies also ignore how such change interacts with information processing characteristics, teacher characteristics, different interventions, and classroom climates. In contrast, developmental longitudinal research studies, in which the same children are repeatedly observed and studied, are one of the most powerful means not only to trace the development of learning in general and LD in particular, but also to obtain data for the construction of focused and succinct definitions of different types of LD.

A major advantage in studying LD from a longitudinal perspective is that there need not be any a priori assumptions made about which children should compose the sample. In fact, the sampling net can be cast widely enough so that children can be selected randomly from the population at large, as early as preschool (or even birth), and then observed over time across a wide range of multiple assessment and teaching contexts. In doing so, descriptions of the attributes of persons who are underachieving academically and socially can be obtained, thus identifying the critical characteristics of different types of LD that are manifested in different ways at different developmental epochs. This strategy allows for an objective test of competing hypotheses vis-a-vis definitional criteria, etiological factors, and issues related to gender and ethnicity. In addition, longitudinal studies also provide a scientific platform to develop early predictors of different types of LD, map the developmental course of specific types of LD, identify commonly co-occurring disorders and secondary behavioral characteristics that develop in response to school failure, and assess the efficacy of different treatments and teaching methods for different types of LD.

In addition to the field's history of conducting research on LD using poorly defined school identified samples, the majority of studies of LD over the past 30 years have attempted to understand the disorder by studying individuals who were grouped according to the broad label of "learning disabilities" without careful attention paid to the specific types of learning disabilities included in the general category and a specific accounting of the characteristics of these disabilities. The general learning disability category is currently composed of seven different types of disabilities to include disabilities in: listening, speaking, basic reading skills, reading comprehension skills, written expression, arithmetic calculation skills, and mathematics reasoning skills. Each of these disability domains are heterogeneous in their own right and quite different from one another with respect to etiology, developmental course, and response to instruction. As Keogh (1993) pointed out, although the use of the broad term "learning disability" is essential for policy and advocacy purposes, selecting children for research studies under this general rubric can confound the interpretation of the results that are obtained.

Over the past decade, NICHD-supported research has concentrated on the study of children and adults with reading disabilities as a specific type of learning disability, and on the study of children and adults who manifest reading disabilities and co-occurring deficits in mathematics and attention. This research focus has been undertaken because reading disabilities are the most common types of learning disabilities, and are extremely deleterious with respect to an individual's educational development, motivation and self-esteem, occupational and vocational success, and other postschool outcomes (Cramer & Ellis, 1996). By focusing initially on reading disabilities, NICHD-supported researchers have now been able to replicate several findings related to the etiology (causes), developmental course, cognitive features, and biological and treatment characteristics of reading disabilities. A brief summary of replicated research points is provided here (the reader is referred to Lyon, 1995a, 1996; Lyon, Alexander, & Yaffe, 1997; Lyon & Moats, 1997, for more comprehensive reviews).

## Selected NICHD Research Findings

Definitional issues continue to be a significant impediment to understanding learning disabilities, particularly with respect to definitions that guide sample selection for research purposes. Specifically, the use of the general term "learning disabilities" in "research" studies may hinder our ultimate understanding of the causes, developmental courses, and outcomes of specific types of disabilities subsumed within the learning disability category. This is primarily because of the substantial heterogeneity inherent within each type of learning disability, and the tendency on the part of researchers to employ ambiguous criteria for the selection of subjects when sampling school-identified or clinic-identified children with learning disabilities. The research community must grapple with the need to address each type of learning disability in its own right in order to arrive at clear definitional statements and a coherent understanding of etiology, diagnosis, prevention, and treatment. This recommendation, which is based on converging findings from several NICHD-supported research centers and projects, does not in any way detract from the need to continue to use the term "learning disabilities" in forging public policy and advocating for the millions of individuals whose lives are affected by learning disabilities (Keogh, 1993). However, progress is being made in understanding reading disability as one type of LD because the definition has been refined (Lyon, 1995b).

Converging evidence from several NICHD research sites indicates that language-based reading disabilities are the most prevalent type of learning difficulty encountered by children in school. This type of reading difficulty is typically reflected in inaccurate and slow decoding and word recognition. This laborious reading of single words frequently impedes the individual's ability to comprehend what has been read, even though listening comprehension is adequate.

Despite the widely held belief that boys are much more likely to have difficulties learning to read than girls, research from several sites indicates that as many females as males have such difficulties. However, more boys are identified by teachers in school, primarily because their behavior and/or activity level brings them more quickly to the teacher's attention.

Although other factors will no doubt be identified as contributing to reading difficulties, deficits in phonological processing reflect a significant impediment to learning to read. Deficits in phonological processing are characterized by difficulties segmenting words and syllables into constituent sound units (phoneme awareness), rapidly naming letters and numbers (lexical access), and remembering verbal items presented in sequence (phonetic recoding in working memory).

Deficits in phonological processing can be identified reliably in late kindergarten and first grade (and later as well), and the presence of these deficits is a strong indicator of future reading difficulties. Deficits in phonological processing appear, in many cases, to be heritable, as shown in family, twin, and molecular genetic studies. Neuroimaging data suggest that poor phonological processing is associated with atypical cortical activation in neural systems that subserve language.

Although relatively reliable assessment procedures to identify children who are at-risk for reading failure now exist, NICHD longitudinal studies show that the majority of children with learning disabilities with deficits in reading skills are not identified until the third grade. This is apparently too late. Approximately 74% of children who are identified after 9 years of age continue to demonstrate reading difficulties throughout their school tenure.

Converging evidence from several NICHD-supported research teams suggests that the most useful interventions for reading disabilities consist of a combination of explicit and direct instruction in phonemic awareness, sound-symbol relationships (phonics), and contextual reading and reading comprehension skills. However, the studies to date also clearly show that instruction in these elements must be systematically integrated and the child provided with substantial practice to develop fluency in single-word and textual reading. In short, direct instruction in phonemic awareness is necessary but not sufficient, and the same holds true for direct instruction in phonics and reading comprehension strategies.

## What We Need to Learn More About

During the next 5 years, the NICHD will continue to encourage prospective longitudinal studies of language and reading disabilities. Incidentally, in 1994, support for NICHD research in reading development and learning disabilities was expanded to include investigations of disabilities in reading comprehension, written language, mathematics, and social behavior. At the same time, the NICHD research program will continue to focus on the study of difficulties learning to read, write, and to develop competencies in arithmetic calculation and mathematics reasoning.

The NICHD will also continue to support neuroimaging and other neurobiological studies that provide a window on the relationship between the developing brain and the ability to learn. We need to better understand how the brain is organized for complex behaviors, and to know more specifically how the child with learning disabilities differs with respect to central nervous system functioning. Within this context, it is critical for us to learn how neurophysiological and neuroanatomical differences are related to genetic factors and to environmental influences within a developmental, longitudinal context.

Over the past 2 decades, NICHD-supported research has focused primarily on the study of children with learning disabilities ranging from 5 years to 18 years of age. The information derived from these studies can now serve as a foundation on which to expand our research initiatives to include studies of children from birth to 5-years of age, and to increase our research efforts with adults with learning disabilities.

Very importantly, we will continue to support basic and applied research programs to understand how different treatment and teaching interventions affect well-defined learning deficits in children and adults with learning disabilities. It is critical that we identify the instructional conditions that must be in place in order to help children and adults develop competencies in academic and social skills. Equally important is the need to better understand how academic skills that are taught componentially (i.e., reading skills) are systematically integrated, transferred, and applied in a fluent fashion in a variety of contexts. We must continue to develop a better understanding about which preventive strategies and remediation tactics are most effective for particular types of learners at different stages of development, in different content areas, and in different settings. It is our view that the ability to prepare professionals to teach children with learning disabilities in optimal ways is dependent on a clear understanding of these conditions.

## POSTSCRIPT: A TRIBUTE TO DR. BARBARA KEOGH

Dr. Barbara Keogh has, and continues to have, a positive influence on the direction and conduct of scientific research in learning disabilities. She has consistently identified and explicated the critical social, political, and scientific issues at the core of learning disabilities in the United States. Moreover, Dr. Keogh has had an ability to articulate in a rational and prescient manner how complex and recursive social, political, and scientific issues can best be understood and accounted for in the development of research practices and research policies. Rather than simply advocate for experimental control of complex ecological variables (e.g., demographics, teaching environments, social environments) in learning disabilities research, Barbara Keogh has taught us that these factors should be defined and studied contemporaneously with cognitive, affective, and academic variables within a longitudinal, developmental context. In doing so, she has changed fundamentally the course of research in this field.

It is through her compelling, albeit quiet and unassuming, style and manner of conceptualizing the scientific and nonscientific forces composing the *Big Picture* that Dr. Keogh strengthens our research efforts and changes the lives of children for the better. She has taught us that educational policies are frequently forged and implemented on the basis of political and economic factors, and through the strength of advocacy, rather than on the shoulders of scientific evidence. She has used her trademark clear and unfettered prose to explain how policies driven by human foibles frequently breed inconsistencies and conflicts in educational practice. Witness, for example, the inherent tension created by the call for high academic standards (Goals 2000) and the realities of classroom inclusion for all students. She has taught that educational policies can be capricious, and in their whimsical implementation give rise to the metaphors of "one size fits all" and the unfortunate persistence of educational pendulum swings. She has observed that teachers remain vulnerable to these predictable, albeit frequently irrational, shifts in federal and local educational policy directives because their preparation can be fragmentary, shallow, and limited with respect to academic content, development, and individual differences.

The complexity inherent in viewing learning disabilities through such a wide scientific and sociopolitical lens has never seemed daunting to Dr. Keogh. It is as if she relishes the opportunity to understand how multivariate ecological contexts (and specific variables) affect children's development and learning, how these interactions take place, and under what conditions. She has taught me (and legions of others) through personal discussions and through her writings that rather than attempts to reduce complexity with rigid experimental controls, we might as well develop an informed amalgam of quantitative and qualitative skills and methods to assess, analyze, and understand it. In no way do I mean to imply that Dr. Keogh eschews principles of experimental design—she is a student and a master of the experimental process. The point is that she has never succumbed to the temptation to force-fit complex research targets (e.g., developing definitions of LD) into narrow designs that inevitably give rise to restrictive and incomplete conclusions. Conversely, she strives to understand developmental phenomena within the real world of children, schools, and learning. Experimental designs are tools, not masters. She asks the tough questions, and then has the brilliance to show us how to answer them using a variety of research strategies and combinations of research strategies. I speak strongly of Dr. Keogh's talent in this arena, because she has taught me that the development of valid research programs and educational policies will indeed rest on research that illuminates the confluence of context, development, and cognition.

Dr. Keogh's thinking and scholarly work has greatly influenced the development of the NICHD Research Program in Learning Disabilities. The conceptual and scientific principles that guide much of the research can be attributed to Barbara Keogh's scholarship, leadership, and commitment to longitudinal, programmatic scientific initiatives. Her vision of how to conduct research in the real world has been instrumental in informing the research programs in learning disabilities at the NICHD, and served as a cornerstone in the development of several NICHD initiatives and research policies in LD. The long-term longitudinal NICHD investments now underway at many sites around the country reflect much of her wisdom, and move forward by her gentle prodding to strive for excellence and rigor in our thinking and our research—to put in motion research efforts that are up to the task of illuminating the nature of development, even when there are no immediate practical payoffs. Yet even in our basic research efforts to forge valid definitions and map the developmental course of different learning disabilities, we are trying to ensure that these basic findings will inform our understanding of what should be done in the classroom. Dr. Keogh stands alone in her ability to meld quantitative and qualitative principles and basic and applied research methods and to conceptualize their application, so that her vision of what constitutes genuine understanding is achieved (Speece & Keogh, 1996). It is my most sincere hope that our work at the NICHD will realize her vision.

I know of no other scientist or professional who is more devoted to the development and welfare of children than is Dr. Barbara Keogh. We are indeed fortunate, as a nation and as a field, that her devotion to improving the lives of children is founded on impeccable integrity, the keenest of intellects, and the courage of a genuine leader. In her unpretentious way, she has guided us away from conventional wisdom when it is neither conventional nor wise. She sees the best in all points of view, and synthesizes these gems so that the whole is clearly greater than the sum of its elements. By the way she does this, everyone wins; and, by her design, so do the children.

## REFERENCES

Cramer, S. C., & Ellis, W. (Eds.) (1996). *Learning disabilities: Lifelong issues.* Baltimore: Brookes.

Fletcher, J. M. (1985). External validation of learning disability typologies. In B. P. Rourke (Ed.), *Neuropsychology of learning disabilities: Advances in subtype analysis* (pp. 187–211). New York: Guilford.

Fletcher, J. M., & Morris, R. (1986). Classification of disabled learners: Beyond exclusionary definitions. In S. J. Cici (Ed.), *Handbook of cognitive, social, and neuropsychological aspects of learning disabilities* (pp. 55–80). Hillsdale, NJ: Lawrence Erlbaum Associates.

Kavanagh, J. F., & Truss Y. (Eds.). (1988). *Learning Disabilities: Proceedings of the national conference.* Parkton, MD: York.

Keogh, B. K. (1983). Classification, compliance, and confusion. *Journal of Learning Disabilities, 16,* 25.

Keogh, B. K. (1986). Future of the LD field: Research and practice. *Journal of Learning Disabilities, 19,* 455–460.

Keogh, B. K. (1987a). Learning disabilities: Diversity in search of order. In M. Wang, M. Reynolds, & H. Wallberg (Eds.), *The handbook of special education: Research and practice* (pp. 221–251). Oxford, England: Pergamon.

Keogh, B. K. (1987b). A shared attribute model of learning disabilities. In S. Vaughn & C. Bos (Eds.), *Research in learning disabilities: Issues and future directions* (pp. 3–18). Boston: College-Hill.

Keogh, B. K. (1993). Linking purpose and practice: Social-political and developmental perspectives on classification. In G. R. Lyon, D. B. Gray, J. F. Kavanagh, & N. A. Krasnegor (Eds.), *Better understanding learning disabilities: New views from research and their implications for education and public policies* (pp. 311–323). Baltimore: Brookes.

Keogh, B. K. (1994). A matrix of decision points in the measurement of learning disabilities. In G. R. Lyon (Ed.), *Frames of reference for the assessment of learning disabilities: New views on measurement issues* (pp. 15–26). Baltimore: Brookes.

Keogh, B. K. (1996). Strategies for implementing policies. In S. C. Cramer & W. Ellis (Eds.), *Learning disabilities: Lifelong issues* (pp. 77–82). Baltimore: Brookes.

Keogh, B. K., & MacMillan, D. L. (1983). The logic of sample selection: Who represents what? *Exceptional Education Quarterly, 4,* 84–96.

Keogh, B. K., Major-Kingsley, S., Omori-Gordon, H., & Reid, H. P. (1982). *A system of marker variables for the field of learning disabilities.* Syracuse, NY: Syracuse University Press.

Lyon, G. R. (1995a). Research initiatives in learning disabilities: Contributions from scientists supported by the National Institute of Child Health and Human Development. *Journal of Child Neurology, 10,* 120–126.

Lyon, G. R. (1995b). Toward a definition of dyslexia. *Annals of Dyslexia, 45,* 3–27.

Lyon, G. R. (1996). The current state of science and the future of specific reading disability. *Mental Retardation and Developmental Disabilities Research Reviews, 2,* 2–9.

Lyon, G. R., Alexander, D. F., & Yaffe, S. (1997). Progress and promise in research in learning disabilities. *Learning Disabilities: A Multidisciplinary Journal, 8,* 1–6.

Lyon, G. R., & Moats, L. C. (1997). Critical conceptual and methodological considerations in reading intervention research. *Journal of Learning Disabilities, 30,* 578–588.

Satz, P., & Morris, R. (1981). Learning disability subtypes: A review. In E. J. Pirozzolo & M. C. Wittrock (Eds.), *Neuropsychological and cognitive processes in reading* (pp. 109–141). New York: Academic.

Speece, D. L., & Keogh, B. K. (Eds.) (1996). *Research on classroom ecologies: Implications for inclusion of children with learning disabilities.* Mahwah, NJ: Lawrence Erlbaum Associates.

# PART IV

## Biographical

# 14 ❦ Multiple Perspectives on the Career of Professor Barbara K. Keogh

**Margaret S. Faust**
*Scripps College*

**Carol Keogh Lindsay**
*North Idaho College*

**Carol E. Smith**
*System Development Corporation*

**Annette Tessier**
*California State University, Los Angeles*

The lives of the contributors to this chapter merged with Barbara Keogh's at different points and in very different circumstances. Throughout the years each has become a colleague and a lifelong friend. It seems appropriate to celebrate Barbara's distinguished career while recognizing also that she is a very family-oriented wife, mother, grandmother, and friend. A straight chronology of her life and times might begin to sound depressingly like an obituary, so an attempt has been made in this portrayal to interweave many facets of her life that we admire and continue to enjoy. Perhaps these reminiscences and selected events provide some clues to the development of a very special woman whose career has inspired this impressive volume.

When Barbara Kolts Keogh was 11 years old, her grandmother took her on a trip around the world. She sailed from Los Angeles to Yokohama on a Japanese liner. She rode rickshaws in Japan, trains through India, and camels in Egypt. She saw the Taj Mahal by moonlight, the Sphinx's sarcophagus by candlelight, and Paris from the Eiffel Tower by daylight. She came home via the *Normandie* to New York City and traveled across the U.S. by train—a bit late for school, but with great material for "How I Spent My Summer Vacation." This may have been the start of her writing career.

Barbara and her younger sister, Carol, grew up in a loving, well-educated family in Glendale, California. Their father, Dr. Robert F. Kolts, was a dedicated physician who headed a medical clinic that served families in an impoverished area of Los Angeles County now known as Watts. Their mother, Carol Willisford Kolts, had been a high school mathematics teacher earlier in her adult life, but like many women of her generation, marriage, family, home and community commitments became her full-time, lifelong occupation. Barbara's parents met when they were students at Glendale High School. Robert Kolts attended USC, and Carol Kolts graduated Phi Beta Kappa from Pomona College. A generation later, Barbara and her sister attended Pomona College, met their husbands, and graduated in 1946 and 1950, respectively.

Throughout her educational career Barbara Kolts was an outstanding student. She attended Glendale public schools from kindergarten through twelfth grade; in high school she was a member of the Honor Society.

She earned a scholarship while an undergraduate at Pomona College, and received the Mabel Wilson Richards Fellowship in Psychology while attending Claremont Graduate School. In 1947, Pomona's Dean of Women wrote:

Miss Kolts ... is an attractive and energetic young woman of superior intelligence. She not only made an excellent record here as a student, but was outstanding in leadership, holding various elective and appointive offices during all of her four years here...She is cooperative and responsible, has a great deal of drive, and yet is sympathetic with and understanding of other people.

In college, Barbara was a member of the Pomona College Women's Glee Club and Choir and of Mortar Board, a national honorary scholastic and service organization. At the end of her third year, she was elected president of the Associated Women Students, which coordinates all women's activities on the campus.

Following her graduation from college, Barbara entered graduate school at Stanford University where she completed requirements for the M.A. degree in psychology in 1 year. Her academic program emphasized courses in psychometrics and clinical psychology, as well as statistics and the psychology of learning. Her master's thesis, completed in 1947, was entitled, "Age and the Recall and Resumption of Interrupted Activities." While at Stanford, she became a member of Sigma Xi, a national honorary, scientific research organization.

From July 1947 to July 1948, she completed a Clinical Psychology Internship in the Department of Child Psychiatry at Stanford University Medical School in San Francisco. There, under the supervision of Katherine P. Bradway, she administered Rorschach and other psychological tests to individual children, and wrote up clinical evaluations. Subsequently, she worked for a year as a Clinical Psychologist for the Alameda County (CA) Juvenile Court and Probation Department. In reference to that time period, Dr. Bradway said:

During the last year Miss Kolts has consulted with me several times about a study of the personality of delinquents in which she has used the Rorschach test. She has done this study entirely on her own initiative with no reference to obtaining credit for it and with no pressure from anyone on her job. She has persisted with it and has shown ingenuity and astuteness in handling the problems involved in the research and in handling the obtained results.

## COMPOSING A LIFE: MARRIAGE, FAMILY, AND CAREER

On August 28, 1949, Barbara Kolts and Jack Keogh were married in the Glendale Congregational Church, the church founded by her grandfather in 1909. Earlier that summer, Barbara had accepted a 1 year appointment as Instructor in Psychology at Pomona College. Barbara and Jack moved to Claremont, and Barbara began teaching while Jack was enrolled in a graduate program in education at the Claremont Graduate School and, concurrently, coached freshman basketball and baseball at Pomona.

During the decade of the 1950s, the Keoghs interwove engaging in professional work, developing a family, and obtaining additional graduate education. Jack taught mathematics and coached basketball in various community colleges and high school districts in California, and he completed his M.A. degree. Barbara gave birth to the Keogh's first child, Kirk, in San Diego in 1952, and their second child, Kelly, in San Francisco in 1954. During the 1955-56 academic year, Barbara worked as a school psychologist in South San Francisco. By 1956, Jack began his doctoral program full-time at UCLA, and the Keoghs moved to the UCLA housing units with their two young children. It is evident that the development of Barbara's professional life, like that of other women of her cohort, "did not follow a linear path, but was a series of improvisations, determined largely by geographic location, financial status, and family needs" (Keogh, 1998, p. 128).

In the fall of 1956, Barbara was in the seventh month of an important developmental project when she applied for a position in the El Segundo Unified School District in Southern California. Dr. Carol E. Smith interviewed Barbara and remembered that her focus in the interview quickly shifted from "Can she do the job?" to "How soon can she start doing it?" Two months after Carol Leigh Keogh was born, Barbara became the district's school psychologist.

The Keoghs returned to Claremont in 1957; Jack was on the faculty in the department of physical education and coached the Pomona College basketball team while completing his doctoral work at UCLA. Barbara began her Ph.D. program in Psychology at the Claremont Graduate School under the chairmanship of Professor W. L. ("Don") Faust, a longtime mentor and friend.

In 1958, Barbara suggested to Carol Smith that the two of them might administer the Bender-Gestalt Test to kindergartners and use the results as a possible predictor of the children's reading skill. Certain theoretical propositions in the psychology of perception made such a predictor seem worth studying, and they soon tested all the kindergarten children in the school district. Because of the equipment they carried and the "fun" drawing tasks they brought, the two were soon recognized in each school by pupils, teachers, and principals, and came to be known as "The Bender Ladies."

Barbara continued her graduate studies and her research with the Bender-Gestalt, and in November 1958 gave birth to a fourth child, Bruce. Jack completed his doctorate in 1959, joined the faculty of UCLA, and the Keogh family moved to Hermosa Beach. (A year later they settled in Manhattan Beach.)

Barbara's doctoral dissertation, *The Bender-Gestalt as a Predictive and Diagnostic Test of Reading Performance* (Keogh, 1963) foreshadowed her subsequent research and writing in its developmental design and utilization of longitudinal data to examine possible relationships between early identification and later achievement in school (in this case, reading). To quote from her dissertation, "The present research focuses upon the relationship between performance on the Bender-Gestalt and reading ability in a longitudinal paradigm by using data on the same children at kindergarten and third grade" (p. 20). Before her dissertation was completed and by the time her degree was granted in 1963, Barbara had developed an ongoing research program and had published three articles on the Bender-Gestalt as a diagnostic test for early identification of problem learners. Her research with the Bender was some of her first work on individual differences, an interest that has been evident throughout her career.

During the academic year 1964–1965, Barbara was a Clinical Research Psychologist at Children's Hospital in Los Angeles. She worked as part of a multidisciplinary team, headed by Dr. Richard Koch, testing, evaluating and making recommendations on case referrals.

By 1965 the Keoghs had four school-age children; both Barbara and Jack had doctorates; and the family went off to Birmingham, England, for Jack's sabbatical leave. The year in England was a productive and enjoyable one for all six Keoghs. Barbara was a USPHS Postdoctoral Fellow at the Centre for Child Study at the University of Birmingham that year.

By the time the Keoghs returned to the United States at the end of the 1965–1966 academic year, Barbara had accepted a full time position as Assistant Professor in the Graduate School of Education at UCLA, and her distinguished career there began. For many years she and her colleague, the late Frank Hewett, worked together closely to develop and strengthen the UCLA Program in Special Education and to apply for funding to attract and support high quality graduate students.

## DEPARTMENTAL AND UNIVERSITY SERVICE

Barbara was Director of the UCLA Special Education Research Program from 1971 to 1976, Co-Director of the UCLA–Office of Education Training Program in Special Education from 1968 to 1978, and Chair of the Program in Special Education much of the time from 1978 to 1988. During that time she was also principal investigator for Project REACH, a 5-year study funded by the Bureau for the Education of the Handicapped, and The Marker Variable Project, under funding from the U.S. Office of Special Education, Department of Education. Since 1985 she has been a Senior Investigator on Project CHILD, a longitudinal study of children with developmental delays and their families, funded by the National Institutes of Child Health and Human Development. Within UCLA Barbara has served as an elective or appointive member on many departmental, Academic Senate, and universitywide committees involving university policies, personnel matters, affirmative action, and ethical issues.

## TEACHING: "CREATING A COMMUNITY OF SCHOLARS"

University classrooms, school administrative offices, therapeutic clinics, educational think-tanks, and state and federal offices of education are but a few settings where one may find UCLA graduates mentored by Professor Barbara Keogh. Not only are many of her former students outstanding educators and researchers, but they are part of a community of scholars where Barbara's influence continues.

A number of Keogh graduates have reported that they find themselves trying to emulate their mentor as well as passing along the scholarly qualities of critical thinking, inquiry, problem solving, persistence, integrity, and respect for individual differences of learning.

To pinpoint some of what the process of learning was like for Barbara's graduate students, it seems pertinent to include recollections from a number of them. The consensus is that "the common denominator of our graduate training was THE SEMINAR." This was the weekly gathering for doctoral candidates to formulate and complete their dissertation studies. Initiation to this august body began with these questions:

1. What are you interested in?

2. What do we know about this area?

3. What have you read, and who are the major contributors?

4. What are some unanswered questions?

5. What specific question would you like to pursue?

6. Why is it important? Who cares?

Thus would begin the shared struggles of the dissertation process, stimulated, guided, prodded, and nurtured by Professor Keogh. As one former student put it, "It made us think, question, clarify and examine all the possible ways to look at a problem. This training continues to influence all I do as a professor of educators." Another graduate said, "I was supported and mentored throughout. I was stretched beyond expectations!" And from yet another, "We not only acquired the tools of research, but we were encouraged to become scholars. Now I am trying to pass that on to my graduate students." The community of former Keogh students (1969–1992), who would like to pay homage to their mentor, adviser, counselor, teacher, and friend, is listed in the Appendix.

One of Barbara's postdoctoral students said, "Professor Keogh was a creative teacher, sensitive listener, and a thoughtful adviser to her graduate students." Her graduate seminar was a model of cooperative learning by students and teacher, with each taking responsibility for his or her own learning and serving as mentor and model for others in the class.

Barbara's own teaching philosophy is revealed, in part, by her citing and endorsing the view expressed by one of her favorite authors, Wallace Stegner, in reference to his teaching of creative writing: "The best teaching … is done by members of the class, upon one another. But it is not automatic, and the teacher is not unimportant. (The teacher's) job is to manage the environment, which may be as hard a job as for God to manage the climate" (cited in Keogh, 1998, p. 132). Barbara then explicated her own pedagogy:

> Consistent with Stegner's comments, over the years at UCLA, I found the most productive activity for students, and my most effective teaching, occurred while using an interactive model in which the key was the joint constructive effort of students and teacher. This is not a didactic model of teaching in which the faculty member structures content and dispenses information. Rather, it is one based in continuing interactions between teacher and student and student and student. (Keogh, 1998, p. 132)

This corresponds closely with the way THE SEMINAR was experienced and recalled by her former students.

Barbara was recipient of the UCLA Distinguished Teaching Award in 1972, and the UCLA Graduate School of Education Haytin Award in 1987. She has been commended publicly for the excellence of her own teaching and for the quality of the students she has trained.

## RESEARCH AND WRITING

Barbara is recognized nationally and internationally as an outstanding scholar/researcher in the field of learning disabilities. She is a Fellow and Founding Member of the International Academy for Research in Learning Disabilities (IARLD), a member of the American Psychological Association, and Fellow of APA's Division 16 (School Psychology) and Division 33 (Mental Retardation). In 1992, she was recipient of the Research Award of the Council for Exceptional Children (CEC). The citation of the CEC award noted:

> Dr. Keogh's research has a positive impact on the delivery of programs and services to exceptional children and youth. Among her research contributions are her efforts to establish marker variables to insure consis-

tency of sampling; her work on children's temperament as a contributor to their school experiences; her efforts in the area of early identification, including the assessment of infants, toddlers, and preschoolers; her study of young children at risk; and her longitudinal studies of developmentally delayed children and their families. Her early work on perceptual and cognitive styles influenced many researchers and helped the field understand how children vary in their approach to problems and tasks and consequently, how teachers can modify tasks so children can learn and retain information. Her insights into the development of high risk children have informed the field of special education over several decades.

One of her former students, a distinguished educator, said, "She has a reputation as a clear thinker who cuts through superfluous rhetoric and tangential issues to get at the heart of the problem being addressed. [She] has been invited repeatedly to contribute chapters to prestigious volumes because of her widely shared reputation as one of the clear thinkers and scholars in the field of LD."

Some examples are her articles in Calfee and Berliner's *Handbook of Educational Psychology* (1996), published by Division 15 of the American Psychological Association and coauthored with Donald MacMillan; in Wittrock's *Handbook of Research on Teaching* (1986), published by the American Educational Research Association; and in Wang, Reynolds, and Walberg's (1988) *Research Integration in Special Education*, published by the National Academy of Education.

From a glance at Barbara's list of publications one can recognize, as Carol Smith pointed out, that "she has moved in a forward and outward direction in her research interests, synthesizing her experiences and integrating everything important within her purview. Nothing seems to have escaped her notice." A colleague in special education wrote that Barbara has "moved" in the focus of her interests "from her early studies of perceptual-motor development (e.g., the Bender), to cognitive tempo, to temperament, to marker variables, to risk factors. All the while, she contributed important pieces on classification, sampling, policy, and other areas." Her current work reflects her strong developmental orientation and sociocultural perspective. Throughout, she has been a major contributor to medical and educational encyclopedias and a frequent reviewer of contemporary works in special education, such as new books, programs, and psychometric tests or batteries of tests.

"No one in the field of LD has had as significant an impact on research as Barbara Keogh" (Vogel, 1987, p. 13). Barbara has brought together medical, educational, and psychological perspectives in proposing recommendations for intervention, policy, and construction of programs for exceptional children and their families. Also, she has played a critical role in identifying points of emerging consensus in the field of learning disabilities, where they exist, while respecting and encouraging a diversity of viewpoints and research approaches to problems that have yet to be resolved.

Her articles have been published in many different scholarly journals, edited volumes, and in medical, psychological, and educational encyclopedias and yearbooks. She was editor of Volumes 1 through 5 of *Advances in Special Education*, (published from 1980 to 1986) and co-author of two books: *Personal Par* (1982) and *A System of Marker Variables for the Field of Learning Disabilities* (1985). In addition, she is co-editor of three recent books on learning disabilities published in 1990, 1992, and 1996. In the Foreword of the 1996 work, Zigler wrote:

> The task undertaken by editors Speece and Keogh and their colleagues is an extremely challenging one...Significantly, the shape of the book itself is in the form of a dialogue, a series of instructive interactions among diverse thinkers and practitioners. The resulting volume is a courageous and remarkably effective effort, and it heralds a new and hopeful era for children with learning disabilities and their teachers, classmates, and families. (p. x)

## ADVOCACY AND PUBLIC SERVICE

Barbara is an effective advocate for disabled persons and others whom she feels are vulnerable or at risk. She has a strong ethical sense and compassion for those who are likely to be overlooked or discriminated against on the basis of race, ethnicity, gender, or disability. A sense of efficacy—the belief that one can make a difference—underlies much of her public service effort. Literally, Barbara takes pen in hand and succinctly writes letters to politicians, university administrators, and editors of journals and newspapers to express her thoughts and feelings about what has been or should be done. Whether expressing praise or outrage, she continues to be an activist who believes that ordinary people can affect public policy and organizational procedures in a significant way, and should try to do so.

In her retirement, Barbara continues to be a member of many boards of private agencies and schools, advisory committees for state and federal government agencies, and consultant for educational and research councils. Recently, she has traveled to France and Argentina in her capacity as member of the Advisory Committee for Exceptional Children and Youth of the U.S. Department of State, Office of Overseas Schools, where she consults about U.S. children who have special needs. On these missions, she seems equally competent dealing with an individual child with special needs; with the child's parents, teachers, and other school personnel; or with State Department officials in Washington, DC.

## REMINISCENCES ON FAMILY LIFE WITH MOTHER: BY HER DAUGHTER, CAROL K. LINDSAY

When writing about one's own mother and the events of our family, the best of biographical intent often becomes somewhat autobiographical. Dictated by the egocentric nature of childhood, we know our mothers in a very singular role—that of our mother. Hence, biography becomes a description of our own life with mother, rather than about our mother's life. The daily routine, which constitutes the majority of our childhood experiences, becomes usurped in memory by novel events. Forgotten are the day-to-day events of life within a family culture, ironically where parental influence is likely to be the greatest. Vacations and out-of-the ordinary incidents are remembered more distinctly than are mundane family rituals such as the evening tucking into bed.

In attempting to reconstruct memories of Keogh family life, all of Barbara Keogh's children echoed the significance of a common theme around which both ordinary and unusual events occurred: that of the role of the ocean in the family character. During most of the years when her four children were young, the Keoghs lived on or near the beach. Swimming, surfing, sailing, body surfing, walks on the strand, and washing inordinate loads of wet, sandy towels were constants in the Keogh family. All her children recall proudly that Barbara was the first member of the family to own and use a surfboard, contributing to a lifestyle for her three boys that centered around their love of surfing. The Keoghs eventually built an enormous surfboard rack in the backyard to accommodate the dozens of teenagers who utilized our home for the before-school and after-school surfing depot and snack bar.

The family's nucleus was comprised of Barbara Keogh's family, her sister's family, her parents, Carol and Robert Kolts, and Jack's mother, Helen Keogh. Humor has been an enduring quality of the Keogh family bond, and many family jokes and pranks have endured over the years. The cousins and their grandparents developed close relationships with each other, and these have been maintained into adulthood. Virtually all holidays were spent together; family tradition was never more strongly regarded than on Christmas Eve, when the Koltses hosted a large gathering for the extended family, representing a very large contingent of relatives. (This festive occasion often caused some initial consternation for the Keogh family, who had to scour the neighborhood for dress shoes and ties for the boys, who generally owned only tennis shoes and thongs.) The highlight of the evening was a visit from Santa in full costume, bearing gifts for all of the many cousins and grandchildren.

Of the novel events of the Keogh family, their trip to England and Europe is one of the most significant. In the fall of 1965, the family moved to England for a sabbatical year where Barbara and Jack were associated with the University of Birmingham, and the children attended English schools. Weekends generally were spent traveling around the country in their Volkswagen van, castle hunting and touring. At the end of the year, joined by a niece, Barbara and Jack took five children, ranging in age from 7 to 14, on a 3-month driving tour of Europe. Although some folks doubted their sanity (and undoubtedly there were times when they were uncertain themselves), the trip was remarkable for all.

Although childhood memories of our mother and family are many, it was not until we children were adults that we became aware of the many roles our mother had maintained during our childhood. Thinking about my own life, I can say that as I began attempting to find some kind of balance between the powerful and important role as a mother and as a teacher of a subject about which I am passionate, I became aware of the enormity of my mother's accomplishments. With my father she raised four children while becoming a distinguished professor and international scholar. All this at a time when she had few female peers who had reached the same level of success, complete with a high level of work demands.

Although as children we may not have been cognizant of the many dimensions of our mother, and as adults may not ever fully recognize the depth and breadth of her accomplishments, all of us clearly recognize and appreciate the wisdom and clarity of her thinking. She serves as a practical and insightful resource into the many challenges of adulthood and family life. Having parents who have raised children and have a strong professional perspective about children's development has provided the Keogh children with many opportunities to benefit from their insights. Barbara is still teased about her comment concerning her first grandchild. Holding her new granddaughter in her arms, and staring at her with as much rapture, love, and awe as a grandparent could possibly feel, Barbara sighed, "Just look at her. She's so neurologically intact!"

The addition of four grandchildren has added a remarkable dimension to the family. Parents have become grandparents, children have become parents, brothers and sisters have become uncles and aunts, and roles exclusive to one generation have become shared by several. Barbara and Jack have established very close relationships with each of their grandchildren, and their home continues to be the nuclear gathering spot for the Keogh family.

## CONCLUDING OBSERVATIONS

The collaborators in this chapter share a deep admiration for Barbara, yet each enjoys a unique relationship with her. Carol K. Lindsay, a teacher of child development, is the Keogh's daughter and mother of two Keogh grandchildren. Annette Tessier was one of Barbara's first doctoral students at UCLA, and since then has been a close colleague in special education. Carol E. Smith was a coauthor with Barbara on several psychological articles as well as a book on golf. Since their association in the El Segundo Unified School District, Carol has become a cherished friend of the whole Keogh family. Margaret S. Faust has known Barbara as a friend since college days, as a fellow psychologist and college professor over many years, and as a postdoctoral fellow under her guidance at UCLA in 1980.

Throughout the years, all four of us have observed and enjoyed many Barbara Keoghs. She's a good sailor, navigator, and a special foredeck crew; a steady and fun traveling companion throughout and around the world; a generous and caring friend; a proud and devoted grandmother; an enthusiastic golfer; a passionate gardener; an avid reader—and we're just talking about her spare-time activities!

With respect to Barbara Keogh's "retirement," a UCLA colleague said, "She has given new meaning to this life stage with her productivity, creativity, and whirlwind writing pace. She still gives of herself so generously to students and colleagues. And all this from someone who claimed to only want to play golf!

Hah!" Her longitudinal research studies continue to captivate her interest and attention. She goes on writing landmark articles, and we have come to expect that she always will.

## APPENDIX A:
## DOCTORAL STUDENTS WHO WORKED WITH
## PROFESSOR KEOGH (1969–1992)

| | |
|---|---|
| Beatrice Babbit | Nancy Lavelle |
| Maurine Ballard-Rosa | Martha Lyon Levine |
| Laurence Becker | Fay Levinson |
| Lucinda Bernheimer | Jack Little |
| Margaret Briggs | Donald MacMillan |
| Nancy Burstein | Ann Maddox |
| Linda Carpenter | Dorothy Major |
| Kenyon Chan | Judith Margolis |
| Ruth Cook | Susan Markowitz |
| Jenni Coots | Michael Moore |
| Steven Daley | Robert Ortiz |
| Melanie Dreisbach | Stella Port |
| Ronald Fischbach | Deborah Priddy |
| Ruth Forer | James Quigley |
| Steven Forness | Cindy Ratekin |
| Patricia Gandara | Patricia Reid |
| Glenda Gay | George Robson |
| Marquita Grenot-Scheyer | Liberato Salandanan |
| Joyce Hagen | Ellen Schneiderman |
| Sherrel Haight | Sue Sears |
| Peter Hall | Janna Siegel |
| Robert Hall | Bruce Smith |
| Nora Jacobs | Saundra Sparling |
| Michelle Pelland Haney | Sandra Sternig-Babcock |
| Philip Hanson | David Sugden |
| Vicki Ann Jax | Sister Phyllis Supanchek |
| Jaana Juvonen | Annette Tessier |
| Susan Major Kingsley | Billy Watson |
| Margie Kitano | Andrea Weiss |
| Paul Klinger | Melinda Wells |
| Barbara Kornblau | Anne Wilcoxen |
| Stevan Kukic | Brenda Wright |
| Maya Laemmel | Barbara Yoshioka |

APPENDIX B: CURRICULUM VITAE

## BARBARA K. KEOGH
Professor of Educational Psychology Emerita
Graduate School of Education & Information Studies
Professor, Department of Psychiatry
University of California, Los Angeles

## Education and Training

| | | | |
|---|---|---|---|
| Pomona College | B.A. | 1946 | Psychology |
| Stanford University | M.A. | 1947 | Psychology |
| Claremont Graduate School | Ph.D. | 1963 | Psychology |

Clinical Psychology Internship, Stanford University Medical School,
     Department of Child Psychiatry                              1947–1948
USPHS Postdoctoral Fellow, Centre for Child Study, the University
     of Birmingham, England                                      1965–1966
Licensed Clinical Psychologist, State of California (PL 1543)

## Professional Experience

Clinical Psychologist, Alameda County Juvenile Court and Probation
     Department                                                  1949–1950
School Psychologist, South San Francisco and El Segundo School Districts
                                                                 1956–1958
Clinical-Research Psychologist, Children's Hospital of Los Angeles
                                                                 1964–1965
Assistant Professor, Associate Professor, Professor, University of California,
     Los Angeles                                                 1966 to date
Director, UCLA Special Education Research Program    1971–1976
Chair, UCLA Program in Special Education             1986–1988
                                      1976–1977, 1983–1984
Co-Director, UCLA-U.S. Office of Education Training Program in Special
     Education                                                   1968–1978
Principal Investigator and Co-Director, Project REACH 1977–1982
Principal Investigator, Marker Variable Project       1977–1980
Senior Investigator, Project CHILD                    1985 to date

## Professional Affiliations

American Psychological Association (Fellow, Divisions 16 & 33)
Council for Exceptional Children

International Academy for Research in Learning Disabilities (Fellow)
Multidisciplinary Academy for Clinical Education

## Professional Service

Member National Advisory Committee on the Handicapped, 1974–1977

Member Professional Advisory Board, the Park Century School, Los Angeles, 1978 to date

Member Professional Advisory Board, the Frostig Center, Pasadena, 1976–1984

Member Professional Advisory Board, Association for Children with Learning Disabilities (ACLD), 1986 to 1989

Member Advisory Board of the Division for Learning Disabilities of the Council for Exceptional Children (DLD), 1970–1974, 1984 to date

Member Advisory Board, Dyslexia Institute, San Jose, California, 1993 to date

Member Professional Advisory Board, National Center for Learning Disablities, 1997 to date.

Reviewer and Consultant, U.S. Office of Education, Bureau of Education for the Handicapped, 1970–1976

Reviewer & Consultant, Maternal and Child Health Division of U.S. Department of HEW, 1972–1974

Consultant, California State Department of Education Research and Evaluation Unit, 1972–1977, 1985

External Evaluator, University of Arizona Department of Special Education, 1980

Ad Hoc Consultant, National Institutes of Health, 1980, 1987–1988, 1994

Consultant, U.S. Department of State Overseas Educational Programs, 1994 to date

Reviewer, Canadian Research Council, 1986, 1988

Reviewer, American Educational Foundation, 1987

Chair, Publication Committee, IARLD, 1994 to date

Co-Chair, Research Committee, Division for Learning Disabilities, CEC, 1992 to 1995

Editorial Board, *Journal of Child Psychology and Psychiatry, European Journal of Special Needs Education, Special Services in the Schools.*

Ad Hoc Reviewer, *Child Development, Developmental Psychology, American Journal of Mental Deficiency, Exceptionality*

## Honors and Prizes

UCLA Distinguished Teaching Award, 1972

Distinguished Visiting Scholar, University of North Carolina, 1980
Gulliami Visiting Scholar, California State University at Los Angeles, 1983
UCLA Graduate School of Education Haytin Award, 1987
Distinguished Alumna Participant, Pomona College Centennial, 1987
Distinguished Visiting Scholar, San Jose State University, 1988
Council for Exceptional Children Research Award, 1992

## Selected Publications

26. Keogh, B. K. (1971). Hyperactivity and learning disorders: Review and speculation. *Exceptional Children, 38*(2), 101–109.

29. Keogh, B. K. (1971). A compensatory model for psychoeducational evaluation of children with learning disorders. *Journal of Learning Disabilities, 4*(10), 544–548.

40. Keogh, B. K., & Becker, L. D. (1973). Early detection of learning problems: Questions, cautions, and guidelines. *Exceptional Children, 40*, 5–11.

54. Keogh, B. K., & Margolis, J. (1976). Learn to labor and to wait: Attentional problems of children with learning disabilities. *Journal of Learning Disabilities, 9*(5), 276–286.

69. Keogh, B. K., & Kopp, C. B. (1978). From assessment to intervention: An elusive bridge. In F. Minifie & L. Lloyd (Eds.), *Communicative and cognitive abilities—Early behavioral assessment* (pp. 523–548). Baltimore, MA: University Park Press.

74. Keogh, B. K., Major, S. M. Reid, H. P., Gandara, P., & Omori, H. (1978). Marker variables: A search for comparability and generalizability in the field of learning disabilities. *Learning Disabilities Quarterly, 1*(3), 5–11.

97. Keogh, B. K. (1982). Children's temperament and teachers' decisions. In R. Porter & G. Collins (Eds.), *Temperamental differences in infants and young children* (pp. 269–279). CIBA Foundation. London: Pitman.

100. Keogh, B. K., & MacMillan, D. L. (1983). The logic of sample selection: Who represents what? *Exceptional Education Quarterly, 4*(3), 84–96.

107. MacMillan, D. L., Keogh, B. K., & Jones, R. (1986). Special educational research on mildly handicapped learners. In M. C. Wittrock (Ed.), *Handbook of research on teaching* (3rd ed., pp. 686–724). New York: MacMillan.

109. Keogh, B. K. (1986). Temperament and schooling: What is the meaning of goodness of fit? In J. V. Lerner & R. M. Lerner (Eds.), *Temperament and social interaction during infancy and childhood. New directions for child development, No. 31* (pp. 89–108). San Francisco: Jossey-Bass.

110. Bernheimer, L. P., & Keogh, B. K. (1986). Developmental disabilities in preschool children. In B. K. Keogh (Ed.), *Advances in special education. Vol. 5. Developmental problems in infancy and the preschool years* (pp. 61–93). Greenwich, CT: JAI Press.

119. Keogh, B. K. (1988). Learning disabilities: Diversity in search of order. In M. Wang, M. Reynolds, & H. Walberg (Eds.), *The handbook of special education: Research and practice.* Oxford, England: Pergamon Press.

137. Keogh, B. K. (1993). Linking purpose and practice: Social/political and developmental perspectives on classification. In D. Gray & R. Lyon (Eds.), *Better understanding learning disabilities: New views for research and their implications for education and policy* (pp. 311–324). Baltimore, MD: Brooks Publishing Company.

142. Keogh, B. K. (1993). A matrix of decision points in the measurement of learning disabilities. In G. R. Lyon (Ed.), *Frames of reference for the assessment of learning disabilities* (pp. 15–26). Baltimore, MD: Brookes Publishing Co.

145. Keogh, B. K. (1994). What the special education research agenda should look like in the year 2000. *Learning Disabilities, Research and Practice, 9*(2), 62–69.

148. Keogh, B. K., & MacMillan, D. L. (in press). Exceptionality. In D. Berliner & R. Calfee (Eds.), *Handbook of Educational Psychology.* Washington, DC: American Psychological Association.

150. Bernheimer, C. P., & Keogh, B. K. (1995). Weaving interventions into the fabric of everyday life: An approach to family assessment. *Topics in Early Childhood Education, 15*(4), 415–433.

155. Keogh, B. K. (1995). Transitions and transactions: The need to study the influence of schooling on students with learning disabilities. *Thalamus, 15*(1), 3–9.

156. Keogh, B. K., Gallimore, R., & Weisner, T. (in press). A sociocultural perspective on learning disabilities. *Learning Disabilities Research and Practice.*

161. Keogh, B. K. (in press). A professional life in context. In L. T. Hashmand (Ed.), *Knowledge, creativity, and moral visions: Careers and lives in psychology.* San Diego: Sage.

## ACKNOWLEDGEMENT

I wish to acknowledge the help of Caroline Beatty, Historical Researcher, in making available material from the Pomona College Archives.

## REFERENCES

Keogh, B. K. (1963). *The Bender-Gestalt as a predictive and diagnostic test of reading performance.* Unpublished doctoral dissertation, Claremont Graduate School, Claremont, CA.

Keogh, B. K. (1988). A professional life in family context. In L. T. Hoshmand (Ed.), *Creativity and moral vision in psychology* (pp. 126–143). Thousand Oaks, CA: Sage.

Vogel, S. A. (1987). Response. In S. Vaughn & C. S. Bos (Eds.), *Research in learning disabilities: Issues and future directions* (pp.13–15). Boston: Little, Brown.

Zigler, E. (1996). Foreword. In D. L. Speece & B. K. Keogh (Eds.), *Research on classroom ecologies: Implications for inclusion of children with learning disabilities* (pp. ix–x). Mahwah, NJ: Lawrence Erlbaum Associates.

# Author Index

# Subject Index

## A

ABCX model, 56, 57
Accountability, 211–216, 256
    programs, 211–213
    in school reform, 237, 238
Acute conditions, 249
Adaptations, 57, 61, 62, 63, 67, *see also*
    Daily routine, sustainability,
    58–63
Adult adaptation, successful, 22, 23,
    27–29
    criteria for ratings of, 27, 28
    protective factors, 24–28
    turning points, 26, 27
Advocacy, 11, 248, 282
Aggression, *see* Behavior problems
Alphabetic principle, 158, 162, 163, *see*
    *also* Reading disabilities, initial
    learning challenges, 158–160
Anterior cingulate, 44
Antisocial behavior, 137–149
Approach, 39
Assessment, *see* Performance assessment
Attention deficit disorders, *see* Attention
    deficit hyperactive disorder, *see*
    *also* Psychiatric disorders,
    138–140
Attention deficit hyperactive disorder
    (ADHD), 143, 144
    long term outcomes, 20–23
Attention, 40
    effortful control of, 40
Attentional orienting, 41
Authoritative definitions, 112–114, 126
    for learning disabled, 112, 113
    for mental retardation, 112

## B

Behavior disorders, 5, *see also* Behavior
    problems, 136, 137

Behavior problems, 136, 137
Bender–Gestalt Test, 277, 278

## C

Children's Behavior Questionnaire, 44
Chronic conditions, 249
Classroom strategies, 33, 42, 43, 47–49
    teacher-student interaction, 47
Comorbidity, 139
    in antisocial behavior, 140–142
    consequences of, 142–146
Concordance among raters, *see*
    Self-concept, and its measure-
    ment
Conduct disorder, *see* Antisocial behavior
Conscience, development of, 43
Constructivism, 200
Contextual factors, 113, 114
    and IQ, 125
Coping, 56, 58, 65–67
Crisis management, 56
Curriculum-based measurement (CBM),
    206, 215

## D

Daily routine, 58–74
    intervention and research implications
    for, 68–74
    literature for, 63–68
    sustainability, 58–63
        ecological features, 59
        values and goals, 59, 60
        personal characteristics 60, 61
Demands, 56
Depression, 145
Depressive disorders, *see* Depression
Development, of temperament, 41–45
Developmental psychopathology, 148
Differentiated instruction, 90
Discrepancy candidates as
    IQ-achievement markers, 124

**303**